GOES HOLLYWOOD

Behind-the-Scenes Stories & Tinseltown Trivia

WEST
SIDE
PUBLISHING

Consultant and Fact-Checker: Susan Doll

Contributing Writers: Jeff Bahr, Susan Doll, James Duplacey, Mary Fons-Misetic, Bill Martin, David Morrow, JR Raphael, Lawrence Robinson, Peter Suciu, Donald Vaughan, James A. Willis

Additional Contributions: Rhonda Markowtiz, Phil Morehart, Bill O'Neal, Stephen Ryder, Jennifer Plattner Wilkinson

Cover Illustration: Dave McMacken

Interior Illustrations: Robert Schoolcraft

Additional Images: Art Explosion, Linda Bittner, Dan Grant, Jupiterimages, Nicole Lee, Retroclipart.com, Shutterstock Images, Elizabeth Traynor

Contents

☆ ☆ ☆ ☆

Hooray for Hollywood!

That's a wrap! It's time to let the fat lady sing and put this baby to bed. We'd like to invite you to enjoy the newest addition to the *Armchair Reader*™ series: *Armchair Reader*™ *Goes Hollywood.*

Hollywood, as we see it, is not so much a place as it is a state of mind. Of course the city exists in California, but the idea of Hollywood—in all its tacky yet glamorous, inspired but trite glory—extends throughout the world.

Everyone seems to have his or her own opinion of Hollywood. Those on the inside often have a cynical viewpoint. Marilyn Monroe famously stated, "Hollywood's a place where they'll pay you a thousand dollars for a kiss and fifty cents for your soul." And author/screenwriter William Faulkner wrote, "Hollywood is a place where a man can get stabbed in the back while climbing a ladder."

But Hollywood also holds an alluring and glamorous mystique for many of us ordinary mortals on the outside who are fascinated by the actions of the rich and famous (and sometimes infamous)—stories so weird, wild, bizarre, and over-the-top that they sometimes seem as fictional as the characters portrayed on the silver screen. With that in mind, we at the *Armchair Reader*™ have compiled a treasure trove of Tinseltown tales for your enjoyment, puzzlement, and all-around reading pleasure. So find your favorite chair (or casting couch), sit back, and prepare to enjoy the show.

Here are some of the coming attractions!

- Beginning in the 1950s, Cary Grant—the epitome of the suave, debonair gentleman—participated in an experimental psychotherapy program that sent him on hallucinogenic trips via LSD.

- Hollywood heartthrob James Dean and 1950s horror hostess Vampira were close friends. There were rumors that they were lovers, but the two were nothing more than kindred spirits.

- Two films that are now considered cinematic classics—*Citizen Kane* and *It's a Wonderful Life*—both tanked at the box office during their initial release.

- *Watchmen,* the 2009 superhero thriller, spent more than 20 years languishing in the development stages. When films spend excessive amounts of time in such purgatory, the process is known as Development Hell.

- Charlie Chaplin was involved in numerous scandals during his lifetime—he was once accused of being a Communist and was also implicated in a paternity case. He made headlines even in death, when his coffin was dug up and held for ransom.

- Katharine Hepburn was once labeled "Box-Office Poison" and was relegated to B-movies in the 1930s. She even left Hollywood for a short time to rethink her career choice.

- There is an urban legend that Billy Bob Thornton is supposedly cursed and anyone who stars in a film with him risks his or her life.

- Many people believe that the action in *The Wizard of Oz* syncs up to the songs on Pink Floyd's album *The Dark Side of the Moon.*

- Believe it or not, the founder of Hollywood actually envisioned it as a preservationist, Christian town free of saloons, bordellos, and other immoral excesses. Oh, how times have changed!

We don't want to spoil the rest of the show, so without further ado, it's time for our feature presentation.

Until next time,

Allen Orso

P.S. If you have any questions, concerns, or ideas pertaining to this book, or if you would like information about other West Side Publishing titles, please contact us at: **www.armchairreader.com.**

Hollywood—A Teetotaling Town?

☆ ☆ ☆ ☆

Few people realize that although Hollywood became the epicenter of the motion picture industry, the city's original planner had something far different in mind. Carousing actors and painted ladies may have been de rigueur in certain towns, but Horace H. Wilcox's haven was never intended to be one of them.

Straight and Narrow

Apart from its abundant sunshine and favorable temperatures, Hollywood seemed perhaps the least likely spot to base an industry that's now well known for

its seedier side. Horace H. Wilcox founded the southern California city not as a progressive hamlet with its eye on an ever-evolving future, but rather as its polar opposite. The city was intended as a preservationist society where modern excesses would not be tolerated. That it turned into something else is a story in itself.

This Is the Place

Wilcox and his wife, Daeida, arrived in Los Angeles from Kansas in the mid-1880s. A real-estate developer of considerable means, the self-made businessman purchased large tracts of land in the southern California region for the purpose of resale. And like any good businessman, he was always on the lookout for more. But in 1887, tragedy struck when the middle-aged couple's only child, a 19-month-old boy, died of typhoid fever. In an attempt to pull themselves out of despair, the couple took peaceful carriage rides into the country. On one of these therapeutic jaunts, Wilcox spied a particularly charming patch of land featuring orange groves and apple orchards. Bordered by the picturesque Santa Monica Mountains, this particular chunk of the Cahuenga Valley struck the developer as the perfect place to start a town. The wheels in Wilcox's head began to spin.

A Town Develops

The formidable challenge of establishing a town would be daunting to most, but Wilcox was well equipped for the task. Crippled by the same disease that had claimed his infant son, Wilcox had become accustomed to overcoming hardships on the way to achieving his goals. Certain of the elements that he desired for his settlement, and those that he did not, Wilcox, a strong advocate of the temperance movement (an organized effort to abolish alcohol backed by people who saw drinking as immoral) got busy. Purchasing a 120-acre expanse for his version of utopia, Wilcox offered free lots to anyone who would construct Protestant churches on the land. His goal was a society free from saloons, bordellos, and red-light districts—excesses that he deemed counterproductive to a clean Christian lifestyle. His wife Daeida came up with the name "Hollywood," although it's believed that she copied it from another woman's estate. Either way, the name stuck and the town began its ascendance to infamy.

Slow Growth

Unfortunately, Wilcox's hopes for an idyllic Protestant community never gained much ground, though efforts to keep the original conservatism lasted until about 1911. Population growth was agonizingly slow—there were never more than a few hundred residents in Wilcox's lifetime—and the return on his investment was disappointingly poor. When he died in 1892, Wilcox was up to his ears in land holdings but surprisingly cash poor. Nevertheless, Hollywood was poised to become one of the most recognizable places on Earth. Unfortunately for the devoted teetotaler, the town's notoriety would come not for its virtues and guiding light of restraint but for something far, far different.

A Giant Arrives

Like a condor taking nest amongst hummingbirds, the motion picture industry swooped down upon Hollywood in 1911. Like Florida before it, Hollywood was chosen for its frost-free climate. But the western locale also offered plenty of wide-open spaces at low prices so that studios could own their own property. Plus, California was known for its varying terrain and landscapes—deserts, mountains, beaches, small towns, urban centers—which allowed for a variety of film genres to be shot within a radius of a few miles. The first studio to set up shop was the Nestor Film Company. Located in a former tavern at the corner of Sunset Boulevard and Gower Street, the modest building would soon be joined by larger studios, which triggered a veritable explosion of commerce. Banks, clubs, restaurants, hotels/motels, movie palaces, and other supporting industries stood at the periphery, ready, willing, and able to feed at the studios' trough of prosperity. Not surprisingly, these new intruders met with considerable resistance and hostility from the town's original residents. Despite such protests, acres of agricultural land gave way to new housing and existing homes were displaced in favor of commercial buildings. The economic infrastructure as well as the local government of Los Angeles was in favor of the burgeoning industry, and they offered incentives to the studios that the political leaders and banking institutions in Florida had not. The message was abundantly clear: The motion picture industry and its mega studios were there to stay. Those opposed would simply have to get out of the way.

Tinseltown

Over time, the once anonymous hamlet in the Cahuenga Valley grew into a movie-making metropolis, with excesses of every sort playing out, on-screen and off. The thought of people openly enjoying alcohol or walking the streets barely clothed would cause Wilcox to turn over in his grave. How ironic that a town of his own creation would act as host to such insidious behavior. Today, the founder's name lives on in a bronze plaque situated at Hollywood and Vine. It reads: "Hollywood was given its name by pioneers Mr. and Mrs. Horace H. Wilcox. They subdivided their ranch in 1887 and called two dirt cross-roads Prospect Avenue and Weyse Avenue." Curiously, the sign mentions nothing of the town's original goal of purity. Within eyesight of the marker stand an assortment of bars, tattoo parlors, and places that "decent" people—those cut from the same cloth as Horace Wilcox—don't talk about. Such, it seems, is the price of progress.

"Strip away the phony tinsel of Hollywood and you find the real tinsel underneath."

—Oscar Levant

Hollywood Firsts

Filmmaking is an ever-evolving process, and Hollywood has certainly seen its share of firsts over the decades. Here are some highlights of inaugural moments from the world of movies.

First Feature-Length Film

The first feature-length film was an Australian Western titled *The Story of the Kelly Gang* from 1906. This tale of Australia's most famous bandit, Ned Kelly, was reportedly about an hour long.

The World's First Movie Theater

The first building designed specifically to show movies was The Nickelodeon in Pittsburgh. It opened in June 1905 and showed three or four one-reel films continuously throughout the day. Within three years, thousands of similar operations, called nickelodeons, had opened around the country.

First Feature Film with Sync-Sound Dialogue

Contrary to popular belief, *The Jazz Singer* (1927) is not the first film with sync sound, which aligns the picture and the soundtrack so that an action and its corresponding sound coincide. The first feature-length film with sync sound was *Don Juan* (1926). However, the only sound in sync in this swashbuckler was the clanking of swords during the duels; the dialogue was conveyed in intertitles. *The Jazz Singer* featured several songs recorded in sync sound and one famous scene of Al Jolson adlibbing some dialogue. Though unplanned and unscripted, this one scene of spoken dialogue caused audiences to line up around the block to see someone speak on film. For that reason, it is often called the first "talkie," though a few shorts from the early 1920s featured sync-sound songs. Confused? Well, there's more. The first all-talkie was *Lights of New York* (1928).

First Movie in Technicolor

In 1935, *Becky Sharp* became the first feature film to be shot in the three-strip Technicolor process, which married negatives shot in red, green, and blue. The movie, starring Miriam Hopkins, influenced the big studios to produce their major films in color. But according to critics, Technicolor made the cast of *Becky Sharp* look like "boiled salmon dipped in mayonnaise" due to the limitations of color technology at the time. Fortunately, the technology improved rapidly.

First Movie Star to Land a Million-Dollar Deal

Roscoe "Fatty" Arbuckle snagged the first big Hollywood payday back in 1921 when Paramount Pictures offered him $1 million a year for a three-year commitment. Think any price could convince a modern Hollywood star to take on the nickname "Fatty"?

First Movie Shown in the White House

The Birth of a Nation (1915) holds the honor of being the first flick to be brought to a president. In 1916, the film was shown to Woodrow Wilson, who was staying out of the public eye at the time, following his wife's death, so he asked to watch the film from the comfort of his own home.

First Movie Shown on a Plane

Movies hit the friendly skies for the first time in 1925. That's when a British Imperial Airways flight screened *The Lost World* for passengers. And no, it wasn't an advance copy of the *Jurassic Park* hit—it was a beautifully crafted silent film based on Arthur Conan Doyle's novel of the same name. *The Lost World* is renowned for using amazing special effects for its time.

First Use of the F-Word in a Movie

The now ubiquitous f-word was first uttered in a film in 1968, in *I'll Never Forget Whatshisname*. Actress Marianne Faithfull shocked audiences when she spoke the four-letter word. For comparison, *Casino* (1995) reputedly had nearly 400 uses of it—but who's counting?

First X-Rated Movie

Ah, how things progressed from that first four-lettered expression. Also in 1968, *Greetings* was the first film to be slapped with an X rating—but not for what you might think. The comedy perfectly captures the attitudes and images of New York's 1960s-era counterculture and its antiwar sentiment, radical views on sex and society, and antiestablishment perspective. It was these characteristics that made the film suitable for adult audiences by the original definition of the X rating. A few years later, after the X rating was appropriated by the porn industry, *Greetings* was given an R rating. The film also featured a young Robert De Niro in his first speaking role.

The Rise and Fall of Fatty Arbuckle

☆ ☆ ☆ ☆

As the saying goes, "The bigger they are, the harder they fall."
And when it comes to early Hollywood scandals, no star
was bigger or fell harder than Roscoe "Fatty" Arbuckle.

The scurrilous affair that engulfed Roscoe "Fatty" Arbuckle (1887–1933) in 1921 remains one of the biggest Hollywood scandals of all time because of its repercussions on the film industry. (It was instrumental in the creation of organized film censorship in Hollywood.) The Fatty Arbuckle scandal rocked the world when it broke, and though few people today know the details, in 2007, *Time* magazine ranked it fourth on its list of the Top 25 crimes of the past 100 years.

As one of Hollywood's first headline-grabbing scandals, it contained all the elements that make a scandal juicy—drunkenness, debauchery, and death. But what made the tawdry tale big was Arbuckle, who himself was big in size (nearly 300 pounds), big in popularity, and, as Tinseltown's highest paid comedian, one of the biggest stars in the Hollywood galaxy at the time.

The Rise

Arbuckle began his career as a child, performing in minstrel shows and sing-alongs. The young entertainer already carried a noticeable girth, but his remarkable singing voice, acrobatic agility, and knack for comedy made him a rising star on the vaudeville circuit.

In 1913, Arbuckle got his big break in film when Mack Sennett hired him on at Keystone Film Company. Arbuckle initially rollicked as one of Sennett's Keystone Cops, but he was soon developing his unique comic persona as the lovable fat man and honing his own slapstick specialties based on the seeming contradiction between his size and graceful agility. By 1914, Arbuckle was teamed with comedienne Mabel Normand for the extremely successful "Fatty and Mabel" shorts, in which the pair offered humorous interpretations of romantic rituals. Arbuckle's charming persona ensured that he always got the girl. He became so adept at working out the duo's physical gags for the camera that he soon took over direction of the films.

In 1917, Arbuckle formed Comique Film Corporation with Hollywood mogul Joseph Schenck, who offered Arbuckle creative control and an astounding paycheck. At Comique, Arbuckle launched the screen career of the great Buster Keaton, who played the rotund actor's sidekick in classic silent comedies such as *Coney Island* (1917), *Good Night, Nurse!* (1918), and *The Garage* (1920).

In 1919, Arbuckle reached unprecedented heights when Paramount Pictures handed him a monstrous three-year $3 million contract to make several feature-length films. But Hollywood's first million-dollar man would have to work like a dog to meet production schedules. So on Labor Day weekend in 1921, a worn out Arbuckle headed to San Francisco for some rest and relaxation.

The Scandal

For the large-living, heavy-drinking Arbuckle, R & R meant a weekend-long bash at the St. Francis Hotel. On September 5, several people joined Arbuckle for a party, including a 26-year-old actress named Virginia Rappe and her friend Maude Delmont. Much has been exaggerated about the sexual exploits of Rappe, but her bad reputation was largely the product of the sensationalized press of the day. However, Delmont was a convicted extortionist known for her penchant for blackmail.

Around 3:00 A.M., Arbuckle left the party for his suite. Shortly thereafter, screams emanated from his room. According to press accounts of the day, several guests rushed in to find Rappe's clothing torn. She hysterically shouted at Arbuckle to stay away from her, supposedly uttering, "Roscoe did this to me." Though very dramatic, Rappe's accusation was most likely untrue and was probably invented to sell newspapers.

The story goes that the shaken Rappe was placed in a cold bath to calm her down and was later put to bed when a doctor diagnosed her as intoxicated. The next day, the hotel doctor gave her morphine and catheterized her when Delmont mentioned that Rappe hadn't urinated in some time.

Delmont later called a doctor friend to examine Rappe, saying that Arbuckle had raped her. He found no evidence of rape but treated Rappe to help her urinate. Four days later Delmont took Rappe to the hospital, where she died of peritonitis caused by a ruptured bladder. Delmont called the police, and on September 11, Arbuckle was arrested for murder.

The Fall

Arbuckle told police—and would contend all along—that he entered his room and found Rappe lying on the bathroom floor. He said he picked her up, placed her on the bed, and rubbed ice on her stomach when she complained of abdominal pain.

Delmont told police that Arbuckle used the ice as a sexual stimulant, and years later, rumors circulated that Arbuckle had raped Rappe with a soda or champagne bottle. Yet, there was no mention of this in the press during the arrest and trial. Instead, police alleged that Arbuckle's immense weight caused Rappe's bladder to rupture as he raped her. But contemporary research speculates that Rappe was probably struck hard in the abdomen, not raped. Whatever the cause, the public—enraged by the extremely sensationalized reports in the newspapers—wanted Arbuckle hanged.

Over the next seven months, Arbuckle was tried three times for the death of Virginia Rappe. The first two ended with hung juries. In the final trial, the jury deliberated for six minutes before declaring Arbuckle not guilty and offering a written apology for the injustice placed upon him.

Arbuckle was exonerated, but the damage was done. In April 1922, the Hays Office, the motion picture industry's censorship organization, which was established in the wake of the scandal, banned Arbuckle's movies and barred him from filmmaking. Although the blacklisting was lifted in December 1922, it would be several years before Arbuckle resumed his Hollywood career. A few years after his acquittal, Arbuckle began directing under the name William Goodrich, and in the early 1930s, RKO hired him to direct a series of comic shorts. In 1933, Vitaphone—part of Warner Bros.— hired Arbuckle to appear in front of the camera again in a series of six sync-sound shorts shot in Brooklyn.

But his revitalized career was short-lived. On June 29, 1933, one day after finishing the sixth film and signing a long-term contract with Warner Bros., Arbuckle died of a heart attack at age 46. Nearly eight decades later, Arbuckle is sadly remembered more for a crime that he *didn't* commit than as the comedic genius he was.

Double Duty

Eddie Murphy and Mike Myers may be the reigning kings of double duty, but many actors have played multiple roles in the same movie. Here are just a few:

- **Nicolas Cage**—Charlie and Donald Kaufman in *Adaptation* (2002)

- **Charlie Chaplin**—Adenoid Hynkel (the Dictator of Tomania) and a Jewish barber in *The Great Dictator* (1940)

- **Bette Davis**—Kate Bosworth and Patricia Bosworth in *A Stolen Life* (1946); Edith Phillips and Margaret DeLorca in *Dead Ringer* (1964)

- **Leonardo DiCaprio**—King Louis XIV and Philippe in *The Man in the Iron Mask* (1998)

- **Michael. J. Fox**—Marty McFly, Marty McFly Jr., and Marlene McFly in *Back to the Future Part II* (1989); Marty McFly and Seamus McFly in *Back to the Future Part III* (1990)

- **Arsenio Hall**—Semmi, Extremely Ugly Girl, Morris, and Reverend Brown in *Coming to America* (1988)

- **Olivia de Havilland**—Terry and Ruth Collins in *A Dark Mirror* (1946)

- **Jeremy Irons**—Beverly and Elliot Mantle in *Dead Ringers* (1988)

- **Danny Kaye**—Edwin Dingle and Buzzy Bellew in *Wonder Man* (1945)

- **Kevin Kline**—Dave Kovic and Bill Mitchell in *Dave* (1993)

- **Jerry Lewis**—Professor Julius Kelp, Buddy Love, and Baby Kelp in *The Nutty Professor* (1963)

- **Lee Marvin**—Kid Shelleen and Tim Strawn in *Cat Ballou* (1965)

- **Hayley Mills**—Sharon McKendrick and Susan Evers in *The Parent Trap* (1961)

- **Jack Nicholson**—President James Dale and Art Land in *Mars Attacks!* (1996)

- **Kim Novak**—Madeleine Elster and Judy Barton in *Vertigo* (1958)

Alleged Celebrity UFO Sightings

It's not just moonshine-swilling farmers in rural areas who claim to have seen UFOs hovering in the night sky. Plenty of celebrities have also reportedly witnessed unidentified flying objects and have been happy to talk about their experiences afterward.

Jimmy Carter
Not even presidents are immune from UFO sightings. During Jimmy Carter's presidential campaign of 1976, he told reporters that in 1969, before he was governor of Georgia, he saw what could have been a UFO. "It was the darndest thing I've ever seen," he said of the incident. He claimed that the object that he and a group of others had watched for ten minutes was as bright as the moon. Carter was often referred to as "the UFO president" after being elected because he filed a report on the matter.

David Duchovny
In 1982, long before he starred as a believer in the supernatural on the hit sci-fi series *The X-Files*, David Duchovny thought he saw a UFO. Although, by his own admission, he's reluctant to say with any certainty that it wasn't something he simply imagined as a result of stress and overwork. "There was something in the air and it was gone," he later told reporters. "I thought: 'You've got to get some rest, David.'"

Jackie Gleason
Jackie Gleason was a comedian and actor best known for his work on the sitcom *The Honeymooners* and his role as Minnesota Fats in *The Hustler* (1961). He was also supposedly a paranormal enthusiast who claimed to have witnessed several unidentified objects flying in the sky. Gleason's second wife, Beverly McKittrick, claimed that in 1974 President Nixon took Gleason to the Homestead Air Force Base in Florida, where he saw the wreckage of a crashed extraterrestrial spaceship and the bodies of dead aliens. The incident had such a profound affect on him that it curtailed his famous appetite for alcohol, at least for a while. Gleason was so inspired by the visit that he later built a house in upstate

New York that was designed to look like a spaceship and was called "The Mother Ship."

John Lennon

In 1974, former Beatle John Lennon claimed that he witnessed a flying saucer from the balcony of his apartment in New York City. Lennon was with his girlfriend May Pang, who later described the craft as circular with white lights around its rim and said that it hovered in the sky above their window. Lennon talked about the event frequently and even referenced it in two of his songs, "Out of the Blue" and "Nobody Told Me," which contains the lyric, "There's UFOs over New York and I ain't too surprised...."

Ronald Reagan

Former actor and U.S. president Ronald Reagan witnessed UFOs on two occasions. Once during his term as California governor (1967–1975), Reagan and his wife Nancy arrived late to a party hosted by actor William Holden. Guests including Steve Allen and Lucille Ball reported that the couple excitedly described how they had just witnessed a UFO while driving along the Pacific Coast Highway. They had stopped to watch the event, which made them late to the party.

Reagan also confessed to a *Wall Street Journal* reporter that in 1974, when the gubernatorial jet was preparing to land in Bakersfield, California, he noticed a strange bright light in the sky. The pilot followed the light for a short time before it suddenly shot up vertically at a high rate of speed and disappeared from sight. Reagan stopped short of labeling the light a UFO, of course. As actress Lucille Ball said in reference to Reagan's first alleged UFO sighting, "After he was elected president, I kept thinking about that event and wondered if he still would have won if he told everyone that he saw a flying saucer."

William Shatner

For decades, the man who played Captain Kirk in the original *Star Trek* series claimed that an alien saved his life. When the actor and a group of friends were riding their motorbikes through the desert in the late 1960s, Shatner was inadvertently left behind when his bike wouldn't restart after driving into a giant pothole. Shatner said that he spotted an alien in a silver suit standing on a ridge and that it led him to a gas station and safety. Shatner later stated in his autobiography, *Up Till Now*, that he made up the part about the alien during a television interview.

Rin Tin Tin to the Rescue

☆ ☆ ☆ ☆

Audiences have always been captivated by furry creatures, going back to the days of small circuses and vaudeville, where trained animal acts were always part of the show. In the silent era of Hollywood, perhaps no animal was as famous or as talented as a dog named Rin Tin Tin. Like his heroic on-screen counterparts, this lovable German shepherd is the center of much Hollywood folklore. Some stories claim he saved a studio from the brink of bankruptcy; others claim he generated more fan mail than human stars. Most of these stories are exaggerated; however, each story reveals the dog's special relationship to the moviegoing public and suggests the magnitude of his stardom. Myth and legend swirl around the famous canine, much like they do around American folk heroes and Hollywood icons.

The German Shepherd that Saved Warner Bros.

"Rinty," as Rin Tin Tin was nicknamed, took an indirect path to movie stardom. Born during World War I at a bombed-out kennel in Lorraine, France, the puppy was amongst a small group of surviving dogs rescued by U.S. Corporal Lee Duncan, who adopted Rin Tin Tin and his sister Nenette (named after French puppets) and took them on an arduous ocean voyage to his home in America. Sadly, Nenette died from canine distemper shortly after her arrival in the States, but Rin Tin Tin forged on. From the start, Rinty's pluck was apparent.

Duncan became fascinated with teaching the young pup tricks. And he knew that he was dealing with a truly special animal; Rin Tin Tin had an innate ability to learn and an athletic prowess that permitted him to leap nearly 12 feet high. The pair frequented the dog show circuit and eventually approached Hollywood studios in search of a contract. The latter proved fruitless until one day in

1922, when the twosome happened upon a Warner Bros. film crew working with a wolf. Take after take had to be reshot as the unruly animal continued to misbehave. As the story goes, Duncan bragged that his dog could do the scene in just one take. The crew initially refused the offer but eventually relented, and Rin Tin Tin was given a shot. One successful scene later, the breakout sensation of *The Man from Hell's River* (1922) was on his way.

Such good fortune had come none too soon for the studio. Warner Bros. was trying to establish itself as a major studio and needed cash flow, a higher profile, and new strategies to make that happen. *The Man from Hell's River* helped give them a success to tout and money to pay off debts incurred during a turbulent time. Subsequent films featuring Rin Tin Tin kept the gravy train rolling and put the studio firmly in the black. In a cutthroat town where countless human actors had failed, Rinty, the German shepherd, prevailed. It was an outcome that Hollywood itself would be hard-pressed to dream up.

Rin Tin Tin starred in 27 successful movies, a feat that earned him the nickname "the mortgage lifter." At the height of his popularity, the canine reportedly pulled down $6,000 per week and attracted 40,000 fan letters per month, though these figures vary based on the source. All suggest he was an animal star of unprecedented magnitude. Fanzines claimed that, like any coddled star, Rinty received his share of perks—a tenderloin steak was his for the barking each day, a delicacy allegedly prepared by his own private chef.

In making a successful transition from silent films to "talkies," the dog won the hearts of millions. Rin Tin Tin's last project was a serial titled *Lightning Warrior* (1931). Later that year, the famous dog retired. Sadly, his "out to pasture" years were short-lived. In 1932, Rin Tin Tin passed away. Legend has it that he died in the adoring arms of his Beverly Hills neighbor, blonde bombshell Jean Harlow. Though Rinty was originally buried in California, Duncan had his remains reinterred in his native France, in *Cimetie're Des Chiens* (a cemetery for dogs) in Paris, as a gesture of honor.

Rin Tin Tin's offspring effectively kept the dog's name alive for years to come, and while successful, they lacked the charisma and special abilities of the original. There were also many imitators at other studios, but they were little more than understudies. There was only one *original* Rin Tin Tin.

Fast Facts: Marilyn Monroe

- Marilyn Monroe was born in Los Angeles on June 1, 1926. The name on her birth certificate was Norma Jean Mortenson, but she was baptized Norma Jean Baker—with her mother's last name—because the identity of her father was considered undetermined.

- Monroe's mother suffered from bipolar disorder and spent much of her life in mental institutions. As a result, Marilyn spent two years of her childhood at the Los Angeles Orphans Home. She also lived in many foster homes as a child.

- Marilyn Monroe was married three times: first, in 1942, to 21-year-old Jim Dougherty. The two had only dated for six months before their wedding, but Marilyn was anxious to escape her unhappy childhood, and her foster parents encouraged her to get married. Monroe and Dougherty divorced in 1946 when Marilyn began to focus on her modeling career. Next, in 1954, she famously married Joe DiMaggio after two years of dating. They divorced nine months later. Finally, Monroe married playwright Arthur Miller in 1956. They stayed together until 1961.

- Monroe signed her first acting contract in August 1946. The deal with 20th Century Fox paid her $125 per week.

- By the time she was a teenager, Marilyn Monroe had very dark blonde hair, which, in black-and-white photographs, sometimes looked brunette. While working as a model in her late teens, she gradually lightened her hair. With the change in hair color, Monroe got more modeling jobs.

- Monroe has been featured in numerous tributes in American culture. Elton John's song "Candle in the Wind" was written in her honor. Her image also graced a commemorative U.S. postage stamp created in 1995.

- Monroe won the Golden Globe for Best Motion Picture Actress for her role in Some Like It Hot (1959). She was also named the *female World Film Favorite at the Golden Globes in 1954 and again in 1962, but she was never nominated for an Oscar.*

- *Contrary to her on-screen persona, Marilyn Monroe loved to read Tolstoy and other classic writers. In fact, while she was under contract at Fox, she was enrolled at UCLA, studying literature.*

- Playboy *magazine has shown plenty of love for MM over the years. The men's magazine first featured Monroe in 1953 as "Sweetheart of the Month" in its debut issue. (Hugh Hefner reportedly paid $500 for the rights to her nude photo—a shot taken seven years prior for which Monroe herself had only received $50.)*

- *Fed up with being typecast as the dumb blonde, Marilyn Monroe defied 20th Century Fox at the height of her popularity and moved to New York City to study with legendary teacher Lee Strasberg at the Actors Studio. Strasberg had enormous respect for her talent as an actress—not her image as a sex goddess.*

- *Though she used the name Marilyn Monroe as early as 1946, she didn't legally take on the moniker until a decade later. Monroe was her mother's maiden name.*

- *Hollywood folklore says that during the production of* Some Like It Hot *(1959) Monroe's notorious habit of being late or not showing up escalated and that when she did show up, she often needed dozens of takes to get even the simplest of lines correct. Few realize that part of the reason for her behavior was due to a miscarriage that occurred during the film's shooting schedule. Monroe was battling a profound depression and was relying on prescription drugs to help her sleep and to wake her up.*

- *Marilyn Monroe completed 29 films during her career. She was working on her last—Something's Got to Give—when she died on August 5, 1962. The film was never released.*

- *Marilyn Monroe is buried at the Corridor of Memories, marker #24, at Westwood Memorial Park in Los Angeles.*

The Weird, Wacky, and Wonderful *Wizard of Oz*

Ah, *The Wizard of Oz*. This movie is to cinema what *Moby Dick* is to literature: essential and timeless, a classic example of an art form at its best. If you haven't seen it . . . but wait—who hasn't seen it? In fact, when considering theatrical releases, rereleases, countless television broadcasts, and relentless video and DVD sales, the film is widely believed to be the most-viewed film in history.

The story behind the making of *The Wizard of Oz* (1939) is almost as entertaining as the movie itself. High drama was everywhere on the set, and legend and lore have only added to the mystique. Read on for some inside info on the movie that's invited millions of viewers to "follow the yellow brick road."

The Story

When L. Frank Baum wrote the book *The Wonderful Wizard of Oz* back in 1900, he had no idea what he was starting. The story follows the adventures of Dorothy Gale, a young girl from Kansas, who, along with her dog, Toto, gets caught up in a tornado and is magically transported to the land of Oz. The book sold tens of thousands of copies to a public who ate up the strange and wonderful tale.

In 1938, MGM bought the rights to the novel and adapted it for film. Many details were changed, including the famous shoes Dorothy wears: in the book, they were silver, not red. But the major difference between the movie and the book is that Baum's Dorothy really *does* go to a place named Oz; MGM felt that making Oz a place Dorothy visits in a dream would better explain the psychological motivations of her desire for love and acceptance. So after countless revisions, the script was finalized and production began.

The Cast

The cast you know and love from the movie wasn't the cast that producers started with. Many, many recasts were made from preproduction until after filming began. Shirley Temple was rumored to be up for the part of Dorothy, and Buddy Ebsen was the original Tin Man. But after suffering an allergic reaction to the silver paint used in the makeup, he was admitted to the hospital, and the role went to Jack Haley instead. Haley was unaware of what caused Ebsen's illness, and the makeup formula was changed to avoid a second disaster. The role of the Wicked Witch originally belonged to Gale Sondergaard, but she quit after execs changed the character from a haughty, glamorous witch to a green-faced old hag. Margaret Hamilton replaced her. And W. C. Fields was asked to play the Wizard, but he reportedly had a scheduling conflict with *You Can't Cheat an Honest Man,* a vehicle designed especially for his talents and thus a better opportunity for him. He was replaced by Frank Morgan.

Once the casting had settled down, the studio likely thought the snags in production were over. Not quite.

The Trouble

Only a few weeks into filming, director Richard Thorpe was fired by MGM. He was replaced by George Cukor, who would soon take on directing *Gone with the Wind* (1939). Cukor never actually filmed any scenes for *Oz* however; he was replaced by Victor Fleming, who was later joined by director King Vidor, who shot the black-and-white scenes. (And you thought the casting was complicated.)

In addition to personnel issues, physical injuries also ran rampant on the set. There was the incident with Ebsen and the makeup, and his replacement, Jack Haley, also endured a serious eye infection because of the makeup. Then, one day while filming, Margaret Hamilton was severely burned during a pyrotechnics accident. When she wasn't recuperating from burns, she was trying not to ingest any of the toxic makeup used to create her witch persona.

And then there were accounts from Judy Garland later in life about the pills administered to her by the studio to keep her weight down. Apparently, the studio plied her with amphetamines to control her weight and increase her productivity. As a result, she battled an addiction to pills the rest of her life, only to have MGM drop her contract during the 1950s because the addiction made her unreliable. In 1969, Garland died of an accidental overdose.

Moreover, the directors, producers, studio heads, songwriters, and scriptwriters all had opinions about the direction of the story, which slowed production and fired up more than a few tempers. Originally, there was a singing contest number in *Oz* in which Dorothy's "hip" vocal style won the hearts of the Munchkins. A group number known as "The Jitterbug" was taken out of the movie after five weeks and thousands of dollars were spent filming it, and, astonishingly, "Over the Rainbow," Dorothy's sweet, sad song (ranked No. 1 on the American Film Institute's list of 100 Greatest Songs in American Films), was also cut from the picture because the studio thought the film was running too long. Producer Arthur Freed and lyricist Harold Arlen, convinced of the song's power, lobbied hard for MGM founder Louis B. Mayer to put it back in. He begrudgingly agreed, which was a smart move because it won the Academy Award for Best Song. The movie itself won an Oscar for Best Original Score and was nominated for Best Picture as well as three technical awards.

The Reception

The film that cost MGM $2.8 million to produce was released in 1939 and made $3 million in its first theatrical run. Because of advertising and distribution costs, that wasn't enough of a profit for the studio to consider it a success, so ten years later, the film was rereleased and earned an additional $1.5 million, which made the producers happy.

But *The Wizard of Oz* is often considered "the movie that television made." In 1956, CBS broadcast the movie to an audience of 45 million viewers—even though most people at the time didn't have color TV sets and therefore never saw the movie's sequences in Technicolor. Three years later, the movie was broadcast again as a two-hour Christmas special and the response was overwhelming. People loved *The Wizard of Oz* so much that the movie was broadcast every year for decades, traditionally around special holidays, first by CBS, then by NBC. You can still catch it on cable channels or just reach into your video or DVD library. *The Wizard of Oz* has enjoyed some of the highest home video/DVD sales in history— millions of people own a copy of one of the many editions available for home viewing.

Howard Hughes

☆ ☆ ☆ ☆

Howard Hughes has been called many things: gifted, eccentric, reckless, crazy. The brilliant billionaire made his fortune in media, aviation, and Hollywood, but his life was tempered by bizarre personal habits and activities.

A Little Texan

Born in 1905, in the suburbs of Houston, Texas, Howard Robard Hughes Jr. was the son of an entrepreneurial oil baron and an overprotective mother. His father pioneered a revolutionary bit for drilling oil and made a fortune with the Hughes Tool Company. His mother, fearing sickness for her son, rushed the boy to the doctor at the slightest hint of illness. If residents of the neighborhood suffered from bouts of colds or flu, she would bundle Howard off to a safe distance until the maladies passed. Not surprisingly, a fear of germs would plague Howard all of his life.

At age 14, Hughes took his first flying lessons, which triggered his lifelong love affair with the great blue yonder. He showed an interest and proficiency in math and engineering and briefly attended classes at Caltech in California and Rice University in Texas. But the unexpected deaths of both of his parents in the early 1920s left Howard rich (he inherited nearly a million dollars) and alone before his 20th birthday.

California, Here He Comes

While attending college in California, Howard was exposed to the Hollywood film industry through his uncle, Rupert Hughes, a screenwriter. This fostered Howard's new-found dream to produce movies. Through shrewd business investments, he managed to parlay his inheritance into a serious fortune, which gave him the means to pursue his interest in films.

In 1925, he married a young woman named Ella Rice, and the newlyweds moved to Los Angeles. His first film production, *Swell Hogan* (1926), was so bad that it was never released, despite his investment of $60,000. But with *Hell's Angels* in 1930, he turned things around. At nearly $4 million in production costs, it was by far the most expensive movie made at the time, and it was loaded with Hughes's favorite subject—airplanes. Although he was pleased with the final product itself, the film had another cost—Rice divorced Hughes. She couldn't deal with his propensity for working up to 36 hours straight and felt completely shut out of his life.

Thereafter, Hughes, ever the tall and handsome Texan, spent time with many Hollywood beauties. At one point or another, he was seen in the company of Katharine Hepburn, Bette Davis, Carole Lombard, Ava Gardner, Ginger Rogers, Terry Moore, and Jean Peters, whom he eventually married in 1957 (and divorced in 1971). And while he was never romantically involved with Jane Russell, when he worked with her on the set of *The Outlaw* (1943), he designed a special bra to emphasize her already ample assets.

Up, Up, and Away

Despite his trysts with Hollywood's leading ladies, Hughes's passion was aviation. Not only was he a self-educated pilot and engineer, he also designed and built record-setting airplanes. His H-1 Racer cracked the airspeed barrier of 352 miles per hour in 1935 with Hughes, of course, at the controls. Within two years, he set the transcontinental speed record, flying from Los Angeles to New York City in just under seven-and-a-half hours. While evidence indicates that the Japanese Zero, German Focke-Wulf, and American Hellcat fighter planes were heavily influenced by the Racer's design, Hughes was unable to secure a military contract to build the plane.

However, during World War II, Hughes designed the XF-11 spy plane; the U.S. Army Air Forces ordered 100 of them but canceled the request when the war ended. On the very first test flight, Hughes crashed the prototype, destroying several homes in the Beverly Hills area and seriously injuring himself. A broken collar-bone, numerous fractured ribs, a collapsed lung, and multiple third-degree burns kept him bedridden for five weeks. Not liking the hospital bed, he called his engineers at Hughes Aircraft and designed a special one over the phone.

Another proposed contribution to the war effort was Hughes's Hercules H-4 cargo plane. With a wingspan of more than 300 feet and a height of nearly 80 feet tall, the eight-engine seaplane was the largest ever built. Although nicknamed the "Spruce Goose," the H-4 was actually built from birch wood, as metal was extremely hard to come by during the war. Like the XF-11, the Hercules was canceled when the war ended, but Hughes did take it out for a test spin in November 1947. The enormous "flying boat" was airborne for nearly a mile, coasting at 135 miles per hour a mere 70 feet above the waters of Long Beach, California. It was the only time the Spruce Goose would fly.

A Restless Tenant

During his career, Hughes owned Trans World Airlines (TWA), as well as RKO movie studios, but when he reached age 60, he began to shun his businesses and live in opulent and luxurious hotels in America, Central America, and the Caribbean. Locating himself in the top-floor penthouse, he would often buy the hotel that rested below his feet. In Las Vegas, Hughes lived in constant fear of radiation from nearby nuclear experiments—going so far as to offer $1 million to President Lyndon Johnson in 1968 if he would stop the atomic tests.

By now, Hughes's germ phobia—along with a longtime addiction to codeine and other painkillers—had led to bizarre habits and rituals. Since the late 1950s, his diet had consisted mostly of fresh whole milk, pecans, chocolate bars with almonds, and bottled water. Unless traveling, he spent his time stark naked in darkened rooms, declining to meet with anyone except his closest aides. He refused to touch anything unless he used a tissue as a barrier between his hands and the object, and he ordered his staff to save his urine in sealed containers. By 1970, his health had deteriorated so much that the once-robust 6'4" Hughes weighed less than 100 pounds. His hair and beard were long, shaggy, and gray; the nails on his fingers and toes were inches long; and his teeth had literally rotted in his mouth. He died of kidney failure in April 5, 1976, aboard a private plane en route to his hometown of Houston.

College Movies

Ah, the old alma mater. If you're feeling nostalgic for your college days, or you've never been to college and want to know what it's like, or you're just looking for some entertaining movies, this list of classic college flicks is a great place to start—no designated driver needed.

Animal House (1978)
This is the comedy that started the trend for anti-establishment college humor and is probably where you should start if you're new to the college flick genre. Starring the late John Belushi as part of a group of misfit frat boys, *Animal House* shows you what happens when fraternities stop being polite . . . and start drinking beer. It's worth mentioning that this film has been deemed "culturally significant" by the National Film Preservation Board and is on the National Film Registry.

Revenge of the Nerds (1984)
The title tells you pretty much all you need to know about this film. Pitted against a harassing fraternity, the nerds of fictional Adams College—you guessed it—take their revenge. Do they get the girls, the fun, and the bragging rights? Grab a brewskie, slap on your favorite pair of nerd glasses, and see for yourself.

Real Genius (1985)
Who says smart kids can't be cool? A young Val Kilmer and his band of uber-smart college friends make their way through heavy science classes, but not without pulling pranks that you wish you'd thought of. There's less drinking in this flick than other college movies, and the female characters are not merely sex objects, but *Real Genius* delivers the college goods nonetheless thanks to the smart direction of Martha Coolidge.

Back to School (1986)
Could this be the first college movie with a message? Perhaps. Stand-up comedian Rodney Dangerfield stars as a self-made millionaire who goes to school to earn the respect of his son, who attends the same college. While the son contends with snobby classmates, Dangerfield's character learns that the value of an education isn't just a path to earning money.

But the message is less important than Dangerfield's outrageous wardrobe and constant barrage of well-timed one-liners.

Rudy (1993)

Based on a true story, *Rudy* follows the college career of Daniel "Rudy" Ruettiger (played by a young Sean Astin), a guy who wanted more than anything to play football for the University of Notre Dame. Trouble is, he doesn't have the right stuff. Or does he? This one might make you cry.

Good Will Hunting (1997)

Devilishly handsome and crazy-smart 20-year-old Will Hunting (born and bred in working-class South Boston) is employed as a janitor at MIT when his high intelligence is discovered by the math department and encouraged by a caring psychologist played by Robin Williams. The title character is brought to life by up-and-coming star Matt Damon, who wrote the film with his real-life best bud and costar, Ben Affleck. This ivy-league movie launched the Matt and Ben craze, in which Damon and Affleck were constantly in the media, culminating in an off-Broadway play by two female playwrights lampooning their tabloid stardom. More importantly, the boys won the Oscar that year for Best Original Screenplay.

Road Trip (2000)

Not a film for the weak-stomached or the uptight, *Road Trip* tells the story of college chums basically running amok. There are sight gags, gross outs, and a lot of decision-making based on the one thing on everyone's mind: sex. Prankster/comedian Tom Green headlines this college film that takes it on the road.

Slackers (2002)

In the movie poster for *Slackers*, a character holds a sign that reads: "When all else fails…cheat." That's the thesis of this movie—one your parents probably shouldn't watch if you're about to go to school. A group of slackers try to take the easy road through college but encounter some trouble along the way. Watch for girls, beer, pranks, and zero homework.

Old School (2003)

Many folks claim their college years were the best times of their lives. In *Old School*, starring Vince Vaughn, Will Ferrell, and Luke Wilson, we see what it might be like to try and relive those days—but without actually going to school. There are plenty of laughs and more than a few gross-out moments in this nontraditional college film.

Film Noir

☆ ☆ ☆ ☆

Hardboiled gumshoes and treacherous dames, pervasive corruption and irresistible temptation, deceit, betrayal, and murder—these are the trappings of film noir, a dark and nihilistic genre of film that evolved in Hollywood in the 1940s and has remained influential ever since.

Film noir was born out of two unrelated modes of storytelling. In the period between the two world wars, American pulp novels by writers such as Raymond Chandler, Dashiell Hammett, and James M. Cain explored a shadowy world of second-rate private detectives and marginalized drifters who were drawn into a web of crime. During that same time, the German film industry was fascinated with a dark style of moviemaking known as Expressionism that featured distorted sets and stark contrasts between light and shadow. Many German filmmakers immigrated to America in the late 1920s and early 1930s, and they and their new Hollywood colleagues applied the Expressionist visual style to those hardboiled American crime dramas. The result was a perfect match of theme and visual style that would come to be known as film noir.

The Conventions

At the heart of every film noir lies a mystery and a protagonist seeking to untangle it. Invariably, the mystery proves to be deeper and more disturbing than it first appeared, and the filmmaker's true purpose in sending the hero on this journey is to reveal the widespread corruption and moral decay that characterizes modern society. To that end, the hero is typically a flawed figure who lacks the capacity to untangle the web of deceit that surrounds him. Instead, he is a pawn to the whims of the conspirators who run the show and doesn't come to fully understand their machinations until it's too late. And his greatest threat comes not from gun-toting thugs or the corrupt powerbrokers who control them but from the beautiful and provocative woman who seduces and betrays him—the femme fatale.

Visually, noir films are characterized by the highly controlled use of lighting. Settings are frequently dominated by shadows that

create a barred motif or weblike pattern, suggesting that the characters are hopelessly trapped. Rain-slicked streets crowded with neon signs become menacing pathways of alternating dark and light, and skewed camera angles suggest a world gone awry. These distorting visual techniques convey the world as an endless maze that offers the characters no chance of escape.

Film noir also often employs nonlinear narrative, meaning that events in the story are revealed to the viewer out of chronological order, which contributes to the disorienting feel of the films. The classic *Out of the Past* (1947) starring Robert Mitchum and Jane Greer—often named as one of the best examples of the genre—makes heavy use of this technique to convey the idea that the characters can never escape their past. *The Killers* (1946), Burt Lancaster's debut film, offers one of the most extreme examples of this. The film opens with the death of the main character and then proceeds to tell the sorry tale that led to his violent end.

The Classics

Though the classic period of the genre lasted less than 20 years (from the early 1940s to the late 1950s), there are plenty of excellent examples for movie buffs to choose from, such as *Double Indemnity* (1944) with Fred MacMurray and Barbara Stanwyck; *Scarlet Street* (1945) starring Edward G. Robinson and Joan Bennett; *The Big Sleep* (1946) with Humphrey Bogart and Lauren Bacall; and *Kiss Me Deadly* (1955) starring Ralph Meeker. Though purists will claim that the only true noirs come from this period, there are also more recent films—often called neo-noirs—that capture the spirit of the genre, such as *Chinatown* (1974), *Body Heat* (1981), *L.A. Confidential* (1997), and *Memento* (2000).

Who's Haunting Hollywood?

Sure, there are literally dozens of maps that will lead you to places where you can see the stars in Hollywood. But where do you go when you want to see the ghosts of the stars? Well, if you're looking for a who's who among Hollywood's ghostly greats, read on . . . if you dare!

Peg Entwistle

The Hollywood sign stands as a beacon of hope for aspiring actors and actresses. Unfortunately, the sign is also the site where down-on-her-luck actress Lillian Millicent "Peg" Entwistle jumped to her death in 1932. Her ghostly apparition is sometimes seen near the sign.

Victor Kilian

Grauman's Chinese Theatre is the place to see all sorts of famous people. And you might even see the ghost of actor Victor Kilian walking along the sidewalk in front of the theater. During his career, Kilian appeared in more than 100 movies, including *Reap the Wild Wind* (1942) and *The Ox-Bow Incident* (1943), and TV shows, such as *The Jeffersons* and *Mary Hartman, Mary Hartman*. In 1979, at age 88, he was murdered by burglars in his apartment near the theater. His killers were never caught, which may be why his ghost cannot rest in peace.

George Reeves

Another ghost said not to rest in peace belongs to "Man of Steel!" George Reeves. Gaining success as TV's Superman, Reeves once owned a home on Benedict Canyon Drive—the very home he was found dead inside, the victim of an apparent self-inflicted gunshot wound. Reeves's spirit is said to be felt throughout the home to this day. Some say it's because he's trying to tell people that he was actually murdered.

Lon Chaney

Known as "The Man of a Thousand Faces" because of his expertise with makeup, Lon Chaney may have frightened millions of moviegoers while he was alive with his roles as the title character in *The Phantom of the Opera* (1925) and Quasimodo in *The Hunchback of Notre Dame* (1923), but he appears to have settled down after death. Although he rarely frightens anyone, his ghost is often seen lurking around Universal Studios' sound stage No. 28, where *Phantom* was shot.

Harry Houdini

He promised his wife that he would return from the dead if at all possible, so it's no surprise that Harry Houdini's ghost is seen at the site of his former home on Laurel Canyon Boulevard. What is surprising is that the house was demolished many years ago, and Houdini's ghost simply wanders around what's left of it.

Rudolph Valentino

It seems that not even death could stop Rudolph Valentino from going on the prowl. The ghost of the eternal ladies man is sometimes seen wandering around the costume department of Paramount Studios, supposedly wearing his costume from *The Sheik* (1921). Valentino is entombed in the Hollywood Forever Cemetery, which butts up against the Paramount lot, perhaps accounting for his wanderings. Others claim he haunts his former residence, Falcon Lair in the Hollywood Hills.

Jean Harlow

She hasn't lived there for many years, but several different owners have claimed to see the ghost of Jean Harlow inside her former residence on North Palm Drive. Apparently, her ghost is most often seen inside her former bedroom.

Orson Welles

Sweet Lady Jane's restaurant on Melrose Avenue was a favorite haunt of actor Orson Welles when he was alive. So it would only stand to reason that his ghost would enjoy hanging out there, too. Patrons often report seeing Welles's ghost sitting in a corner. Sometimes, he simply makes his presence known with the smell of cigars and brandy.

Montgomery Clift and Marilyn Monroe

Montgomery Clift and Marilyn Monroe worked together on *The Misfits* (1961), Monroe's last completed film, and legend has it that they're still working together in the afterworld, offering up a spooky double-bill at the Hollywood Roosevelt Hotel. Clift's ghost makes its home in Room 928, which the actor occupied for several months during the filming of *From Here to Eternity* (1953). As for the ghost of MM, it is often seen in a mirror that hangs near the elevators. Apparently, at one time, the mirror hung in a room that was a favorite of the blonde bombshell.

Hitchcock and Stewart

Few Hollywood pairings seem less likely than Alfred Hitchcock and Jimmy Stewart. Director Hitchcock was "The Master of Suspense" who plumbed the depths of the human psyche, while Stewart had built his career playing the simple, inarticulate everyman who is the moral center of the film. But at a pivotal moment in Stewart's career, the pair surprised audiences by turning the actor's image on its head in four dark suspense films.

The mere mention of director Alfred Hitchcock's name is enough to send shivers down the spines of many moviegoers. The true master of the suspense film, Hitchcock thrilled audiences time and again with his tension-filled tales of murder and intrigue, such as *The Lady Vanishes* (1938), *Notorious* (1946), and, of course, *Psycho* (1960). On the other end of the entertainment spectrum, in the 1930s, actor Jimmy Stewart established a star image for himself, portraying naive young men with wholesome American values in various feel-good films including *The Shopworn Angel* (1938), *You Can't Take It with You* (1938), and *Destry Rides Again* (1939). Teaming up the two of them would seem like cinematic folly, yet the four pictures they made together included some of each man's finest work.

A New Star Image

The timing of this pairing is critical to understanding its success. The films were made over a ten-year period from 1948 to 1958, as the country was adjusting to the aftermath of World War II. Social unrest, the Cold War, and increasing consumerism created a less homogenized and more complicated society after World War II, changing the conventions of films and the tastes of audiences. In addition, Stewart was in his early forties, and his daring exploits as a decorated bomber pilot in the Army Air Corps had been well publicized. So the notion of him portraying a stammering naïf simply didn't sit well with the actor, who felt the audiences would no longer accept him in this type of role.

Stewart did appear in several lighthearted or sentimental films in the late 1940s, such as the well-known Christmas classic *It's a Wonderful Life* (1946) and the screwball comedy *You Gotta Stay Happy* (1948), but even in those films his character had at least a touch of cynicism or worldliness that was largely absent from his prewar roles. In his collaborations with Hitchcock, he moved beyond even this, taking on flawed characters with a decidedly dark edge.

In *Rope* (1948), the first Hitchcock–Stewart collaboration, Stewart played a professor whose pet theory holds that a superior man is entitled to live beyond the normal restraints of society. Two callous students test this theory by committing a senseless murder and flaunting it to their friends. While Stewart's character is appropriately shocked at their pointless and misguided act, the macabre subject matter of the film represented a major shift for the actor.

In their next film, *Rear Window* (1954), Stewart played a self-centered, commitment-phobic bachelor, who, laid up at home with a broken leg, thinks he witnesses a murder while spying on his neighbors to pass the time. Obsessed with proving his neighbor's guilt, he risks his girlfriend's life to find the truth. *The Man Who Knew Too Much* (1956) put Stewart in a more recognizable role as an everyman whose family becomes embroiled in an assassination plot. But in the duo's final film, *Vertigo* (1958), Stewart played a private detective who loses himself in a dark obsession with a woman who resembles his lost love.

Stewart embraced this more sophisticated star image in other films as well, playing a hard-nosed reporter in the realistic crime drama *Call Northside 777* (1948) and various rough Western heroes in a series of films with director Anthony Mann. But the characters he created under the hand of Hitchcock remain the most disturbing and provocative roles of his career.

Hitchcock and Stewart Filmography:
Rope (1948)
Rear Window (1954)
The Man Who Knew Too Much (1956)
Vertigo (1958)

Boo-Boos on the Big Screen

It doesn't matter how big the budget or how many star names appear in a movie, just about every feature contains some kind of goof or continuity error. Whether it's something as simple as a camera reflected in a window or a change in an actor's clothing from one take to the next, few movies are perfect. Usually during a single viewing of a movie, few, if any, members of the audience are likely to notice such minor slipups. But thanks to rabid fans and a DVD player's pause button, no mistake goes unnoticed for long. Here are some goofs from a few popular movies, though they're no reflection on the quality of each film.

I Am Legend (2007)
This film focuses on the story of a lone human (Will Smith) left on Earth after a widespread plague. However, in the film's establishing scenes—which were meant to show a desolate and deserted New York City—people are clearly visible walking near buildings in one panning shot.

The Dark Knight (2008)
In the opening scene of the popular sequel to *Batman Begins* (2005), as the Joker and his gang are robbing the Gotham City bank, the shadow of the Steadicam operator can be seen as he passes the vault door. Later in the same sequence, as the bus leaves the bank, the camera is visible in the reflection of the window.

During a couple of scenes in the movie, a sign that reads "Sweet Home Chicago" is clearly visible. Much of the film was shot in the Windy City.

Another error occurs later in the movie. After the chase scene through the streets of Gotham, Jim Gordon, wearing a distinctive pair of glasses, puts a shotgun to the Joker's head. A few seconds later, Gordon opens the armored car door to let out Harvey Dent. He is still wearing glasses but clearly a different pair this time.

Mamma Mia! (2008)
Some might say that the biggest mistake made in this movie was letting Pierce Brosnan sing. But there are also a couple of noticeable continuity

errors. During the scene in which Meryl Streep's character sings "Mamma Mia," the amount of dirt on the knees of her dungarees changes with each shot. During the dancing scene on the beach, the decanter and ice bucket sitting on the bar also appear to move as the camera angles change.

Slumdog Millionaire (2008)
Even this Academy Award-winning Best Picture isn't free of errors. Early in the movie, when Salim and Jamal are hustling tourists at the Taj Mahal, Jamal is given a new $10 bill. Eagle-eyed viewers will note that this scene is supposed to be set in 2002, even though the new bill shown wasn't issued until 2006.

Another factual mistake involves the cricket match being played on a TV in the background of one scene. It would take a real enthusiast of the sport to pick this one up, but the match shown between India and South Africa was actually played in Belfast, Ireland, although the commentator says that it is being played in the Wankhede Stadium in Mumbai.

Here's an easier mistake to spot: When Jamal stands at the front gate of Javed's house and tells the guard that he is the new dishwasher, his shirt changes from a dark, long-sleeved button-up to a light blue, short-sleeved button-up. When the guard lets him in and Jamal enters the house, he is back to wearing the long-sleeved shirt.

WALL-E (2008)
Continuity errors are not limited to live-action movies. In the animated feature WALL-E, when the title character adds the Zippo lighter to his collection, he carefully places it facing out. When he rotates the shelf unit after he meets EVE, the lighter is no longer there. Later, though, when EVE reaches for it, the lighter has returned.

Another error occurs in the scene in which WALL-E first meets the cleaner robot. The tread marks WALL-E leaves on the floor are pointing in the wrong direction.

Wanted (2008)
In Wanted, starring Angelina Jolie, a typo made its way onto a prop. The killing order papers shown on-screen begin with the words, "I Hereby Acknowedge."

The Black Dahlia

☆ ☆ ☆ ☆

One of the most baffling murder mysteries in U.S. history began
innocently enough on the morning of January 15, 1947. Betty
Bersinger was walking with her young daughter in the Leimert
Park area of Los Angeles, when she spotted something lying
in a vacant lot that caused her blood to run cold. She ran to a
nearby house and called the police. Officers Wayne Fitzgerald
and Frank Perkins arrived on the scene shortly after 11:00 A.M.

A Grisly Discovery

Lying only several feet from the road, in plain sight, was the naked
body of a young woman. Her body had numerous cuts and abrasions, including a knife wound from ear to ear that resembled a
ghoulish grin. Even more horrific was that her body had been
completely severed at the midsection, and the two halves had been
placed as if they were part of some morbid display. That's what disturbed officers the most: The killer appeared to have carefully posed
the victim close to the street because he wanted people to find his
grotesque handiwork.

Something else that troubled the officers was that even though
the body had been brutally violated and desecrated, there was very
little blood found at the scene. The only blood evidence recovered
was a possible bloody footprint and an empty cement package with a
spot of blood on it. In fact, the body was so clean that it appeared to
have just been washed.

Shortly before removing the body, officers scoured the area for a
possible murder weapon, but none was recovered. A coroner later
determined that the cause of death was from hemorrhage and shock
due to a concussion of the brain and lacerations of the face, probably
from a very large knife.

Positive Identification

After a brief investigation, police were able to identify the deceased
as Elizabeth Short, who was born in Hyde Park, Massachusetts, on
July 29, 1924. At age 19, Short had moved to California to live with

her father, but she moved out and spent the next few years moving back and forth between California, Florida, and Massachusetts. In July 1946, Short returned to California to see Lt. Gordon Fickling, a former boyfriend, who was stationed in Long Beach. For the last six months of her life, Short lived in an assortment of hotels, rooming houses, and private homes. She was last seen a week before her body was found, which made police very interested in finding out where and with whom she spent her final days.

The Black Dahlia Is Born

As police continued their investigation, reporters jumped all over the story and began referring to the unknown killer by names such as "sex-crazed maniac" and even "werewolf." Short herself was also given a nickname: the Black Dahlia. Reporters said it was a name friends had called her as a play on the movie *The Blue Dahlia,* which had recently been released. However, others contend Short was never called the Black Dahlia while she was alive; it was just something reporters made up for a better story. Either way, it wasn't long before newspapers around the globe were splashing front-page headlines about the horrific murder of the Black Dahlia.

The Killer Is Still Out There

As time wore on, hundreds of police officers were assigned to the Black Dahlia investigation. They combed the streets, interviewing people and following leads. Although police interviewed thousands of potential suspects—and dozens even confessed to the murder—to this day, no one has ever officially been charged with the crime. More than 60 years and several books and movies after the crime, the Elizabeth Short murder case is still listed as "open." We are no closer to knowing who killed Short, or why, than when her body was first discovered.

There is one bright note to this story. In February 1947, perhaps as a result of the Black Dahlia case, the state of California became the first state to pass a law requiring all convicted sex offenders to register themselves with a local law enforcement agency.

In the end, it seems that Elizabeth Short's death helped her achieve the fame and lasting recognition that she was searching for but was unable to attain in life.

Pop Quiz: Movie Taglines

A tagline is a short, concise phrase designed to generate interest and intrigue in a film. Without a creative tagline, a movie might tank at the box office. See if you can match the famous movie to its tagline.

1. "In space, no one can hear you scream."

2. "They're heeeere!"

3. "Just when you thought it was safe to go back in the water...."

4. "They'll never get caught. They're on a mission from God."

5. "Fear can hold you prisoner. Hope can set you free."

6. "They're here to save the world."

7. "A lot can happen in the middle of nowhere."

8. "Nothing on Earth could come between them."

9. "Why so serious?"

10. "Yule crack up!"

11. "For some, it's the last real taste of innocence, and the first real taste of life. But for everyone, it's the time that memories are made of."

12. "The adventure of a lifetime, the summer of their dreams...the dog of their nightmares."

13. "His whole life was a million-to-one shot."

14. "He was never in time for his classes.... He wasn't in time for his dinner.... Then one day...he wasn't in his time at all."

15. "Have the time of your life..."

16. "A 3,000-mile chase...That blazes a trail of TERROR to a gripping, spine-chilling climax!"

17. "Get ready for rush hour."

18. "He is afraid. He is totally alone. He is 3 million light years from home."

19. "He's good. She's good. He's just Duckie."

Answer choices:

A. *Alien* (1979)

B. *Back to the Future* (1985)

C. *The Blues Brothers* (1980)

D. *The Dark Knight* (2008)

E. *Dirty Dancing* (1987)

F. *E.T.: The Extra-Terrestrial* (1982)

G. *Fargo* (1996)

H. *Ghostbusters* (1984)

I. *Jaws 2* (1978)

J. *National Lampoon's Christmas Vacation* (1989)

K. *North by Northwest* (1959)

L. *Poltergeist* (1982)

M. *Pretty in Pink* (1986)

N. *Rocky* (1976)

O. *The Sandlot* (1993)

P. *The Shawshank Redemption* (1994)

Q. *Speed* (1994)

R. *Stand by Me* (1986)

S. *Titanic* (1997)

Answer Key: 1. A; 2. L; 3. I; 4. C; 5. P; 6. H; 7. G; 8. S; 9. D; 10. J; 11. R; 12. O; 13. N; 14. B; 15. E; 16. K; 17. Q; 18. F; 19. M

You Can't Do that on Television . . . But Apparently You Can in the Movies

When directors push the envelope, audiences react in one of two ways: They line up in protest or they line up for tickets. Whatever happens, if you build a controversial movie, they will come. Cinema's most controversial movies have caused a stir based on their explicit treatment of sex, violence, politics, and religion. Those hot-button topics didn't scare off the directors of the films on this list—they served as inspiration.

A Clockwork Orange (1971)

Director Stanley Kubrick was never one to shy away from shocking visual imagery in his films. Adapting Anthony Burgess's once-censored novel gave Kubrick the opportunity to take his frightening imagery to new levels. Scenes of "ultraviolence" disturbed much of the mainstream public but in different ways: In Britain and the United States, teens were arrested for "copycat" crimes such as rape, battery, and vandalism after seeing the movie. Kubrick was so appalled that he withdrew the film from release in the UK, where he lived. It was unavailable there until after he died in 1999. *Clockwork* was originally rated X, but after Kubrick altered about 30 seconds of violent footage, it was given an R rating upon its rerelease in America in 1973. While it was still rated X, it was nominated for four Oscars but did not win any.

The Exorcist (1973)

Many people don't take too kindly to images of young girls engaged in sexual situations. More than a few folks don't much care to see religious iconography—like a crucifix, for example—being used anywhere other than in worship. In this horror film, a young girl possessed by the devil is driven to commit vile acts upon herself with a crucifix. This and other controversial imagery caused religious groups to picket and complain, calling *The Exorcist* "pure evil committed to celluloid," especially after the film received only an R rating. Legal cases against the film for indecency and obscenity jammed the courts for several months, but none of them held up.

Monty Python's Life of Brian (1979)

Though the members of the Monty Python comedy group argue that they never set out to make fun of Jesus Christ, *Life of Brian* certainly lampoons religion. Brian Cohen, a simple Jewish guy, is mistaken for the messiah and hilarity ensues—in one scene, a choir of crucifixion victims sing and whistle a cheery tune. Folks of all denominations picketed the film in the United States and the UK, and Norway, Italy, and Ireland banned it outright.

Blue Velvet (1986)
David Lynch has always been a filmmaker with a preference for dark material, surrealistic imagery, and perverted characters. Blue Velvet is a dark, twisted film that uncovers the sleaze, perversion, and depravity just under the surface of a fictional small town in America. The film was criticized for its violence against women, including a scene in which Dennis Hopper's nitrous-sniffing character repeatedly beats and sexually degrades his girlfriend, played by Isabella Rossellini. Some of Rossellini's nude scenes, in which she grovels while completely naked in a public setting, are raw, even by today's standards. Their disturbing quality made the film one of Lynch's most controversial.

Do the Right Thing (1989)
In America, discussing racial discord is risky—it's a topic many would like to avoid altogether. Not Spike Lee. In this groundbreaking film set in Brooklyn on the hottest day of the year, the tensions between races in the neighborhood reach a fevered pitch. The movie's unhappy ending, in which people DO NOT learn to live in harmony, sparked a million conversations about prejudice, racism, and violence, many of them as heated as the film itself.

Basic Instinct (1992)
When Sharon Stone goes into the police station to be questioned by the authorities in this psychological sex-thriller, she gives them a little more than expected. While being questioned, she crosses her legs, exposing the fact that she is not wearing underwear. Male viewers of the R-rated picture went wild over the shot of Stone's, er, most private part. If you blink, you'll miss it, but that split-second shot has become part of movie folklore and has since been parodied in other films. Director Paul Verhoeven already had a reputation for shaking things up in terms of the sex scenes in his films, but the controversy at the time involved the depiction of the main character as a murderous bisexual. Gay activists feared Stone's character would cater to homophobia and incite violence against homosexuals. Protests were staged across the country and in Canada by gays and feminists, pitting director Verhoeven and screenwriter Joe Eszterhaus against each other over how to rectify the situation.

Natural Born Killers (1994)
Oliver Stone's film about lovers Mickey and Mallory, who go on a murder spree across the country, was an indictment of the tabloid media that romanticizes violence to attract viewers or sell papers. However, the director's depiction of their crimes, which used fast-paced editing, surreal imagery, and hyper-stylized film techniques, did the very thing that he accused the media of doing. The film almost received an NC-17 rating, but Stone made enough cuts at the behest of the ratings board to ensure an R rating. The controversy came when a real-life couple claimed to have been influenced by the film and went on a crime spree across the South, killing and wounding several people.

Kids (1995)
Kids today, eh? Parents of teenagers who saw this film were given a rude, frightening wake-up call. A bleak portrait of a group of teens in New York City, this film chronicles the drug use, sexual misadventures, and reckless activities of these kids using documentary filmmaking techniques, which made it all seem so real. Film critics praised the realistic film for its rawness; many viewers weren't so sure and protested the movie, labeling it pornography.

The Passion of the Christ (2004)
For the first time in cinematic history, the story of Christ's crucifixion was re-created with all the gory details. Mel Gibson's film divided fundamentalists (many of whom were split on his use of explicit imagery) and nonreligious viewers alike (some of whom accused the film of being anti-Semitic, especially after Gibson's father made controversial remarks to the press). Rumors of sexism plagued the movie as well, but the box-office receipts proved that everyone was watching: Passion brought in an unprecedented $26 million on its first day in theaters.

Brokeback Mountain (2005)
Heath Ledger and Jake Gyllenhaal made movie history when they took on the roles of Ennis and Jack, two cowboys who fall in love with each other while herding cattle on Brokeback Mountain. Never before had a main-stream studio picture taken on love between two men as earnestly as this Ang Lee-directed feature. Also, Ennis and Jack were cowboys—iconic characters representing America's mythic self, which offended purists of the Western genre. Protesters howled and boycotted, critics and gay rights activists cheered, and the Academy granted the film three Oscars—Best Director, Best Original Score, and Best Screenplay.

The Little Tramp Gets Railroaded

☆ ☆ ☆ ☆

Best known for his "Little Tramp" character, Charlie Chaplin was one of the greatest comedic actors of all time. He gave the world classic films such as *The Gold Rush* (1925), *Modern Times* (1936), and *The Great Dictator* (1940), in which he lampooned Adolf Hitler.

Chaplin was involved in numerous scandals during his lifetime, including spurious allegations that he was a Communist. But his most publicized embarrassment was a paternity case brought against him in 1943 by actress Joan Barry, with whom he had been involved.

An investigation resulted in Chaplin being charged with violating the Mann Act, which made it a crime to transport women across state lines for "immoral purposes." However, attorney Jerry Giesler, who had defended Errol Flynn against a similar charge, easily got Chaplin off the hook, noting that the actor didn't need to take Barry from California to New York for sex—he could have enjoyed her company "for as little as 25 cents carfare."

The paternity charge, however, was more problematic. Chaplin was advised that using a high-powered attorney such as Giesler in the paternity suit might make him look guilty, so he hired competent, low-key representation. This proved to be a mistake. Barry's attorney waxed eloquently over the need to "stop Chaplin in his lecherous conduct," and Chaplin was ultimately declared the father of Barry's child and ordered to pay support despite a blood test that proved that he couldn't possibly be the child's father.

The paternity trial effectively ended America's love affair with Chaplin. He left the United States in 1952 and then settled in Switzerland, where he made a few more movies and wrote new scores for several of his earlier silent films. Chaplin returned to America only once after that—to receive an honorary Academy Award in 1972.

Incidentally, Chaplin fathered 11 children in his lifetime—a son with his first wife Mildred Harris (the baby died after only a few days); two sons with his second wife, actress Lita Grey; and three sons and five daughters with his fourth wife, actress Oona O'Neill. Chaplin became a father for the last time at age 73. He died in 1977 at age 88.

Extra Credit

☆ ☆ ☆ ☆

Extras have been an integral part of moviemaking since the art form really took off at the turn of the 20th century. Usually working in anonymity, extras play many roles, from the thousands of soldiers necessary for a convincing battle scene to the harried stranger walking down the street while the main characters talk.

Extra! Extra!

The first movie to boast a "cast of thousands" was Luigi Maggi's Napoleonic masterpiece *Il Granatiere Roland* (1910), which reportedly employed 2,000 extras. A similar number was also used in Charles Weston's *The Battle of Waterloo* (1913), which was Great Britain's first movie extravaganza.

That's nothing, however, compared to the nearly 300,000 Indian extras featured in the funeral scene in *Gandhi* (1982). Approximately 200,000 people were summoned to Delhi's ceremonial mall via loudspeaker and ads in newspapers and television. They were supplemented with 94,560 contracted performers, who were paid less than a dollar each. The funeral scene was filmed in a single day—the 33rd anniversary of Gandhi's funeral—using 11 camera crews, which shot a total of 20,000 feet of film, more than the entire footage of the 188-minute movie. On-screen, the sequence ran just over two minutes.

Other movies that used huge numbers of extras include *War and Peace* (1967) (120,000); *Around the World in 80 Days* (1956) (68,894); *Ben-Hur* (1959) (50,000); and *Metropolis* (1927) (36,000, including 1,100 bald men for the Tower of Babel sequence).

Soldiering On

Soldiers are often hired as movie extras, especially for battle scenes. One of the most bizarre uses of soldiers as extras was for the filming of *Kolberg* (1945), among the last motion pictures filmed in Nazi Germany. The movie, which started production in 1943, told the story of Napoleon's siege of the town of Kolberg. Legend has it that 187,000 German soldiers were pulled from the front lines to fill

crowd scenes—despite the fact that Germany was on the verge of defeat.

Speaking of Nazis and extras, all of the German concentration camp guards in Samuel Fuller's World War II flick *The Big Red One* (1980) were played by Jews. The sequence was filmed on a military base in Israel, and the "guards" were Israeli soldiers hired by the production.

Career Boosters and Curtain Calls

A surprising number of movie stars got their start as extras, including Gary Cooper, Marlene Dietrich, Clark Gable, Jean Harlow, Sophia Loren, Marilyn Monroe, Rudolph Valentino, and Loretta Young. Most interesting of all, however, is David Niven, whose first Hollywood movie role was supposedly as a Mexican in a Western. Niven was an extra in 26 films before hitting the big time and establishing himself as a debonair gentleman.

Similarly, many of Hollywood's earliest stars ended their careers as extras, when they were forced out of the limelight by a voice that was unacceptable for talkies, an image that faded with age, or lack of support from a studio or agent. Their numbers include the original screen vamp Theda Bara; Western star Franklyn Farnum; Francis Ford, brother of director John Ford; and Julanne Johnston, who once played opposite Douglas Fairbanks.

Extras are rarely remembered after a film in which they appear is released. But their presence adds texture to every scene they're in. So the next time you watch a movie, pay more attention to that nondescript guy in the crowd. He could be The Next Big Thing.

- *Blow-up dolls were used for much of the background crowds in* Seabiscuit *(2003). The script called for 7,000 extras—a number too costly for the film's budget—so a production assistant came up with the idea of having inflatable people fill the void. Computer effects helped them look a little livelier.*

From the Land Down Under

Though Australia produced one of the world's first feature films (The Story of the Kelly Gang, 1906), actors from the "Land Down Under" were decidedly absent from Hollywood for decades—the one exception being Tasmania's Errol Flynn, who is remembered for his dashing good looks, wild personal life, and swashbuckling portrayals of Robin Hood and Captain Blood. Finally, in the 1980s, the Aussie film industry charged onto the global scene, led by director Peter Weir and leading man Mel Gibson. Since then, a steady stream of top-notch film professionals from Australia (and New Zealand) have become major players in Hollywood.

Eric Bana
After enjoying a decade as one of Australia's top television comedians, Eric Bana made his American debut in the intelligent action drama *Black Hawk Down* (2001). He capitalized on his brooding good looks with high-profile roles in *Hulk* (2003), *Troy* (2004), *Munich* (2005), and *The Time Traveler's Wife* (2009).

Cate Blanchett
Born in Melbourne, Cate Blanchett studied economics and art history in college but found her true calling after appearing as an extra in an obscure Egyptian film. She began a well-received stage career that led to television work and an Oscar-nominated role as the Queen of England in *Elizabeth* (1998). She has since appeared in such major films as *The Lord of the Rings* trilogy (2001–2003) and *The Curious Case of Benjamin Button* (2008), and her portrayal of Katharine Hepburn in *The Aviator* (2004) earned her an Academy Award.

Russell Crowe
Russell Crowe got his first glimpse of show business early in life. His parents worked as caterers in the Australian film industry and occasionally brought him along to the set. The Aussie hunk had been acting in Australian TV and films for more than 20 years before he made his Hollywood debut in the quirky Western *The Quick and the Dead* (1995). After that, he quickly vaulted to Hollywood's A-list with his portrayal of a tough 1950s cop in *L.A. Confidential* (1997), and his Oscar-winning performance as a betrayed Roman general in *Gladiator* (2000) secured his superstar status. Though notorious for his explosive temper

offscreen, he has softened his tough-guy image with dramatic roles in films such as *The Insider* (1999) and *A Beautiful Mind* (2001).

Mel Gibson

Mel Gibson was born in New York but moved to Australia with his family as a child. He became an international sensation with his portrayal of "Mad Max" Rockatansky in a trio of action films set in post-apocalyptic Australia. He later took Hollywood by storm, first as an actor in the blockbuster *Lethal Weapon* series (1987–1998), and then as a director of films such as *Braveheart* (1995), *The Passion of the Christ* (2004), and *Apocalypto* (2006).

David Gulpilil

Instantly recognizable for his lean frame and distinct features, David Gulpilil is one of the few Aboriginal actors to gain worldwide attention. His skill as a traditional dancer earned him a primary role in the British film *Walkabout* (1971) when he was just 15. Since then, he's appeared in a number of other internationally successful films, including *The Right Stuff* (1983), *Crocodile Dundee* (1986), and *Australia* (2008).

Paul Hogan

For many Americans, Paul Hogan epitomizes the rugged but easygoing charm that Australia seems to offer. He started his career as a comedian on a talent show on Australian TV and went on to become one of the nation's most-beloved funny men. America's first glimpse of him came through a series of tourism ads ("I'll slip an extra shrimp on the barbie for you") before he enjoyed his blockbuster turn in *Crocodile Dundee* (1986).

Hugh Jackman

Hugh Jackman began his career as a respected actor in Australian theater and television. He gained instant cache in America with his portrayal of the comic-book antihero Wolverine in *X-Men* (2000) and has since headlined in *Swordfish* (2001), *Van Helsing* (2004), and *Australia* (2008) and reprised his role as a razor-clawed mutant in *X-Men Origins: Wolverine* (2009). Ruggedly handsome, Jackman was also named *People* magazine's Sexiest Man Alive in 2008.

Peter Jackson

New Zealand native Peter Jackson pursued his passion for movies even as a child, making frequent use of the family's 8-mm camera to shoot films with his friends. He developed a cult following for his gore-filled offerings such as *Bad Taste* (1987), *Meet the Feebles* (1989), and *Dead Alive* (1992) and then surprised critics with *Heavenly Creatures* (1994), his sensitive account of a real-life murder from the 1950s. He then gained worldwide recognition as the director of the ambitious and wildly successful *Lord of the Rings* trilogy (2001–2003), which earned him three Oscars for the third film, *The Return of the King* (2003).

Nicole Kidman

Born in Hawaii to globe-trotting Australian parents, Nicole Kidman returned to her folks' native land as a child and studied acting. As a teen, she appeared in Australian films and television, and in 1989, she drew international attention in the thriller *Dead Calm* alongside Sam Neill. But Hollywood really took notice after Kidman costarred with soon-to-be husband Tom Cruise in *Days of Thunder* (1990) and then again in *Far and Away* (1992) and *Eyes Wide Shut* (1999). After a volatile breakup with Cruise in 2001 (which was much covered in the tabloids), she ably took on challenging roles in *The Others* (2001), *The Hours* (2002), and *Cold Mountain* (2003).

Baz Luhrmann

Baz Luhrmann developed a distinct visual style working as a creative director in Australian theater and opera. In 1992, he won international attention by bringing that style to the quirky film fable *Strictly Ballroom*. His next two films, *Romeo + Juliet* (1996) and *Moulin Rouge!* (2001), were lavish updates of classic stories noted for their imaginative visuals and innovative use of music.

Peter Weir

Peter Weir established himself as a gifted director with his eerie, dreamlike Australian films *Picnic at Hanging Rock* (1975) and *The Wave* (1977). His later work, known for its focus on introspective characters who find themselves at odds with their surroundings, helped several big-name action and comedy stars cross over to dramatic roles, including Mel Gibson (*Gallipoli*, 1981), Harrison Ford (*Witness*, 1985), Robin Williams (*Dead Poets Society*, 1989), and Jim Carrey (*The Truman Show*, 1998).

Bizarre Names of Celebrities' Children

Following their creative instincts and propensity to shock, some celebrities have saddled their kids with some truly strange names. Here's a sampling of offspring that carry the burden:

Magician Penn Gillette & Emily Gillette	Moxie CrimeFighter (Daughter)
Jason Lee & Beth Riesgraf	Pilot Inspektor (Son)
Gwyneth Paltrow & Chris Martin	Apple (Daughter)
Sylvester Stallone & Sasha Czack	Sage Moonblood (Daughter)
	Seargeoh (Son)
Shannyn Sossamon & Dallas Clayton	Audio Science (Son)
Rob Morrow & Debbon Ayer	Tu Morrow (Daughter)
Director Robert Rodriguez & Elizabeth Avellan	Rocket (Son)
	Racer (Son)
	Rebel (Son)
	Rogue (Son)
	Rhiannon (Daughter)
Forest Whitaker & Raye Dowell & Keisha Whitaker	Ocean (Son)
	Sonnet (Daughter)
	True (Daughter)
Bruce Willis & Demi Moore	Rumer (Daughter)
	Scout (Daughter)
	Tallulah Belle (Daughter)
Director Paul Anderson & Milla Jovovich	Ever Gabo (Daughter)
Rachel Griffiths & Andrew Taylor	Banjo (Son)

Casablanca

☆ ☆ ☆ ☆

*Nearly seven decades after its initial release,
Casablanca (1942) remains one of the most popular and
critically acclaimed motion pictures ever made.*

What Almost Was

The story, despite its World War II backdrop, is really one for the
ages, a thrilling tale of lost love and personal sacrifice to which
everyone can relate. And the casting couldn't have been better.
Humphrey Bogart as disillusioned nightclub owner Rick Blaine and
a radiant Ingrid Bergman as his former love, Ilsa, are simply riveting
to watch. Add Claude Rains as the corrupt but endearing Captain
Louis Renault; Paul Henreid as Victor Laszlo, Ilsa's resistance-
fighter husband; and Dooley Wilson as Sam, the nightclub's resident
pianist, and you have an almost perfect picture—which is a miracle,
really, considering *Casablanca*'s chaotic creation.

Based on an unproduced play titled *Everybody Comes to Rick's*
written by Murray Burnett and Joan Alison, *Casablanca* came very
close to bearing absolutely no resemblance to the beloved film
everyone knows today. Early in the process, it was rumored that
Ronald Reagan was being considered for the role of Rick, and
Warner Bros. wanted Hedy Lamarr to play Ilsa. But she was unavailable for loan-out from MGM, which kept her off the picture. Most
startling of all, the movie's signature song, "As Time Goes By," was
almost cut from the picture.

Luckily, the fates intervened and *Casablanca*, which was directed
by Michael Curtiz, came to star Bogart and Bergman. But the
filming was anything but easy. Howard Koch, one of the writers,
described the movie as "conceived in sin and born in travail."
Several key roles had yet to be cast when production began, and the
script was in various stages of completion even as shooting began.
Indeed, much of the script was written on the fly, with pages often
delivered in the morning for that day's filming.

But perhaps most surprisingly of all, the cast didn't know how the
movie would end until the final scene was filmed.

Studio Rush

Many of the problems were the result of Warner Bros.' decision to rush the film into production to capitalize on America's recent involvement in World War II. In fact, had the play upon which the movie was based been evaluated by studio readers just a few weeks earlier than it was, there was a very good chance it would have been rejected due to lack of interest.

But once approved, Warner Bros. went all in on *Casablanca*. The film's final budget came in at around $950,000. Bogart, who was red hot following *The Maltese Falcon* (1941), received $3,500 per week, while Bergman received $3,125 per week. The highest-paid actors were Conrad Veidt and Claude Rains, who received $5,000 weekly to play Major Strasser and Captain Renault, respectively. The lowest paid main performer was Wilson, who received just $500 per week. On top of it all, the studio ponied up a then-record $20,000 for the screen rights to *Everybody Comes to Rick's*.

Propelled by a tremendous wave of patriotism among American filmgoers, the studio's investment paid off in spades. Warner Bros. had originally intended to release the film in 1943 but rushed it to select theaters just 18 days after Allied troops reclaimed the real-life Casablanca from the Germans in November 1942. The film received more free publicity when Franklin Roosevelt, Winston Churchill, and Josef Stalin held a summit in Casablanca that just happened to coincide with the film's general release on January 23, 1943.

Award Winner

Casablanca was also a hit at the Academy Awards, winning Oscars for Best Screenplay, Best Picture, and Best Director. No one was more surprised than Curtiz, who didn't even have a speech prepared.

Today, *Casablanca* remains a perennial favorite. In 1989, it was selected for preservation in the Library of Congress's National Film Registry, and in 1998, it was named the second greatest movie ever made (behind *Citizen Kane*) by the American Film Institute.

- *Director Michael Curtiz, as well as Conrad Veidt, Peter Lorre, Paul Henreid, and other bit players in* Casablanca, *had all fled the Nazis in their native lands before coming to the United States.*

You Did NOT Just Say That!

Hollywood isn't always the lovefest it appears to be. When giant egos collide, the put-downs start flying. Here are some of the most colorful:

"Working with [Julie Andrews] is like being hit over the head with a Valentine's card."
—*Christopher Plummer on his* The Sound of Music *costar*

"A day away from Tallulah Bankhead is like a month in the country."
—*Publicist Howard Dietz*

"Bogie's a hell of a nice guy until 11:30 P.M. After that he thinks he's Bogart."
—*Restauranteur Dave Chasen*

"Most of the time he sounds like he has a mouth full of wet toilet paper."
—*Critic Rex Reed on Marlon Brando*

"If you were more of a woman, I would be more of a man. Kissing you is like kissing the side of a beer bottle."
—*Laurence Harvey to French actress Capucine during the filming of* Walk on the Wild Side *(1962)*

"He looks as though his idea of fun would be to find a nice cold damp grave and sit in it."
—*Critic Richard Winnington on actor Paul Henreid*

"When [Gary Cooper] puts his arms around me, I feel like a horse."
—*Clara Bow*

"The best time I ever had with Joan Crawford was when I pushed her down the stairs in *What Ever Happened to Baby Jane?*"
—*Bette Davis*

"As much sex appeal as Slim Somerville. . . . I can't imagine any guy giving her a tumble."
—*Producer Carl Laemmle on young Bette Davis*

"I knew Doris Day before she was a virgin."
—*Pianist, composer, actor Oscar Levant*

"She is not even an actress, only a trollop."
—*Gloria Swanson on Lana Turner*

62

"[James Dean] was a hero to the people who saw him only as a little waif, when actually he was a pudding of hatred."
—*Elia Kazan, who directed Dean in* East of Eden

"Before [Burt Lancaster] can pick up an ashtray, he discusses his motivation for an hour or two. You want to say, 'Just pick up the ashtray, and shut up!'"
—*Actress Jeanne Moreau*

"If people don't sit at [Charlie] Chaplin's feet, he goes out and stands where they're sitting."
—*Screenwriter Herman Mankiewicz*

"He's the kind of guy that, when he dies, he's going up to heaven and give God a bad time for making him bald."
—*Marlon Brando on Frank Sinatra*

"It's like kissing Hitler."
—*Tony Curtis on kissing Marilyn Monroe, his costar in* Some Like It Hot

"The ham of hams."
—*Writer/director Allan Dwan on Nelson Eddy*

"I've got three words for him: 'Am. A. Teur'."
—*Charlie Sheen, commenting on Colin Farrell's reputation as Hollywood's latest bad boy*

"If he wants to see *Chicago*, I've left him two tickets; one adult, one child."
—*Brooke Shields on Tom Cruise's relationship with Katie Holmes*

"She runs the gamut of emotions from A to B."
—*Writer Dorothy Parker on Katharine Hepburn's performance in the Broadway play* The Lake

"A fellow with the inventiveness of Albert Einstein but with the attention span of Daffy Duck."
—*Critic Tom Shales on Robin Williams*

"[Dean] Martin's acting is so inept that even his impersonation of a lush seems unconvincing."
—*Critic Harry Medved*

"[Steven] Spielberg isn't a filmmaker, he's a confectioner."
—*Director Alex Cox*

The Subtle Censors

We're all familiar with the movie industry's voluntary film rating system—G, PG, PG-13, etc. But how did this system get started, and why does it cause such controversy among filmmakers?

The 1960s, of course, were a time of social upheaval and cultural change. One part of that change occurred in the movie industry, where young filmmakers began incorporating harsh language and frank depictions of sex and violence in films such as *Who's Afraid of Virginia Woolf?* and *Blow-up*, both released in 1966. Worried about backlash from parents and socially conservative groups and the ever-present threat of government censorship, Jack Valenti, the new head of the Motion Picture Association of America, devised a voluntary rating system intended to cue parents to potentially objectionable content in films. Unveiled in 1968, the system used letter ratings to indicate age-appropriateness of films—G for general audiences, M for mature audiences (i.e., teens), R for restricted, and X for adults only. The association relied on a board of average parents who screened every film that was submitted and voted on its rating.

Tweaking the System

At first, the system was generally well received, but over time changes were made. Some parents were confused about the difference between M and R, so the M rating was eventually changed to PG, for parental guidance suggested. In the early 1980s, after many people objected to the violence in PG-rated films such as *Indiana Jones and the Temple of Doom* (1984) and *Gremlins* (1984), the industry came up with the PG-13 ("Parents Strongly Cautioned") rating to signify films that might be too harsh for children under 13. A few years later, they replaced the X rating with NC-17. At first, the X rating had properly been used to identify films with strong adult themes, like 1968's *Midnight Cowboy* (the only X-rated film to win an Oscar for Best Picture). But it was soon tainted by the burgeoning pornography industry, which, although separate from the Hollywood industry, still used the X rating as a marketing tool to tout the salaciousness of porn films, so much so that filmmakers were averse to having their work given what had become a tawdry label. NC-17 is still a problematic rating though, as many theaters refuse to show movies with this rating, and many media outlets will not accept advertising for them, making it nearly impossible for these films to succeed financially. It is quite common for filmmakers to reedit their work in order to get an NC-17 rating changed to R or an R rating changed to PG-13; *Natural Born Killers* (1994) and *Boys Don't Cry* (1999) are well-known examples of this practice.

Still Imperfect

The controversy over the rating system involves more than the question of how it affects the final version of a film. Many industry professionals have criticized the system for its secrecy. The identity of the board members who rate the films has been kept carefully guarded, prompting many to question whether they truly represent average parents. The ratings board does not publish the criteria they use to judge films or tell filmmakers precisely why they rated an individual movie as they did, and many feel their decisions can be arbitrary. Even more controversial, there seems to be a clear tendency for the raters to be much more strict about sex than they are about violence. Many academic studies have shown that parents weigh these two issues in exactly the opposite way, expressing more concern about their moviegoing children seeing brutal murders than romantic trysts. Moreover, studio-backed films, which have the industry backing to be resubmitted to the ratings board over and over again until the desired rating is obtained, have an unfair advantage over independent films. Indie filmmakers don't have the resources or the connections to keep resubmitting until their films get a more commercial rating.

In 2006, filmmaker Kirby Dick blew the lid off the ratings board in *This Film Is Not Yet Rated*. The fascinating documentary uses interviews with filmmakers and clips from rated films to reveal questionable biases in the board's rulings, and it also reveals the identity of the board members, which were ferreted out by a pair of private detectives hired by the filmmakers.

Monster Movies

Eating brains. Toppling skyscrapers. Emerging from swamps. It's all in a day's work for a monster. There are all types of monsters within the horror genre, so that means there are all kinds of ways to be frightened by the fanged, the undead, the giant, etc. Check out these essential monster flicks and learn the language of "Arrrrgggghh!!!"

Nosferatu (1922)
Probably the scariest film on this list—and maybe one of the creepiest films ever—*Nosferatu* is the first adaptation of Bram Stoker's *Dracula* and a must-see monster movie. German director F. W. Murnau uses good old-fashioned makeup and camera tricks such as low-key lighting, symbolic set design, tilted camera angles, and reverse photography to create a world that still chills, thrills, and freaks you out. And all of that without a single spoken word—the film is a classic of the silent era.

Frankenstein (1931)
Among the most recognized images in popular culture is that big green guy with the screws in his neck—that would be Frankenstein's monster. When you compare director James Whale's film to Mary Shelley's allegorical tale, it's a little melodramatic (Dr. Frankenstein's famous "It's alive! It's alive!" line is a good example), but it's still one of the top monster movies and a landmark moment in cinematic history.

King Kong (1933, 1976, and 2005)
The American Film Institute has ranked the 1933 version of *King Kong* by Merian C. Cooper and Ernest Schoedsack among the 50 best films of the 20th century. The stop-motion animation of a huge gorilla running amok in New York City still stands the test of time for ingenuity—and nobody screams like Fay Wray does when the beast gets ahold of her on top of the Empire State Building. Peter Jackson's 2005 remake does the story justice, though—we recommend a double feature.

The Wolf Man (1941)
This is one classic monster movie in which the monster is part human. *The Wolf Man*, played with sympathy by Lon Chaney Jr., is "born" when he tries to save a damsel in distress and is bitten by a werewolf in the process. Savagery and pathos ensue in this strangely touching tale of

man-gone-wild and the tragic life he's doomed to lead. Several sequels came after the release of this movie, including *Frankenstein Meets the Wolf Man* (1943), the first of the crossover monster flicks. The two monsters duke it out—in a castle on a dark and stormy night, naturally.

The Beast from 20,000 Fathoms (1953)
When a prehistoric dinosaur/mutant lizard is unfrozen somewhere in the Arctic, all hell breaks loose. The creature decides to wreak havoc on New York City. Why? Because he's a monster, that's why! *Fathoms,* which started the creature-feature subgenre with a bang, features a limited level of special effects that seem downright charming by today's computer-generated imagery (CGI) standards.

The Creature from the Black Lagoon (1954)
Universal Studios was responsible for many monster movies, and *The Creature,* directed by Jack Arnold, was its last in the classic, kitschy, creature-feature subgenre, which came and went in the 1950s. The story isn't anything new: monster discovered, monster angered, monster gets girl, monster is fought and relinquishes girl, monster dies . . . *or does it?* But the film's psychological subtext about sexual sublimation and jealousy gives this movie a depth that makes it a classic. If you like your monsters soaking wet, you'll love this story starring the weird-looking Gill Man.

Godzilla: King of the Monsters (1954)
Japan's Toho Studios struck radioactive gold with *Gojira,* a dark thriller about a gigantic dinosaur, roused by atomic bombs, that screams and stomps his way out of the ocean to crush the city of Tokyo and melt anything in his path with his atomic breath. Given Japan's first-hand experiences with the A-bomb, *Gojira* is even more gloomy and frightening than one might expect. Sure, the monster is just a guy in a rubber suit stomping on miniature buildings, but Eiji Tsuburaya's eerie effects cinematography make the lizard seem several hundred feet tall. Hollywood caught on to *Gojira's* smashing box-office success and adapted the picture for American audiences. Thoughtful dubbing, some clever rejiggering of existing footage, and smartly done new sequences with Raymond Burr as an American reporter in Tokyo helped make the newly titled *Godzilla: King of the Monsters* a sensation when it was unleashed in America in 1956. The *Godzilla* franchise has continued for more than 50 years, alternately silly and serious, but no follow-up has ever matched the original's mix of monster thrills with post-World War II political and scientific paranoia.

The Blob (1958)

Does all this human blood make me look fat? The star of this surprisingly satisfying monster flick isn't Steve McQueen, though the young actor does a fine job. No, the wiggling, jiggling mass of protoplasm is the real stunner in this cult classic. Like many films in the genre, *The Blob* is more silly than it is scary—but who wouldn't enjoy watching people get eaten by what looks like a big wad of chewing gum?

Q: The Winged Serpent (1982)

A rash of ritual sacrifice has brought Quetzalcoatl— the ancient dragonlike Aztec deity—out of dormancy to terrorize lower Manhattan. The enormous, leathery, flying lizard is nesting in a craggy loft atop the Chrysler Building, where she keeps the bones of victims plucked from window-washing jobs and the rooftops of skyscrapers, along with her precious egg grown big enough to incubate a Volkswagen. David Carradine squawks as the hard-boiled cop out to end Q's dive-bombing reign of terror. Full of silly humor and gory ideas that only half work, director Larry Cohen's haphazardly edited movie is also obsessed with bird iconography: post office eagles, fried chicken restaurant mascots, and avian architectural motifs. There's even a cameo by squat baseball star Ron Cey, a man affectionately known as The Penguin. He has no dialogue, but neither does the creature that's flapping around eating New Yorkers.

Cloverfield (2008)

In contemporary monster flicks like *Cloverfield*—the first original monster movie to come along in decades—computer-generated imagery takes the place of actors in costumes or stop-motion animation. But the theme of a big scary beast terrorizing a city remains the same. Is the creature an allegory for America's fear of terrorism? Many viewers thought so; others just liked the convincing special effects and the movie's pseudo-documentary style, which made it seem as though this monster disaster had really happened to real New Yorkers who kept their digital video cameras rolling... for as long as they could.

Wedding Bells for Jim Nabors and Rock Hudson?

☆ ☆ ☆ ☆

A lot of outrageous Hollywood couples have gotten hitched over the years, but Jim Nabors and Rock Hudson? That rumor was rampant in the 1970s, and Hudson went to his grave trying to live it down.

The story apparently started as a joke that quickly became an urban myth. According to Hudson, the instigators were a gay couple living in California who often promoted their annual parties with wacky invitations. One year the notice read: "You are cordially invited to the wedding reception of Rock Hudson and Jim Nabors." And a lot of people took it seriously.

The obviously whimsical invitation was distributed all over the country and eventually found its way into a movie magazine. Other publications picked up on it, and off it went.

The joke took a jarring toll on Hudson and Nabors, who were friends but nothing more. In fact, once the rumor started to spread, the men realized they could never again be seen in public together without giving it legitimacy.

Hudson was especially hard-hit. He had always made an effort to keep his sexual preference a secret, lest it negatively affect his career. In fact, at the time the rumor surfaced, Hudson was just beginning a long and successful stint on the television show *McMillan & Wife* (with Susan Saint James), a gig that depended on his "wholesome" reputation. It wasn't until the mid-1980s, when he was diagnosed with AIDS, that Hudson went public with his homosexuality.

Nabors, too, had a lot to lose. He had been horribly typecast because of his role as Gomer Pyle on *The Andy Griffith Show* and *Gomer Pyle, U.S.M.C.*, and was struggling to reinvent himself. Scandalous rumors of an alleged marriage to a man were the last things he needed.

Celebrity gossip certainly isn't new, but this lingering tale proves that it still dies hard.

The Launching Pad

Ensemble pieces that become popular among film-going enthusiasts are often successful because they combine a solid script and plausible plot with well-drawn, intricate characters that need only a few lines of dialogue to establish their personality. A few of them also catapulted the careers of some of Hollywood's biggest stars.

Citizen Kane (1941)
Orson Welles's fictionalized fable, which was a thinly veiled account of the life, love, and legend of media magnate William Randolph Hearst, was a box-office failure but later became a critically acclaimed masterpiece. Featuring Welles and his troupe of theatrical Mercury Players, the film helped introduce future fan favorites such as Joseph Cotten, Agnes Moorehead, Paul Stewart, and Ruth Warrick to the moviegoing masses.

The Dirty Dozen (1967)
In this World War II drama from director Robert Aldrich, a group of military misfits are spared a date with the executioner to take part in a death-defying mission. This cinematic study of racism, individualism, and patriotism launched the film careers of former gridiron great Jim Brown, versatile actor Donald Sutherland, and singer Trini Lopez, and it introduced Telly Savalas and John Cassavetes to mainstream audiences.

American Graffiti (1973)
George Lucas's loving tribute to lost innocence, cars, cruising, and late-night radio introduced a new generation of fans to the talents of rock 'n' roll pioneers like Bill Haley, Buddy Holly, and Wolfman Jack. It also jump-started the careers of Paul LeMat, Richard Dreyfuss, Charles Martin Smith, Harrison Ford, Cindy Williams, and Suzanne Somers.

Taps (1981)
A military academy mutiny provides the dramatic backdrop for this gritty drama that examines the bond of brotherhood and the military mentality. An army of young talent that included Tom Cruise, Sean Penn, Timothy Hutton, Billy Van Zandt, Evan Handler, and Giancarlo Esposito helped bring the drama to life.

Diner (1982)

The first installment in Barry Levinson's Baltimore trilogy, which also included *Tin Men* (1987) and *Avalon* (1990), this coming-of-age comedy tells the tale of a group of high school buddies who reunite for a wedding and contemplate life, love, and liberty. This classic comedy awoke audiences to the talents of Mickey Rourke, Paul Reiser, Kevin Bacon, Ellen Barkin, and Steve Guttenberg.

Fast Times at Ridgemont High (1982)

Writer Cameron Crowe, who later directed *Jerry Maguire* (1996) and *Almost Famous* (2000), posed as a high school student to research this sly observation of early '80s teen culture and the educational system that tried to nourish them. The original stoned-slacker saga featured early film roles by Sean Penn, Jennifer Jason Leigh, Judge Reinhold, Phoebe Cates, Forest Whitaker, Nicolas Cage, Anthony Edwards, and Eric Stoltz.

The Big Chill (1983)

Lawrence Kasdan's comedy chronicles a group of long-separated college chums who reunite for the funeral of a friend and reassess their commitment to their careers and to each other. The film helped launch the career of Meg Tilley and made relative newcomers Glenn Close, Kevin Kline, and Tom Berenger box-office big shots. The film might have helped boost Kevin Costner's career too had his scenes not been deleted.

The Outsiders (1983)

Francis Ford Coppola's adaptation of S. E. Hinton's novel about teenage angst, rival gangs, and the bonds of friendship didn't quite pack the punch of the novel. It did, however, open the door for a stock of talented young actors, including Matt Dillon, Ralph Macchio, Patrick Swayze, Emilio Estevez, and C. Thomas Howell and also starred Tom Cruise.

The Right Stuff (1983)

This impressive film documented the birth of the American space program, the selection of the seven original *Mercury* astronauts, and the perplexing paranoia that characterized the Cold War era. Based on the best-selling book by Tom Wolfe, the film adaptation proved newcomers Levon Helm, Sam Shepard, Ed Harris, Scott Glenn, and Fred Ward indeed had the right stuff.

Thomas Ince:
A Boating Excursion Turns Deadly

☆ ☆ ☆ ☆

Film mogul Thomas Ince joins other Hollywood notables for a weekend celebration in 1924 and ends up dead. Was it natural causes or one of the biggest cover-ups in Hollywood history?

The movie industry has been rocked by scandal throughout its history, but few incidents have matched the controversy and secrecy surrounding the death of Thomas Ince, a high-profile producer and director of many successful silent films. During the 1910s, he set up his own studio in California where he built a sprawling complex of small homes, sweeping mansions, and other buildings that were used as sets for his movies. Known as Inceville, the studio covered several thousand acres, and it was there that Ince perfected the idea of the studio system—a factory-style setup that used a division of labor amongst large teams of costumers, carpenters, electricians, and other film professionals who moved from project to project as needed. This system, which allowed for the mass production of movies with the producer in creative and financial control, would later be adopted by all major Hollywood film companies.

Down on his luck by the 1920s, Ince still had many influential friends and associates. In November 1924, newspaper magnate William Randolph Hearst offered to host a weekend birthday celebration for the struggling producer aboard his luxury yacht the *Oneida*. Several Hollywood luminaries attended, including Charlie Chaplin and Marion Davies, as well Louella Parsons, then a junior writer for one of Hearst's East Coast newspapers. But at the end of the cruise, Ince was carried off the ship on a medical gurney and rushed home, where he died two days later. A hastily scribbled death certificate blamed heart failure.

The Rumors Fly

Almost immediately, the rumor mill churned out shocking and sordid versions of the incident, which were very different from the official line. A Chaplin employee, who was waiting at the docks when the boat returned, reportedly claimed that Ince was suffering from a gunshot wound to the head when he was taken off the *Oneida*. Could he have been the victim of a careless accident at the hands of a partying Hollywood celeb? Perhaps, but film industry insiders knew of complex and passionate relationships among those on board, and a convoluted and bizarre scenario soon emerged and has persisted to this day. As it turns out, Davies was Hearst's long-time mistress, despite being almost 34 years his junior. She was also a close friend of the notorious womanizer Chaplin. Many speculate that Hearst, enraged over the attention that Chaplin was paying to the young ingenue, set out to kill him but shot the hapless Ince by mistake.

Certain events after Ince's death helped the rumors gain traction. Ince's body was cremated, so no autopsy could be performed. And his grieving widow was whisked off to Europe for several months courtesy of Hearst—conveniently away from the reach of the American press. Louella Parsons was also elevated within the Hearst organization, gaining a lifetime contract and the plum assignment as his number-one celebrity gossip columnist, which she parlayed into a notoriously self-serving enterprise. Conspiracy theorists believe that she wrangled the deal with Hearst to buy her silence about the true cause of Ince's death.

Lingering Mystery

Was Ince the victim of an errant gunshot and subsequent cover-up? If anyone in 1920s California had the power to hush witnesses and bend officials to his will in order to get away with murder, it was the super rich and powerful Hearst. But no clear evidence of foul play has emerged after all these decades. Still, the story has persisted and even served as the subject for *The Cat's Meow*, a 2002 film directed by Peter Bogdanovich, which starred Kirsten Dunst as Davies and Cary Elwes as the doomed Ince.

What's in a Name?

A good movie title should compel moviegoers to line up for tickets on opening weekend. So it's surprising to find out that some of Hollywood's biggest hit movies started out with very different names.

Blade Runner (1982)

Ridley Scott's futuristic sci-fi classic starring Harrison Ford as a policeman tracking down human-looking cyborgs was based on the Philip K. Dick novel *Do Androids Dream of Electric Sheep?* The movie adaptation initially kept the same title, but the studio considered it too long and "uncommercial," so it pushed for a change. Before settling on *Blade Runner*, however, the movie was known by a variety of other titles including *Android, Mechanismo,* and *Dangerous Days*.

Field of Dreams (1989)

W. P. Kinsella's book *Shoeless Joe* was the source material for this poignant story of redemption about an Iowa farmer (Kevin Costner) who builds a baseball diamond in his cornfield because he heard a voice. He is surprised and pleased to learn that the spirit of disgraced ballplayer Shoeless Joe Jackson inhabits the field. The film's producers were content to use the novel's title for their film adaptation, but according to their marketing departments, the title confused test audiences. The "shoeless" part of the title suggested the story of a homeless person, while those who were familiar with the real Shoeless Joe thought Costner would be playing him. This is one case where Hollywood actually improved on a book's title, because the film proved so inspirational that the real Iowa cornfield used for location shooting has attracted movie tourists who were touched by the story.

Pretty Woman (1990)

In 1990, this hugely popular romantic comedy made a star out of Julia Roberts and resurrected the career of Richard Gere. But it was nearly a very different movie with a very different title. Originally called *3,000*—in reference to the amount of money Gere's character pays Roberts's character (a prostitute) to spend the weekend with him—the script was first written as a dark drama about prostitution. Even after it was reworked as a romantic fairytale, the title *3,000* remained until test audiences complained that it sounded like a story about hookers in outer space.

While considering songs for the film, director Garry Marshall came across Roy Orbison's 1964 hit "Oh, Pretty Woman" and the new title was sealed.

Unforgiven (1992)
This film, which Clint Eastwood directed, produced, and starred in, won four Oscars and is widely considered one of the greatest Westerns ever made. The script, however, had been bouncing around Hollywood for nearly 20 years before Eastwood picked it up, during which time it carried the less-than-snappy title *The Cut Whore Killings*. During production, the movie's working title was changed to *The William Munny Killings* before Eastwood finally settled on the more succinct *Unforgiven*.

While You Were Sleeping (1995)
In this romantic comedy, Sandra Bullock plays a Chicago subway employee who has a serious crush on a man who loses consciousness for several days after a fall, thus the original title of the film—*Coma Guy*. Disney wisely decided to change the somber-sounding title when they realized that, in 1991, *Dying Young* had proved a box-office disappointment, despite the fact that its star—Julia Roberts—was at the height of her game. Studio execs figured that couples looking for a romantic escape would probably avoid a movie with words like *dying* or *coma* in the title, so they went with *While You Were Sleeping* instead, and it grossed $81 million—more than twice as much as *Dying Young*.

G.I. Jane (1997)
This Disney flick starring a very buff Demi Moore as a female Navy SEAL recruit carried several different titles before its release in 1997. The film would have been titled *In Pursuit of Honor* or *Navy Cross* had Disney not eventually paid several hundred thousand dollars to purchase the rights to use the name G.I. Jane from toy company Hasbro.

American Pie (1999)
The title *American Pie* probably doesn't immediately make you think "teenage sex comedy," but the title proved hugely successful for the movie. The original script carried the more apt, but far too lengthy title *Teenage Sex Comedy that Can Be Made for Under $10 Million that Your Reader Will Love, But the Executive Will Hate*. When Universal purchased the project the title was changed to *East Great Falls High*, but the final decision came down to a choice between *American Pie* or *Comfort Food*. Perhaps it was executives looking ahead to the possibility of having sequels called *Comfort Food 2* and *Comfort Wedding* that helped cement their decision.

The Hollywood Sign Girl

☆ ☆ ☆ ☆

In the 1930s, Millicent Lilian "Peg" Entwistle was a young, aspiring actress in New York when she was lured to Hollywood by two West Coast producers, Homer Curran and Edward Belasco, who asked Entwistle to costar in their play, *The Mad Hopes*. With dreams of finally hitting the big time, Entwistle moved to Hollywood. Although the play was a success, it closed on schedule on June 4, 1932, at which time Entwistle signed a one-movie deal with RKO Pictures and began working on the film *Thirteen Women* (1932). Several

months later, test screenings for the film produced very negative comments, many of which were directed at Entwistle. RKO held back the film from general release while the director heavily edited the picture, deleting many of Entwistle's scenes in the process. According to those close to her, Entwistle took this to mean that she was a failure and would never succeed in Hollywood.

On Friday, September 16, 1932, Entwistle said she was going to meet some friends, but instead, she made her way to the top of Mount Lee. After placing her personal belongings at the base of the Hollywood sign, she used a workman's ladder to climb to the top of the "H" and jumped to her death. She was only 24 years old. The suicide note found in her purse read simply:

"I am afraid I am a coward. I am sorry for everything. If I had done this a long time ago, it would have saved a lot of pain. P.E."

Thirteen Women officially opened after Entwistle's death, and while it did not get good reviews, her name was never mentioned. Her uncle speculated to the press after her death that she was disappointed by not being able to impress the movie industry, and the rumors spiraled from there. The real cause of her decision to end her life remains a mystery, but to this day, Entwistle's suicide symbolizes Hollywood's ability to smash the dreams of so many aspiring actors and actresses.

Pop Quiz: The Bond Baddies

James Bond films are universally known for offering up incredible stunts, beautiful women, and witty one-liners. But perhaps more than anything else, Bond fans love the diabolical villains and bizarre plots that the supercool secret agent perennially foils. In this quiz, match the Bond baddies with their maniacal schemes.

Answer Choices: Ernst Stavro Blofeld; Elliot Carver; Dr. Kananga; Emilio Largo; Max Zorin

1. In *Thunderball* (1965), this top SPECTRE agent, played by a well-known Italian writer, director, and actor, threatens to detonate stolen nuclear warheads in unspecified Western cities.

2. In *Diamonds Are Forever* (1971), this Bond baddy uses a laser-equipped satellite to blackmail the world's superpowers by threatening to destroy their military hardware. As the head of the criminal organization SPECTRE, he is Bond's most frequent nemesis.

3. This villain from *Live and Let Die* (1973) leads a double life and plans to flood the illegal drug market with an especially addictive form of heroin. Bond dispatches him by force-feeding him a pellet of compressed CO_2 gas.

4. In *A View to a Kill* (1985), this supersmart but psychopathic computer mogul—a product of genetic manipulation—intends to trigger an earthquake to wipe out Silicon Valley so he can become the sole supplier of microchips to the computer industry.

5. In *Tomorrow Never Dies* (1997), this media mogul takes over a secret military communications system to feed misinformation to the British navy, with the intent to start a war with China that his journalists can then cover exclusively.

Answer Key: 1. Emilio Largo; 2. Ernst Stavro Blofeld; 3. Dr. Kananga; 4. Max Zorin; 5. Elliot Carver

Fast Facts: Leading Ladies

- Katharine Hepburn was actually born on May 12, 1907, though for years, she gave November 8, her deceased older brother's birth date, as her own as a way to ensure that he was not forgotten.

- Bette Davis was born Ruth Elizabeth Davis. When she started her acting career, studio executives wanted her to take on the name Bettina Dawes. But Davis refused to adopt the name, saying that it sounded too much like "between the drawers."

- Elizabeth Taylor was the first star to get a million-dollar paycheck. She scored the big bucks for her role in Cleopatra (1963).

- Grace Kelly gave up her glamorous acting career to become a real-life princess when she married the Prince of Monaco in 1956. The couple had three children.

- Ingrid Bergman's 5-foot-10-inch frame made things challenging for some of her shorter male costars. Some men, including Humphrey Bogart who was 5'8", had to use lifts in their shoes so they wouldn't appear too short next to her.

- Julia Roberts, the soon-to-become "pretty woman," played clarinet in her high school band.

- Ava Gardner may have been known for her beauty, but she hardly had a ladylike reputation. A reporter once described her language as being "like a sailor and a truck driver...having a competition." He also said she threw a champagne glass at him during an interview.

- *Meryl Streep almost went to law school. She applied, but when she overslept and missed her interview, she took it as a sign that law school wasn't where she belonged.*

- *Katharine Hepburn's mother was a renowned suffragette who championed birth control before women even had the right to vote, while her father was a well-known urologist who spoke out against venereal disease in an era when few people acknowledged that it was a problem.*

- *Elizabeth Taylor is one of only two women who, in the same year, won an Oscar for playing a prostitute. In 1961, Taylor received the Best Actress award for her role in* BUtterfield 8. *That same year, Shirley Jones won Best Supporting Actress for her role in* Elmer Gantry.

- *There is a rose named after Ingrid Bergman. The Ingrid Bergman rose is a highly fragrant, dark red tea rose.*

- *In 1984, Julia Roberts auditioned for a role on the TV soap opera* All My Children. *She was shot down, and the role went to Melissa Leo.*

- *By the time she was 30, Meryl Streep had won a Tony, an Emmy, and an Oscar.*

- *An entire museum exists solely to showcase Ava Gardner memorabilia. The Ava Gardner Museum is located in Smithfield, North Carolina.*

- *Grace Kelly starred in only 11 feature films in her career, and three of them were for Alfred Hitchcock. That means more than a quarter of her film work was for "The Master of Suspense."*

- *Julia Roberts was reportedly offered the super-sexy leading role in the 1992 thriller* Basic Instinct, *but she turned it down, thus allowing Sharon Stone to make it her own.*

Before Hollywood Was Hollywood

☆ ☆ ☆ ☆

For decades, the city of Hollywood, California, has been synonymous with the American film industry. But studios didn't take over this West Coast town until after World War I, and America had a thriving film industry for many years before that. So where did all those early films get shot?

Movie Migration

Few communities have such an indelible association with a creative industry as Hollywood has had with American film. But in the early days of moviemaking, Tinseltown did not yet exist. Fledging film studios were scattered across the country, with many of them located in the large population centers of Chicago, New York City, and New Jersey.

These early film companies did not have the sprawling studios that would be built on the West Coast. Indeed, many relied heavily on location shooting, which was fine in late spring, summer, and early fall, but the heavy snows and bitter cold of the forbidding northern winters limited the ability to shoot year-round. As the demand for filmed entertainment grew in the early 1900s, studios began sending entire troupes to various parts of the South to work during the winter months. Florida quickly became a favored location. The "Sunshine State" was largely underdeveloped at this time, so land and labor were cheap. The state also offered a stunning array of landscapes—rolling hills in the Panhandle, open prairies in the central region, exotic swamplands in the south, and pristine beaches all around.

In 1908, the Kalem Company sent one of the first of these winter troupes to Jacksonville, Florida, and many other film companies soon followed. Located on the Atlantic coast, the growing community welcomed the high-profile industry—and the jobs it brought—with open arms. Local government offered tax breaks and smoothed the way for real estate transactions. Merchants embraced the studios as favorite customers, ensuring that they had ample supplies of paint, lumber, tools, and electrical materials. They even special-ordered unusual props for the studios. And the general public was thrilled to have a chance to see "flickers" being made firsthand.

Within a few short years, Jacksonville was the permanent home to a cluster of film studios, both established and new, that supplied the country with much of its filmed entertainment. Some of the era's biggest stars, including action star Kathlyn Williams and Western hero Tom Mix, worked in the area. Other performers who would eventually become household names also got their start in Florida, such as comedian Oliver Hardy. And the Norman Studios, one of the most prolific and successful producers of films with black actors for black audiences, called Jacksonville its home. The city seemed poised to become the film capital of America, and of the world, but alas, it was not meant to be.

Worn Out Welcome

Jacksonville residents soon grew prickly over the inconsiderate practices of their new neighbors. Street closures for location shooting were a common and annoying occurrence. Filmmakers often worked on Sundays, when they could arrange access to banks and stores that were closed for the day, and the idea of working on the Sabbath offended traditional sensibilities, especially when it involved a staged car chase or gun battle. Even the city government got annoyed when unscrupulous filmmakers would call in false fire alarms in order to get free footage of fire trucks racing through the streets. In the mayoral election of 1917, a reform candidate ran and won on promises of reining in the studios, and Jacksonville soon became far less hospitable to the industry. Some Florida studios managed to hang on for a few years, but by the early 1920s, most had fled to the nation's new movie mecca on the West Coast, and Jacksonville was relegated to an important but little-remembered footnote in the history of American film.

Offscreen Accomplishments

*Most actors are famous for the movies in which they appear.
Typically less well known are their non-Hollywood accomplishments,
some of which are quite impressive. Consider the following:*

Lionel Barrymore

Academy Award-winner Lionel Barrymore, the star of *Grand Hotel* (1932)
and *Dinner at Eight* (1933), as well as the *Dr. Kildare* film series,
composed a symphony titled *Tableau Russe,* part of which was featured
in the 1941 film *Dr. Kildare's Wedding Day.*

Wallace Beery

Wallace Beery, who won a Best Actor Oscar for *The Champ* (1931),
once held the world record for the largest black sea bass ever caught.
He hooked the 515-pound behemoth off Catalina Island in 1916. Beery's
record stood for 35 years.

Chief John Big Tree

Chief John Big Tree, who costarred with John Wayne in *Stagecoach*
(1939) and *She Wore a Yellow Ribbon* (1949), was also the model for
the 1912 Indian head nickel.

Rossano Brazzi

Rossano Brazzi, who costarred in *Three Coins in the Fountain* (1954),
The Barefoot Contessa (1954), and *South Pacific* (1958), among many
other films, was at one time the featherweight boxing champion of Italy.

Lon Chaney

Lon Chaney startled the world with his portrayals in the silent-screen
versions of *The Hunchback of Notre Dame* (1923) and *The Phantom of
the Opera* (1925), for which he designed his own makeup. Chaney also
wrote the entry on theatrical makeup for the *Encyclopedia Britannica*.
The article has been reworked through various editions.

Bebe Daniels

Bebe Daniels, whose acting career began with the 1910 version of
The Wonderful World of Oz (in which she played Dorothy Gale), was a
reporter for the BBC during World War II. She was the first female
civilian to land in Normandy after D-Day.

Irene Dunne

Irene Dunne, who received five Academy Award nominations for Best Actress (but never won), was an alternate delegate at the 12th session of the U.N. General Assembly in 1957.

Clint Eastwood

Clint Eastwood, one of Hollywood's most stalwart leading men and most respected directors, was elected mayor of Carmel, California, in 1986. His first act as mayor was the legalization of ice cream parlors. The Carmel City Council wanted to ban ice cream sales within the city limits because they felt ice cream was making the sidewalks sticky. This is the kind of silly bureaucracy that made Eastwood decide to run for mayor in the first place. He accomplished much during his two-year tenure but decided not to run for a second term.

Ethan Hawke

As a child actor and teen heartthrob, Ethan Hawke worked hard to be taken seriously as an actor. He also worked hard as an author of fiction, penning two books, *Ash Wednesday* and *The Hottest State*. Many actors write or cowrite their biographies, but Hawke's modest success in the fiction world suggests that he's the real deal.

Hedy Lamarr

Exotic Austrian beauty Hedy Lamarr played sultry women of mystery and was once billed as "the most beautiful woman in the world." And like her name implies, Hedy had a good head on her shoulders: Together with composer George Antheil, she developed the idea of switching frequencies in order to create torpedo radio signals that could not be jammed by the Nazis. The idea was not practical until transistors made the switching of frequencies easy, and now the concept has applications in cell phone technology and satellite communications. In 1997, she was acknowledged at the Computers, Freedom, and Privacy Conference for "blazing new trails on the electronic frontier."

Steve Martin

"Wild and crazy guy" Steve Martin is also a knowledgeable art connoisseur. Martin has been collecting 20th-century American art since he was 21 years old and has amassed an important albeit eclectic collection that he lends to museums for exhibitions. Tops in his collection are two major works by Edward Hopper—*Hotel Window* and *Captain Upton's House*—which toured the country in a Hopper retrospective in 2008–2009.

Rebel with a Curse:
James Dean and "Little Bastard"

☆ ☆ ☆ ☆

From the moment James Dean first walked onto a Hollywood set, countless people have emulated his cool style and attitude. When Dean died in a car crash in 1955 at age 24, he was immortalized as a Hollywood icon. Perhaps this is partly due to the strange details that surrounded his death. Did a cursed car take the rising star away before his time?

How Much Is that Porsche in the Window?

In 1955, heartthrob James Dean purchased a silver Porsche 550 Spyder, which he nicknamed "Little Bastard." Dean had the number "130" painted on the hood and the car's saucy name on the back.

Dean drove the Porsche to his mechanic for a quick tune-up on the morning of September 30, before heading to a race he was planning to enter. The car checked out, and Dean left, making plans to meet up with a few friends and a *Life* magazine photographer later that day.

Everyone who knew Dean knew he liked to drive fast. The movie star set out on the highway, driving at top speeds in his beloved Porsche. He actually got stopped for speeding at one point but got back on the road after getting a ticket.

Soon after, when the sun got in his eyes and another car made a quick left turn, Dean couldn't stop in time. Screeching brakes, twisted metal, and an ambulance that couldn't make it to the hospital in time signaled the end of James Dean's short life.

You Need Brake Pads, a New Alternator, and a Priest

Within a year or so of Dean's fatal car crash, his Porsche was involved in a number of unusual—and sometimes deadly—incidents. Were they all coincidental, or was the car actually cursed?

Consider the following:

Two doctors claimed several of Little Bastard's parts. One of the docs was killed and the other seriously injured in separate accidents. Someone else purchased the tires, which blew simultaneously, sending their new owner to the hospital.

The Fresno garage where the car was kept for a while after Dean's death was the site of a major fire. The California State Highway Patrol removed the car from Fresno, figuring they could show the charred remains of Dean's car to warn teenagers about the dangers of reckless driving. When the vehicle transporting the remains of the car crashed en route to the site, the driver was thrown from his vehicle and died.

The display the Highway Patrol produced was incredibly popular, of course, but it also turned out to be dangerous. A young boy looking at the car had his legs crushed when three of the cables holding the vehicle upright suddenly broke, bringing the heavy metal down onto the boy's body. When the car left the exhibit, it broke in half on the truck used to haul it away and killed a worker involved in the loading process.

In 1959, a new owner attempted to display the car. Though it was welded together, legend has it that the car suddenly broke into 11 pieces. The following year, the owner had finally had enough and decided to have the Porsche shipped from Miami back to California. Little Bastard was loaded onto a sealed boxcar, but when the train arrived in L.A., the car was gone. Thieves may have taken the car, sure, but there were reports that the boxcar hadn't been disturbed. Whether or not the car was cursed, with all the trouble it caused, perhaps it was for the best that it finally disappeared.

More Boo-Boos on the Big Screen

Moviemakers aren't perfect, and sometimes their mistakes end up slipping by unnoticed into the final cut. Here are some errors and oversights that dedicated movie sleuths have picked out over the years.

Back to the Future (1985)
In this fan favorite, Eric Stoltz, who was originally cast as Marty McFly, is seen driving the DeLorean as it's being chased by terrorists. The filmmakers didn't bother reshooting the scene after Michael J. Fox took over the part.

Forrest Gump (1994)
This multiple Oscar-winning picture is known for special effects that weaved the title character (played by Tom Hanks) into some historical settings. However, in a scene from the early 1970s, a *USA Today* newspaper is shown, even though *USA Today* didn't make its debut until 1982.

Apollo 13 (1995)
In this Ron Howard film, the daughter of Tom Hanks's character—astronaut Jim Lovell—is seen holding a copy of The Beatles' album *Let It Be*. However, the *Apollo 13* mission took place in April 1970, and the *Let It Be* album wasn't released until May 8 of that year.

Twister (1996)
In the widescreen version of *Twister*, you can see a crew member's hand manually turning a windmill. (The windmill was supposedly being blown by wind gusts as a tornado moved into the area.)

Sling Blade (1996)
In *Sling Blade* (1996), when Karl (Billy Bob Thornton) and Vaughan (John Ritter) are talking in a diner, a watch on Vaughan's wrist appears and disappears throughout the sequence.

A Beautiful Mind (2001)
In this Oscar-winning picture directed by Ron Howard, Alfred Nobel's name is misspelled Noble on a nameplate.

How to Become a Movie Extra

Q: So what are movie extras?

A: Movie extras or "background performers" are people who speak no lines into the camera but are essential for crowd scenes and other large-scale scenes. They're the people who walk by on the sidewalk while the stars are saying their lines, fill a restaurant to make it look busy, or make up the crowd at a sporting event.

Q: What kind of skills does a movie extra need?

A: Patience and an ability to behave "naturally." Acting skills don't matter because there are no lines to memorize. Age and education don't matter, and to a large extent, looks don't matter either. Filmmakers just want people who look "normal" to populate the background of a scene rather than anyone who looks overly distinctive and might distract the viewer from what the stars are saying. For example, someone with a bright pink mohawk probably won't get asked to walk behind the star in a bustling hospital scene.

Q: Why patience?

A: Movie shooting schedules can be very long. You might be asked to shoot the same scene over and over for an entire day. Alternately, you might be asked to do one quick take and then have to sit around waiting for the rest of the day. Keep a book or a crossword puzzle handy so that you have something to do during all the downtime. Soundstages are usually cold, as well, so bring a jacket, and wear comfortable shoes—there can be a lot of standing around.

Q: How difficult is it to find work as an extra?

A: Hundreds of movies are produced every year, and most need extras. In Los Angeles, the Central Casting Corporation has been supplying extras since 1926. If you do not live in L.A., sign up with a reputable casting agency in the city closest to you or check for casting calls in trade publications such as *Backstage*. Just remember to always arrive on time, never look at the camera, and don't pester the stars for autographs. And when the movie comes out, you'll get to see yourself on the big screen!

Fast Facts: Star Wars

- *Released in 1977, the first* Star Wars *movie cost just over $11 million to make, compared to $113 million for* Star Wars: Episode III—Revenge of the Sith *(2005) produced nearly 30 years later.*

- *In the late 1990s, remastering and reediting* Star Wars *for its 20th anniversary edition cost nearly as much as it did to make the original movie.*

- *The first U.S. theater run for the original* Star Wars *pulled in $215 million.*

- *The first-ever* Star Wars *trailer began showing a full six months before the movie came out. Vague taglines such as "the story of a boy, a girl, and a universe" and "a billion years in the making" were meant to build up buzz before the film's debut.*

- *The first* Star Wars *film was originally going to be titled* The Star Wars, *but George Lucas decided to drop the introductory article. The movie's full title,* Star Wars: Episode IV: A New Hope, *was not used on posters, promotions, or publicity until the film was rereleased in 1981.*

- *George Lucas was initially set to receive about $165,000 for the making of* Star Wars. *But when production costs rose, he waived his fee in exchange for 40 percent of the box-office returns. That, combined with a lucrative merchandising deal and his foresight into snagging creative control and full merchandising rights for the sequels, made him millions.*

- *The filmmaker who directed* Scarface *(1983) cowrote the opening crawl text at the beginning of* Star Wars. *Brian De Palma helped pen the words: "It is a period of civil war. Rebel spaceships, striking from a hidden base, have won their first victory against the evil Galactic Empire...."*

- *The actors who played C-3PO and R2-D2—Anthony Daniels and Kenny Baker, respectively—are the only two people credited with appearing in all six of the* Star Wars *movies.*

- *Daniels' C-3PO costume was precision engineered and fit very tightly. If he moved too much, the pieces of the suit cut into him. On the first day of shooting, walking in the costume resulted in a great many scrapes, cuts, and abrasions—a persistent problem throughout the shoot.*

- *After Harrison Ford tested for the part of Han Solo, he had the edge for the role, though early in the project, Lucas had decided he didn't want to use anyone he had directed in the past. The potential candidate list included Kurt Russell and Christopher Walken, among others.*

- *Jodie Foster and Cindy Williams auditioned for the role of Princess Leia, along with Linda Purl, Terry Nunn, and many others. Foster and Nunn were rejected because they were under 18 at the time.*

- *The character of Luke Skywalker went through many incarnations during script development. In the original treatment for the* Star Wars *script, which was written in 1973, Luke Skywalker was a general assigned to protect a rebel princess. In a later version, his name was Kane Starkiller, and he was a half-man, half-machine character who is friends with Han Solo. Later, he evolved into the young man closer to the character we are familiar with, but his name was Luke Starkiller. Just before shooting began, Lucas decided that the name might remind people of murderers like Charles Manson (who was literally responsible for killing stars), so the name was changed to Luke Skywalker.*

- *The stormtroopers' weapons in* Star Wars *were retooled military weapons from the 1940s.*

Citizen Kane

*Orson Welles was considered a genius of the stage at
an early age. He became infamous after his shockingly
real radio broadcast of* War of the Worlds. *But* Citizen
Kane, *his debut as a filmmaker, made him a legend.*

Is *Citizen Kane* (1941) the greatest movie ever made? The question
usually begets a spirited debate, but *Citizen Kane* has been praised
by almost every major film critic who ever compiled a Top Ten list
and by the prestigious American Film Institute, which, in 1998,
ranked *Kane* number one on its list of the Top 100 Movies ever
made. In 1989, the Library of Congress honored *Citizen Kane* by
selecting it for preservation in the National Film Registry.

Nearly everything about *Citizen Kane* is remarkable, from its
unique storytelling framework to director Orson Welles's use of
flashbacks, narrative point of view, and deep-focus cinematography
to the film's groundbreaking makeup, which seemed
to age its principal actors by decades.

A Hollywood Novice

Interestingly, wunderkind Welles,
just 25 when *Citizen Kane* was
released, had almost no background
in moviemaking when RKO Pictures
lured him to Hollywood with an unprec-
edented two-picture deal, in which Welles and his Mercury Theatre
company would receive $100,000 for their first film, plus 20 percent
of the profits after cost. On Broadway, Welles had already made a
name for himself (and for his Mercury Theatre company) as a daring
stage director, and he had achieved infamy in the wake of his *War of
the Worlds* radio broadcast in 1938. The latter in particular attracted
Hollywood's attention. At RKO, Welles was free to make any film
project he wanted with no studio interference, as long as he kept
the budget under $500,000. This left Welles free to produce, direct,
write, and star in his own projects, giving the director a level of
creative control that was absolutely unheard-of in the studio system
of the era.

Welles's first two projects never got off the ground because of either budgetary or casting issues. For his third attempt, Welles chose *Citizen Kane,* which he cowrote with Herman Mankiewicz. It told the story of a newspaper magnate who bore a striking resemblance to real-life newspaper publisher William Randolph Hearst. Over the years, the Hearst connection has been greatly exaggerated. But in painting this critical portrait of an American captain of industry, Welles's tale did use elements exceedingly similar to Hearst's life.

Welles cast himself as Charles Foster Kane, filling the rest of the cast with favorites from his Mercury Theatre troupe, including Joseph Cotten and Agnes Moorehead. RKO capped the film's budget at $723,000, though the final tally was around $800,000.

Hearst Unhappy

Welles attempted to make *Citizen Kane* in relative secrecy, closing the set to all but those involved in the production. But when a disgruntled RKO employee sent a script to Hearst's New York office, the rich old man was livid. He vowed to do everything in his power to stop the production and ruin Welles. Louella Parsons, Hearst's number-one Hollywood columnist, pressured RKO with threats of bad publicity for *Kane,* in addition to no publicity for the studio's other films. And at one point, MGM studio head Louis B. Mayer offered RKO $800,000 to destroy Welles's negatives—probably at the behest of Hearst—but RKO declined.

Though considered a classic today, *Citizen Kane* did not do well during its initial release. Hearst's wealth and power had diminished somewhat by 1941, but he influenced his syndicate of newspapers to suppress any mention of the film's premiere. (According to Welles in an interview in the mid-1960s, he ran into Hearst once in the elevator of the building in San Francisco where the movie was being premiered. Welles cheekily offered Hearst free tickets, but the newspaper mogul refused to even acknowledge him. But Welles was known for spinning a good yarn, so the story may have been the great director's attempt to add to his own legend.)

Despite Hearst's campaign, *Citizen Kane* was nominated for nine Academy Awards. However, when the nominations were read, the film was roundly booed by insiders who disliked Welles for his arrogance, his cushy deal at RKO, and the bad publicity he stirred up for the movie industry. Nonetheless, Welles and Mankiewicz would share the Oscar for Best Screenplay. But the award did little to boost the film's take at the box office. After a year, RKO shelved the picture, which came out $150,000 in the red.

Critical Accolades

Orson Welles's debut masterpiece would gain newfound respect in the 1950s. In 1956, when *Kane* was rereleased in theaters, a whole new audience found itself entranced by Welles's movie magic and American critics delivered the praise that had eluded the film during its original release. Movie lovers began to understand that *Citizen Kane*'s flashback structure, in which multiple characters offer contradictory details about Kane's life, was not only inventive but also a complex statement about the relativity of truth. The film's striking look, largely a product of cinematographer Gregg Toland's talent and innovation, utilized deep-focus photography unseen in Hollywood films of the time. In addition, the movie's obtuse angles, expressionist lighting, and experimental sound effects advanced the story as much as its spoken dialogue did. Add it all to Welles's self-conscious use of stock footage and faked newsreel reports, and *Citizen Kane* begins to look like the first truly modern American film. To this day, film buffs enjoy dissecting *Kane* scene by scene. Over the years, numerous books have detailed its continuing cinematic influence. *Citizen Kane* has become as monumental as its own title character.

As for the sled upon which the entire story revolves, two copies were burned during the making of the film. Famed director Steven Spielberg purchased the third sled at a 1982 auction for more than $60,000. Said Spielberg at the time: "... [It] will go over my typewriter to remind me that quality in movies comes first."

- *During* Citizen Kane's *picnic scene, a winged black creature—possibly a pterodactyl—can be seen flapping through the background. This recycled footage was most likely borrowed from one of several previous RKO productions.* King Kong *(1933),* Son of Kong *(1933), and* Creation *(1931)—an unfinished and unreleased early attempt at a* Kong-*like adventure film—are the leading candidates.*

Oscar-Winning Films

Anagrams are new words or phrases made by rearranging the letters of the original word or phrase. Check out the new phrases made by rearranging the letters of these Oscar-winning films.

All the President's Men	Ah, spilled resentment
Apocalypse Now	Swoop anyplace
Barry Lyndon	Nobly ran dry
Bonnie and Clyde	Bandy indolence
Chariots of Fire	A historic offer
Gone with the Wind	Two entwined high
Good Will Hunting	Unwilling hot dog
The Lord of the Rings	Short, frightened, lo!
The Madness of King George	Throne gagged, knifes some
Man on Wire	Air men won
Million Dollar Baby	Abominably ill lord
Mr. Smith Goes to Washington	Senator might swing smooth
The Poseidon Adventure	Inundated, hope to serve
The Red Violin	Loved, inherit
Schindler's List	End stirs, chills
Shakespeare in Love	Ophelia's keen saver
The Silence of the Lambs	Cellmate, he fibs, honest!
Slumdog Millionaire	India's ill, glum Romeo
There Will Be Blood	Robbed the oil well
The Towering Inferno	Entering fire; hot now!
Walk the Line	Knelt awhile
What Dreams May Come	Some academy warmth

Diamond Dreams

Baseball's relaxed pace combined with its rich tapestry of myth and folklore make it a natural canvas for tall tales enmeshed with true stories. Here are a few essential films that examine the character, charisma, and culture of America's national pastime.

The Pride of the Yankees (1942)
This classic baseball film tells the sentimental story of Lou Gehrig, baseball's Iron Horse, whose career and life were cut short by the disease that would carry his name. The film, which was nominated for 11 Oscars, is notable for Gary Cooper's impassioned portrayal of Gehrig, including his emotional farewell speech. Babe Ruth plays himself in the film.

Bang the Drum Slowly (1973)
The unlikely relationship between a star pitcher (Michael Moriarty) and his dying, dull-witted catcher (Robert De Niro) provides the dramatic backdrop for this examination of friendship, forgiveness, and understanding that goes beyond statistics on a score sheet. De Niro's performance as the terminally ill backstop showed a softer side to an actor best known for grittier roles.

The Natural (1984)
Barry Levinson's cinematic adaptation of the Bernard Malamud novel faithfully captures the mood, atmosphere, and nostalgic feel of the book. As the story of a superbly talented baseball player who is given a second chance at life, love, and legend, the film features commanding efforts by Robert Redford and Glenn Close and was nominated for four Oscars.

Bull Durham (1988)
One of the most popular baseball movies ever made, this fanciful tale examines the relationship between a baseball groupie, a stud pitcher, and a grizzled veteran catcher. By combining racy romance, bullpen humor, and uncanny insights into the inner workings of the game, director, writer, and former professional ballplayer Ron Shelton created a timeless classic.

Eight Men Out (1988)
Independent filmmaker John Sayles offered up this remarkable and realistic portrayal of the Black Sox scandal and the "fixed" 1919 World Series. Poetic dialogue, fierce attention to detail, and an uncompromis-

ing examination of the scandal make this film one of the more genuine observations of the murky side of America's pastime.

Field of Dreams (1989)
As much a story of the relationship between father and son as an examination of the mystical magic of baseball, this film paints a poignant portrait of baseball's ability to reunite, regenerate, and rejuvenate those who fall captive to its spell. Based on W. P. Kinsella's novel *Shoeless Joe*, it features a passionate performance by Burt Lancaster in one of his last film appearances.

Pastime (1991)
This seldom-seen gem is a poignant period piece that tells the story of the friendship between an aging pitcher trying to hang on for one more year and a young African American rookie trying to overcome prejudice, pressure, and expectations. The importance of the message is solidified by the participation of Hall of Famers such as Ernie Banks, Bob Feller, Duke Snider, Don Newcombe, and Harmon Killebrew.

A League of Their Own (1992)
This fictionalized account of the All-American Girls Professional Baseball League uses humor, realistic action, and an all-star cast to recount the struggles of the women left behind while the men fought overseas during World War II. Geena Davis, Madonna, Rosie O'Donnell, and Tom Hanks lend their talents to this charming tribute to sacrifice and sport.

61* (2001)
This lovingly constructed drama directed by lifelong Yankees fan Billy Crystal revolves around the day-to-day trials and tribulations of Roger Maris as he attempts to break Babe Ruth's single-season home run record. Barry Pepper (*The Green Mile*, 1999) is particularly effective in portraying the ups and downs of Maris's pursuit.

The Rookie (2002)
The Rookie tells the true tale of schoolteacher Jim Morris, who made his major-league debut with the Tampa Bay Devil Rays at age 35. Dennis Quaid is quietly effective as Morris, whose fairy-tale ascent from the classroom to the diamond reminds everyone that dreams are definitely worth pursuing.

Classic vs. Method Acting

Picture this: A solitary figure runs by you, sweat dripping from his brow as he labors beneath the searing sun. Undeterred by the burden, he pushes on in his quest, seemingly oblivious to any and all who observe him. Could this be a marathon runner embarking on a grueling training run? It could be. Then again, it might be a determined actor sufficiently preparing for an upcoming scene. "Method" actors often approach their roles with such immersion. Through the years, waves of method-trained actors have invaded Hollywood. And they've arrived to the shock and amazement of more traditional actors not so smitten by the technique.

Method to the Madness

While the Method may sound mysterious and, when taken to extremes, can often appear bizarre, there's actually good solid theory behind it. Based on "the System," which was devised in the 1920s by Russian theater director Konstantin Stanislavski, the technique utilizes one's personal senses, memories, and experiences to better interpret a character. Examples are as varied as the roles being attempted. For instance, an actor hoping to exhibit grief might conjure up painful memories of personal loss and fold the physical aspects of human grief into his performance. Another looking to convey wonderment might recall an especially joyous occasion. Method techniques find actors signing on for boxing lessons before portraying fighters, conjuring a bad mood to help approximate sullen characters, and slipping into meditative states to express a character's sense of calm. While certain acting techniques can be clearly described and practiced, the Method cannot. It is as personal as each actor and role undertaken and, consequently, can be quite hard to teach.

Forming a Following

Since followers of method acting draw off tangible memories and practiced events to get inside their characters, you could say that the acting appears to be nonacting. The illusion is that actors actually become their characters. Method acting became prominent in film during the early 1950s with the emergence of the legendary Actors Studio—a Manhattan-based school founded by Elia Kazan, Cheryl Crawford, and Robert Lewis and operated under the tutelage of famed acting teacher Lee Strasberg from 1951 to 1982. Since the studio opened its doors in 1947, Hollywood heavyweights such as Al Pacino, Marlon Brando, Marilyn Monroe, James Dean, Robert De Niro, Paul Newman, and Joanne Woodward have gotten in touch with their inner voices, thus adding their names to the burgeoning ranks of method-trained stars. The Actors Studio became famous for developing the Method, but it's not the only training ground for this style of acting. Other proponents of this approach include Stella Adler and Richard Boleslavski, and still others offer a modified version of method techniques. This form of training has become so widespread that many of today's top actors, including Sean Penn and Johnny Depp, list method training on their résumés. For those actors captivated by the technique, there seems to be no other way to approach the art. Nevertheless, there are some actors not quite so swayed by the Method's charms.

Make Like a Tree...and *Leave!*

While filming *The Sheltering Sky* (1990), Academy Award nominee John Malkovich practiced a decidedly non-method acting approach. In between takes, Malkovich caught up on his needlepoint—a far cry from the search for "motivation" thought mandatory by method actors. When the cameras started to roll, Malkovich suddenly transformed. His masterful performance went on to win him much critical acclaim.

Sir Laurence Olivier, considered by some to be the finest actor in the world, came straight to the point in regards to the Method: "All this talk about the Method. The Method! *What* method?" he demanded. "I thought each of us had our *own* method!" In keeping with his convictions, Olivier reportedly teased method actor Dustin Hoffman while the pair was filming *Marathon Man* in 1976. When a bedraggled, motivation-searching Hoffman arrived on the set without sleeping for two days (to prepare for a scene in which his character was physically tortured), Olivier was ready for him. "Why don't you just act?!" the veteran performer chided.

Steven Spielberg

☆ ☆ ☆ ☆

One of the most commercially and critically successful directors in film history, Steven Spielberg has changed the way we see movies. Blending chills and thrills with moral messages and unforgettable stories, Spielberg films boldly announce themselves. Read on for more about this influential director's life and times and the films that helped shape cinema in the second half of the 20th century.

Spielberg Start-up

As a kid growing up in Cincinnati, Ohio, little Steven Spielberg (born in 1946) knew he wanted to work in the movies. He made his earliest films with his dad's 8mm camera and won his first film-making prize at age 13. By that time, Steven and his family had moved to Phoenix. Around age 17, Spielberg raised $500 to write and direct his first "feature" film, called *Firelight.* The picture, which was shown in his local movie theater, made a $100 profit and later inspired *Close Encounters of the Third Kind* (1977).

After high school, Spielberg applied to the University of Southern California to study in an acclaimed film program. He was turned down not one but three times. After a brief stint at California State University at Long Beach, Spielberg dropped out and moved to Hollywood.

Still in his early twenties, Spielberg found a chance to direct a few movies on his own, including the short film *Amblin'* (1968), which hinted at some of the interests that the director would later revisit: aliens, the desert, and the classic hero quest story line. *Amblin'* got the attention of a Universal bigwig, and Spielberg became the youngest director ever to sign a major long-term contract with a Hollywood studio.

His time with Universal and other studios throughout the late 1960s and early '70s often resulted in television work. In 1970, Spielberg landed his first project as a director with part of the pilot for *Night Gallery,* which starred veteran movie star Joan Crawford. The high point of his television work was a 1971 made-for-TV movie titled *Duel,* about a mysterious trucker who pursues and terrorizes an average guy, played by Dennis Weaver. The theme was one

Spielberg would return to again and again—an ordinary man caught up in extraordinary circumstances. It wasn't until 1974, however, that Spielberg's star truly began to rise. He directed Goldie Hawn in *The Sugarland Express,* a movie based on a true story about a husband and wife who take back their son and go on the run from the law. It was this film that made people in Hollywood sit up and take note; but it was the young director's next film that really grabbed the whole world's attention.

The B.D.O.C. (Biggest Director On Campus)

In 1975, movie audiences were introduced to a very big, very angry shark. In what would become what many consider the world's first blockbuster, *Jaws* terrorized filmgoers around the globe and became the first film in the United States to earn more than $100 million in first-run box-office receipts. This was largely due to the decision to give *Jaws* a wide release. Before this, movies were released slowly, a few cities at a time; *Jaws* opened in more than 400 theaters on the same day. All in all, Spielberg's hit grossed close to $490 million worldwide, was nominated for numerous Academy Awards (including Best Picture), won several of the coveted statuettes, and forever changed the way movies are marketed and distributed. It also put director Steven Spielberg on the map for good.

The auteur's next project was *Close Encounters of the Third Kind* (1977), a film that allowed him to explore one of his favorite subjects: alien visitors on Earth. The movie was a critical and commercial success and earned Spielberg his first Best Director nomination. Over the next few years, Spielberg experienced a few missteps: *1941* (1979), a World War II farce, was a big-time flop, but everyone would forgive him when he teamed up with George Lucas to bring a character named Indiana Jones to life on the big screen.

Raiders of the Lost Ark was unleashed in 1981 and, to this day, is considered by many to be *the* quintessential action-adventure film. Starring the handsome Harrison Ford as archeologist/adventurer Indiana Jones, *Raiders* paid homage to the cliffhanger serials of a bygone Hollywood era. Audiences loved the film almost as much as Spielberg's next project: *E.T.: The Extra-Terrestrial* (1982).

The story of a young boy and his alien friend, *E.T.* stunned audiences around the world. The movie excited the imagination, offered humor and heart-wrenching drama, and, true to most Spielberg flicks, contained lots of really cool special effects. Nominated for buckets of awards, the film garnered critical praise from nearly all camps and surpassed *Star Wars* (1977) as the highest-grossing movie of all time—a record that would stand for nearly 15 years. If there was any doubt that Steven Spielberg was the most gifted director of the last half of the 20th century, *E.T.* took care of that.

The next years for Spielberg were almost too dizzyingly successful to comprehend. A second *Indiana Jones* picture, *Indiana Jones and the Temple of Doom,* was released in 1984, before Spielberg moved on to producing mega-popular '80s movie classics *Gremlins* (1984) and *The Goonies* (1985). Spielberg gave audiences *The Color Purple* (1985), starring Oprah Winfrey and Whoopi Goldberg, and *Empire of the Sun* (1987), both successful book adaptations that were largely critically acclaimed. In 1988, he produced the colossal hit *Who Framed Roger Rabbit,* which earned more than $329.8 million at box offices worldwide. In 1989, Spielberg nearly topped himself when he directed and produced *Indiana Jones and the Last Crusade* and served as executive producer on *Back to the Future Part II,* both of which were blockbuster hits.

Spielberg in the '90s: Does This Guy Ever Sleep?

Much of the early 1990s found this prolific director working in television animation. He did a lot of producing in the animation genre (*Tiny Toons Adventures, Animaniacs, Pinky and the Brain,* etc.), but in 1993, he returned to live-action filmmaking with one of his most financially successful pictures ever: dinosaur thriller *Jurassic Park.* That same year, Spielberg showed his somber, serious side with *Schindler's List,* a lengthy, black-and-white film based on a true story about the Holocaust. *Schindler's List* won the director his first Best Picture and Best Director awards. In 1994, Spielberg signed on to produce the hugely popular television series *ER* and, along with David Geffen and Jeffrey Katzenberg, founded DreamWorks, a production company responsible for more box-office wins than we've got room to list.

Saving Private Ryan (1998), Spielberg's return to gripping, historical drama, was an epic World War II search-and-rescue story that earned him his second Best Director Oscar.

Looking to the Future

The first decade of the new millennium saw Spielberg bounce from movies based on true stories to sci-fi and other works of fiction. *Artificial Intelligence: AI* (2001), the story of a childlike android, whose programming allows him to feel love, came as a result of Spielberg's friendship with legendary filmmaker Stanley Kubrick, who had been developing the story since the early 1970s. Kubrick shared his ideas for the movie with Spielberg, and after Kubrick's death, Spielberg took on the project. Reviews were somewhat mixed, but no one could deny the director's unique vision.

Also in 2001, Spielberg revisited the topic of World War II, this time as an executive producer for the hugely successful television miniseries *Band of Brothers*. Spielberg has focused mostly on producing during the latter part of the decade, but he still directed some memorable films, including *Catch Me If You Can* (2002), *War of the Worlds* (2005), and *Munich* (2005), which was nominated for five Oscars for its depiction of the true story of 11 Israeli athletes who were murdered by a Palestinian terrorist group during the 1972 Olympics.

In 2008, Spielberg released the much-anticipated fourth installment in the *Indiana Jones* series: *Indiana Jones and the Kingdom of the Crystal Skull*. It received generally favorable reviews, was nominated for several awards, and took in more than $700 million worldwide at the box office.

Steven Spielberg is not without his detractors. But it cannot be denied that the director's impact on the business of filmmaking is indelible or that millions have been moved, scared silly, or delighted by his work. Where Spielberg will go next with his career in film is anyone's guess. Though he and his partners sold DreamWorks in late 2005, we can bet that he'll revisit favorite themes. And the passion with which he approaches every project will likely keep us buying tickets to his movies for quite some time.

"I dream for a living."

—Steven Spielberg

Bombs Away: Monumental Box-Office Flops

An astronomical budget or an A-list cast doesn't always guarantee a movie's box-office success. Here's a look at some of Hollywood's more notable cinematic bombs.

Doctor Dolittle (1967)
Cost: $18 million; Box-office take: $9 million

Rex Harrison starred in 20th Century Fox's attempt to match the success of Disney's musical fantasy *Mary Poppins* (1964). Production costs soared thanks to numerous on-location shooting problems, upkeep for more than 1,500 live animals, and the fabrication of pricey props like an eight-ton mechanical Great Pink Sea Snail. Critics panned *Doctor Dolittle*, and audiences stayed away in droves. Ironically, the film garnered nine Oscar nominations and two wins for Best Special Effects and Best Original Song ("Talk to the Animals").

Can't Stop the Music (1980)
Cost: $20 million; Box-office take: $2 million

Talk about bad timing. This musical extravaganza aimed to cash in on both the disco craze and the popularity of 1976 Olympic champion Bruce Jenner. Unfortunately, *Can't Stop the Music* was released long after both disco and Jenner were passé. Incredibly, millions of dollars were spent publicizing the PG flick as mainstream entertainment despite its sophisticated sexuality. The production company incorrectly assumed that audiences would enjoy watching the Village People perform their homoerotic anthem "Y.M.C.A." accompanied by a chorus line of bikini-clad babes, naked men showering, and people frolicking in a hot tub.

Heaven's Gate (1980)
Cost: An estimated $44 million; Box-office take: $3.5 million

United Artists gave Oscar-winning director Michael Cimino (*The Deer Hunter*, 1978) unfettered artistic control and a star-studded cast for *Heaven's Gate*, a film based on the Johnson County War, a range war between large ranch owners and small homesteaders in 1890s Wyoming.

But Cimino blew six times the original $7.5 million budget by creating elaborate sets; shooting convoluted action scenes; doing repeated retakes; and shooting only during the time of day when the sun is setting. The result was a five-and-half hour monstrosity that was edited to about half that time, released in a few cities, strongly criticized, pulled from theaters, reedited and shortened, rereleased, and universally panned—all in the span of six months. Heads rolled at United Artists after *Heaven's Gate* became the biggest financial flop in cinematic history up to that time.

One from the Heart (1982)
Cost: $26 million; Box-office take: $637,000

After directing gripping cinematic dramas like *The Godfather* (1972) and *Apocalypse Now* (1979), Francis Ford Coppola decided to make a musical romance about a couple who temporarily break up and enjoy brief flings. Ignoring the film's $2 million budget, Coppola poured millions of dollars into elaborate sets, technical effects, and complex lighting schemes—all of which overpowered the characters, making it difficult to care about their romance. Annoyed by critics who panned his attempt at a lighthearted and whimsical musical, Coppola pulled the movie from theaters after only two weeks.

The Postman (1997)
Cost: $80–100 million; Box-office take: $17.6 million

If at first you don't succeed, try, try again. Or in Kevin Costner's case, flop, flop again. Costner's post-apocalyptic cash-draining epic *Waterworld* (1995) tanked in the States but eventually made money thanks to better worldwide box-office receipts. No such luck for *The Postman,* in which Costner plays a lone-wolf hero whose symbolic quest to deliver 15-year-old mail restores hope to a futuristic American town gripped by totalitarianism. *The Postman* was shunned by audiences the world over, who drew little hope from the film's excessive three-hour run time and poor script.

Town & Country (2001)
Cost: $90–120 million: Box-office take: $6.7 million

Town & Country is a comedy about midlife crises and marital infidelity, but the bosses at New Line Cinema weren't laughing when it became a total box-office bust. The film took three years and twice the original budget to make as the perfectionism of lead star Warren Beatty reportedly led to multiple script rewrites, recastings, and reshoots. After a rumored 13 postponements, the film finally opened—only to be trashed by critics and ignored by audiences. Mercifully, it was pulled from the theaters after just four weeks.

The Adventures of Pluto Nash (2002)
Cost: $100 million (estimated); Box-office take: $7 million

This film had all the makings of a hit. It boasted a strong cast of supporting and cameo roles, as well as megastar Eddie Murphy cast in the title role. Plus, the film was directed by Ron Underwood, whose previous works *Tremors* (1989), *City Slickers* (1991), and *Mighty Joe Young* (1998) enjoyed critical and box-office success. And it had really good—and really costly—special effects. Unfortunately, audiences were not amused by Murphy as a futuristic moon-dwelling ex-con nightclub owner on the run from intergalactic mobsters with his space-suit clad gal pal (Rosario Dawson) and obsolete robot friend (Randy Quaid) in tow.

Gigli (2003)
Cost: $54 million; Box-office take: $6.1 million

Columbia Pictures was certain that casting Ben Affleck and Jennifer Lopez, who at the time were red-hot A-list superstars and a real-life couple, would guarantee the box-office success of *Gigli*. Oops. Lopez was thoroughly unconvincing as Ricki, a man-hating, lesbian-leaning assassin/mobster. Worse was Affleck's character incessantly trying to get Ricki to switch teams and sleep with him (which, of course, she did). But nothing could save the vacuous plot and badly written script. Now considered one of the worst films ever made, *Gigli* was in and out of theaters in just three weeks.

Zyzzyx Road (2006)
Cost: $2 million; Box-office take: $20

Producer Leo Grillo had to meet minimum domestic release obligations for the Screen Actors Guild before carrying out his plan to distribute *Zyzzyx Road* abroad. He showed the flick for six days in a rented Dallas theater, and then pulled it. The film, about a family man accountant (Grillo) who has a brief fling with a temptress (Katherine Heigl) who later runs around the Nevada desert trying to escape her psychotic boyfriend (Tom Sizemore), currently holds the dubious distinction as the lowest-grossing film of all time.

Always a Bridesmaid . . .

For these nominated but ultimately neglected actors, directors, and technical staff, the standard cliché "It's an honor just being nominated" is all that remains after the envelopes have been opened.

He Won Liz's Heart but Not Oscar's

Acclaimed actor Richard Burton (*Cleopatra*, 1963; *Who's Afraid of Virginia Woolf?*, 1966), known for marrying Elizabeth Taylor twice, went winless at the Academy Awards despite being nominated seven times.

Ostracized by Oscar

Irish-born thespian Peter O'Toole (*Lawrence of Arabia*, 1962; *Goodbye, Mr. Chips*, 1969) has seen his name listed on eight Best Actor ballots but has yet to receive one of the gold-plated pieces for an on-screen performance. He has, however, received a Lifetime Achievement Award.

Dinner but No Dessert

Influential Swedish director and screenwriter Ingmar Bergman (*The Seventh Seal*, 1957; *Fanny and Alexander*, 1982) inspired the term "Bergmanesque" as a means of describing films that emulate his unique cinematic vision. In 2006, *Time* magazine named him the world's greatest living director. However, he never brought home the gold, despite nine nominations before his passing in 2007.

Statue Shutouts

The Turning Point (1977), which starred Anne Bancroft, Shirley MacLaine, and Mikhail Baryshnikov, had 11 grabs at Academy Award greatness, but at the end of the night, the cast and crew left empty-handed. Steven Spielberg's drama *The Color Purple* (1985), which was based on Alice Walker's Pulitzer Prize-winning tome and starred Whoopi Goldberg, Danny Glover, and Oprah Winfrey, also received 11 Academy Award nominations but became the second film to go 0 for 11 at the Oscars.

And the Winner Is...

The all-time record for Academy Award nominations without ever sniffing the sweet smell of success goes to . . . sound mixer Kevin O'Connell (*Terms of Endearment*, 1983; *A Few Good Men*, 1992), who has been nominated for an Oscar 20 times but has yet to hear his name called when the envelope is opened.

River Phoenix

☆ ☆ ☆ ☆

River Phoenix was a rising star whose career was cut short at age 23.
Still, he is considered one of the greatest actors of his generation.

Difficult Beginnings

Some kids seem destined to become stars—River Phoenix wasn't one
of them. River Jude Bottom was born in a log cabin in Oregon on
August 23, 1970. Arlyn Dunetz and John Bottom named their eldest
child for a "river of life" reference in the Hermann Hesse novel
Siddhartha. His middle name is from The Beatles song "Hey Jude."

   Young River and his family lived in various communes during his
childhood. In 1972, they settled within a cult called the Children of
God. There, the family members became missionaries and traveled
throughout Latin America for several years. Money was always tight,
and River and his siblings—at that point there was brother Joaquin
and sisters Rain and Liberty (another sister, Summer, would be born
in 1978)—frequently had to perform on the streets just to eat. In the
late 1970s, the family stowed away on a boat and moved to Florida,
taking on the surname Phoenix to mark its new beginning.

Back to the States

The family's stay in Florida would not last long. River and Rain's success in local talent shows convinced John and Arlyn to pack up their
old station wagon and head for L.A. in 1979. There, a talent agent
signed River and found him work in TV commercials. Then, in 1982,
he was cast in a new television series called *Seven Brides for Seven
Brothers.* That role led to guest appearances on more popular
shows, such as *Family Ties,* and in TV movies, including one in
which he played a young Robert Kennedy Jr.

Big Screen Transition

River Phoenix made his leap to the big screen in 1985, playing a
young genius in the film *Explorers.* Next came his role as Chris
Chambers in the classic film *Stand By Me* (1986), which was followed by *The Mosquito Coast* (1986), *Little Nikita* (1988), and

Running on Empty (1988), the latter of which earned him an Oscar nomination. In 1989, he landed the role of young Indy in Steven Spielberg's blockbuster *Indiana Jones and the Last Crusade.*

But the turning point for Phoenix, both professionally and personally, came with the 1991 film *My Own Private Idaho.* The Gus Van Sant film catapulted the teen heartthrob to the rank of a true Hollywood star—but it is also believed to have marked the start of Phoenix's battle with drugs.

The Final Night

River Phoenix's career had never been hotter. He followed up *Idaho* with *Dogfight* (1991) and *Sneakers* (1992), and although his acting career was thriving, his personal life was beginning to unravel.

It all came to a head on October 30, 1993, when River Phoenix and his girlfriend Samantha Mathis, along with his brother Joaquin and sister Rain, went to the Viper Room, a Hollywood nightclub owned by Johnny Depp. Phoenix—an accomplished musician who, along with Rain, played in a band called Aleka's Attic—had brought along his guitar with hopes of performing. Shortly after his arrival, however, he began vomiting and having trouble breathing. As he tried to leave the club, he collapsed on the sidewalk and began having a seizure. Paramedics rushed him to the hospital where he died of heart failure in the early morning hours of October 31, 1993. An autopsy found cocaine, heroin, and other drugs in Phoenix's system. The official cause of death was accidental "acute multiple drug intoxication." River Phoenix was just 23 years old.

Continuing Memories

Fans and the Hollywood community were stunned by the young actor's sudden death. Phoenix was an animal rights activist and an environmentalist, and he appeared to be an advocate for healthy living—he was a vegan and would not wear animal products, such as leather—so the nature of his death shocked many.

At the time of his death, Phoenix was filming *Dark Blood,* which was never finished nor released. Phoenix was also set to film *Interview with the Vampire* with Tom Cruise. Christian Slater, who was recast in the role, donated his salary from the film to several of Phoenix's favorite charities, including Earth Save and Earth Trust.

Scorsese and De Niro

☆ ☆ ☆ ☆

Hollywood has many tales of great actor-director pairs producing important films. But the collaborations between Martin Scorsese and Robert De Niro are truly unique, resulting in a remarkable collection of some of the greatest films and most unforgettable (and unpleasant) characters in Hollywood history.

The Ultimate Antiheroes

Robert De Niro and Martin Scorsese both grew up as products of the tough streets of New York City in the 1940s and '50s. When they were introduced by director Brian De Palma at a party in the early 1970s, they found they had much in common. Scorsese decided to cast De Niro in his next film *Mean Streets* (1973), which perfectly captured the gritty life of small-time criminals in New York City and launched both men on the path to superstardom. The two would go on to achieve remarkable accomplishments separately, and Scorsese would even pair up on multiple films with other actors, such as Harvey Keitel, Daniel Day-Lewis, and Leonardo DiCaprio. But there is no question that some of Scorsese's finest work has come in the movies he's done with De Niro.

Scorsese and De Niro's second collaboration, *Taxi Driver* (1976), offered a chilling glimpse into the world of a disturbed New York City cabbie, who feels isolated and disgusted by the uncaring nature of his urban environment, so he commits a horrific act of violence. Scorsese's deft direction and De Niro's phenomenal portrayal combined to create one of the most complex and haunting protagonists ever to appear on film.

Raging Bull (1980), the biopic of New York boxer Jake La Motta, was a risky undertaking—shot in black and white and featuring a main character who was persistently repugnant. It performed poorly at the box office, but it earned De Niro an Academy Award and is now widely considered one of the greatest American films of all time. It also served to solidify the pair's place among the greatest actor-director combinations in film history.

The dark satire *The King of Comedy* (1982) also fared poorly on the financial front and was largely glossed over by critics. This peculiar character study focuses on Rupert Pupkin, a socially awkward misfit who clings pitifully to the dream of becoming a stand-up comedian and eventually resorts to kidnapping in pursuit of his shot at the big time. Pupkin engenders little sympathy for much of the film, until the final scene in which the audience finally hears his self-revealing comedy routine.

The Characters

By the mid-1980s, a consistent pattern had been established for Scorsese–De Niro protagonists. The featured characters were, to put it mildly, difficult to like or identify with. In fact, many bordered on being repulsive. A great many other films, of course, focus on dark, complex characters or flawed antiheroes who reflect the shortcomings of the societies in which they live. But *Taxi Driver*'s Travis Bickle, *The King of Comedy*'s Rupert Pupkin, *Cape Fear*'s Max Cady, and the gangsters in *GoodFellas* (1990) and *Casino* (1995) represent some of the darkest and most wrenching explorations of the human psyche ever offered in the guise of popular entertainment.

Scorsese consistently explores the nature of the Hollywood hero, who often uses violence to resolve conflict. Because we identify with traditional heroes, we accept the violence when an attractive, morally upright protagonist uses it, even if he commits an illegal act. However, when Scorsese's protagonists commit similar acts of violence, we are repulsed by them. In this subtle way, the director forces us to think about our acceptance of violence through identification with movie heroes.

Scorsese and De Niro Filmography:

Mean Streets (1973)	*The King of Comedy* (1982)
Taxi Driver (1976)	*GoodFellas* (1990)
New York, New York (1977)	*Cape Fear* (1991)
Raging Bull (1980)	*Casino* (1995)

Pop Quiz: The Name Game

Celebrities are notorious for changing their names for one reason or another. Here are a few that played the name game and won. See how well you do matching up each famous actor with his or her birth name.

Stage Name	Birth Name
1. Alan Alda	A. Alphonso D'Abruzzo
2. Woody Allen	B. Byron Barr
3. Tom Berenger	C. Margarita Carmen Cansino
4. Michael Caine	D. Jacob Cohen
5. Joan Crawford	E. Dino Crocetti
6. Tony Curtis	F. Michael John Douglas
7. Rodney Dangerfield	G. Ramon Gerardo Antonio Estevez
8. Dale Evans	H. Arthur Andrew Kelm
9. Peter Finch	I. Allen Stewart Konigsberg
10. Cary Grant	J. Archibald Leach
11. Rita Hayworth	K. Lucille Fay LeSueur
12. Tab Hunter	L. Joseph Levitch
13. Michael Keaton	M. Maurice Micklewhite
14. Jerry Lewis	N. William Mitchell
15. Dean Martin	O. Thomas Michael Moore
16. Roy Rogers	P. Bernard Schwartz
17. Martin Sheen	Q. Leonard Slye
18. Barbara Stanwyck	R. Frances Octavia Smith
19. Gig Young	S. Ruby Stevens

Answer Key: 1. A; 2. I; 3. O; 4. M; 5. K; 6. P; 7. D; 8. R; 9. N; 10. J; 11. C; 12. H; 13. F; 14. L; 15. E; 16. Q; 17. G; 18. S; 19. B

A Sign of the Times

☆ ☆ ☆ ☆

For more than 80 years, aspiring actors from all over the world have climbed to the top of Mount Lee in the Hollywood Hills. Their mission? To touch the famous HOLLYWOOD sign for good luck in their acting careers. Few realize that this iconic sign was originally constructed as an advertisement for a housing development.

"Now THAT'S a Billboard!"

In 1923, *Los Angeles Times* publisher Harry Chandler was searching for a way to promote his new real estate development, Hollywoodland. Instead of a traditional billboard, Chan-

dler wanted something bigger—a lot bigger—so he plunked down $21,000 to have Thomas Goff, owner of the Crescent Sign Company, create what he considered a giant advertisement: a sign placed on top of Mount Lee.

Using wood and sheet metal, the sign would spell out HOLLYWOODLAND. Each letter would be roughly 50 feet tall and 30 feet wide and would incorporate nearly 4,000 20-watt light-bulbs to illuminate the sign in sections—first *HOLLY,* then *WOOD,* and finally, *LAND.*

On July 13, 1923, the HOLLYWOODLAND sign was officially dedicated and lit for the first time. Albert Kothe was appointed the sign's caretaker, which meant that he was in charge of looking after the sign and, of course, changing all those lightbulbs.

The original plan was to remove the sign once all the plots in the development had been sold. But this coincided with the emergence of Hollywood as the epicenter of the American film industry, as well as the elevation of studio heads and major stars into America's "aristocracy" and the boom of nightclubs and restaurants on Sunset Boulevard. Thus, the sign took on meaning beyond its original intent. And years later, even after the development was filled, the sign was deemed so enormous and awe-inspiring that it was allowed to stay.

Signs of Deterioration

By the mid-1940s, the sign had deteriorated so much that it had become an eyesore. The Los Angeles Parks Department and the Hollywood Chamber of Commerce joined forces to save the sign, but it was a massive undertaking. To cut costs, it was decided that the sign would no longer be illuminated. Also, the letters *L*, *A*, *N*, and *D* were removed so that the sign reflected the city of Hollywood rather than the Hollywoodland subdivision.

Of course, it didn't help that the elements were taking their toll on the sign. The first *O* splintered in half. Then, the third *O* and the *D* both fell over. And during the 1940s, in a bizarre twist of fate, an intoxicated Albert Kothe lost control of his vehicle and crashed headlong into the *H,* destroying it.

Over the next few decades, the sign continued to be damaged. An arsonist burned off part of the second *L*. In 1973, a group of pranksters, who apparently had a love for a certain green leaf, changed the sign to read HOLLYWEED. So by the end of the 1970s, there were serious discussions about demolishing the sign for good—which might have happened if help had not come from an unexpected source.

I'd Like to Buy a Vowel, Please

In 1978, *Playboy* magazine creator Hugh Hefner held a fund-raiser at his Los Angeles Playboy Mansion to raise money to replace the HOLLYWOOD sign. Hef asked people to step forward and pay roughly $28,000 to "adopt" a letter, and, when all was said and done, the list of donors couldn't have been more diverse:

H—Terrence Donnelly (newspaper publisher)

O—Giovanna Mazza (Italian movie producer)

L—Gene Autry (singer/actor)

L—Les Kelley (creator of the *Kelley Blue Book*)

Y—Hugh Hefner (*Playboy* magazine creator)

W—Andy Williams (singer)

O—Warner Bros. Records

O—Alice Cooper (singer)

D—Dennis Lidtke (businessman)

Using the money raised, nine 45-foot-high letters, ranging from 31 to 39 feet wide, were created out of steel. The new sign was unveiled on November 14, 1978. The Chamber of Commerce sold the original letters for a grand total of $10,000 to private collector Tony Wood.

The Sign Today

Today, the Hollywood Sign Trust, a nonprofit organization, handles the security, maintenance, and upkeep of the sign. In 2000, in an effort to cut down on potential vandalism, the Los Angeles Police Department installed a motion-activated security system around the sign, as well as several closed-circuit cameras, which were paid for by the Trust. Now, anyone coming within 50 yards of the sign will immediately be detected. The Hollywood Sign Trust relies solely on contributions from individuals and sponsorships from businesses to maintain the sign, which requires considerable upkeep. In addition to security issues, the sign is always in danger of deterioration from the elements (rain, smog, wind). In the early 2000s, the Trust repaired minor damage and then recoated the entire sign.

And while the original letters were believed to have been destroyed, in 2005, they were found inside a storage unit belonging to businessman Dan Bliss. In what was clearly a sign of the times, Bliss put the letters for sale on eBay. The winning bidder, sculptor Bill Mack, paid $450,000 for them. Mack plans to use them as a canvas onto which he'll paint portraits of famous movie stars, many of whom were first lured to Hollywood by the sign itself.

Los Angeles residents, tourists, and movie lovers alike are all captivated by an unmistakable allure that the sign still holds after so many decades. It is a potent symbol that represents everything— both fun and tragic—that Hollywood stands for. It represents the lost dreams of those who wanted to become stars but didn't make it, as well as the future dreams of today's young hopefuls; it reminds us of the glamorous facade of the dream factory as well as the illusion and sham behind that facade. It is at once uniquely American yet it attracts tourists from all over the world. The sign beckons the dreamer in all of us because we all want to believe that the movies are still magic and that dreams of stardom still come true.

Military History vs. Hollywood History

Movies are not history and should not be judged as such. But some films at least attempt to get the key details right. Sometimes the names have been changed to protect the innocent (or even the guilty). Sometimes the facts have been "revised" to make a story line more believable or entertaining or to convey a larger point or a universal truth. Here are a few war films that raise the bar in terms of entertainment; how each stands up to the actual history is another case entirely.

The Charge of the Light Brigade (1936)
Few know much about the 19th-century Crimean War fought between the Russians and a handful of European countries, so this highly inaccurate portrayal of the most famous part of the war often goes unnoticed. Rather than relying on actual history as their source, the scriptwriters used Alfred, Lord Tennyson's narrative poem of the same name, which lionizes the 600 British killed during a famous charge at the Battle of Balaclava. The climactic charge includes many acts of bravery, lots of galloping horses, and a great deal of action; it also suggests that the battle lasted several hours, although the actual charge included only 7 minutes and 30 seconds of heavy gunfire.

They Died with Their Boots On (1941)
Errol Flynn makes a dashing General George Armstrong Custer as he bravely fights to the finish at the Battle of Little Big Horn. Flynn's screen image as a cocky swashbuckler fit Custer's real-life tendencies toward being a dandy. But the real-life atrocities that Custer committed against the Native Americans are omitted in this version of Hollywood history, as are the general's foolish decisions that led up to the battle. Still, if you consider when the film was made—just prior to America's entry into World War II—you'll understand that it was meant to propagate U.S. military might rather than serve as a history lesson.

The Bridge on the River Kwai (1957)
This Oscar-winning movie's ending is cinematic magic—and actually pure fantasy. Although a real bridge was built over the Mae Klong River by conscripted Asian laborers and Allied prisoners of war, most of this story, in which a British colonel supervises his soldiers as they build the bridge for the Japanese, is fictional. In fact, the suffering of the soldiers was

actually far worse than depicted on-screen, and at no time did any senior POWs aid in the effort as shown in the film. And finally, in reality, an aerial bombing destroyed the bridge, not a commando raid, as the film implies.

The Alamo (1960)

The story of the 1836 Battle of the Alamo has been remade many times, even as recently as 2004, but the 1960 version stands out because it was John Wayne's directorial debut. It does earn kudos for its two-thirds-scale replica of the real mission, which was so well designed that it has been used in several other films depicting this key battle for Texas independence. Nevertheless, the film is guilty of several inaccuracies, particularly in regards to the ending. Davy Crockett—who was from Tennessee, not Kentucky as the film suggests—did not retreat to the powder magazine with a torch and blow it up in defiance. In all likelihood, he surrendered and was executed by Santa Ana, who may have been jealous of Crockett's celebrity. Jim Bowie was not put in the chapel because he was wounded, as shown in the film; he was actually sick from typhoid. And Sam Houston never visited the Alamo before the battle, though he is shown arriving in grand fashion at the beginning of the film. Wayne's interest in the story of the Alamo likely had more to do with his anticommunist fervor than any real desire for an accurate portrayal of history. Crockett's dialogue about believing in the values of a republic and the film's presentation of the Alamo as a defense of freedom were representative of Wayne's own beliefs.

The Guns of Navarone (1961)

Based on a novel by Alistair MacLean, this story of espionage and sabotage on a German-occupied Greek island has been reduced to rip-roaring action and adventure. The film starts out strong and believable, thanks to solid acting and impressive use of vintage World War II gear, but the focus on the double crosses, escapes, guerrilla fighting, and a truly explosive conclusion—with the guns of Navarone blown sky-high and tumbling down the side of a cliff—was clearly more important to the filmmakers than historical accuracy.

Lawrence of Arabia (1962)

A bit light on action for many war movie buffs, this Academy Award winner for Best Picture is about as epic as they come. The film tells a deeply emotional story and features sweeping vistas, and while Peter O'Toole's performance as Colonel T. E. Lawrence suggests that the real man was also larger than life, the truth is a bit disappointing. It is likely that the Turks never knew his name—let alone had a bounty on his head—and his role in the Palestine Front during World War I is vastly overdramatized. A line in the movie that called these actions "a side-show to a sideshow" may have best summed up Lawrence's real-world role. Yet strong performances make for a classic film that could arguably be better than the actual history.

The Great Escape (1963)

Very loosely based on an actual Allied escape from a German POW camp, this film escaped a bit from reality for the sake of international marketing. The real breakout was fully a British affair, yet the film neatly adds a few Americans into the mix, including star Steve McQueen. And although McQueen's legendary escape over a barbed wire fence via motorcycle is pure fantasy, it stands as a symbol of American rebellion in the face of pure oppression, as does his continual tossing of a baseball in his cell to annoy the Germans.

Gettysburg (1993)

Media mogul Ted Turner, an American Civil War buff, produced this epic screen version of Michael Shaara's novel *The Killer Angels*. Originally slated as a TV miniseries, this story of the bloodiest battle of the Civil War was shot in part on the actual Gettysburg battlefield and further benefited from the aid of thousands of Civil War reenactors who volunteered their time to participate in the massive battle scenes. Screenwriter Ronald Maxwell took pains to include some of the actual words and speeches of the battle's famous participants. The film even showed Pickett's Charge in real time. Although picky historians might find small-scale inaccuracies, this four-hour film may well be one of cinema's most truthful interpretations of the historical battle.

U-571 (2000)

Events are sometimes changed to protect the innocent, but *U-571*'s biggest crime is that some events were changed at the expense of the real wartime heroes. This film suggests that it was a secret American mission that captured the infamous German Naval Enigma machine. But in fact, it was the British Royal Navy that captured the device in May 1941, nearly seven months *before* the United States entered the war. In addition to the Americanized plot, there are aspects of submarine design and capabilities that are not accurate or are distorted to create tension and suspense.

Frances Farmer: Tortured Soul

☆ ☆ ☆ ☆

*When Frances Farmer's life spiraled out of control, the results
proved devastating. Institutionalized for many years, the
troubled actress miraculously fought her way back to the top.
Unfortunately, her demons accompanied her every step of the
way. She made very few films, but her story is remembered as a
cautionary tale about the dark side of the Hollywood star system.*

Hitting the Big Time

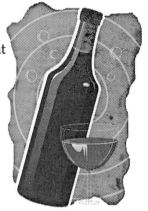

When moviegoers watched *Come and
Get It* (1936), a film starring the effervescent
flaxen-haired beauty Frances Farmer
(1913–1970), they couldn't have guessed
that in a few short years, the star would
decline into a mentally tormented, alcohol-
addicted figure. Certainly Farmer herself
was unaware of the cruel fate that awaited
her. Up to that point, the actress's ascent to
stardom had gone according to plan. After
studying at the University of Washington
as a journalism and drama major, Farmer left her Seattle home and
headed off to Hollywood. There she secured a seven-year contract
with Paramount Pictures and was groomed for major stardom. While
under Paramount's employ, Farmer was loaned out to the Samuel
Goldwyn Company for the making of *Come and Get It,* a drama that
proved the perfect vehicle to highlight Farmer's prodigious talents.
Critics raved about Farmer's dual mother/daughter performance in
the film. And director Cecil B. DeMille referred to the actress as
the "screen's outstanding find of 1936." With this early victory acting
as impetus, the 23-year-old Farmer thought she had the world on a
string. Unfortunately, her good fortune would not last.

Downwardly Mobile

For the stage-trained Farmer, 1937 would bring further success.
Fulfilling a dream that she'd had since first getting the acting bug,

Farmer moved to New York City to work on the stage, joining the famed Group Theatre. She was cast in the production of *Golden Boy* and received praise for her portrayal of the emotionally charged Lorna Moon. She stayed with the production into its off-Broadway run.

But in 1939, things started to unravel for Farmer. Erratic behavior and an ever-increasing drinking habit began to take its toll on her. By the early 1940s, she had returned to Hollywood, but directors and producers took note of Farmer's sudden unreliability and responded in kind. By 1941, Farmer was no longer treated as a major player and was relegated to B-movies—the unimportant second features on a double bill. Then in 1942, the bottom completely fell out. Confronted with a severely unstable actress who regularly fueled her mental demons with alcohol, the studio pulled the plug on her contract. Farmer's downward spiral was firmly on track.

The Snake Pit

In January 1943, Farmer was reportedly involved in a physical alter-cation with a studio hairdresser. After being arrested for her role in the assault, Farmer was placed in the custody of psychiatrist Thomas H. Leonard. The doctor determined that the uncooperative actress was "suffering from manic-depressive psychosis," a diagnosis that has since been contested. Farmer was then transferred to Rockhaven Sanitarium in La Crescenta, California, thus beginning an on/off ordeal of forced institutionalization that lasted for several years. In her autobiography *Will There Really Be a Morning?*, which was largely written by a longtime friend, Farmer recalled the horrors that she was subjected to as a patient in various sanitariums. Tales of shock treatments that did far more harm than good, hydrotherapy (submerging the patient in icy cold water for hours at a time), her use as an unwitting pawn to test unproven drugs, and even gang rape at the hands of hospital orderlies abound in her first-person account of those tortured years, but perhaps nothing is more heartbreaking than Farmer's realization that her own mother signed her commitment papers. It is believed that the actress was hospitalized against her will three separate times during the 1940s, spending a total of five years in mental institutions. Finally, in 1950, Farmer was released for good.

A Career Almost Resurrected

While Farmer's life easily could have continued its downward spiral, it didn't. In fact, it rebounded to a degree that seems improbable given her severe mental history, problems with addictions, and the tortures that she had endured. Starting small, Farmer first took a job working in a Seattle hotel laundry to help support her parents. After a failed marriage in 1954, she moved to Eureka, California, and found work at a photo studio. In 1957, a lucky break came when a talent scout rediscovered the actress and helped revive her career. Appearances on *The Ed Sullivan Show* and *This Is Your Life* led to a series of television dramas. Farmer's biggest break came in 1958, when she became hostess of *Frances Farmer Presents,* an afternoon movie/interview show on an NBC affiliate in Indianapolis. The show held the No. 1 position for six straight years, but in a nod to her first mental downfall, Farmer's demons ultimately resurfaced. After Farmer fell back into the throes of alcoholism, the station pulled the plug on her show in September 1964.

A Bottle in Front of Me

While various sources have suggested that Farmer received a frontal lobotomy during her stay in a mental hospital, evidence does not support the claim. The 1978 book *Shadowland,* a purportedly factual account of her life that author William Arnold now calls "fictionalized," was largely responsible for popularizing the myth. Subsequent accounts of Farmer's treatments released by Western State Hospital have mostly laid this to rest. Certainly her successful stint as a television interviewer belies the limited capabilities of a person who has undergone a lobotomy. What cannot be debunked, however, was Farmer's dependency on alcohol. For most of her post-institution life, the actress fought a battle with the bottle, and the bottle usually won. Farmer's final years were spent operating a number of small businesses. The spell that the actress had once held over Hollywood had all but vanished and had been replaced by the lingering, silent hell of anonymity. In 1970, Frances Farmer developed esophageal cancer and quietly passed away at age 56. Her demons would torture her no more.

Actors Say the Darndest Things

They may make a living reading lines, but sometimes Hollywood actors are just as famous for what they say off-camera. Check out these memorable quotes.

"I don't want people to know what I'm actually like. It's not good for an actor."

—*Jack Nicholson*

"I enjoy being a highly overpaid actor."

—*Roger Moore*

"I am not the archetypal leading man. This is mainly for one reason: As you may have noticed, I have no hair."

—*Patrick Stewart*

"The exciting part of acting—I don't know how else to explain it—are [sic] those moments when you surprise yourself."

—*Tom Cruise*

"Now I can wear heels."

—*Nicole Kidman, following her divorce from Tom Cruise*

"There are two types of actors: those who say they want to be famous and those who are liars."

—*Kevin Bacon*

"Just standing around looking beautiful is so boring."

—*Michelle Pfeiffer*

"With two movies opening this summer, I have no relaxing time at all. Whatever I have is spent in a drunken stupor."

—*Hugh Grant*

"I veer away from trying to understand why I act. I just know I need to do it."

—*Ralph Fiennes*

"It was definitely different from kissing a girl. He had a bunch of stray hairs on his lip."

—*Jason Biggs, on his intimate scene with Seann William Scott in* American Wedding (2003)

"I carried my Oscar to bed with me. My first and only three-way happened that night."

—*Halle Berry*

"Once you've been really bad in a movie, there's a certain kind of fearlessness you develop."

—*Jack Nicholson*

"People have been so busy relating to how I look, it's a miracle I didn't become a self-conscious blob of protoplasm."

—*Robert Redford*

"I'm staggered by the question of what it's like to be a multimillionaire. I always have to remind myself that I am."

—*Bruce Willis*

"Heartthrobs are a dime a dozen."

—*Brad Pitt*

"I have a love interest in every one of my films—a gun."

—*Arnold Schwarzenegger*

"I tell you what really turns my toes up: love scenes with 68-year-old men and actresses young enough to be their granddaughter."

—*Mel Gibson*

"The really frightening thing about middle age is the knowledge that you'll grow out of it."

—*Doris Day*

"Acting is the most minor of gifts and not a very high-class way to earn a living. After all, Shirley Temple could do it at the age of four."

—*Katharine Hepburn*

"Life is a tragedy when seen in close-up, but a comedy in long-shot."

—*Charlie Chaplin*

"I stopped believing in Santa Claus when I was six. Mother took me to see him in a department store, and he asked for my autograph."

—*Shirley Temple*

"When choosing between two evils, I always like to pick the one I've never tried before."

—*Mae West*

The Hippest of the Hip: The Rat Pack

In the early 1960s, after picking up the mantle from Humphrey Bogart, Frank Sinatra formed a close-knit fraternity of entertainers who conquered film, television, the nightclub circuit, and the recording industry while casually establishing the definition of cool for their era.

During the 1950s, Humphrey Bogart, David Niven, Spencer Tracy, and Cary Grant were among the biggest stars in Hollywood, and they were also the best of friends. They brought as much vigor to pursuing their social activities as they did to their careers and soon earned a reputation for enjoying long nights of partying. After one particularly indulgent binge, they staggered back to Bogart's house only to be met by the icy glare of Bogie's wife, Lauren Bacall, who purportedly muttered that they looked like a pack of rats. Soon the press was referring to the garrulous group as the Rat Pack, and they embraced the label proudly. Over the years, various other stars floated in and out of the mix, including Judy Garland, Katharine Hepburn, and Frank Sinatra. After Bogart's death in 1957, the group drifted apart, only to be reinvented by Sinatra around 1960 as the suave crooner began to reach the apex of his career.

The New Rat Pack

Sinatra's clique was a boys-only club anchored by singers Dean Martin and Sammy Davis Jr., comedian Joey Bishop, and actor Peter Lawford, with actress Shirley MacLaine as sort of an honorary member or mascot. Though they typically referred to themselves as The Clan, the press was so persistent in applying the familiar moniker that this 1960s incarnation of cool has become, for many, the one and only Rat Pack.

The group is perhaps best known for a series of shows they did together in Las Vegas in the 1960s. Moving from nightclub to nightclub, they put their hard-drinking, chain-smoking, skirt-chasing lifestyle on display and served it up with a chaser of talent, charisma, and charm that made them the envy of America. Columnist Ralph

Pearl summed up the reaction to their routine by frowning at the too-casual jokes about sex, race, and religion but admitting, "I'd be a fat, old hypocrite if I said I didn't enjoy their act. It's like eavesdropping on a stag party." They became the must-see show on The Strip and forever cemented their reputations as the kings of Sin City. Sometimes, marquees would list all of their names in order. Others would read "Frank and Sammy… Maybe Dean, Maybe Joey." Or they might simply proclaim, "They're Here!"

To the Big Screen and Beyond

With Sinatra's backing, the Rat Pack carried their success onto the silver screen in a series of buddy pictures that also exploited their natural camaraderie. The spirit of the group was best captured in *Ocean's Eleven* (1960), a hip caper movie about several war buddies who rob five Las Vegas casinos in a single night. In *Sergeants 3* (1962), a freewheeling adaptation of *Gunga Din* (1939), the raucous group saves the U.S. Cavalry from an ambush in the Old West. And *Robin and the Seven Hoods* (1964) presents the group, with Bing Crosby added for good measure, as likable gangsters in Prohibition-era Chicago.

Sinatra's gang was also known for exerting its influence outside the entertainment industry. They indirectly supported the civil rights movement by refusing to play any Vegas hotels that were segregated, essentially forcing the integration of the town through their star power. They also became actively engaged in John F. Kennedy's presidential campaign. But their social, political, and professional activities never interfered with their pursuit of a good time. While filming *Sergeants 3* in desolate Monument Valley, Utah, the group reportedly brought in a group of prostitutes and paid them as extras out of the film's budget. Though the Rat Pack is long gone, they are still remembered for their unique brand of hip hedonism that bridged the staid 1950s and the counterculture of the 1960s in a way no one else could have.

• *Joey Bishop, who passed away on October 17, 2007, was the last surviving member of the Rat Pack.*

Dog Movies

Whether it's Benji saving the day or Marley ruining it, dogs have starred in movies for decades. Stories of man's best friend strike a chord with audiences who can always relate to the love between human and canine. Although there have been plenty of movies that featured animated dogs (Scooby Doo, Bolt, etc.), our list focuses on the movies that star actual dogs in roles that made them famous. This way to your trailer, Fido....

Lassie Come Home (1943)

No list of dog movies would be complete without *Lassie*, now would it? Perhaps no dog has been the subject of more films, books, or television shows and specials than this beloved pooch. The first of the *Lassie* pictures, *Lassie Come Home*, starred an especially brilliant rough collie named Pal in the title role. Pal and his offspring played Lassie in numerous films and TV shows in the years that followed. *Lassie Come Home*, the story of a dog who finds her way home against the odds, also features an all-star cast of humans, including Roddy McDowall, one of the most talented child actors of all time.

The Return of Rin Tin Tin (1947)

This film is just one of the many starring one of several German shepherds known as Rin Tin Tin. The original dog was found by American serviceman Lee Duncan in a bombed-out French town just after World War I. The talented canine dazzled audiences with his intelligence and ability to do tricks. Before long, he shot onto the Hollywood scene, and over the next few decades it seemed there was always a *Rin Tin Tin* movie to be found. This one stars a young Robert Blake (*In Cold Blood*, 1967) as a war orphan brought out of his shell by Rinty.

Old Yeller (1957)

In this time-honored picture set in post-Civil War Texas, a young boy and his dog, Old Yeller, have many fantastic adventures together through the years. When Old Yeller gets rabies from a wolf bite after saving members of his human family from attack, he must be put down. The person who does the job? You probably guessed it already, but we won't spoil it for you. You might feel like bawling your eyes out.

The Shaggy Dog (1959)
This boy-turns-into-a-dog comedy is the forerunner of a long line of Disney canine-themed movies that came after it. The plot is weird but funny: A teenage boy is transformed into a sheepdog and (with the help of his father) must reverse the spell that got him into trouble. Hollywood veteran Fred MacMurray invigorated his career by playing everyone's favorite father in Disney films during this time frame, and this film reveals his genuine warmth and humor. The cast also features a whole stable of Disney child actors who were extremely popular in their day, including Tommy Kirk, Annette Funicello, Tim Considine, and Kevin Corcoran, and they made this film a hit with family audiences.

Benji (1974)
Many dogs that land feature films are purebreds; not Benji. A mangy mutt is the hero in this and numerous other Benji-centric films that have been produced over the years. A classic brilliant-dog-saves-the-day picture, *Benji* tells a heartwarming story that even involves a doggie love affair. But don't worry—this film is about as family-friendly as you can get.

Where the Red Fern Grows (1974)
The story of Billy and his two hounds, Old Dan and Little Ann, is one that many kids read in junior high. The movie version does the beloved book proud—maybe better. The whole story unfolds as a flashback and comes full circle by the end, which is when you'll need a box of tissues.

White Fang (1991)
A young Ethan Hawke stars in this cherished Jack London story about a Yukon prospector (Hawke) and the semi-feral but oh-so-lovable wolf/dog that he befriends. White Fang, as he calls his canine companion, is never far from trouble or danger—sometimes he saves the day, sometimes he's part of the problem. This action-filled Disney film features good production values and an excellent supporting cast.

Marley & Me (2008)
Based on a best-selling memoir by author John Grogan, this tearjerker centers on "the world's worst dog," Marley, a yellow Labrador. Starring Owen Wilson and Jennifer Aniston as the owners of this lovable-but-impossible pet, the movie follows the trials, tribulations, and lessons learned as the family grows over the years. *Marley & Me* set a record upon its release for drawing the biggest Christmas Day box-office take in history: $14.75 million.

The Birth of a Nation

☆ ☆ ☆ ☆

D. W. Griffith's epic The Birth of a Nation *may be one of the most racist films ever made, but its role in the development of cinema cannot be overstated. Despite its controversial story line revolving around the Civil War and the Reconstruction era, film critics and scholars have praised it, and in 1992, it was even deemed "culturally significant" and was selected for preservation in the Library of Congress's National Film Registry. It also had the honor of being the first film ever shown at the White House.*

Exactly how does a film that lionized the founding of the Ku Klux Klan, preached white supremacy, and perpetuated African American stereotypes earn such kudos? Partly because the 1915 film—which was based on the then-popular Thomas Dixon Jr. novel and stage play *The Clansman*—is a compendium of techniques innovated by director D. W. Griffith that have become staples in modern filmmaking.

It might be hard to imagine, but *The Birth of a Nation* was the first true Hollywood blockbuster, earning roughly $60 million by the 1920s—equal to more than $660 million today. Its success proved to film producers and industry insiders that audiences would actually be interested in a feature-length movie more than three hours long in an era when 15-minute one-reelers were the norm.

Much More than Just Racist Propaganda

While the film is remembered for its sweeping footage of Klan riders on horseback, it was also among the first films to take advantage of such innovative techniques. Griffith pioneered many film techniques while working on this picture, chief among them the methods of classic film editing still used today. The groundbreaking director divided his scenes into a variety of shots, with each one having a purpose and function. From extreme long shots of battlefields to medium shots of characters interacting to the expressive close-ups of star Lillian Gish, the variety of shots helped direct the audience's attention and emotions. Arguably the most famous technique used in the film was parallel editing, in which Griffith cut back and forth between two or more scenes to suggest simultaneous action, such as when the KKK is riding to rescue the heroine and her family. Combined with Griffith's use of fast pacing, the technique provided a sense of immediacy that audiences found exciting. This approach is still a staple of editing today.

Other influential techniques found in *The Birth of a Nation* include tracking shots, in which the camera moves to follow the action, providing a sense of energy and excitement. When the protagonist, the Little Colonel, bounds the length of the battlefield hoisting his army's flag and then thrusts the flag into the mouth of the enemy's cannon, the camera tracks alongside him, making the action seem more dynamic and heroic. Billy Bitzer, Griffith's cameraman extraordinaire, was on the back of a flatbed truck with his simple silent-film camera as it sped across the field alongside the actor. The smoothness of the shot, even by today's standards, is a testament to Bitzer's expertise in crude circumstances.

In addition, the film includes the use of color tinting for mood; primitive night photography; editing transitions such as dissolves, fades, and irises; and a modern, naturalistic approach to acting. *The Birth of a Nation* starred several of Griffith's discoveries, who helped him pioneer a more natural approach to acting than that of stage actors who worked in the movies. Lillian Gish, Mae Marsh, Henry B. Walthall, and Wallace Reid gave nuanced performances that influenced subsequent generations of actors.

As an early example of a feature-length film, *The Birth of a Nation* is also notable for its narrative complexities. Most movies were still one- or two-reelers in 1914 when Griffith conceived the script. But the film's monumental scale, clever intertwining of epochal events and small human moments, and mixture of historical and fictional characters make for sophisticated storytelling.

However, as a result of the film's content, Griffith was branded a racist, an allegation that he took to heart. His next film, *Intolerance: Love's Struggle Throughout the Ages* (1916), which was also more than three hours long, preached against the evils of cultural intolerance. A complete flop, the film's massive sets of ancient Babylon towered over Hollywood for decades—a monumental reminder of Griffith's vision and box-office failure.

Not Quite the Best Picture

It featured a strong cast and solid performances and had the makings of being one of the best pictures of that particular year. And the Oscar goes to... one of the other nominees. In fact, you might be surprised that some films that have become timeless classics did not bring home the gold. Of course, they say it's an honor just to be nominated....

In 1935, *The Thin Man* lost to *It Happened One Night*.

In 1938, *A Star Is Born* and *The Awful Truth* lost to *The Life of Emile Zola*.

In 1940, *The Wizard of Oz* lost to *Gone with the Wind*.

In 1941, *The Grapes of Wrath* lost to *Rebecca*.

In 1942, *Citizen Kane* and *The Maltese Falcon* lost to *How Green Was My Valley*.

In 1943, *Pride of the Yankees* lost to *Mrs. Miniver*.

In 1947, *It's a Wonderful Life* lost to *The Best Years of Our Lives*.

In 1949, *The Treasure of the Sierra Madre* lost to *Hamlet*.

In 1951, *Sunset Boulevard* lost to *All About Eve*.

In 1952, *A Streetcar Named Desire* lost to *An American in Paris*.

In 1957, *The Ten Commandments* and *Giant* lost to *Around the World in 80 Days*.

In 1959, *Cat on a Hot Tin Roof* and *The Defiant Ones* lost to *Gigi*.

In 1964, *How the West Was Won* lost to *Tom Jones*.

In 1978, *Star Wars* lost to *Annie Hall*.

In 1982, *On Golden Pond* and *Reds* lost to *Chariots of Fire*.

In 1990, *Born on the Fourth of July* lost to *Driving Miss Daisy*.

In 1991, *GoodFellas* lost to *Dances with Wolves*.

In 1999, *Saving Private Ryan* lost to *Shakespeare in Love*.

In 2006, *Brokeback Mountain* lost to *Crash*.

The Curious Friendship of Cary Grant and Randolph Scott

Today, gay characters are commonplace on television and in the movies, and stars are more likely to openly acknowledge their sexual orientation. But during the Golden Age of Hollywood, when star images were carefully guarded by the studios, public perceptions regarding gay lifestyles could be quite biased. If a Hollywood star was so inclined, he hid the fact for fear that it would ruin his career. Nevertheless, whispers and rumors persisted.

The Gossip Mill

During the Golden Age of Hollywood, when the major movie studios kept actors under contract, personas were constructed for these stars, which they were expected to play on and off the screen. The studios were adamant that nothing be done to ruin or damage those carefully groomed personas, so they had publicity departments with press agents who fed free stories and photographs to fan magazines, which propagated the images of the major stars and presented their best sides. Any aspects of their lives that did not fit their image were hidden behind the studios' carefully orchestrated promotion and propaganda.

Occasionally, an arrest, messy divorce, or scandal slipped through the gears of the star-making machine, but sometimes even those problems were covered up. The wild cards in this system were gossip columnists and nosy reporters, and it was this faction of the Hollywood dream machine that circulated veiled rumors about Cary Grant and Randolph Scott.

Closer than Close

The two actors met on the set of *Hot Saturday* (1932) and formed a quick friendship. A short time later they acquired a Malibu beach house and moved in together—supposedly to save money. Dubbing the beach house "Bachelor Hall," the pair threw lavish parties and, according to witnesses, generally reveled in each other's company. They lived in this fashion, off and on, for several years, and during that time, suspicious tongues took to wagging. Had the two really paired up to save on expenses, as had been put forth, or was something more salacious occurring? The idea of the two living together to split expenses wasn't as far-fetched as it might have seemed. Stars under contract to studios did not make the millions they do now. They made weekly salaries that went up only at the discretion of the studio. It wasn't unheard-of for up-and-coming actors to move in together. Yet something about the way Grant and Scott looked at each other suggested something deeper than friendship, at least to those who'd observed them up close.

Gossip columnist Jimmie Fiddler began to make veiled remarks about Grant and Scott's roommate status, and studio press agents only aggravated the situation when they tried to present the pair as the town's most eligible bachelors. Much later, gossip queen Hedda Hopper tried to "out" Grant in her column, but various people within the industry rallied around him, and Hopper backed off. The curious part was that neither man seemed much disturbed by the whisperings going on behind his back. In fact, each seemed indifferent to the potential backlash that might arise from their living arrangement.

So, were Grant and Scott gay? It depends on whom you choose to believe. Many friends and colleagues thought the two were indeed gay. Director George Cukor supposedly revealed in interviews that the two were more than friends, and that Scott was willing to admit to it.

Perhaps They Were

In William Mann's book *Behind the Screen: How Gays and Lesbians Shaped Hollywood, 1910–1969,* photographer Jerome Zerbe tells of "three gay months" spent in Hollywood taking photos of the pair, in which he implies that the two were gay or bisexual, based upon his lengthy observations. Fashion critic Richard Blackwell went Zerbe one better, claiming to have slept with both actors.

But Then Again . . .

On the "perhaps not" side, Grant more than once declared that he "had nothing against gays, I'm just not one myself." A book entitled

Whatever Happened to Randolph Scott, penned by Scott's adopted son Christopher, puts forth similar, albeit somewhat predictable, denials about the famous duo's relationship. And director Budd Boetticher, who worked with Scott during the 1950s in some of the actor's most memorable Westerns, emphatically denied any rumors of the alleged romance. Further confusing the matter, Grant walked down the aisle a total of five times, and Scott took the plunge twice.

For their part, the actors let the insinuations slide past them the way a veteran actor sidesteps a bad review. If the two were gay or bisexual, they seemed rather comfortable with it. If they weren't, well, that too appeared to be okay. The most puzzling thing, however, was the fact that the Hollywood gossip machine couldn't or wouldn't bring them down. Did the actors' prodigious charm and drop-dead good looks neutralize writings about their offscreen romance? Had their studios suppressed information that proved conclusively that the two were gay? Were the actors just incredibly lucky? In Hollywood, anything seems possible, so any or all of these scenarios might be plausible. One thing is for certain: If their relationship took place in this day and age, there'd likely be no shame in admitting which team the boys were playing for.

More important are the films the two actors left behind and the ideals their screen personas represented. Grant's sophisticated, articulate, and well-mannered gentleman was the perfect comic foil for boisterous costars, providing audiences with classic films known for their snappy dialogue and sharp wit, including *The Philadelphia Story* (1940), *His Girl Friday* (1941), and *The Bishop's Wife* (1947). Scott's image as the stoic Western hero who always retains his integrity was used to great effect by Boetticher in *Ride Lonesome* (1959) and Sam Peckinpah in Scott's last film, *Ride the High Country* (1962). Each represented an ideal of masculinity that overshadowed their personal sexual preferences, whatever they were.

- *To escape an unhappy home life, Cary Grant ran away as a teenager and joined the Bob Pender comedy troupe, where he learned to dance, perform acrobatics, stilt-walk, and pantomime. The experience gave him a lifelong agility, physical grace, and poise that suited his star image.*

Resurrected!

Any career has its twists and turns, bends and breaks. And while many actors have risen to the top of the Hollywood heap and then fallen out of the spotlight, only a few climb back up the ladder of success to the penthouse after dropping into the basement. Here are a lucky few who resurrected their careers after the business turned its back on them.

Robert Downey Jr.

In 1996, Robert Downey Jr.'s drug problems came to a head when police arrested him for drug possession and weapons charges. But this did not end the troubles of the respected star of *Less Than Zero* (1987) and *Chaplin* (1992). A short time later, he was cited for trespassing and drug possession again. Numerous rehab stints failed, and eventually, he was jailed twice and did a year of hard time. After jail, Downey continued to act in secondary roles, and finally, in 2003, he kicked his drug habit. By 2008, his career had turned around with a starring role in *Iron Man* and an Oscar-nominated performance in *Tropic Thunder.*

Jackie Earle Haley

A charismatic child star who elicited cheers as the delinquent-turned-champ in *The Bad News Bears* (1976) and the mischievous Moocher in *Breaking Away* (1979), Haley drifted into obscurity, surviving by delivering pizzas and refinishing furniture. In 2006, he commanded critical acclaim as a paroled sex offender in *Little Children,* a role that resurrected his career and earned him an Oscar nomination. In 2009's *Watchmen,* Haley starred as one of a group of superheroes in director Zack Snyder's adaptation of the comic book of the same name.

Katharine Hepburn

It's hard to believe that Katharine Hepburn was once dubbed "box-office poison," but a series of bombs in the 1930s prompted her to leave Hollywood to rethink her career. In 1940, she plucked a prize plum when she lobbied MGM to turn *The Philadelphia Story*—which she'd successfully starred in on Broadway—into a film vehicle for her. The movie earned her an Oscar nomination and a place among the Tinseltown elite. She went on to garner nine more Academy Award nominations, including wins for *Guess Who's Coming to Dinner* (1967), *The Lion in Winter* (1968), and *On Golden Pond* (1981).

Dennis Hopper

Dennis Hopper's ascension to the top with *Easy Rider* (1969) was followed by a meteoric descent in the 1970s. A string of box-office flops in the early '70s combined with well-documented drug use and unstable behavior forced him to retreat to his home in New Mexico. Eventually, he returned to acting in European films, and in 1986, he returned to prominence with a pair of captivating performances in *Blue Velvet* and *Hoosiers.* He's continued to earn accolades as both a crafty director and an expressive character actor.

Jack Palance

After nabbing Best Supporting Actor nominations for *Sudden Fear* (1952) and *Shane* (1953), the outspoken and cantankerous Jack Palance spent the majority of the 1960s and '70s appearing in forgettable foreign films interspersed with sporadic TV appearances. After years mired on the B-list, the former professional boxer struck Oscar gold as Curly, a brash and bold cattle wrangler in *City Slickers* (1991).

Mickey Rourke

After captivating audiences with gritty performances in secondary roles in *Body Heat* (1981), *Diner* (1982), and *Rumble Fish* (1983), Mickey Rourke starred in several successful films during the 1980s, including *9 1/2 Weeks* (1986) and *Barfly* (1987). But his difficult behavior on the set coupled with his erratic offscreen antics affected his status as a sought-after leading man. His ill-fated romances, plastic surgery to change his looks, and stint as a professional boxer made Hollywood execs shun him for lead roles. He continued to nab secondary roles in lackluster films throughout the 1990s and early 2000s. Then, in 2005, his performance in the CGI-heavy *Sin City* won him critical acclaim. And in 2008, Rourke returned to stardom in *The Wrestler,* which earned him a Golden Globe and an Academy Award nomination for Best Actor.

John Travolta

After starring in *Saturday Night Fever* (1977) and *Grease* (1978), two of the most successful movies of the 1970s, John Travolta spent much of the mid-1980s out of the limelight, relegated to substandard schlock such as *The Experts* (1989) and *Chains of Gold* (1991). But when director Quentin Tarantino tapped Travolta to star in *Pulp Fiction* (1994), he regained his status as a cool customer. Since then, he's delighted audiences in *Get Shorty* (1995), *Face/Off* (1997), and *Hairspray* (2007).

Alfred Hitchcock

☆ ☆ ☆ ☆

*Born in London in 1899, Alfred Joseph Hitchcock became the
most recognizable director in Hollywood history, not only for
his commanding presence but also in regard to his cinematic
style. Known as "The Master of Suspense," he made, on average,
about one movie per year in a career that spanned more than
50 years. His influence in the world of cinema is unparalleled.
Here's a little more about everyone's favorite Hitch.*

Hitch: The Younger Years

Hitchcock's films were largely
suspense-filled, psychological
thrillers with gallows humor
that attracted audiences with
their subject matter and dark
visual imagery. He had a gift for
transforming familiar characters
and ordinary-looking locations into
frightening stories about the moral

failings that lurk in all of us and the evil hidden in the everyday world.

The son of a greengrocer in a working-class London neighborhood, Alfred was the only child of strict parents. When Hitch left
school, he pursued a career as a draftsman, but became increasingly
interested in movies. In 1920, with some experience as a designer
under his belt, he got a job doing title cards (the intertitles that
contain the dialogue and text between the scenes of a silent film) for
a Hollywood studio called Famous Players–Lasky, which had an
office in London. It was the beginning of his illustrious film career.

Stepping Up

Hitch put in time doing art direction work and quickly climbed his
way up the ranks at the studio, becoming an assistant director in
1922. After some uncredited work, he got his first directorial assignment with *The Pleasure Garden* (1925). Sadly, none of the initial
projects embarked upon by the fledgling director took off. It wasn't

until 1927 that he had a hit—*The Lodger: A Story of the London Fog* was a commercial success and put Hitch on the map. Two years later, he directed Britain's first "talkie," a thriller called *Blackmail*. The story of a woman who suffers pangs of guilt for killing a would-be rapist, *Blackmail* foreshadowed Hitchcock's mature style.

In 1934, Hitchcock garnered international attention with *The Man Who Knew Too Much,* followed by *The 39 Steps* the next year. His approach to the thriller was established by this time, and he became adept at using a plot device he liked to call the MacGuffin— the thing in the story that the characters are concerned with (important papers, secret microfilm, uranium) but the audience doesn't really care about because they are wrapped up in the suspense and the motivations of the characters.

By the end of the 1930s, the rotund English director had made quite the name for himself as a significant auteur. It was time to take on Hollywood.

Hollywood Loves Hitchcock

In 1939, mega-producer David O. Selznick offered Hitchcock a deal. Selznick had just made cinematic history producing the record-breaking, Oscar-winning epic *Gone with the Wind.* It gave the producer even more power, so when he offered Hitch a seven-year contract, it was clear that Selznick would have a significant amount of control over the director's work, which was par for the course in Hollywood at the time. It was not an arrangement that sat well with Hitch, but he agreed to the terms; he finally had Hollywood money with which to make his movies.

The first picture of the partnership was *Rebecca* (1940), a Gothic melodrama that starred Sir Laurence Olivier and Joan Fontaine. The movie was a critical and commercial hit, and when Oscar time rolled around, *Rebecca* won Best Picture. Hitch didn't win for Best Director, but it secured his reputation in Hollywood.

Hitch's Heyday

Throughout the 1940s, Hitchcock worked tirelessly, making movies that used familiar filmmaking techniques and typical conventions. Yet with his exquisite craftsmanship, the films were like works of art. He also toyed with audience expectations in regard to the casting, using leading man Cary Grant in a sinister role in *Suspicion* (1941), for example. Classic Hitch titles such as *Lifeboat* (1944) and—the director's personal favorite—*Shadow of a Doubt* (1943) were made during this time, complete with his expressive use of light and shadows, carefully worked-out compositions, and oblique angles.

But if Hitch had a golden age, it was the 1950s. The list of films he made reads like a "best of" list: *Dial M for Murder* (1954), *Rear Window* (1954), *To Catch a Thief* (1955), a remake of *The Man Who Knew Too Much* (1956), and *Vertigo* (1958). Hitch worked multiple times with Jimmy Stewart and Cary Grant as well as leading lady Grace Kelly. His favorite female archetype was the cool, sophisticated blonde, whom he often used as the lead character and even the protagonist. These films featured his key themes: the presence of evil in the everyday world, the deceptive nature of appearances, and the idea that we are all guilty of something. Hitchcock's most famous plotline—the story of the falsely accused man—was epitomized by the film that topped the decade, *North by Northwest* (1959).

By the 1950s, color film was the norm. Hitchcock used it to his advantage when it suited him, but he still had a fondness for the expressive nature of black and white, which was evidenced by one of his major masterpieces: *Psycho* (1960).

Later Years

Considered his most famous films, *Psycho* and *The Birds* (1963) mixed suspense with anxiety-inducing soundtracks by legendary composer Bernard Herrmann. *The Birds* chronicles an infestation of avian creatures that are terrorizing a California town, while *Psycho* offers a warning about the darkness that exists in all of us through the character of Norman Bates. As Norman says, "We all go a little mad sometimes... haven't you?"

Hitch made two more significant works, *Marnie* (1964) and *Frenzy* (1972), but when his health started to decline, his output began to suffer. In 1976, the undisputed "Master of Suspense" made his last film, *Family Plot,* before dying of kidney failure in 1980.

TV Shows that Grew Up to Be Movies

Directors and producers are constantly scouring local bookstores and wading through stacks of scripts on their desks searching for what will become their next blockbuster. But sometimes, inspiration comes while they're lounging on the sofa watching television. Here are a few popular TV shows that made their way to the big screen:

The Addams Family	McHale's Navy
The Avengers	Miami Vice
Babylon 5	Mighty Morphin Power Rangers
Batman	Mission: Impossible
The Beverly Hillbillies	The Mod Squad
Bewitched	The Muppet Show
The Brady Bunch	My Favorite Martian
Car 54, Where Are You?	Popeye
Charlie's Angels	The Saint
Dragnet	Sex and the City
Dudley Do-Right	Sgt. Bilko
The Dukes of Hazzard	The Simpsons
Flipper	Starsky and Hutch
The Fugitive	Star Trek
Get Smart	S.W.A.T.
The Honeymooners	The Transformers
Inspector Gadget	The Twilight Zone
I Spy	Twin Peaks
Leave It to Beaver	The Untouchables
Lost in Space	The Wild, Wild West
Maverick	The X-Files

Albert Dekker's Gruesome Demise

☆ ☆ ☆ ☆

When a veteran actor is found dead in his apartment,
compromised circumstances unleash a wave of speculation.

Sex-O-Rama

If you enter "kinky Hollywood sex" into an Internet search engine,
(which we don't recommend, by the way) you probably won't find
a reference to Albert Dekker. Yet, when Dekker, the star of *Doctor
Cyclops* (1940) and *The Killers* (1946), died tragically more than
40 years ago, his body was found in a state that greatly pushed the
envelope of accepted sexual mores of the time. When the seasoned
thespian took his final bow at age 62, he left even the most jaded
observers slack-jawed in disbelief.

Who Was Albert Dekker?

Born in Brooklyn, New York, in 1905, Albert Dekker was a highly
respected character actor who had been trained for the stage. After
a solid career on Broadway, in which he appeared in *Grand Hotel*
and *Parnell* in the early 1930s, he moved to Hollywood. Interested
in politics, Dekker held the Democratic seat in the California State
Assembly from 1944 to 1946. However, his life was not without tragedy. In the early 1950s, Dekker was one of many victimized by the
accusations of Joseph McCarthy, which resulted in the actor's return
to the stage. Also, his son John died from an accidental gunshot
wound. But by the 1960s, Dekker had returned to Hollywood.

Macabre Discovery

On May 5, 1968, when Dekker's fiancée Geraldine Saunders was
unable to reach him by telephone, she drove to his Hollywood apartment and found a number of notes left on his door by concerned
friends. After summoning the building's manager, Saunders entered
the residence. What she saw sprawled before her was enough to
make her lose consciousness. Dekker was dead, that was for certain,
but the way that he had died was most disturbing. Kneeling nude in
his bathtub, the actor wore a hangman's noose around his neck and

sported a hypodermic needle in each arm. Suggestive words such as *whip* and *slave* were scrawled on his body in red lipstick, and a rubber-ball bit was stuffed in his mouth, with the metal chains from the bit tied behind his head. Blindfolded by a scarf, Dekker was attached to three leather straps that terminated in a hitch. These, in turn, were hooked to a strap that was held in Dekker's hand. Completing the bizarre picture were a pair of handcuffs around each wrist (with keys inserted) and obscene drawings on his abdomen.

All Choked Up

After a brief investigation, detectives concluded that Dekker had committed suicide. However, finding little evidence to support that theory, Los Angeles County Coroner Thomas Noguchi ruled the death an "accidental death, not a suicide." Some of Dekker's friends rejected both findings. They suspected murder even though the death scene showed no signs of forced entry or a struggle, although according to some reports, some camera equipment and cash were missing. Dekker's fiancée also insisted that the actor was murdered. She guessed that the killer was "someone he knew and let into the apartment." But coroner Noguchi rejected the idea of foul play in favor of accidental strangulation by "autoerotic asphyxia." The coroner explained that this solitary sexual act often features blindfolds, cross-dressing, and handcuffs. This appeared to be the case with Dekker.

A Sexual Pioneer

After his death, Albert Dekker became even more famous, but unfortunately, his heightened fame was for all the wrong reasons. Dekker's last film, *The Wild Bunch,* was released posthumously in 1969. The Western featured a group of desperados who had little use for conformity or rules. The film, directed by Sam Peckinpah, is now considered a masterpiece of editing and one of Hollywood's most provocative revisionist Westerns. It was a notable final film and a fitting epitaph considering the mode of Dekker's death.

In 2009, actor David Carradine was found dead in a similar embarrassing state. The circumstances surrounding Carradine's death invited speculation along the same lines as Dekker's demise. Sadly, both actors' deaths overshadowed their talents and accomplishments.

Play It Again, Ronald

☆ ☆ ☆ ☆

One of the most enduring Tinseltown myths is that Ronald Reagan was under serious consideration for the role of Rick Blaine in Casablanca *(1942)—a character forever associated with Humphrey Bogart.*

It turns out that the Reagan-as-Rick story was a clever publicity stunt perpetrated by Warner Bros., but no actor other than Humphrey Bogart was ever considered for what would become one of cinema's most iconic roles. The rumor started when the publicity department at Warner Bros. planted a false press release in the *Hollywood Reporter* on January 5, 1942, announcing that Ronald Reagan and Ann Sheridan were set to costar in *Casablanca*, which was still in the script stage at the time.

Why would a major studio intentionally plant such a falsehood? To protect its property—in this case, Ronald Reagan. Under the old system, studios such as Warner Bros. worked hard to keep the names of their best talent in the public (and professional) eye. Planting false news items in the industry press and elsewhere was an easy way to accomplish this.

Interestingly, Reagan couldn't have appeared in *Casablanca* even if the role of Rick Blaine had been up for grabs. He was a second lieutenant in the Army Reserve, and Warner Bros. had been getting deferments for him for several months. But when the United States entered World War II on December 8, 1941, there was no question that the actor would be called up for active duty long before *Casablanca* began filming in April 1942. And that's exactly what happened.

- *Ronald Reagan was not the only star leaked as the possible lead in* Casablanca. *George Raft—known for playing gangsters—was also floated as a contender but was never seriously considered.*

20 Memorable Nicknames

Match the actor with his or her sobriquet.

1. Ursula Andress
2. George Arliss
3. Brigitte Bardot
4. John Barrymore
5. Jack Benny
6. Clara Bow
7. Francis X. Bushman
8. Lon Chaney
9. Robert De Niro
10. Clark Gable
11. Betty Grable
12. Jean Harlow
13. Bob Hope
14. Carmen Miranda
15. Rita Moreno
16. Mary Pickford
17. Norma Shearer
18. Sylvester Stallone
19. Lupe Velez
20. John Wayne

A. America's Sweetheart
B. Bobby Milk
C. The Brazilian Bombshell
D. The Duke
E. The Feet
F. The First Gentleman of the Screen
G. The First Lady of the Screen
H. The Girl with the Million Dollar Legs
I. The Great Profile
J. The Handsomest Man in the World
K. The Ice Maiden
L. The Italian Stallion
M. The It Girl
N. The Man of 1,000 Faces
O. The King of Hollywood
P. The Meanest Man in the World
Q. The Mexican Spitfire
R. Old Ski Nose
S. The Original Platinum Blonde
T. The Sex Kitten

Lights, Camera, Technicolor!

☆ ☆ ☆ ☆

*Moving pictures were astonishing to the audiences
who first saw them, and with the coming of color,
all of a sudden, movies looked like real life.*

Tripping the Shutter

The marvel of moving pictures was first demonstrated in 1878 by
Eadweard Muybridge, who set up a series of 24 still cameras at
a racetrack in Palo Alto, California. The shutter of each camera
was connected to a string; as a horse galloped by, the strings were
tripped, and each camera captured an image. Muybridge fashioned
a crude process to project the images in sequence and demonstrated
his process in San Francisco in 1880.

In 1891, Thomas Edison set up a lab in West Orange, New Jersey,
and patented a 35mm motion picture camera called the Kinetograph.
In 1900, Edison hired Edwin S. Porter, a camera technician, who
quickly realized that entire stories could be told with film, and he
proceeded to do just that. Major film studios opened in Chicago,
New York City, and other parts of the country, but by the mid-teens,
most filmmakers had settled in sunny southern California.

Problems Persist

As the film industry continued to grow, several issues remained. The
cinema was silent, and images were black and white—hardly realistic.
During the 1920s, feature films were usually accompanied by live
piano or organ music as action unfolded on the screen. Some studios
tried to enhance the visual experience by hand-tinting certain scenes
in various washes of color.

Color movies had been tried with limited success in England.
Known as Kinemacolor, the process involved special cameras and
projectors that used black-and-white film with two colored filters.
But the result was questionable, producing fringed and haloed
effects that distracted from the projected image. Even so, more than
50 American films had been produced with the Kinemacolor process
by the late teens.

The Color of Money

Technicolor picked up where Kinemacolor left off. Three chemical and mechanical experts named Kalmus, Comstock, and Wescott, recognizing the need for a realistic color film stock, created the Technicolor Company in 1915 (taking Tech from their alma mater, Massachusetts Institute of Technology). Their two-color dye process gained limited use for some sequences in epics from the 1920s, including *The Ten Commandments* (1923), *Ben-Hur* (1925), *The Phantom of the Opera* (1925), and *The King of Kings* (1927). By the end of the 1920s, the two-color process had reached talking pictures with *On with the Show!* (1929).

Still, Technicolor was garish and didn't look real. Kalmus convinced Walt Disney to try a refined three-color Technicolor process on his animated short *Flowers and Trees* (1932). The result was a breathtaking success: an Academy Award for Disney and a contract to produce all future Disney films in Technicolor (which remained in force until the Hollywood Technicolor plant closed in 1975).

The new Technicolor process used a series of filters, prisms, and lenses to create a red, a blue, and a green strip. The three were then combined, and the result was a three-strip print. The success of this film stock was not lost on Hollywood, as budgets were increased to allow for color productions. While black-and-white features such as *Citizen Kane* (1941), *Casablanca* (1942), and *The Treasure of the Sierra Madre* (1948) became classics of the 1940s, Technicolor had already become part of the visual story in landmark films such as *The Wizard of Oz* and *Gone with the Wind*, both released in 1939.

Aging Somewhat Gracefully

By the 1950s, television had taken a large bite out of moviegoing America. To fight back, Hollywood tried gimmicks such as wide screens (CinemaScope and VistaVision, for example) and three-dimensional projection (3-D). Technicolor continued to thrive and was used for 3-D features including *House of Wax* (1953) and *Dial M for Murder* (1954). But by the 1970s, the cost of making Technicolor films had become very high, and the dye process was too slow to serve the country's theaters with enough prints. *The Godfather* (1972) and *The Godfather: Part II* (1974) were among the last American films to use the Technicolor process.

When Stunts Become Deadly

When it comes to on-camera stunts, A-list actors depend on specially trained doubles to do the dangerous work. Sometimes, though, things go very wrong, and even the most experienced stunt professionals have no way of recovering. Here are a few examples.

The Crow (1993)

It wasn't a stuntman who died during the making of *The Crow* but the lead actor himself. The title character, played by Brandon Lee, son of the late, great kung-fu star Bruce Lee, gets shot by a drug dealer lurking in his apartment. Tragically, the handgun used in the scene had a real bullet lodged in its barrel, which was propelled out by the force of the blank. Lee was hit in the abdomen and died later that day—just a few days before the movie wrapped. The filmmakers ended up finishing the movie with a combination of doubles and computer enhancement.

The Dark Knight (2008)

Heath Ledger wasn't the only person from *The Dark Knight* who died tragically. Special effects technician Conway Wickliffe died while filming a test run for a Batmobile stunt. Wickliffe was on a camera truck traveling parallel to the Batmobile when the driver of the vehicle missed a turn and clipped a tree with the side of the truck that the camera and Wickliffe were on. Wickliffe was fatally injured by the impact.

Million Dollar Mystery (1987)

A stunt veteran known for flawless performances lost his life while filming this movie. Dar Robinson—who, legend has it, had never broken a single bone in nearly 20 years of stunt work—was performing a motorcycle stunt when he lost control of the bike and drove over a cliff.

Noah's Ark (1928)

Three extras died during the Great Flood scene in *Noah's Ark* when they became trapped in the water and drowned. Some sources claim that John Wayne was actually among the extras in the scene.

Red Cliff (2008)

Director John Woo—the filmmaker behind action flicks such as *Face/Off* (1997) and *Mission: Impossible II* (2000)—made his first Chinese film in 16 years with *Red Cliff*. During the filming, however, a stunt involving a collision between two boats started a massive fire that claimed the life of 23-year-old stuntman Lu Yanqing.

The Skywayman (1920)
Stunt pilots Ormer Locklear and Milton "Skeets" Elliott died on the final day of filming for The Skywayman. The two were attempting to perform a dive in an airfield filled with oil rigs. Blinded by movie lights, which crew members had failed to turn off at a designated point in the stunt, the aerialists crashed while trying to pull out of the maneuver.

Steel (1979)
A fall designed to kill a character in Steel ended up killing the stuntman performing it. In the scene, stuntman A. J. Bakunas falls from a construction site. In the original take, Bakunas jumped from the ninth floor and landed without trouble. But because he wanted to reclaim the record for the world's highest stunt fall, he asked to reshoot the fall, jumping from the 22nd floor. During the second attempt, the airbag Bakunas landed on broke upon impact, and he died from his injuries the next day.

Top Gun (1986)
If you think the high-flying maneuvers in Top Gun looked dangerous, that's because they were. In fact, stunt pilot Art Scholl died while flying one of the movie's jets over the Pacific Ocean. Scholl was engaging in a spin maneuver when he lost control of the aircraft and crashed into the water.

Twilight Zone: The Movie (1983)
Three actors died during a notorious stunt for Twilight Zone: The Movie. Veteran actor Vic Morrow and child actors My-Ca Dinh Le and Renee Shin-Yi Chen were running from a helicopter during a Vietnamese battle scene. When a pyrotechnic explosion damaged the chopper's tail, it spun out of control, crashed sideways, and decapitated Morrow and My-Ca Dinh Le, then landed on top of Renee Shin-Yi Chen. Several crew members, including director John Landis and a stunt organizer, were indicted on various counts of involuntary manslaughter, but they were acquitted.

XXX (2002)
This Vin Diesel blockbuster was jam-packed with stunts, but one in particular stands out for catastrophic reasons. Stuntman Harry O'Connor was parasailing over a bridge in Prague when he hit a pillar and died. O'Connor had already completed the stunt once without incident and was doing a second take when the accident occurred.

Roman Polanski

☆ ☆ ☆ ☆

In 1969, director Roman Polanski was in the news when his pregnant wife, actress Sharon Tate, was brutally murdered by the followers of Charles Manson. Eight years later, Polanski made headlines again, this time for a scandal of his own.

In 1977, the famed director of movies such as *Rosemary's Baby* (1968) and *Chinatown* (1974) was hired to photograph 13-year-old aspiring model Samantha Geimer for *Vogue* magazine. Allegedly, 43-year-old Polanski plied the girl with champagne and antianxiety medication, then had sex with her. As part of a plea bargain, Polanski pleaded guilty to unlawful sexual intercourse, and, in exchange, prosecutors dropped other charges such as furnishing a controlled substance to a minor.

Initially, the judge ordered a 90-day jail term for the director to undergo a psychiatric evaluation. He was officially released after 42 days. Polanski's lawyers expected he would receive probation at sentencing, but they got wind that the judge was going to suggest imprisonment and possible deportation. So prior to sentencing, where he faced up to 50 years in jail, Polanski skipped bail. The filmmaker, who was still a French citizen, relocated to Paris, where under French law he was safe from extradition to the United States. Because he fled before sentencing, the original charges remained pending.

Despite frequent legal attempts to dismiss the case, Polanski remained a fugitive and lived in self-imposed exile from the United States for more than 30 years. When he won the Best Director Oscar for *The Pianist* in 2003, actor Harrison Ford collected the award at the ceremony on his behalf.

Then in September 2009, Polanski was arrested when he entered Switzerland to accept a lifetime achievement award at the Zurich International Film Festival. He spent two months in a Swiss jail, until late November when he was released after paying $4.5 million bail. Polanski was placed on house arrest at his luxurious Swiss chalet and was required to wear a monitoring bracelet. As of this writing, U.S. authorities continue their efforts to get Polanski extradited, while his lawyers attempt to get the case dismissed.

Carole Lombard

☆ ☆ ☆ ☆

Carole Lombard was at the height of her career
when she died in a plane crash outside of Las Vegas.
Even today, fans still mourn her passing.

Lombard appeared in her first film, *A Perfect Crime,* in 1921 at age 13 and costarred in more than 20 silent comedies during the 1920s. She signed with Paramount in 1930 and starred in several movies that showcased her skills at both drama and comedy, including *It Pays to Advertise* (1931), *Twentieth Century* (1934), and *My Man Godfrey* (1936), a screwball comedy for which she received her only Academy Award nomination. In 1931, Lombard married actor William Powell, who was 16 years her senior, but the couple amicably divorced two years later. In 1939, she married the newly divorced Clark Gable, with whom she had been having a not-so-secret affair.

In January 1942, Lombard traveled to her home state of Indiana for a war bonds rally, during which she sold more than $2 million worth of bonds. Turning to her fans, Lombard said, "Before I say goodbye to you all, come on and join me in a big cheer! V for Victory!" The crowd erupted in applause.

On January 16, at 4 A.M., Lombard and her mother boarded a plane to return to Hollywood. Less than half an hour after refueling in Las Vegas, the DC-3 on which Lombard was flying crashed into a mountain, killing all 22 people onboard.

The Army offered to give the 33-year-old actress a military burial, and the Hollywood Victory Committee sought to build a memorial in her honor. However, Gable declined both requests and had Lombard and her mother interred at Forest Lawn Memorial Park in Glendale, California, per Lombard's wishes.

What's in a Name?

*Actors commonly change their names to something more
glamorous. Sometimes, the change is as simple as altering
a single letter, such as Warren Beatty (born Warren Beaty).
In other cases, the story is much more interesting.*

Doris Day
Born Doris von Kappeloff, the singer/actress was renamed Doris Day by
bandleader Barney Rapp, for whom she sang "Day After Day." Her
biggest movies include *The Pajama Game* (1957), *Teacher's Pet* (1958),
and *Pillow Talk* (1959). She was nominated for an Academy Award for
her role in the latter.

Judy Garland
A popular child actress, Garland entered this world as Frances Ethel
Gumm. Her stage name, which was reportedly suggested by entertainer
George Jessel, came from the Hoagy Carmichael song "Judy" and the last
name of Chicago theater critic Robert Garland. Best remembered as
Dorothy in *The Wizard of Oz* (1939), Garland also starred in *Meet Me in
St. Louis* (1944), *The Harvey Girls* (1946), *Easter Parade* (1948), and
A Star Is Born (1954), the latter of which earned her an Oscar nomination.

Judy Holliday
No one played ditzy blondes better than Judy Holliday, who was born
Judy Tuvim—*tuvim* being the Hebrew word for holiday. Her film career
began in 1938, with an unbilled bit in Orson Welles's comedy short *Too
Much Johnson,* and ended in 1960 with *Bells Are Ringing.* In between,
Holliday starred in several rollicking comedies, including *Born Yesterday*
(1950) (for which she won an Academy Award), *The Marrying Kind*
(1952), and *It Should Happen to You* (1954).

Rock Hudson
The epitome of rugged, Hudson was born Roy Scherer Jr. He received
his screen name from his agent, Henry Willson, who, according to
Hollywood legend, combined the Rock of Gibraltar and the Hudson River.
Hudson made his first movie in 1948 (an uncredited role in *Fighter
Squadron*) and was soon in high demand. His best-known movies include
Giant (1956), which earned him an Academy Award nomination;

A Farewell to Arms (1957); *Pillow Talk* (1959); and the cult favorite *Seconds* (1966).

Buster Keaton
One of the greatest comedic actors and directors in movie history, Keaton was known to his family as Joseph until he tumbled down some stairs as a baby. Family friend Harry Houdini reportedly remarked to Keaton's dad, "That was some buster your boy took!" Keaton starred in and directed or codirected dozens of comedies over the years, including *The Boat* (1921), *Cops* (1922), *Sherlock Jr.* (1924), and *The General* (1927).

Carole Lombard
Best remembered for her beauty, her acting, and her marriage to Clark Gable, Lombard was known simply as Jane Alice Peters before she hit the big time. When it came time to choose a more glamorous moniker, her studio, Fox Films, named her Carol Lombard. Later, she added the e for luck. Her better-known films include *My Man Godfrey* (1936), *Nothing Sacred* (1937), *Mr. & Mrs. Smith* (1941), and *To Be or Not to Be* (1942).

Groucho Marx
Groucho, a comedy legend whose films still make audiences laugh, was born Julius Marx. His stage name and those of his brothers, Chico, Harpo, Zeppo, and Gummo, were inspired by the names in a popular comic strip called *Mager's Monks*, in which all the characters' monikers ended in *o*. The Marx Brothers' most beloved movies include *Animal Crackers* (1930), *Monkey Business* (1931), *Horse Feathers* (1932), *Duck Soup* (1933), and *A Night at the Opera* (1935). Groucho also hosted the popular television game show *You Bet Your Life* from 1950 to 1961.

Marilyn Monroe
Still an icon more than 45 years after her death, Marilyn Monroe was simply known as Norma Jean Baker (or, by her married name, Norma Jean Dougherty) before the 20th Century Fox talent director renamed her after one of his favorite performers, Marilyn Miller. Monroe was the maiden name of Norma Jean's mother. The blonde bombshell starred in a string of popular movies during her relatively brief career, including *Gentlemen Prefer Blondes* (1953), *The Seven Year Itch* (1955), and *Some Like It Hot* (1959), for which she won a Golden Globe award.

Jaws

☆ ☆ ☆ ☆

Originally released in 1975, the movie Jaws *single-handedly made millions of people nervous about putting so much as a toe in the ocean. That was due mainly to director Steven Spielberg's filming technique, which played on the audience's fear of the unknown. Spielberg hadn't originally planned on shooting the movie that way, but he was forced to improvise when the star of the show—a mechanical shark—simply refused to work.*

Spielberg Dives In . . . And Bites Off More than He Can Chew

It all started in late 1973, when director Steven Spielberg picked up a galley proof of something simply labeled *Jaws* from the desk of producer David Brown. Spielberg didn't know it at the time, but he had just picked up the adaptation of the immensely popular novel by Peter Benchley about a killer great white shark that wreaks havoc on a tiny New England town. Spielberg loved what he read and immediately had visions of a giant shark leaping out of the water, teeth bared, and attacking people as they swam for their lives. Benchley's vivid descriptions of the shark swimming through the water also made it clear to Spielberg that the shark would be the star of the show. There was only one problem: No one had ever used a live great white shark as an actor before.

So Spielberg began reaching out to shark experts to see what, if anything, live sharks would be capable of doing on cue. After being all but laughed out of the aquarium, Spielberg came to the conclusion that he'd have to create a mechanical shark to play the lead role. But once again, there was a problem: No one had ever created a mechanical shark before.

Anybody Know How to Build a Killer Shark?

Production designer Joe Alves was given the undesirable job of hunting down someone who could build a fully operational, 25-foot great white shark.

Most people thought this would be impossible to create, but Alves heard whispers that if anyone could create such a beast, it would be special effects guru Bob Mattey, who was responsible for creating the giant squid used in the film *20,000 Leagues Under the Sea* (1954). After meeting with Alves, Mattey was so convinced that he could create the shark that he agreed to come out of retirement.

Building the Perfect Killing Machine

Mattey was hired to create three 25-foot mechanical sharks. Two of them were "half-sharks" and were completely open on one side (one on the left side, the other on the right) to make them easier to manipulate when only one side of the shark needed to be filmed. The third shark created was a "full shark," which would serve as the star of the film. Spielberg named this shark "Bruce" after his personal lawyer, Bruce Raymer. Finally, a single dorsal fin that could be pulled along the surface of the water was also built.

All in all, it took about three months to create the sharks, which forced Spielberg to move ahead with filming scenes that did not include the beast and allowed the actors time to flush out their characters and create an ensemble approach to their performances. In order to speed up production time, it was decided that whenever a shark's mechanics needed to be tested, it would be done on dry land. This would prove to be a huge mistake.

Once complete, the sharks were shipped from California to Martha's Vineyard, Massachusetts, where filming was already well under way. Bruce the shark would then be mounted to a special framework on the ocean floor, and pneumatic equipment attached to the framework would allow Bruce to be raised and lowered on a 30-foot crane arm. Or so everyone thought.

Meet Flaws, The Great White Turd

Once the mechanical sharks arrived in Martha's Vineyard, Bruce was placed on a boat and brought out to sea. After a quick check to make sure all of the mechanics were working, Bruce was placed into the ocean for the very first time—and promptly sank to the bottom of Nantucket Sound. Professional divers had to be called upon to retrieve the shark.

Only then did the entire crew realize that the salt in the seawater was corroding the hydraulics used to move the shark. In fact, the saltwater was literally eating through the fake "skin" used to cover the sharks' bodies. The ocean waves were also knocking the beast around. For the next few days, as designers scrambled to fix things, Spielberg tried to film around what the crew was now calling "Flaws the Shark." But when days turned into weeks and the shark still wasn't working, Spielberg got so frustrated that he started referring to it as "The Great White Turd" because it only wanted to float on the water's surface or sink to the bottom of the ocean.

It took until August 1974—almost five months into shooting— before Bruce finally came up out of the water and worked properly (barely) in what would become known as the "You're Gonna Need a Bigger Boat" scene. But after the scene, the shark stopped working again. And at that point, even though they had reworked the script several times to film around the mechanical shark, the only scenes remaining were the ones that starred Bruce. And with the weather about to turn cold, it looked as though a broken mechanical shark was going to sink the whole project—until Spielberg got an idea that would change his vision for the entire movie.

"Shark's Eye View"

In Benchley's original novel, readers meet the shark before the first attack. But Spielberg decided that since Bruce was making him wait a long time, he'd make the audience wait, too.

When it became clear to Spielberg that the mechanical shark wasn't going to work as planned, he knew that he needed another approach to showing this underwater villain. It was then that he realized that it could be really scary *not* to see the shark. Recalling the production years later, Spielberg remarked that it was then that the film went from a "Japanese Saturday matinee horror flick to more of a Hitchcock, the-less-you-see-the-more-you-get thriller."

Now that Spielberg didn't need to rely on Bruce the shark anymore, he could use creative ways to let the audience know where the shark was. In one scene, the shark's location is marked by the broken section of dock that the killer fish is dragging behind it. And in the final showdown between man and beast, the shark's arrival is signaled by floating yellow barrels that have been harpooned into the shark. No giant teeth, no fins cutting through the water. Just a couple of floating barrels. And the audience was terrified!

Spielberg also decided to drop the camera angle down to the shark's level, either underneath or parallel to the water level. He felt that putting the audience at water level would make them feel as though they, too, were in danger of being attacked by the shark.

When filming finally wrapped, Spielberg took a look at what he had and was amazed. Despite Bruce's malfunctions and his late appearance in the movie, *Jaws* still managed to frighten audiences with suspense and their own fear of the unknown. In fact, Spielberg still contends that had he used more footage of Bruce, the film would not have worked as well. Of course, there was also John Williams's simple yet effective score which, with little more than two notes, foreshadowed trouble. *Dun-nuh, dun-nuh.*

A Trendsetter

By the time *Jaws* was released in June 1975, Universal had spent hundreds of thousands of dollars on a media blitz. That, combined with the picture's simultaneous release in 409 theaters, helped make the film an immediate sensation. During the summer of 1975, *Jaws* took in $129 million at the box office, making it the first-ever summer blockbuster. More importantly, the film's success influenced the major studios to use the blockbuster approach in releasing their films. Studios began to bank on releasing one or two blockbusters per year in order to generate enough profit to make and release the other films on their schedules. Major genre films, such as comedies or action flicks, were designated for summer release, while serious films were relegated to the fall or winter. Product tie-ins, such as T-shirts, action figures, and other merchandise, became part of the equation for a successful release. And releasing films nationwide on opening weekend became the norm; in other words, big-budget, large-scale films were released in hundreds of theaters on opening weekend instead of staggering the release, which was the norm prior to *Jaws.* For better or worse, the film with the big bite changed Hollywood practices forever. Not bad for a movie starring a broken mechanical shark.

Fast Facts: Buster Keaton

- *Keaton spent his entire childhood performing with his mother and father in the family vaudeville act in which he was constantly heaved, hurled, and hoisted across the stage. During this era, he learned many of the physical skills he later employed in his silent films, including mimicry, stuntwork and falls, and costuming. He never attended school, but he learned to read while on the road.*

- *Keaton's first film was* The Butcher Boy *(1917), in which he costarred with Roscoe "Fatty" Arbuckle, one of the silver screen's first superstars.*

- *Keaton learned about filmmaking while working on Arbuckle's shorts, which were made for producer Joseph Schenck. When Arbuckle moved to Paramount, Keaton took over Schenck's Comique Films (later called Buster Keaton Productions). Keaton perfected his comic persona and learned how to direct comedy for cinema on the shorts he made for Schenck.*

- *Buster Keaton, Charlie Chaplin, and Harold Lloyd were the three top comedians of Hollywood's silent era.*

- *In 1923, Keaton made his first feature-length comedy,* The Three Ages, *a spoof of D. W. Griffith's* Intolerance.

- *Keaton's comedy included large-scale stunts and gags, often involving vehicles and buildings, which he performed with remarkable grace and agility. His stunts were not only remarkable but dangerous. While working on* Sherlock Jr., *he broke his neck when gallons of water spilled on top of him as part of a gag. He got up and walked away as scripted in order to finish the scene correctly, broken neck and all.*

- *Known as "The Great Stone Face," Buster Keaton is instantly recognizable by his trademark porkpie hat.*

- *After his Civil War opus* The General *flopped at the box office in 1927, Keaton sold his studio and the rights to his films (and essentially his soul) to MGM. Chaplin and Lloyd continued to enjoy great success and immeasurable wealth, while Keaton endured years of financial problems as well as creative failures because of MGM's inability to use him to his best advantage.*

- *In a case of art imitating life, Keaton appeared as a down-on-his-luck silent screen star who plays bridge with Gloria Swanson in Billy Wilder's* Sunset Boulevard *(1950). Although he was reportedly paid only $1,000 and mutters just one line in his brief cameo, Keaton's performance was a brilliant character study of lost dreams and shattered illusions.*

- *Keaton also appeared as an aging comedian in Chaplin's* Limelight *in 1952. It was the only time in their careers that the two great stars appeared together.*

- *In 1959, Buster Keaton was finally appreciated by Hollywood when he was awarded with an honorary Oscar.*

- *In 1965, Keaton starred in a silent short called* The Railrodder *for the National Film Board of Canada. Wearing his trademark porkpie hat, he rode the rails and traveled from one end of Canada to the other on a motorized handcar, performing gags similar to those that made him a box-office star in the 1920s. It was the last silent movie of his illustrious career.*

- *Although it was completed before* The Railrodder, *the last film released starring Keaton was Richard Lester's* A Funny Thing Happened on the Way to the Forum. *The film didn't hit movie screens in North America until October 16, 1966, almost nine months after Keaton had passed away.*

- *Buster Keaton's last public performance—and appearance—was at a star-studded salute to Stan Laurel hosted by Dick Van Dyke that aired on TV in November 1965. He died two months later on February 1, 1966.*

Universal Studios: The Horror Factory

☆ ☆ ☆ ☆

Any sincere discussion of cinematic horror must begin with the terrifying quartet of Dracula *(1931),* Frankenstein *(1931),* The Mummy *(1932), and* The Wolf Man *(1941). Firmly entrenched in pop culture for more than 70 years, all four films were produced by Universal Studios—Hollywood's horror factory.*

Established in 1912, Universal initially specialized in melodramas and action-oriented films, such as Westerns. In 1923, however, Lon Chaney, one of the studio's biggest silent stars, was featured in the first of Universal's pantheon of horror films based on literary works: *The Hunchback of Notre Dame,* an adaptation of Victor Hugo's novel. Two years later, Chaney again shocked audiences with his portrayal of the grotesquely disfigured Erik in *The Phantom of the Opera.*

Bela and Boris

In the late 1920s and early 1930s, several directors, actors, and crew members from the German film industry immigrated to America and went to work at Universal. Most had worked in German Expressionism, which they introduced to Hollywood through low-key lighting techniques, set design preferences, and a penchant for visual symbolism. This was the birth of the American horror genre as we know it.

In 1931, Universal produced a movie that was pure horror— *Dracula,* starring Bela Lugosi as the tuxedo-wearing bloodsucker. Also in 1931, Boris Karloff frightened moviegoers in *Frankenstein,* which was a tremendous success that spawned several sequels, including *Bride of Frankenstein* (1935) and *Son of Frankenstein* (1939).

The following year, Karl Freund, Germany's greatest cinematographer, tried his hand at directing *The Mummy,* with Karloff as Im-Ho-Tep, the ancient being who comes back to life in modern Egypt. The exquisite high-contrast lighting, odd angles, and symbolic use of shadows defined the classic horror genre for decades. *The*

Mummy was so successful that it resulted in several sequels, including *The Mummy's Tomb* (1942) and *The Mummy's Curse* (1944).

In 1933, Universal again turned to classic literature for inspiration with *The Invisible Man,* starring Claude Rains as the demented Dr. Jack Griffin. And in 1941, Lon Chaney Jr. found himself covered with yak fur as *The Wolf Man,* a role that defined his career.

Monster Mash-Up

In 1943, Universal pitted two of its most famous monsters against each other in *Frankenstein Meets the Wolf Man.* The two creatures appeared to die at the end, but neither stayed dead for long. The studio resurrected them in *House of Dracula* (1945) and again in the horror comedy *Abbott and Costello Meet Frankenstein* (1948).

Universal also produced many lesser-known but still notable fright flicks, including *Murders in the Rue Morgue* (1932), *The Old Dark House* (1932), *The Black Cat* (1934), and *The Invisible Woman* (1940).

The Frightening '50s

The 1930s and '40s were the glory years for Universal monsters, but the studio continued to give horror audiences what they craved. One of its biggest hits of the 1950s was *The Creature from the Black Lagoon* (1954), which birthed two sequels: *Revenge of the Creature* (1955) and *The Creature Walks Among Us* (1956). Other memorable Universal monster movies of the '50s featured sci-fi elements, such as *It Came from Outer Space* (1953) and *Tarantula* (1955), as well as several Abbott and Costello comedies in which the duo met everyone from the Invisible Man to Dr. Jekyll and Mr. Hyde.

He Created a Monster

Much of the success of Universal's most fearsome fiends must be credited to makeup artist Jack Pierce, who created the unique look for Bela Lugosi's Dracula, the many incarnations of Frankenstein's monster, Lon Chaney Jr.'s Wolf Man, and Boris Karloff's Mummy. Pierce also did impressive work on *The Invisible Man, The Old Dark House,* and *Werewolf of London* (1935), among many others. Had it not been for Pierce's creative vision and talent, Boris Karloff might never have become the personification of Frankenstein's horrifying creation, nor Lon Chaney Jr. the world's most famous werewolf.

Civil War Movies

Since its inception, Hollywood has been enamored with the Civil War. From early silent films to modern-day blockbusters, here are some movies that have featured the war's glory and despair.

The Birth of a Nation (1915)
Directed by film pioneer D. W. Griffith and based on the Thomas Dixon Jr. novel *The Clansman*, *The Birth of a Nation* depicts abolitionist Northerners and slaveholding Southerners in pre–Civil War times. Starring Lillian Gish, Walter Long, and Henry B. Walthall, the story journeys through the war and into Reconstruction, where the Ku Klux Klan is born to "restore order" in the South. Regarded by most modern viewers as a divisive film that supports racism and the Klan, this silent classic nonetheless remains a giant among cinema historians and critics for its technical innovations.

The General (1927)
Starring, cowritten, and codirected by Buster Keaton—"The Great Stone Face"—this film is considered one of the greatest silent comedies of all time. The film is set during the Civil War and depicts the true story of Andrews's Raid. Keaton stars as a train engineer in the Confederate South who loses his locomotive—*The General*—along with his fiancée to Union spies. One acclaimed scene involves Keaton removing a railroad tie from the tracks while perched on the train's cowcatcher.

Gone with the Wind (1939)
Undeniably the most lavish and bold cinematic statement on the Civil War and Reconstruction period, this movie was based on the Pulitzer Prize-winning novel by Margaret Mitchell. At its core, the movie, which stars Clark Gable, Vivien Leigh, Olivia de Havilland, Leslie Howard, and Hattie McDaniel, follows a love story in the Confederate South. A rising crane shot of hundreds of wounded and dead Confederate soldiers in the Atlanta railroad yard following the crushing siege of the city stands as one of Hollywood's most memorable scenes.

A Southern Yankee (1948)
This comedy stars Red Skelton as a would-be Union spy who ventures deep into Confederate territory and falls for a Southern belle. One famous sight gag, designed by Buster Keaton, has Skelton walking a battlefield between North and South—half-dressed as a Northerner and half-dressed as a Southerner, carrying a two-sided flag. Once the wind changes direction, however, his cover is blown.

The Horse Soldiers (1959)
Directed by film legend John Ford, this movie stars William Holden and Constance Towers, as well as John Wayne, who plays a Union cavalry colonel who leads his troops deep into Confederate territory to sabotage supply and transportation lines. It is based on the true story of Grierson's Raid, which took place in Mississippi in April 1863.

Glory (1989)
This winner of three Academy Awards, which stars Matthew Broderick, Denzel Washington, Cary Elwes, and Morgan Freeman, highlights the story of the 54th Massachusetts Volunteer Regiment, one of the first formal U.S. Army units to be made up entirely of black soldiers. The climax of the film depicts the Battle of Fort Wagner in July 1863, during which the 54th showed great courage and bravery while suffering heavy casualties, convincing many skeptics that black soldiers had a significant contribution to make toward the war effort.

Gettysburg (1993)
Based on *The Killer Angels*, Michael Shaara's Pulitzer Prize-winning novel, *Gettysburg* details the definitive three-day battle with a cast that includes Jeff Daniels, Tom Berenger, Martin Sheen, and Stephen Lang. This four-hour film was shot on-site at many of the actual battle locations, including Devil's Den and Little Round Top.

Cold Mountain (2003)
A romance set at the end of the Civil War, this award-winning film starring Jude Law, Nicole Kidman, and Renée Zellweger follows a wounded Confederate soldier returning to his home in North Carolina. As he makes his trek to reunite with his sweetheart, he crosses paths with memorable people and events.

Screwball Comedy

☆ ☆ ☆ ☆

What do you get when you pair a zany heiress with a straitlaced working stiff? In Hollywood, the combination invariably results in witty banter, broad physical humor, and romantic sparring—all the makings of a screwball comedy.

In the Beginning...

When Columbia Pictures released *It Happened One Night* in 1934, there's no doubt that they expected it to do well. With charismatic young stars Clark Gable and Claudette Colbert and capable young director Frank Capra, it seemed destined to succeed. But the quirky romantic comedy exceeded all expectations, dominating the box office and becoming the first film to win all five of the major Academy Awards: Best Actor, Best Actress, Best Director, Best Writing, and the coveted Best Picture. The film thrust Capra, Gable, and Colbert to the top of Hollywood's A-list and launched a whole new genre that would become the dominant form of film humor for the next decade—the screwball comedy.

The inspired story features a rebellious socialite who runs away from her domineering father and teams up on the road with a down-on-his-luck reporter who's only slightly less conniving than she is. The pair find romance and, along the way, lampoon a variety of social institutions through their outrageous schemes and misadventures.

Defining Screwball

Technically, a screwball comedy is defined by its combination of three forms of humor—farce, slapstick, and romantic comedy. *It Happened One Night* had all three as well as a battle-of-the-sexes relationship between the leading characters and the all-important theme of social satire or class conflict between the rich and the working class. The latter is an important convention considering the genre was developed during the Depression. In the coming years, the genre would bring in other standard elements, such as rapid pacing, sophisticated and witty banter, mistaken or concealed identity, gender-role reversal, and wacky supporting characters. Later screwballs also put the woman much more firmly in control. In classic films like *Bringing Up Baby* (1938) with Katharine Hepburn and Cary Grant, the leading lady frustrates the perplexed male lead through a series of misadventures, maneuverings, or misunderstandings or through her unconventional personality, which jars him out of his complacency and guides him into her arms. In other examples like *His Girl Friday* (1940), starring Grant and Rosalind Russell, the lovebirds are more evenly matched in their sparring.

A number of actors became known for their work in screwball comedies, particularly Colbert and Grant, as well as Jean Arthur, Carole Lombard, Irene Dunne, Joel McCrea, and William Powell. And they worked with stellar directors on these films, including George Cukor, Howard Hawks, and Ernst Lubitsch. But the undisputed king of the genre is writer and director Preston Sturges, whose most significant accomplishments include *The Lady Eve* (1941) with Henry Fonda and Barbara Stanwyck, *Sullivan's Travels* (1941) starring McCrea and Veronica Lake, and *The Palm Beach Story* (1942) with Colbert and McCrea. Sturges raised the genre's satire, class differences, and dialogue to a new level of zaniness, which made him more strongly associated with the screwball comedy than any other filmmaker.

A Lasting Influence

The screwball comedy remains one of the most distinctive genres Hollywood has ever produced, and although the genre faded in the 1940s, it has continued to exert a major influence on comic films over the decades. Billy Wilder's *Some Like It Hot* (1959) and the Doris Day–Rock Hudson marital comedies from the 1960s owe a debt to these earlier madcap films. And every so often, a modern version will make its way into theaters, such as *What's Up Doc?* (1972) and *The Main Event* (1979). George Clooney has made attempts to recapture the spirit of these classic films with *Intolerable Cruelty* (2003), where he matches wits with Catherine Zeta-Jones in divorce court, and *Leatherheads* (2008), which has him squaring off against Renée Zellweger during the early days of professional football. Actress Sandra Bullock, with her willingness to sacrifice her beauty for a good pratfall, comes closest to a modern-day screwball actress as evidenced in *Forces of Nature* (1999) and *The Proposal* (2009).

Movie Records

Since the first feature film was put to celluloid, directors and producers have been trying to get people to come see their films—and that means outdoing the other guy. Maybe their heart-wrenching love story is more tragic. Maybe their explosions are more destructive. Maybe their casts are more famous, their budget bigger, and their kissing scenes longer. When movies set records, people pay attention. Here are a few notable record-setters.

Single Most Expensive Prop: Pirate ship in *Pirates* (1986)

Roman Polanski is definitely a risk taker. For this film starring Walter Matthau, several million dollars were spent on a to-scale Spanish pirate galleon. Sadly, the movie tanked and most people never saw it.

Highest-Grossing Movie Ever: *Titanic* (1997)

This romantic story set on the large, doomed ship grossed more than $1.84 billion worldwide. It didn't matter that everyone knew how the movie would end—they came in droves to see the romance between Leonardo DiCaprio and Kate Winslet, the impressive re-creation of the disaster, and the historically accurate set design.

Movie with the Most Crashed Police Cars: *Blues Brothers 2000* (1998)

When the original *Blues Brothers* came out in 1980, the film held the record for crashing the most police cars in a single movie—between 30 and 60, according to director John Landis. That record stood for nearly 20 years until the second *Blues Brothers* movie smashed up a reported 76 cars.

Actor Who Does the Most Kissing in a Single Film: John Barrymore in *Don Juan* (1926)

Pucker up, ladies: Hollywood folklore has it that Barrymore, a Don Juan both on and off the screen, kissed Mary Astor and Estelle Taylor 127 times in this famous silent film...and that's just counting smooches planted on his leading ladies. When you add lip-locks he handed out to the supporting cast, the final tally comes in at 191!

The Most Extras: *Gandhi* (1982)
Today, CGI gives filmmakers the ability to create football fields full of virtual people if they need them for a battle scene. But before CGI, directors actually had to use real people. The horror! For *Gandhi*, 300,000 extras were used for the funeral scene. We hope there were enough bathrooms!

Longest Movie Ever: *The Cure for Insomnia* (1987)
Directed by John Henry Timmis IV, this movie clocks in at 5,100 minutes—that's 3 days and 13 hours! The film consists of poet L. B. Groban reading a poem he wrote. That's right. One poem. Almost four days. Who needs more popcorn?

The Most Costumes in a Single Film: *Quo Vadis* (1951)
This epic film, which is set in Ancient Rome, required 32,000 costumes, which ate up the majority of the film's budget. They don't make 'em like they used to.

Most Best Actress Awards: Katharine Hepburn
This screen legend's career spanned more than 70 years, and, in that time, she received 12 Best Actress nominations and won four of the coveted statuettes.

Actor in the Most Movies: Tom London
Never heard of him, you say? London's record-setting career spanned 56 years. He began making films in 1903 and stopped in 1959, racking up more than 2,000 roles, according to *Guinness World Records*. London played everything from leading man to supporting actor to random extra in his astonishing array of film credits.

Longest End Credits: *Who Framed Roger Rabbit* (1988)
A whopping 743 names roll at the end of this Toontown adventure. Perhaps Jessica Rabbit had hair and makeup to thank?

Most Tedious Makeup Job: Rod Steiger, *The Illustrated Man* (1960)
There have been some humdinger movie costumes that took a long time for actors to put on, but none took longer than this one. Steiger sat in the makeup chair for ten hours each time he came to the set.

Ray Harryhausen: Master of Illusion

☆ ☆ ☆ ☆

*Though you may not recognize his name, Ray Harryhausen
is revered among fantasy film fans. Through the laborious
process known as stop-motion animation, the special effects
wizard has brought to life numerous dinosaurs, a giant
octopus, a monster from Venus, and everything in between.*

As a teenager, Harryhausen was enthralled by *King Kong* (1933).
He marveled at the giant gorilla's lifelike movements and eventually
struck up a friendship with Kong's animator, Willis O'Brien, who
taught Harryhausen the tricks of the trade. Harryhausen's first professional job was animating George Pal's Puppetoon shorts for Paramount Pictures. After a stint in the Army Signal Corps, he teamed
up with O'Brien to make *Mighty Joe Young* (1949), a big-gorilla flick
that starred Terry Moore and Ben Johnson.

From there, Harryhausen was hired by Warner Bros. to animate
the giant dinosaur that rampaged through New York City in
The Beast from 20,000 Fathoms (1953), a gig that cemented his
reputation as one of the best animators in the business. He soon
found himself at Columbia Pictures, where he created the special
effects for a variety of innovative science-fiction films, including
It Came from Beneath the Sea (1955), *Earth vs. the Flying Saucers*
(1956), *20 Million Miles to Earth* (1957), *Mysterious Island* (1961),
and *First Men in the Moon* (1964).

But it was Harryhausen's lifelong love of mythology that led to
some of his most acclaimed films, including three movies featuring
Sinbad the Sailor. His crowning achievement, however, was *Jason
and the Argonauts* (1963), which featured a remarkable sequence
involving seven sword-swinging skeletons. Though it lasts just a few
minutes on-screen, the scene took Harryhausen more than four
months to animate.

Clash of the Titans (1981), which starred Laurence Olivier and
Harry Hamlin, was Harryhausen's final film. In 1992, the master
animator received the Gordon E. Sawyer Award—an honorary
Academy Award—in recognition of his remarkable career.

Little Rascals with Big Troubles

Our Gang *was a popular prepubescent posse of rogues, rascals, and scamps that appeared in more than 200 short films over the course of 20 years. During the 1950s, the series was sold to television and rechristened* The Little Rascals, *and it ran in syndication for decades. Most of the 41 actors who portrayed the troublesome tykes went on to live rich and resourceful lives. However, for some of the motley mites, tragedy, turmoil, and tribulation marked their adult years.*

Matthew "Stymie" Beard
Beard costarred in numerous *Our Gang* shorts in the 1930s, but he started using drugs in adulthood and eventually spent time in jail for possession and dealing. He finally kicked his heroin habit in the 1960s and enjoyed a minor comeback as an actor, appearing on television shows, such as *Starsky and Hutch,* and in small roles in several critically acclaimed miniseries. He died in 1981.

Scott "Scotty" Beckett
A prodigious talent who joined the Rascals in 1934, Beckett became one of Hollywood's top child actors after leaving the *Our Gang* family in 1936. Beckett appeared in such notable films as *Dante's Inferno* (1935), *Charge of the Light Brigade* (1936), and *King's Row* (1942). But his childhood success didn't translate into adult employment, and he spent the last ten years of his life in a self-destructive spiral. He died of an apparent drug overdose in 1968 at age 38.

Robert Blake
One of the most famous and successful members of the *Our Gang* clan, Robert Blake appeared in 40 episodes of the series from 1939 to 1944 under the name Mickey Gubitosi. Later, he appeared as a regular in the Red Ryder film series. After serving in the U.S. Army, Blake became a noted movie actor, starring in such well-regarded films as *In Cold Blood* (1967) and *Tell Them Willie Boy Is Here* (1969). He also played the title character on the TV series *Baretta* from 1975 to 1978. But his career and personal integrity suffered a serious blow when he was arrested and charged with murdering his wife in 2001. Although he was acquitted of murder, he was found responsible for her death in a civil trial and was ordered to pay $30 million in damages to her children.

Norm "Chubby" Chaney

Chubby was a *Little Rascals* regular from 1929 to 1931. After leaving the troupe, he continued to gain weight without growing any taller. It was determined that he suffered from a glandular ailment, a malady that eventually led to his death in 1936 at age 21. He was the first *Our Gang* alumnus to pass away.

Richard "Mickey" Daniels Jr.

Daniels was a regular in the *Our Gang* series of shorts from 1922 until 1926. After he left the series, Daniels was part of another series for Hal Roach, *The Boy Friends.* As an adult, he quit acting and eventually became a construction worker. Despite appearing in several highly publicized *Our Gang* reunions, Daniels's death from cirrhosis of the liver in 1970 at age 55 went unnoticed by fans and film historians until 1991, when a researcher discovered records detailing his demise.

Darla Hood

A regular in the Gang from 1935 until 1941, Hood retired from movies at that time, returned to school, and graduated with honors from Fairfax High in Hollywood. As an adult, she resurrected her career by lending her voice to TV commercials and scoring a minor hit in 1957 with the song "I Just Wanna Be Free." She died in 1979 at age 47 after contracting hepatitis following minor surgery.

Bobby "Wheezer" Hutchins

Wheezer was an *Our Gang* member from 1927 to 1933 and appeared in more than 60 of the Hal Roach–produced film shorts. After outgrowing his role, he retired from acting, graduated from high school, and joined the Army Air Corps. The 20-year-old cadet was only days away from graduating from flying school when the B-26 Marauder aircraft he was attempting to land crashed on May 17, 1945.

Billy "Froggy" Laughlin
Froggy, whose nickname stemmed from his gravelly voice, joined the *Our Gang* family in the final years of their existence, appearing in 29 of the crowd-pleasing comedies between 1940 and 1944. He returned to school as a teenager and was working his morning paper route when a truck rammed into his motor scooter on August 31, 1948. At age 16, he was the youngest of the *Our Gang* family to die.

Jay R. "Freckle Face" Smith
Freckle Face was a steady contributor to the *Our Gang* series until 1929. At age 14, he retired from acting and later served in the U.S. Army and ran a retail paint business in Hawaii. In 2002, at age 87, Smith was murdered by a transient that he'd befriended. His body was eventually discovered in the desert near Las Vegas.

Carl "Alfalfa" Switzer
Carl Switzer was among the most popular and fondly regarded *Our Gang* alumni. A staple of the group from 1935 until 1940, he forged a fortuitous and formidable career as an adult character actor, appearing in such notable films as *It's a Wonderful Life* (1946), *Pat and Mike* (1952), and *The Defiant Ones* (1958). Despite that success, he also had difficulty dismantling his demons. In January 1959, he was shot and killed in a bizarre argument over an unpaid $50 debt and a missing hunting dog. He was just 31 years old.

Billie "Buckwheat" Thomas
Buckwheat, who was a member of *Our Gang* from 1934 until the series' demise in 1944, was one of the few African American members of the group. He appeared in 97 productions, including all 52 of the *Our Gang* films produced by MGM, the studio that assumed control of the series in 1938. After leaving the show, Thomas worked as a film technician until his death of a heart attack in 1980 at age 49. Ten years later, he was the subject of an odd controversy when the investigative program *20/20* aired an interview with an imposter—a grocery store clerk in Arizona—who claimed to be the "real" Buckwheat.

Frankie and Annette

☆ ☆ ☆ ☆

When two teen idols joined forces in a series of low-budget films glorifying teen life and the California beach scene, a pop-culture phenomenon was born. In the 1960s, Frankie and Annette were the reigning king and queen of the beach scene.

American International Pictures (AIP) got its start cranking out sensationalized low-budget films in the 1950s aimed at America's growing teen audience. Its early films, such as *Reform School Girl* (1957) and *I Was a Teenage Werewolf* (1957), capitalized on social concerns about juvenile delinquency by depicting teens as dangerous outsiders who rejected the conventions of American society. Using the profits from those efforts, AIP branched into films with less controversial themes and more mainstream appeal. By the early 1960s, AIP had switched gears to make movies about clean-cut, wholesome youths who knew how to have fun but still reinforced the American ideal. Pairing crooner Frankie Avalon with former Mouseketeer Annette Funicello, the company produced a series of madcap surf-and-sand adventures featuring carefree teens cavorting on California's beaches, starting with *Beach Party* in 1963.

The Formula

These beach films typically offered up a consistent three-strand narrative: First, the two lead characters, Frankie and DeeDee, would engage in a series of encounters in which they'd argue, then make up, most often over Frankie's reluctance to commit to their relationship. Then, the couple and their friends would band together to confront the recurring character of Erik Von Zipper (played by Harvey Lembeck), the inept head of a motorcycle gang. Finally, an interloping adult, who represented "the establishment" and held a general disdain for teen beach culture, would have to be put in his place. In *Beach Party,* for example, an anthropologist stakes out the beach to study the kids' "primitive mating rituals," while in *Beach Blanket Bingo* (1965), a publicist attempts to exploit the youngsters to promote his latest celebrity client. In each film, these simple stories were punctuated by raucous dance sequences, one-off gags involving secondary characters, and musical numbers by popular performers such as Dick Dale and a young Stevie Wonder.

Though Frankie and Annette were the center of most of the films, they were supported by a recurring cast of friends. Jody McCrea regularly appeared as a dimwitted surfer named either Deadhead or Bonehead, and a rotating series of young actresses took on the role of a sexually provocative beach bunny named Animal. The films typically featured a comedian from the era in a supporting role, such as Don Rickles or Morey Amsterdam. The establishment heavy would generally be portrayed by a veteran actor such as Keenan Wynn or Bob Cummings, and legendary stars, including Buster Keaton and Peter Lorre, made frequent cameos.

The Spinoffs

The AIP pictures were so successful that several other companies tried to copy the formula for their own beach films, but none had the lasting impact of the Frankie and Annette series. AIP tried its own variations by sending Frankie off on his own as *Sergeant Deadhead* in 1965 and by pairing the star couple in a 1966 cross-country race adventure called *Fireball 500.* Of course, the carefree and innocent nature of the genre couldn't hold up against the political awareness of the late 1960s counterculture movement, and the beach party had come to an end by 1966. And in 1987, when Avalon and Funicello teamed up again to star in a parody called *Back to the Beach,* which received only lukewarm reviews, it was clear that the beach films were a product of a very specific moment in American pop culture history. But there's no question that Frankie and Annette remain the reigning couple of the California beach scene.

Frankie and Annette Filmography:

Beach Party (1963)	*How to Stuff a Wild Bikini* (1965)
Muscle Beach Party (1964)	*Fireball 500* (1966)
Bikini Beach (1964)	*Back to the Beach* (1987)
Beach Blanket Bingo (1965)	

Making a Mockery of Things

Just as its name implies, a mockumentary is a film that is part mockery and part documentary. Traditionally, these are fiction films posing as documentaries that chronicle real events. Mockumentary filmmakers tend to use handheld cameras and purposely frame scenes haphazardly, use inadequate lighting, and let their subjects go out of focus, all to help sell a film's fake authenticity. So, without further ado, here are some of the most popular mockumentary movies ever made.

The Rutles: All You Need Is Cash (1978)
Monty Python's Eric Idle expanded his popular *Saturday Night Live* skits about an English pop band into a full-length feature film centering around The Rutles—a band that was clearly a parody of The Beatles. Cameos by Paul Simon, Mick Jagger, and even real-life Beatle George Harrison helped add an air of credibility to the film.

Cannibal Holocaust (1980)
Not a true mockumentary, this horror exploitation film features a framing device in which an anthropologist finds film footage shot by documentary filmmakers who have gone missing while searching for Amazonian cannibals. When the anthropologist returns to New York, he screens the recovered footage for a group of TV executives, and these scenes, detailing the "documentarists'" jungle ordeal, make up the bulk of the film. Upon its release, *Cannibal Holocaust* shocked and offended audiences with its gruesome violence and realistic gore. Only a few scenes, particularly those depicting the abuse and death of several animals, were authentic. But outraged Italian authorities—convinced that director Ruggero Deodato had actually killed or maimed four actors in front of rolling cameras—seized prints of the film, banned it from theaters, and arrested Deodato. Murder charges were eventually dropped, though Deodato and four others involved in the production received suspended sentences for obscenity and violence.

Zelig (1983)
Presented as a straightforward documentary, *Zelig* features director Woody Allen as the title character, a man from the 1920s with the unique ability to take on the personality and appearance of anyone he is near. Archival footage was expertly spliced together to make it appear

as though Zelig interacted with the likes of Adolf Hitler, Lou Gehrig, Charlie Chaplin, and Herbert Hoover. *Zelig* paved the way for *Forrest Gump* (1994) a decade later.

This Is Spinal Tap (1984)

If there is a king among mockumentaries, *This Is Spinal Tap* wears the crown. Following the exploits of a heavy metal band called Spinal Tap, the film features veteran comic actors in key roles, who created memorable characters that audiences still quote. Rock bands everywhere were convinced that *they* were the inspiration for the movie. The fact that Michael McKean, Harry Shearer, and Christopher Guest all sang and played their instruments helped sell the ruse, too, though it was director Rob Reiner's spoofing of rockumentary-style interviews and ludicrous rock band conventions that made it seem real.

The success of *This Is Spinal Tap* influenced cowriter Christopher Guest to write several follow-up mockumentaries, including *Waiting for Guffman* (1996), *Best in Show* (2000), and *A Mighty Wind* (2003).

Man Bites Dog (1992)

This Belgian film centers on two filmmakers following the exploits of Ben, a serial killer. This mockumentary also crossed over and became a commentary on violence in the media, which earned it the SACD (International Critic's Prize) at the 1992 Cannes Film Festival before it was even released to mass audiences.

The Blair Witch Project (1999)

Purportedly pieced together out of footage recovered from cameras manned by three student filmmakers who disappeared in the Maryland woods while filming a documentary about an urban legend, *The Blair Witch Project* broke all records for independent movies. During shooting, the actors were never told exactly what the movie was about and were simply told to hike through the woods and film everything that happened. So the fear in their eyes and voices was real. The film's mock home-movie-style footage was the ultimate in realism, enhancing the tension created by what the audience hears but cannot see.

Some believe that *Blair Witch* was inspired by a similar independent mockumentary, *The Last Broadcast*, which had been released the previous year.

Drop Dead Gorgeous (1999)

A camera crew shoots the behind-the-scenes machinations of a small-town beauty contest in this comedy that skews pageant culture and rural life. You wouldn't think a movie starring established actors like Kirsten Dunst, Denise Richards, and Kirstie Alley would convince people that they were actually part of a documentary about a small-town beauty contest. But it did.

Incident at Loch Ness (2004)

In this mockumentary, legendary German director Werner Herzog is seen boarding the boat *Discovery IV* and reluctantly taking part in an expedition in search of the Loch Ness Monster, which ends in disaster. Cinematographer John Bailey, also on board, is making his own documentary about Herzog. Director Zak Penn, along with cowriter Herzog, raises the bar for mockumentaries by making it almost impossible to detect which footage is staged. *Incident at Loch Ness* achieves some humor and a few cheap thrills while also inviting viewers to question the "realism" of all documentaries. As a side note: Owners of the DVD were only let in on the secret that the film was fake after unlocking a hidden alternate commentary.

Behind the Mask: The Rise of Leslie Vernon (2006)

This horror film about horror films involves aspiring filmmakers who shoot a documentary about Leslie Vernon, a character who is studying to become "the next great horror psycho slasher." Unbeknownst to those behind the camera, Vernon is planning for them to spend some time being filmed themselves.

Borat: Cultural Learnings of America for Make Benefit Glorious Nation of Kazakhstan (2006)

In what can only be described as guerilla movie making, Sacha Baron Cohen never breaks character as Kazakh journalist Borat Sagdiyev, who travels to America to film his own documentary. Alternately hilarious and offensive, *Borat* led viewers everywhere to wonder what was real and what was staged.

For Some, Acting Just Isn't Enough

Movie stars are talented people. And sometimes that talent transcends the silver screen and transmits over the airwaves too. Here are some songs by a few stars who tried their luck in the music biz as well.

"Ballad of Thunder Road" by Robert Mitchum

This tune, cowritten and sung by Mitchum, was intended to be the theme song to the movie *Thunder Road* (1958). But when Mitchum decided that there was no place for it in the film, he released it as a single in conjunction with the movie. However, it is never actually heard in the film.

"Tammy" by Debbie Reynolds

This *Singing in the Rain* (1952) costar had the best-selling single by a female artist in 1957, thanks to this ditty from *Tammy and the Bachelor*.

"Purple People Eater" by Sheb Wooley

Wooley, who appeared in *High Noon* (1952), *Giant* (1956), and *Hoosiers* (1986), had a No. 1 hit in 1958 with this oddball ode to a man-munching monster.

"Old Rivers" by Walter Brennan

The winner of three Academy Awards, this quivering and gravelly voiced actor hit the Top Five with this ballad in 1962.

"Johnny Angel" by Shelley Fabares

In 1962, while portraying Mary Stone on *The Donna Reed Show,* Fabares recorded this hit tune aimed at teen girls. She went on to appear in three Elvis Presley films and later costarred on the popular sitcom *Coach.*

"MacArthur Park" by Richard Harris

As an actor, Richard Harris was nominated for an Academy Award for his roles in *This Sporting Life* (1963) and *The Field* (1990). He also scored a No. 1 hit with this seven-and-a-half-minute pop tune in 1968.

"Wanderin' Star" by Lee Marvin

This song, from the movie *Paint Your Wagon,* was recorded by actor Lee Marvin and became a No. 1 hit in England in 1970.

"Basketball Jones" by Cheech and Chong
Hemp-hewn hipsters added musical parody to their comedic repertoire with this bouncy canticle in 1973, which reached No. 15 on *Billboard*'s Top 100 charts.

"Let Her In" by John Travolta
The former Sweathog and future *Saturday Night Fever* fave hit the Top Ten with this piece of fluff in 1976.

"King Tut" by Steve Martin
The banjo-strumming wild and crazy guy cashed in on the King Tut craze with this tune that hit the Top 20 in 1978.

"Rocket Man" by William Shatner
The star of the original *Star Trek* TV series sang this Elton John classic at the 1978 Sci-Fi Awards, where it was caught on tape for posterity.

"Party All the Time" by Eddie Murphy
This Rick James-penned tune hit the charts in 1985 and was once voted the eighth-worst song of all-time by *Blender* magazine.

"Heartbeat" by Don Johnson
In 1986, the future star of *Harley Davidson and the Marlboro Man* (1991) and *Guilty as Sin* (1993) rode his *Miami Vice* popularity to No. 5 on charts with this guitar-laden tune.

"She's Like the Wind" by Patrick Swayze
The star of *Dirty Dancing* (1987) and *Ghost* (1990) had a Top Ten hit with this ballad that he cowrote and sang for the *Dirty Dancing* soundtrack.

"Looking for Freedom" by David Hasselhoff
The timing of this 1989 song made it a hit in Eastern Europe. Pop music lovers in that part of the world embraced the Hasselhoff tune as an anthem just as the fall of communism began.

"Acid Tongue" by Jenny Lewis
Teen idol and star of more than a dozen movies in the 1990s, the cofounder of indie rockers Rilo Kiley released this gem in 2008.

"Anywhere I Lay My Head" by Scarlett Johansson
The *Lost in Translation* (2003) star released an album of Tom Waits tunes to mixed reviews in 2008.

Ed Wood Could and Did: The Odd Genius of Ed Wood

☆ ☆ ☆ ☆

For years, he was considered the worst director in the history of cinema, but oddly, in recent decades, his work has gained new respect. Despite the shaking sets, loopy lighting, awkward editing, questionable casting, abhorrent acting, incoherent dialogue, and overall cinematic calamity, the films of Ed Wood are now regarded as entertaining glimpses into the mind of Hollywood's greatest B-movie oddball.

The strange saga of Edward Davis Wood Jr. began naturally enough, with his birth on October 10, 1924, in Poughkeepsie, New York. Allegedly, the junior Wood's mother desperately wanted a daughter, so she dressed her son in girls' clothing until the young lad reached puberty. Aside from acquiring a fetish for angora sweaters and a tendency to wear female finery, Wood had a fairly normal childhood. He was not a homosexual cross-dresser but a heterosexual who just happened to prefer frilly undergarments to cotton briefs. Wood loved movies, worked as an usher in the local cinema as a teen, and carried a Kodak "Cine Special" camera wherever he went.

In 1942, Wood signed up for the Marine Corps and fought in World War II, where he took a slew of slugs in the leg that left him permanently maimed. He also lost a pile of pearly whites when he was on the receiving end of an enemy's rifle butt. After the war, he returned stateside, joined a traveling freak show in which he played a bearded lady and, in 1947, eventually made his way to Hollywood.

The Knock on Wood

In Tinseltown, Wood wrote scripts for a couple of low-budget TV Westerns that were quickly forgotten. Despite these failures, he was commissioned to direct an exploitation film based on the life of transsexual Christine Jorgenson, which was eventually released under the title *Glen or Glenda* (1953) and proved to be Wood's big break.

Wood, who gained notoriety for resurrecting the career of Bela Lugosi by casting the star of *Dracula* (1931) in three of his movies, went on to create more than a dozen unique pieces of cinematic history. These "epics" include *Plan 9 from Outer Space* (1959), often described as the worst movie ever made; *Jail Bait* (1954); *Bride of the Monster* (1955); *Night of the Ghouls* (1959); and *The Sinister Urge* (1960). The common denominators in each of Wood's films are technical mishaps and outrageous continuity errors, crude special effects, erratic and outlandish dialogue, eccentric casts, bizarre plot elements, and, of course, their failure to make any kind of impact at the box office.

The Steep Decline

By the 1960s, Wood's career had taken a serious nosedive—which wasn't exactly a severe drop—and he was forced to write sex novels and dabble in pornography in order to survive. A heavy drinker—his pen name was Akdov Telmig (vodka gimlet spelled backward)—he died penniless and forgotten in 1978 at age 54.

In the 1980s, the advent of film festivals revolving around bad movies revived the work of Ed Wood, catapulting the eccentric director to a level of fame unattained during his lifetime. In 1994, Tim Burton and Johnny Depp teamed up to make the film *Ed Wood,* a loving tribute to one of Hollywood's kookiest writers and directors.

- *Wood's girlfriends and wives often helped out with his movies. His first wife, Norma McCarty, costarred in* Plan 9. *Second wife Kathy O'Hara served as art director on* Night of the Ghouls. *And girlfriend Dolores Fuller costarred in* Glen or Glenda, Jail Bait, *and* Bride of the Monster *before becoming a songwriter, composing tunes such as "Rock-a-Hula Baby" for Elvis Presley, among others.*

Ed Wood Films

Over the years, the films of director Ed Wood have become cult classics. Here are a few that are so bad they're good... or not.

Glen or Glenda (1953)
Originally intended as a sexploitation film about the life of famous transsexual Christine Jorgenson, this movie became a study of sexual tolerance when Jorgensen refused to be involved. Starring Bela Lugosi and Wood's real-life girlfriend Dolores Fuller, the film was supposedly shot in just four days at a cost of $26,000 and is renowned for Lugosi's off-the-wall performance and gibberish-filled dialogue.

Jail Bait (1954)
Wood once again enlisted Dolores Fuller to star in this homage to the crime thrillers of the 1940s and the time-tested cliché that "crime does not pay." This cinematic clunker features plastic surgery, blackmail, and illegal handguns. Former bodybuilding champ and future *Hercules* star Steve Reeves made his first silver screen appearance in the film.

Bride of the Monster (1955)
Wood claimed that the underlying theme of this low-budget horror flick, which was originally titled *Bride of the Atom*, is that "beauty is really in the eye of the beholder." Bela Lugosi stars as a mad scientist who attempts to create an army of "atomic" supermen. Former professional wrestler Tor Johnson and Loretta King are also featured.

Plan 9 from Outer Space (1959)
Wood's "masterpiece" was filmed in 1956 but didn't hit theaters until 1959. This meandering combination of horror and sci-fi boasts stock footage, plastic flying saucers, and the last existing footage of Bela Lugosi. TV horror-film hostess Vampira is featured, along with Tor Johnson and legendary drag queen John "Bunny" Breckenridge.

The Sinister Urge (1960)
Shot in Wood's usual roughshod fashion, this gem tackles the steamy underbelly of the pornography business. Technically incompetent—mic booms are evident; the sets shake when doors are slammed—and almost without plot, the acting here is so wooden it's an insult to quality timber. Wood makes a cameo as a man in a fight.

Sidney Poitier

☆ ☆ ☆ ☆

Lead roles of substance for African Americans were relatively scarce when Sidney Poitier made his Hollywood debut in the early 1950s. But his inherent talent and quiet dignity helped open doors for black actors to land roles that were not disdainful stereotypes. This also made him one of the most iconic actors of his generation.

Although born in Miami, Florida, in 1927, Poitier lived most of his childhood in the Bahamas. In his mid-teens, his father sent him back to Miami to live with his brother, but shortly thereafter, at age 16, Sidney headed to New York City. While working as a dishwasher, he auditioned for the American Negro Theater but was rejected because of his Bahamian accent. After curbing his accent by mimicking the voices on the radio, he joined the American Negro Theater, where he honed his craft and took acting lessons. He eventually worked as an understudy for Harry Belafonte in the play *Days of Our Youth,* which led to a small role in a production of *Lysistrata.* It was an inauspicious debut—Poitier flubbed his lines and ran off the stage in a panic. Nonetheless, the American Negro Theater saw something special in Poitier, whose career took off despite that early case of nerves.

Hollywood Comes Calling

Poitier made his film debut in *No Way Out* (1950), playing a doctor harassed by a racist who blames Poitier's character for the death of his brother. The reviews were positive, and the young actor found himself working steadily throughout the '50s in such memorable films as *Cry, the Beloved Country* (1952), *The Blackboard Jungle* (1955), *Porgy and Bess* (1959), and *The Defiant Ones* (1958), the latter for which he earned an Oscar nomination for Best Actor.

The 1950s established Poitier as an actor of notable talent. However, it was in the 1960s that he helped open doors for other black actors. In 1961, Poitier starred as Walter Younger in the film adaptation of Lorraine Hansberry's play *A Raisin in the Sun*, a role he had cultivated on Broadway. Two years later in *Lilies of the Field* (1963), he played an ex-GI searching for better opportunities who decides to help a group of German nuns build a church. The role earned Poitier his first Oscar and made him the first African American to win an Academy Award for Best Actor.

Poitier made even more dramatic strides in Hollywood in the 1960s, playing a journalist in *The Bedford Incident* (1965), a school teacher in *To Sir, With Love* (1967), and Detective Virgil Tibbs in the Norman Jewison-directed crime drama *In the Heat of the Night* (1967), a role he reprised in the sequel, *They Call Me Mister Tibbs!* (1970). It was also in 1967 that Poitier costarred with Spencer Tracy and Katharine Hepburn in the social drama *Guess Who's Coming to Dinner*, in which his character is engaged to a white woman.

An Accidental Director

Poitier's career continued apace in the 1970s. He costarred with his good friend Harry Belafonte in the Western *Buck and the Preacher* (1972), a film he found himself directing after a falling out with the original director. It wasn't a job Poitier particularly wanted, and both he and Belafonte asked the studio to hire a replacement. But studio execs liked what Poitier was doing and encouraged him to finish the film. As a result of that experience, Poitier went on to direct several other movies over the ensuing years, including *Uptown Saturday Night* (1974), *A Piece of the Action* (1977), and *Stir Crazy* (1980).

Poitier slowed down a bit in the decades that followed but still landed a few juicy roles, including Supreme Court Justice Thurgood Marshall in the made-for-TV movie *Separate But Equal* (1991).

In addition to the Academy Award he received for *Lilies of the Field,* Poitier has been awarded numerous honors for both his acting and his work for civil rights. In 1992, he received the American Film Institute's Lifetime Achievement Award. In 2000, he received the Screen Actors Guild Lifetime Achievement Award and also published his life story, *The Measure of a Man: A Spiritual Autobiography.* He was awarded the NAACP's Hall of Fame Award in 2001, and the following year, he received an honorary Academy Award for his amazing career in front of and behind the camera.

Inside Jokes in Animation

Moviemakers love sneaking their own inside jokes and references into films, and animation is the perfect place to pull it off. Here are some subtle examples that you might not have noticed.

- In *Who Framed Roger Rabbit* (1988), when Eddie walks into a Toontown restroom, graffiti on a wall in the background reads: "For a good time, call Allyson Wonderland." The message originally had a phone number next to it that was rumored to have belonged to either Disney CEO Michael Eisner or then-Disney chairman Jeffrey Katzenberg. The digits were removed for the home-video release.

- "A113" is seen on a license plate in *Toy Story* (1995), referenced in a jail cell block number in *The Incredibles* (2004), and heard as a flight number in an airport announcement in *Toy Story 2* (1999). "A113" is the room number of the animation department at the California Institute for the Arts, where numerous Pixar animators trained.

- In *Aladdin* (1992), when the genie looks at his cookbook to see whether he can turn Aladdin into a prince, he briefly pulls Sebastian from *The Little Mermaid* (1989) out of the pages.

- Mickey Mouse makes some brief appearances in *The Little Mermaid* (1989), but you have to know where to look. First, a Mickey outline pops up in a scroll that Ursula hands to Ariel. It's hidden in the middle of some words on the page. Then, when the animals are working to break up the wedding, a woman with black hair appears on the screen. Her hair forms the shape of Mickey's head.

- Mickey Mouse makes a cameo of sorts in *The Lion King* (1994), too: In the middle of "Hakuna Matata," when Timon pulls a bug out of a knothole, the creature is wearing Mickey Mouse ears.

- When *The Lion King* was released, overzealous watchdog groups accused Disney animators of inserting a racy message into the movie.

It happens in the scene in which Simba collapses on a cliff right after he talks to Timon and Pumbaa about stars. A puff of dust flies up, and if you look closely, it forms three letters. Some people thought it said "SEX," but it actually says "SFX"—the name of the special-effects team that put the scene together.

- In *Toy Story*, the Pixar people paid tribute to the company's original founder, George Lucas. The scene where Buzz is knocked out of the window features numerous references to Lucas's first *Indiana Jones* flick, *Raiders of the Lost Ark* (1981), including the film's music.

- *Toy Story* also slipped in a little homage to *The Lion King*. If you listen when Slinky is stuck on the back of a garbage truck, "Hakuna Matata" plays on the car radio for a few seconds.

- Pixar referenced some of its smaller, less-famous film shorts within *Toy Story*. When Woody holds a staff meeting, books behind him bear the titles of two of Pixar's previous works: *Red's Dream* (1987) and *Knick Knack* (1989). A red desk lamp also appears, as a nod to *Luxo Jr.*, Pixar's first short film.

- In *Toy Story 2*, Andy has a calendar in his room that shows the characters from *A Bug's Life* (1998).

- Disney's animated feature *Tarzan* (1999) gave a subtle shout-out to a 1950s-era Disney short called *In the Bag* (1956). While Turk is tearing up the explorer's camp, two apes replicate a move called the "bump-bump step" from the film made four decades earlier.

- Pixar has an ongoing gag with a Pizza Planet truck. The fake restaurant's delivery vehicle has appeared somewhere in every Pixar movie, though it's sometimes hard to spot. In *Finding Nemo* (2003), for example, the truck zooms by the dentist's office toward the end of the film. Blink and you might miss it.

- Buzz Lightyear made a cameo (of sorts) in *Finding Nemo*. During the scene in the dentist's waiting room, a Buzz action figure is sitting on the floor.

- *Finding Nemo* also looked into the future: Animators slipped in a quick shot of Mr. Incredible—from the upcoming Pixar film *The Incredibles*—during the same dentist office scene. The muscular fellow is shown on a comic book that a patient is reading.

Grauman's Chinese Theatre

☆ ☆ ☆ ☆

When stars get down and dirty at this well-known
Hollywood landmark, they really get down and dirty.

Curious Doings

A stroll along the 6900 block of Hollywood Boulevard often reveals
a puzzling sight. Throngs of people apparently bereft of anything
better to do kneel along the sidewalk staring intently at the ground.
Newcomers may wonder if these pedestrians are searching for a lost
contact lens or misplaced earring. They aren't. Since 1927, millions
of starstruck fans have made the pilgrimage to Grauman's Chinese
Theatre simply to see impressions of their favorite stars' hands and
feet embedded in the sidewalk, along with their signatures.

A Visionary Settles in Hollywood

Sidney Patrick Grauman (1879–1950) was the epitome of today's
mover and shaker. Striking out (quite literally) in search of a fortune
during the Klondike Gold Rush, the prospector eventually hit pay
dirt in Hollywood with a series of grand movie theaters. In 1918,
Grauman erected his first movie palace on Broadway in Los Angeles,
christening it the Million Dollar Theater. Marveling at its ornate
facade done up in Spanish Rococo style, visitors immediately knew
that this was no ordinary theater. Inside, it was decorated in a spectacular, eclectic, "fantasy" design. The theater enjoyed overnight
success due to its breathtaking style, as well as a gala opening that
included Hollywood royalty, such as Roscoe "Fatty" Arbuckle,
Charlie Chaplin, Douglas Fairbanks, and Mary Pickford. It remains
in its original location to this very day.

Themed for Success

Spurred on by this triumph, in 1922 Grauman opened his second
themed Tinseltown theater, The Egyptian. Like its predecessor, The
Egyptian, located at 6712 Hollywood Boulevard, wowed visitors with
its structural distinctiveness, beauty, and panache and entertained
guests with first-run films. Unlike the Million Dollar Theater, The

Egyptian also featured a forecourt where Grauman accentuated the Egyptian theme with enormous four-foot-wide columns, murals, a tiled fountain, and pots filled with exotic plants. The forecourt was edged by Middle Eastern-style shops and by guards standing in Egyptian-like costumes. It was at this location that Grauman staged Hollywood's first massively scaled movie premieres, inviting the press, stars, and fans alike to partake in the Hollywood experience. The theater, now fully restored, harkens back to that long-gone era of moviemaking magic. The Egyptian's opening coincided with the release of *Robin Hood,* starring Douglas Fairbanks and Wallace Beery. With a red carpet leading the way from limousine to theater and klieg lights signaling that a genuine happening was under way, a procession of stars filed in to see the movie.

The night was a smashing success. This star power was clearly evident to Grauman, who made a mental note of the phenomenon for future reference. His next great palace would not only feature a wealth of stars, it would also boast a "concrete" permanence that none of the others could match.

East Meets West

Grauman's Chinese Theatre made its debut on May 18, 1927. Featuring 90-foot-high coral red columns, huge temple bells, and carved dragons, the $2 million theater was Grauman's most opulent offering. The decor also included a couple of "heaven dogs," which are canine statues in the style of the Ming Dynasty (1403–1643). Heaven dogs were believed to ward off evil spirits and were used to protect important tombs in China during that time period. Perhaps the dogs have helped to keep the theater going decade after decade.

The Chinese Theatre's "Forecourt of the Stars" was its chief distinction over its predecessors. The concept was simple: movie stars would appear for "footprint ceremonies" in which they would set their feet and hands into wet cement. Then they would autograph these sidewalk casts for posterity. Grauman theorized that people would come in droves to see the physical impressions of their favorite stars, and he was right. Millions visit Grauman's each year for this reason.

Stooping Stars

Since 1927, when Douglas Fairbanks, Mary Pickford, and Norma Talmadge set the first casts, more than 200 celebrities have knelt down to leave their mark.

The "Who's Who" list includes Marilyn Monroe, Jimmy Stewart, Shirley Temple, Judy Garland, John Wayne, Elizabeth Taylor, Cary Grant, Bing Crosby, Jean Harlow, Rock Hudson, Bette Davis, Clark Gable, Paul Newman, and scores of others. Stars are generally selected for this honor based on the popularity of a recent hit movie. For example, Monroe and Jane Russell were asked to leave their "mark" after *Gentlemen Prefer Blondes* (1953) made a big splash.

Sometimes stars leave more than their hand- and footprints, especially if they're famous for a specific gimmick or attribute. George Burns and Groucho Marx were seldom seen without a cigar because it was part of their comedy shtick, so both of them immortalized their trademark stogies in cement. Tough guy John Wayne offered a fist print in lieu of both handprints, while Jimmy Durante and Bob Hope, who were famous for their oddly shaped noses, left—you guessed it—nose prints! More recently, the cast of the *Harry Potter* movies left imprints of their magic wands.

In 1973, theater magnate Ted Mann purchased the famed building and renamed it Mann's Chinese Theatre. In 2000, a couple of movie studios purchased the theater through a separate company to add to their other theater holdings. "Mann's" had never sat well with native Angelinos, so the name was changed back to Grauman's in 2002. In 2009, the studios decided to sell their theater holdings and put Grauman's on the market. However, protected as a historical landmark, it will remain a popular theater and tourist attraction no matter who buys it.

Despite the oodles of venerated names plastered in its forecourt, when it comes to celebrity pop art, the fact is that one can't get much lower than this. Just ask any fan who's thrown out his or her back trying to get closer to the stars.

Hollywood's Jaded Souls

"Hollywood's a place where they'll pay you a thousand dollars for a kiss and fifty cents for your soul."

—*Marilyn Monroe*

"I'll never understand the animal, the machine of Hollywood business. And I don't want to understand it. It's like joining a club, a clique, just because everyone else is in it. You don't have any particular interest in it, and it has nothing to do with who you are as a person. You just join it because it's the thing to do."

—*Johnny Depp*

"Hollywood is a place where a man can get stabbed in the back while climbing a ladder."

—*William Faulkner*

"The execs don't care what color you are. They care about how much money you make. Hollywood is not really black or white. It's green."

—*Will Smith*

"Hollywood died on me as soon as I got there."

—*Orson Welles*

"It's a scientific fact. For every year a person lives in Hollywood, they lose two points off their IQ."

—*Truman Capote*

"I can't talk about Hollywood. It was a horror to me when I was there and it's a horror to look back on. I can't imagine how I did it. When I got away from it, I couldn't even refer to the place by name."

—*Dorothy Parker*

"Working in Hollywood does give you a certain expertise in the field of prostitution."

—*Jane Fonda*

"Hollywood amuses me. Holier-than-thou for the public and unholier-than-the-devil in reality."

—*Grace Kelly*

"They've great respect for the dead in Hollywood, but none for the living."

—*Errol Flynn*

Gone with the Wind

☆ ☆ ☆ ☆

The year 1939 is a very special one for movie buffs. Among the great films that premiered that year were The Wizard of Oz; Mr. Smith Goes to Washington; Stagecoach; Wuthering Heights; Goodbye, Mr Chips... *and a little Civil War story called* Gone with the Wind.

Margaret Mitchell's sweeping tale of love and loss in the war-torn South was one of the year's most anticipated movies, and the behind-the-scenes story of its creation is as remarkable as the film itself. Though now considered a classic, *Gone with the Wind* was a huge gamble for the film's producer, the legendary David O. Selznick, whose reputation and career hinged on its success.

Selznick optioned the rights to *GWTW* in 1936 for $50,000 (an unheard-of fee for the first book by an unknown author) and spent the next three years bringing it to the screen. His first challenge was finding just the right performers to play Rhett Butler and Scarlett O'Hara, characters that had developed a very devoted following among readers. According to movie fan magazines, Clark Gable was the obvious choice for Rhett, but the rugged actor initially turned down the role because of the high public expectation and his insecurity about his acting ability.

Grabbing Gable

Louis B. Mayer helped Selznick secure Gable for *GWTW* by quietly convincing the actor's estranged wife to grant him a divorce so he could marry his true love, Carole Lombard. Mayer knew that the divorce would cost Gable a sizable sum, so he gave him a little nudge by offering him a $100,000 bonus to play Rhett Butler.

Finding the right actress to play Scarlett O'Hara proved even more difficult. Nearly every leading lady in Hollywood coveted the part, and Selznick screen-tested many of them, including Paulette Goddard, Katharine Hepburn, Lucille Ball, Carole Lombard, and Bette Davis. As a publicity stunt, he even started a national talent search for Scarlett. Though Selznick never intended to make his selection from the thousands of unknowns who auditioned, the search did help fill at least one role—Alicia Rhett as India Wilkes.

After looking at every pretty face in Hollywood, Selznick finally chose Vivien Leigh, a British actress who had initially caught the producer's eye in the movie *Fire Over England.* Selznick's early interest in Leigh and her ultimate selection were kept a closely guarded secret, and filming on *GWTW* had actually begun when Leigh was signed to the part.

One Problem After Another...

Casting *GWTW* had been difficult, but not nearly as difficult as crafting Mitchell's 1,037-page novel into a manageable screenplay. Over a three-year period, numerous writers took a stab at the project, including Pulitzer Prize-winning playwright Sidney Howard, F. Scott Fitzgerald, and Ben Hecht, who went back to Howard's original. Selznick rewrote scenes as the film was shooting, making him one of the principal writers as well. Though many talented people contributed to the script, only Howard received a screenwriting credit.

Several individuals also had a hand in directing *GWTW.* George Cukor was Selznick's first choice, but he was fired shortly after filming began and was replaced by Victor Fleming, who had just finished directing *The Wizard of Oz.* When Fleming left due to an alleged nervous breakdown, Selznick replaced him with Sam Wood, who had directed *Goodbye, Mr. Chips.* But shortly after Wood took the reins, a recovered Fleming returned, and the two men found themselves codirecting the movie.

Gone with the Wind was in turmoil throughout its five-month shooting schedule. Long hours and constant changes to the script exhausted the cast and crew; personality conflicts often made the set an unhappy place to work; and cost overruns dug deep into MGM's pocket. Industry observers began questioning Selznick's ability to bring Mitchell's massive novel to the silver screen, and even Selznick had some doubts toward the end, but his belief that *GWTW* would be a masterpiece kept him going.

The Four-Letter Word Worth Fighting For

When filming wrapped, Selznick faced one last problem: Rhett's response to Scarlett when she asks what she'll do if he leaves her: "Frankly, my dear, I don't give a damn." It's one of the most famous lines in movie history, but it was almost cut from the film.

The Motion Picture Production Code strictly prohibited the use of profanity, so Rhett's line had been changed in retakes to "My dear, I don't care" to appease the Code office. Deciding whether to allow the original version or the retake confounded the Code office for several weeks, especially after Selznick came up with repeated examples of the word *damn* in popular magazines and newspapers. When a test audience in Santa Barbara complained that they were disappointed because the original line had been changed, Selznick appealed to Will Hays, the head of the Motion Picture Producers and Distributors Association. Hays overturned the initial ban on the word *damn* and allowed Selznick to include the original line after meeting with the Motion Picture Association Board to amend the Code to allow profanity if "it is a quotation from a literary work."

Box-Office Bonanza

Gone with the Wind opened in December 1939 to huge attendance and glowing reviews. It went on to win Academy Awards for Best Picture, Best Actress, Best Supporting Actress, Best Director, and Best Screenplay, among others. The award for Best Supporting Actress was particularly significant because its recipient, Hattie McDaniel, became the first African American to win an Oscar. McDaniel was so overcome with emotion when her name was announced that she burst into tears.

Gone with the Wind is rightly considered one of the greatest motion pictures ever made, but the film turned out to be a curse for Selznick, who struggled for the rest of his career to produce a movie of equal grandeur.

- GWTW *made Vivien Leigh a star in America, but she worked hard for it, putting in 125 days with only a few days off. In contrast, Clark Gable worked 71 days, Olivia de Havilland worked 59 days, and Leslie Howard, who played Ashley Wilkes, worked only 32 days.*

Question-able Movies

*Here's a handful of films whose titles are questions—
from the ridiculous to the sublime. . . .*

1. *Are Parents People?* (1925)

2. *Brother, Can You Spare a Dime?* (1975)

3. *Daddy's Dyin'. . . Who's Got the Will?* (1990)

4. *Dude, Where's My Car?* (2000)

5. *Has Anybody Seen My Gal?* (1952)

6. *O Brother, Where Art Thou?* (2000)

7. *Shall We Dance?* (2004)

8. *They Shoot Horses, Don't They?* (1969)

9. *What About Bob?* (1991)

10. *What Ever Happened to Baby Jane?* (1962)

11. *What's So Bad About Feeling Good?* (1968)

12. *What's the Matter with Helen?* (1971)

13. *What's Up, Doc?* (1972)

14. *What's Up, Tiger Lily?* (1966)

15. *When Did You Last See Your Father?* (2007)

16. *Where Are My Children?* (1916)

17. *Where Were You When the Lights Went Out?* (1968)

18. *Who Is Harry Kellerman and Why Is He Saying Those Terrible Things About Me?* (1971)

19. *Who's Afraid of Virginia Woolf?* (1966)

20. *Whose Life Is It Anyway?* (1981)

21. *Who's That Girl?* (1987)

22. *Why Worry?* (1923)

Animal Rights in Hollywood

☆ ☆ ☆ ☆

*Throughout motion picture history, animals have taken it on
the chin. Regular abuse was the sad reality of their Hollywood
existence until a series of laws helped right the wrongs.*

A Profitable Fur Trade

During the early days of filmmaking, a laissez-faire attitude existed
within the motion picture industry. Like any organization in its
infancy, rules and regulations regarding accepted practices were
made up on an as-needed basis. Not surprisingly, mistreatments and
abuses occurred, particularly for Hollywood's performance animals.
As a furry subgroup without a voice, animals were treated as producers and directors saw fit. With eyes firmly fixed on the financial
bottom line, filmmakers treated animals as little more than props.
With the exception of a few breakout performers like Rin Tin Tin
and Jackie the Lion, animal treatment bordered on the appalling.

Horsing Around

Shocking examples of mistreatment to animals, both on-screen and
off, were enough to give an animal lover nightmares. Horses were
tripped, shocked, and run ragged. When a scene called for a horse
to fall, wires were strung around its ankles or through its hooves,
and a vicious yank did the job. During the making of *The Charge
of the Light Brigade* (1936) and *Ben-Hur* (1959), it is believed that
31 horses were killed or euthanized after being wire-tripped.

Advocates Step In

To get a horse to plunge off a cliff, the animal was blindfolded and
sent down a heavily greased metal tilt chute dangling high above a
waterway. After a grisly tilt chute accident claimed a horse's life in
Jesse James (1939), the animal-welfare group American Humane
damned Hollywood for its brazen mistreatment of animals. Hoping
to sidestep bad press, Hollywood bigwigs made swift changes. In
1940, provisions were added to the Production Code to include
the prohibition of trip wires, branding, and tilt chutes. Also, if a

film featured scenes with animals, a representative from American Humane's Film & TV Unit had to be invited to the set. It was a step in the right direction.

One Step Forward . . . Two Steps Back

During the 1950s, the constitutionality of Hollywood's Production Code was challenged by the Supreme Court. Unfortunately, this led to the gradual weakening and eventual dissolution of the office that enforced the animal code, and American Humane's ability to observe film sets was revoked. Once again, Hollywood was free to treat animals as it pleased. Some moviemakers did self-police and treat their animals properly, but others were not nearly as kind.

And so, animal abuses continued for decades. *Apocalypse Now* (1979) and *Heaven's Gate* (1980) each featured incidents where animals were killed, with the latter including a scene in which a saddle was blown from a horse's back by an explosion, injuring the animal so severely that it had to be euthanized. *Heaven's Gate* also featured genuine cockfights (illegal in California and most other U.S. states) as well as intentional chicken beheadings. With such outright gore taking place virtually unchallenged, many actors and crew members clamored for change. It finally came in 1980 with an amendment to the Screen Actors Guild/Producer's Agreement. The newly implemented rules once again authorized American Humane's Film & TV Unit to oversee the treatment of animals in film and gave the organization the power to grant or deny the end credit: "No animals were harmed in the making of this film."

A Dicey Future

Today, computer-generated imagery often acts as a stand-in for stunts deemed too risky for an animal to perform. Nevertheless, the question of animal rights in Hollywood lingers. Recently, chimpanzee trainers have come under fire for abusing their simian charges during and after their film days. Pending lawsuits will attempt to sort it all out, but one thing seems certain: Because animals can't speak for themselves, they require the protective advocacy of concerned humans. It is a fact as true now as it was in moviemaking's golden era.

8 of the Most Depressing Movies Ever

If you find crying at the movies to be an oddly cathartic experience, feel free to use this list to curate your own movie marathon. Featuring lost love, death and dying, or good old pain and suffering, the following movies are widely recognized as being total downers. But sometimes that can be a good thing! Just don't expect to be very good company for a few days afterward.

Bambi (1942)

Think you're too cool to cry over a cartoon deer? Think again. This animated Disney classic ranks high on the list of depressing movies thanks to a famous scene involving Bambi, his mom, and a hunter in the woods. A surprisingly poignant film, *Bambi* is one kids' movie that will leave you crying like a baby.

Old Yeller (1957)

If there's a dry eye in the house at the end of this Disney classic, check that person's pulse—he or she may not have a heart. The story of a boy, his dog, and a heartbreaking decision, *Old Yeller* is a vintage family film based on a book by Fred Gipson. The silver screen adaptation depicts the story at its sentimental, heart-wrenching best.

They Shoot Horses, Don't They? (1969)

If a movie takes place during the Great Depression, you can bet it's going to be pretty bleak. This Sydney Pollack-directed masterpiece tells the tale of 1930s-era dance marathons, where contestants pushed themselves beyond fatigue and reason in order to win desperately needed cash. Jane Fonda delivers a powerhouse performance, and the movie garnered several Academy Award nominations and a win for Gig Young, the sleazy dance marathon emcee.

Love Story (1970)

This oft-referenced story of young love starts out simply: Boy meets girl, boy and girl fall in love, boy and girl make out a lot and do wacky stuff like play football in the snow. Life gets more complicated when the beautiful Jennifer's health begins to decline. Some folks say it's too schlocky to take seriously, but *Love Story* was a massive hit when it opened and continues to top lists of classic tearjerkers. The movie's theme song, "(Where Do I Begin?) Love Story," was a huge hit on the pop music charts at the time, and the famous quote "Love means never having to say you're sorry" is straight from the script.

Beaches (1988)
Gripping drama or sentimental tearjerker? Chick flick or movie with mass appeal? When everyone's sobbing at the end of *Beaches*, who really cares? Bette Midler and Barbara Hershey star as friends who go through everything together—love, divorce, children...and cancer. We'll leave it at that. Tissues, please!

Schindler's List (1993)
We could easily come up with a list of movies strictly dealing with the Holocaust—one of the most depressing events in history—and this one would rank at the top of that list. Steven Spielberg's dramatic tale of one man's efforts to save as many Jews as possible during World War II perfectly encapsulates the horror and the tragedy of the Holocaust. Liam Neeson and Ralph Fiennes turn in remarkable performances in this account of one of the darkest times in human history.

Dancer in the Dark (2000)
Pop in this DVD and sit back for a two-and-a-half-hour descent into bummerville. Lars von Trier directs Icelandic singer Bjork in a story about Selma, an immigrant mother who works in a factory and is trying to make enough money to pay for an operation to save her son's eyesight, which is fading due to a genetic condition that is slowly eroding her own vision. If that's not depressing enough to make you want to jump off a bridge, we're not sure what is.

My Dog Skip (2000)
Have the tissues handy for this tearjerker based on a memoir by Pulitzer Prize-winning author Willie Morris. In this story about a Jack Russell terrier named Skip and the lifelong friendship with his owner, the now grown-up Willie recalls the warmth and rascally personality of Skip over the years, how the dog saved him in times of trouble and always cheered him up, even after returning from the Vietnam War in bad physical and mental shape. We don't want to spoil anything, but *My Dog Skip* is on the list of Most Depressing Movies Ever for a reason. Nobody lives forever, you know....

The Curse of Billy Bob Thornton

☆ ☆ ☆ ☆

*By and large, actors tend to be a pretty superstitious bunch.
Even so, if you're an aspiring actor and are offered a role in
a Hollywood movie, you might want to scan the cast list just
to make sure Billy Bob Thornton's name isn't on it.
If it is, consider passing on the role because, according to
a bizarre legend, Billy Bob Thornton is cursed, and sharing
a scene with him might cause injury and even death.*

Origins of a Curse

No one's really sure when the Billy Bob curse originated, but most
believe it first reared its ugly head right around the time Thornton
hit it big in the film industry with the release of *Sling Blade* (1996),
which he wrote, directed, and starred in. On February 27, 1998, less
than two years after costarring in the hit film with Thornton, actor
J. T. Walsh died suddenly of a heart attack at age 54.

Though many knew him only as a character named Ernest, actor
Jim Varney was always looking for roles that would expand his acting
repertoire. And so, in the late 1990s, Varney signed on for a role in
Daddy and Them (2001), another film that Thornton wrote,
directed, and starred in. Varney completed the film but died of lung
cancer on February 10, 2000, before the movie was released.

Curse Schmurse

Curse or no curse, as the 21st century began, Thornton decided to
focus on his acting and put writing and directing on the back burner.
In late 2002, he took the lead role in *Bad Santa*, which was set for a
Christmas 2003 release. John Ritter, one of Thornton's costars in the
movie, would not live to see its debut, though, as he died unexpectedly from an aortic dissection on September 11, 2003.

On January 22, 2008, the world mourned the loss of 28-year-old
actor Heath Ledger, who died tragically of an accidental drug
overdose. Curse believers were quick to point out that Ledger
and Thornton had worked together on the Oscar-nominated movie
Monster's Ball (2001).

Then, in the summer of 2008, *Bad Santa* became the first movie to claim two victims from the alleged curse when, in addition to John Ritter, actor Bernie Mac passed away at age 50 from complications from pneumonia.

Another recent victim of the Billy Bob curse was actress Natasha Richardson, who costarred with Thornton in 2002's *Waking Up in Reno*. On March 18, 2009, Richardson died suddenly of an epidural hematoma after falling while skiing. She was 45 years old.

Last and certainly not least is actor Patrick Swayze, who also shared the screen with Thornton in *Waking Up in Reno*. Swayze passed away on September 14, 2009, at age 57, after a courageous battle with pancreatic cancer.

Is the Curse Losing Strength?

Obviously, not everyone who has been involved in a Billy Bob Thornton movie has met an untimely death. So even if Thornton is indeed cursed, a few lucky actors have managed to work with him and live to tell the tale.

For example, in July 2008, rising star Shia LaBeouf—Thornton's costar in *Eagle Eye* (2008)—was involved in an auto accident during which the vehicle he was traveling in flipped upside down and landed on its roof. LaBeouf walked away from the accident with only minor injuries.

The following month, actor Morgan Freeman, who costarred with Thornton in the film *Levity* (2003), was involved in a serious car accident in Mississippi. Freeman's injuries were critical enough that he had to be airlifted to a hospital, but he did make a full recovery.

So what does Billy Bob think of this alleged curse? So far, he isn't talking, but he's probably not worried about it. After all, the curse would have to be pretty powerful to shake a man who survived a marriage to Angelina Jolie.

- *During his short-lived romance with Angelina Jolie, Thornton and his beloved actually wore vials of each other's blood around their necks as a symbol of their devotion to each other.*

Stars on 45s

Songwriters have always been intrigued and infatuated with Hollywood. Here are some songs about the stars of the silver screen written by their musically gifted brethren who can relate to the acclaim and acrimony that come with fame and fortune.

"James Dean" by The Eagles

The southern California country rockers included this tribute to the pop icon and star of *Rebel Without a Cause* (1955) on their 1974 album *On the Border*. The lyric "too fast to live, too young to die, bye, bye" is a catchphrase used to describe life in the Hollywood fast lane.

"The Right Profile" by The Clash

Troubled and talented actor Montgomery Clift, whose face was severely disfigured in an auto accident in 1957, was saluted by this English quartet of punk rockers who readily identified with Clift's brooding, sensitive acting technique and refusal to play the Hollywood game despite the cost to his career. Included on the group's seminal 1979 release *London Calling,* the song mentions three of the actor's most memorable movies: *Red River* (1948), *From Here to Eternity* (1953), and *The Misfits* (1961).

"Candle in the Wind" by Elton John

This tragic yet uplifting tribute to Marilyn Monroe was originally released in 1973. It features profound lyrics by Bernie Taupin, who borrowed the title from a phrase used to describe 1960s blues-belter Janis Joplin, who, like Monroe, lived a troubled life and suffered an untimely death. Elton John performed a similar version of the song, aptly renamed "Goodbye England's Rose," at Princess Diana's funeral.

"Bette Davis Eyes" by Kim Carnes

Kim Carnes originally rejected this tribute to the Grande Dame of American film, but the raspy-throated warbler won a Grammy for Record of the Year for the song in 1982. Davis was a vocal supporter of the tune, which describes her uncanny ability to silence a room and command instant attention with a simple glance from her large, seductive eyes.

"Man on the Moon" by R.E.M.
This tribute to comedian Andy Kaufman, the star of *In God We Tru$t* (1980), *Heartbeeps* (1981), and the TV series *Taxi*, is from the Athens, Georgia, quartet's 1992 album *Automatic for the People*. It contains references to Kaufman's surprisingly good Elvis impersonations as well as his ill-fated and nearly fatal wrestling career.

"City Lights" by Lou Reed
Former Velvet Underground frontman Lou Reed borrowed the title from one of Charlie Chaplin's most accomplished films and used the actor's forced exodus from Hollywood as a metaphor for loss, loneliness, and love in this tune that was released in 1979. Chaplin, a British citizen, was accused of un-American activities by FBI director J. Edgar Hoover and was banned by the attorney general from reentering the United States when he tried to return in 1952 after a trip abroad promoting his film *Limelight* (1952).

"Bela Lugosi's Dead" by Bauhaus
In 1979, British gloom-and-doom rockers Bauhaus recorded this nine-minute drone to the memory of Hollywood's most famous Dracula. Often regarded as the first gothic-rock record to be committed to vinyl, the song has been covered by more than a dozen other artists, including The Buzzcocks and The Dream Disciples.

"Rosanna" by Toto
In 1982, Toto recorded this passionate platitude to actress Rosanna Arquette (*Desperately Seeking Susan*, 1985), who was dating keyboard player Steve Porcaro at the time. It peaked at No. 2 on the charts and earned the group a Grammy for Record of the Year.

"Kiss Them for Me" by Siouxsie and the Banshees
British post-punk band Siouxsie and the Banshees wrote this song about Jayne Mansfield, the bouncing blonde bombshell and silver screen sex symbol who was killed in a grisly automobile accident in 1967. "Kiss Them for Me"—which was named after a 1957 movie that starred Mansfield and Cary Grant—was included on the band's 1991 album *Superstition*. The title of the tune also refers to Mansfield's three children, who were in the car when it crashed but miraculously escaped serious injury.

Gene Siskel: A Critical Myth

★ ★ ★ ☆

Contrary to a widespread rumor, famed film critic Gene Siskel did not insist that he be buried with his thumb pointing up.

Few in the specialized field of film criticism have been as well known or respected as Gene Siskel, who penned countless movie reviews for the *Chicago Tribune* and later teamed up with fellow critic Roger Ebert of the *Chicago Sun-Times* on the popular television show *At the Movies*.

The show was famous for its movie rating system of "thumbs up–thumbs down," which became the duo's critical trademark. Shortly after Siskel's death in 1999 from complications following brain surgery, a story started to circulate that, among other provisions, Siskel's will stipulated that he be buried with his thumb pointing skyward.

Siskel's thumbs had made him internationally renowned, a legacy that he may have wanted to take to his grave. The rumor raced through the Internet in the form of a fake UPI news story that noted Siskel's unusual request. It read, in part: "According to public records filed in chancery court in Chicago, Gene Siskel asked that he be buried with his thumb pointing upward. The 'Thumbs Up' was the Siskel–Ebert trademark."

The story continued: "'Gene wanted to be remembered as a thumbs-up kind of guy,' said Siskel's lawyer. 'It wasn't surprising to me that he'd ask for that. I informed his family after his death, but he didn't want it made public until after his will had been read.'"

The faux article carries all of the marks of a typical urban legend. Most telling is its failure to identify Siskel's attorney by name, an omission that no legitimate news organization would make.

The magazine *Time Out New York* investigated the rumor and set the record straight, reporting on July 15, 1999: "A glance at the will, now on file with a Chicago court, makes clear that there are no digit-placement requests in [Siskel's] last wishes."

Gridiron Glory

Coordinated chaos. Graceful brutality. Passionate pledges. Locker room locutions. Hail Marys and Immaculate Receptions. These are just some of the characteristics that make football America's most-watched sport. Those same traits make the game a natural subject for the silver screen. Here are a few essential football films that honor and reflect the grit, guts, and glory of the gridiron.

The Galloping Ghost (1931)
If you want to see real football on the big screen, then catch this 12-part serial, which features real-life football legend Red Grange as himself. The story is sentimental and hackneyed, but that matters little when you consider that Grange is not only playing football but also doing his own stunts—jumping out of planes, engaging in fisticuffs, and doing other acrobatics. Fans of football should jump for joy at the chance to see one of the sport's legends in action.

Knute Rockne All American (1940)
Pat O'Brien and Ronald Reagan star in this biographical ode to the University of Notre Dame's football program and the legendary coach who inspired his troops to win with dignity and live with respect. The film is famous for Reagan's "Win one for the Gipper" speech, a slogan that he used while campaigning for George H. W. Bush in 1988.

Brian's Song (1971)
This touching made-for-TV movie documents the relationship between Chicago Bears teammates Gale Sayers and Brian Piccolo. The poignant story tells the tearful tale of Piccolo, whose life and career were cut short by cancer. Watch for the athletic performances of Billy Dee Williams as Sayers and James Caan as the stricken Piccolo.

The Longest Yard (1974)
This hard-hitting blend of comedy, drama, and pathos captures the brutality of a gridiron grudge match between prison inmates and the guards who make their life inside the walls miserable. Burt Reynolds

plays the star quarterback, but Eddie Albert steals the show as the maniacally perverse warden.

Black Sunday (1977)
Though technically this is a film about terrorism, not tackling, the impact of the sport on the American psyche and the importance of Super Bowl Sunday as a cultural event are the key plot points of this superbly crafted thriller. Starring Bruce Dern as a deranged blimp pilot and Robert Shaw as an Israeli intelligence officer, the film says more about football than most movies that feature the game in a starring role.

North Dallas Forty (1979)
This was the first football film to realistically tackle the sticky issue of drug use—both recreational and prescribed—in the sport. The movie also explores the pain threshold needed to compete, the lengths players will go to and the methods they will use to prepare for game day, and the consequences involved. Nick Nolte stars as a hobbling wide receiver struggling to stay competitive.

Rudy (1993)
This sentimental and emotionally moving film is based on the real-life story of Daniel "Rudy" Ruettiger, an undersized student from Joliet, Illinois, who accomplished his lifelong dream of attending the University of Notre Dame and playing football for the Fighting Irish. Despite a poor academic record and a slight 5'6" frame, Rudy overcame both his scholastic and physical shortcomings to graduate from the university and play in one game for the Irish. The film focuses on Rudy's competitive spirit, tenacity, perseverance, and positive outlook.

Jerry Maguire (1996)
Writer/director Cameron Crowe examines the business side of professional sports and the complex relationship between athlete and agent in this perceptive film starring Tom Cruise and Cuba Gooding Jr. The actual on-field action is secondary to the story line. However, the film's primary focus of uncovering football's unique—and sometimes unfair—system of recognizing talent and rewarding performance is sharply dissected.

Any Given Sunday (1999)
Oliver Stone's brutal montage, with its nerve-jarring kaleidoscope of images, upset purists. But it does capture the game's coordinated chaos, archaic atmosphere, and steamy underbelly of corruption and

collusion. Al Pacino stars as a traditionalist coach at the back end of a legendary career while Jamie Foxx plays the upstart quarterback with a mind—and method—of his own.

Remember the Titans (2000)
Racial tension, personal prejudices, and the unifying force of football take center stage in this carefully crafted adaptation based on the true story of the newly integrated football program at T. C. Williams High School in Alexandria, Virginia. Denzel Washington stars as Coach Herman Boone, whose staunch determination and dignified leadership helped solidify the team, temper the town, and take home the title.

Friday Night Lights (2004)
This poignant portrayal of football as religion in the small Texas town of Odessa also touches on the underlying current of social injustice, class conflict, racial tension, and personal politics that permeate the proceedings. At the heart of the matter, however, is the game itself, and it is depicted with distinguished flair. Billy Bob Thornton and country superstar Tim McGraw highlight the strong cast.

Invincible (2006)
This film depicts the remarkable story of Vince Papale, a respected track-and-field athlete, who, despite never playing a down of college football, went on to enjoy a three-year career with the NFL's Philadelphia Eagles. In 1976, at age 30, Papale was working as a bartender and substitute teacher when he attended a professional tryout, which eventually earned him a spot with the Eagles. Mark Wahlberg captures the spirit and earnest dedication of Papale, and Greg Kinnear is effective as Coach Dick Vermeil.

We Are Marshall (2006)
This true story of redemption and revitalization describes the rebirth of the Marshall University football program after the majority of the team and its staff were killed in a 1970 airplane crash. Though some may find the film sentimental and simplistic in its approach, it does capture the honest yet complex role that the game played in healing the university and the town.

How to Get Your Dog in the Movies

Q: What skills does a dog need to get a role in a movie?

A: Every pet owner thinks his or her dog is the cutest, the smartest, and the best trained, but there's more to it than just being able to sit and roll over on command. The dog needs a great deal of specific training. To be used in a movie, your dog needs to be comfortable obeying hand commands in unfamiliar locations, under the glare of hot lights and surrounded by dozens of strangers. In some situations, owners cannot be on set with their animals, so your dog must be able to take commands from a stranger. If you feel confident that your pooch possesses all the skills to become a movie star, you must ask yourself: Are you ready to be the owner of a celebrity dog?

Q: So the owner needs special skills as well?

A: Show business can be just as competitive for canine actors as it is for human ones. As the owner, are you able to attend an audition or turn up on the set with your dog at a moment's notice? Movie schedules can be long with plenty of downtime spent waiting for your dog's scene to shoot. This might be all right if you're retired and have a lot of spare time but not so convenient if you have a full-time job.

Q: How much can a dog earn?

A: Depending on Fido's skills and talents, payment can range from $100 to $500 per day.

Q: Where do I start?

A: First, you should check out the American Humane organization (www.americanhumane.org), which protects animals on sets. You should know something about this watchdog group because it will be watching out for your dog's welfare. Once you've done your homework, take some photos and video clips of your dog and contact an animal-talent agent. It's also a good idea to contact local film schools to see if any student filmmakers need your dog's services. They may not be able to pay much, but it's a good way to get Fido some on-set experience and make sure that acting really is for him. Some dogs prefer to curl up with their owners while they watch a movie on TV rather than actually be part of the cast.

Fast Facts: Leading Ladies

- *Katharine Hepburn may have been shy about revealing her age, but she wasn't shy about her body. On one occasion, she allegedly walked around a movie studio in her underwear (in the modest era of the 1930s) when someone from the costume department took her slacks away. She refused to put on any other clothes until her pants were returned.*

- *In 1982, Bette Davis told* Playboy *magazine that she had worked as a nude model in her younger years, stating that an artist had created a statue of her that was featured in a public place in Boston. However, the statue has never been located or identified.*

- *Liz Taylor, who has suffered from numerous health problems during her life, was even pronounced dead once. Doctors made the mistaken declaration while Taylor was sick with pneumonia during the filming of* BUtterfield 8 *(1960).*

- *In 1993, Grace Kelly became the first American actress ever depicted on a U.S. postage stamp. That same year, Monaco released a stamp bearing her likeness. In the United States, she was listed as Grace Kelly, while in Monaco, the stamp called her Princess Grace.*

- *Meryl Streep was both a cheerleader and a homecoming queen during her high school years.*

- *Ingrid Bergman battled to keep her birth name after becoming an actress. Early in her career, producers looked at re-branding her Ingrid Berriman or having her use her married name, Ingrid Lindstrom.*

- *Ava Gardner did her own singing in* The Killers *(1946). However, most of her other films dubbed the vocals for her songs. In* Showboat *(1951), Gardner's singing voice wasn't used in the film, but it made it onto the soundtrack album.*

Thelma Todd: Suicide or Murder?

☆ ☆ ☆ ☆

During her nine-year film career, Thelma Todd costarred in dozens of comedies with the likes of Harry Langdon, Laurel and Hardy, and the Marx Brothers. Today, however, the "Ice Cream Blonde," as she was known, is best remembered for her bizarre death, which remains one of Hollywood's most enduring mysteries.

Sins Indulged

Todd was born in Lawrence, Massachusetts, in 1906 and arrived in Hollywood at age 20 via the beauty pageant circuit. Pretty and vivacious, she quickly became a hot commodity and fell headlong into Tinseltown's anything-goes party scene. In 1932, she married Pasquale "Pat" DiCicco, an agent of sorts who was also associated with gangster Charles "Lucky" Luciano. Their marriage was plagued by drunken fights, and they divorced two years later.

For solace, Todd turned to director Roland West, who didn't approve of her drinking and drug use, but he could not stop her. With his help, Todd opened a roadhouse called Thelma Todd's Sidewalk Café, located on the Pacific Coast Highway, and the actress moved into a spacious apartment above the restaurant. Shortly after, Todd began a relationship with gangster "Lucky" Luciano, who tried to get her to let him use a room at the Sidewalk Café for illegal gambling. Todd repeatedly refused.

On the morning of December 16, 1935, Todd was found dead in the front seat of her 1934 Lincoln Phaeton convertible, which was parked in the two-car garage she shared with West. The apparent cause of death was carbon monoxide poisoning, though whether Todd was the victim of an accident, suicide, or murder remains a mystery.

Little evidence supports the suicide theory, outside the mode of death and the fact that Todd led a fast-paced lifestyle that sometimes got the better of her. Indeed, her career was going remarkably well, and she had purchased Christmas presents and was looking forward to a New Year's Eve party. So suicide does not seem a viable cause, though it is still mentioned as a probable one in many accounts.

The Accident Theory

However, an accidental death is also a possibility. The key to her car was in the "on" position, and the motor was dead when Todd was discovered by her maid. West suggested to investigators that the actress turned on the car to get warm, passed out because she was drunk, and then succumbed to carbon monoxide poisoning. Todd also had a heart condition, according to West, and this may have contributed to her death.

Nonetheless, the notion of foul play is suggested by several incongruities found at the scene. Spots of blood were discovered on and in Todd's car and on her mouth, and her nose was broken, leading some to believe she was knocked out then placed in the car to make it look like a suicide. (Police attributed the injuries to Todd falling unconscious and striking her head on the steering wheel.) In addition, Todd's blood-alcohol level was extremely high—high enough to stupefy her so that someone could carry her without her fighting back—and her high-heeled shoes were clean and unscuffed, even though she would have had to ascend a flight of outdoor, concrete stairs to reach the garage, which was a 271-step climb behind the restaurant. Investigators also found an unidentified smudged handprint on the left side of the vehicle.

Two with Motive

If Todd was murdered, as some have suggested, who had motive? Because of her wild lifestyle, there are several potential suspects, most notably Pasquale DiCicco, who was known to have a violent temper, and "Lucky" Luciano, who was angry at Todd for refusing to let him use her restaurant for illegal activities.

Despite the many questions raised by the evidence found at the scene, a grand jury ruled Todd's death accidental. The investigation had been hampered by altered and destroyed evidence, threats to witnesses, and cover-ups, making it impossible to ever learn what really happened. An open-casket service was held at Forest Lawn Memorial Park, where the public viewed the actress bedecked in yellow roses. After the service, Todd was cremated, eliminating the possibility of a second autopsy. Later, when her mother, Alice Todd, died, the actress's ashes were placed in her mother's casket so they could be buried together in Massachusetts.

Pop Quiz: Movie Taglines—Take Two

Taglines can often either make or break a movie. If the tagline is creative and clever, it will intrigue audiences and draw them in; at the same time, a dull tagline might keep moviegoers away. How many movie taglines can you match up with their famous films?

1. "Mischief. Mayhem. Soap."

2. "Sleep all day. Party all night. Never grow old. Never die. It's fun to be a vampire."

3. "...look closer."

4. "Scaling the Cliffs of Insanity, battling rodents of unusual size, facing torture in the Pit of Despair. True love has never been a snap."

5. "The night HE came home!"

6. "The mission is a man."

7. "Makes *Ben-Hur* look like an epic."

8. "He's out to prove he's got nothing to prove."

9. "They only met once, but it changed their lives forever."

10. "The man lived by the jungle laws of the docks!"

11. "Cute. Clever. Mischievous. Intelligent. Dangerous."

12. "Your future is in his hands."

13. "The scariest comedy of all time!"

14. "You don't assign him to murder cases. You just turn him loose."

15. "A little knowledge can be a deadly thing."

16. "I see dead people."

17. "This is Benjamin. He's a little worried about his future."

18. "An offer you can't refuse."

19. "Check in. Relax. Take a shower."

Answer Choices

A. *American Beauty* (1999)

B. *The Breakfast Club* (1985)

C. *Dirty Harry* (1971)

D. *Fight Club* (1999)

E. *The Godfather* (1972)

F. *The Graduate* (1967)

G. *Gremlins* (1984)

H. *Halloween* (1978)

I. *The Lost Boys* (1987)

J. *The Man Who Knew Too Much* (1956)

K. *Monty Python and the Holy Grail* (1975)

L. *Napoleon Dynamite* (2004)

M. *On the Waterfront* (1954)

N. *The Princess Bride* (1987)

O. *Psycho* (1960)

P. *Saving Private Ryan* (1998)

Q. *The Sixth Sense* (1999)

R. *The Terminator* (1984)

S. *Young Frankenstein* (1974)

Hollywood Goes to War

☆ ☆ ☆ ☆

During World War II, Hollywood and the U.S. War Department joined forces to create a juggernaut of entertainment and propaganda that played a critical role in the war effort and also just happened to produce some of the finest films of the Golden Age.

In the late 1930s and early 1940s, the American public was intently focused on the growing conflict among nations around the world. With help from the Soviet Union, China was defending itself against an invasion by the Japanese Empire; France, Britain, and other European countries were unsuccessfully fighting the aggressive incursions of the German and Italian war machines. Should the United States get involved, and if so, to what extent?

Responding to the widespread interest in these events, Hollywood released a number of popular films that clearly favored the cause of the Allies, such as *Confessions of a Nazi Spy* (1939) and *A Yank in the RAF* (1941). Many elected officials grew concerned that these films might tilt popular opinion toward entry into the war, so much so that a Congressional committee pressured the major studio heads with threats of censorship if they didn't tone down the messages in their films. Two months later, Pearl Harbor was bombed, and the U.S. government did a complete about-face, embracing Hollywood as an integral part of the war effort. The federal Office of War Information essentially became a coproducer of Hollywood war films, reviewing and approving scripts, weighing in on the final cuts, providing military personnel to serve as technical advisors, and arranging for location shooting on army and air force bases. The government even provided tanks, fighter planes, weapons, and other military hardware for props.

The War-Era Formula

Bataan and *Air Force,* both released in 1943, were two of the first combat films to come out of this collaboration between the studios and the military. *Air Force* established a clear formula that would be followed by many other war-era films, touting teamwork, training, and superior technology as the keys to victory. The films eschewed big-name stars in favor of using ensemble casts that represented diverse ethnic and socioeconomic groups from American society banding together for the good of the nation. They also pointedly extolled the effectiveness of the new technologies available to America's soldiers—from hand grenades and flamethrowers to the portable communications devices of infantrymen and the complex systems of a B-17 bomber—as a way to inspire confidence in the nation's military might. As the war dragged on and civilians became more knowledgeable about both the mechanics and the horrors of the war, combat films focused more on the sacrifices and struggles made by the individuals fighting the good fight. Heroes on the homefront were given their due as well: In *Saboteur* (1942) an ordinary factory worker brings a German operative to justice, while *Tender Comrade* (1943) chronicles the hardships stoically borne by several female factory workers who share an apartment while their husbands are fighting overseas. Even after the hostilities ended, Hollywood followed through by addressing the difficult adjustment to life during peacetime, as in *The Best Years of Our Lives* (1946).

Times Change

Heroic films about the war remained a fixture into the early 1960s, as did the mutually beneficial relationship between the film industry and the military. But with the Vietnam War prompting many Americans to rethink their views on armed conflict, audiences became more receptive to movies that laid bare the futility of war, such as *Catch-22* (1970) and *Kelly's Heroes* (1970). Little question remains, though, that the World War II-era films greatly boosted morale among soldiers and civilians alike and left future generations of movie buffs with enduring classics such as *Casablanca* (1942) and *They Were Expendable* (1945).

Small Screen Starts

Stardom rarely comes easy in Hollywood. Most actors labeled an "overnight success" have actually spent many years honing their craft, often in bit parts on easily forgettable television shows. Indeed, a surprising number of today's movie superstars—including several Academy Award winners—actually got their start on the small screen before making the transition to motion pictures. Here are just a few:

Halle Berry

Halle Berry won a Best Actress Oscar for her performance in *Monster's Ball* (2001) and has costarred in three *X-Men* movies as well as the James Bond thriller *Die Another Day* (2002). She also starred in the impressive biopic *Introducing Dorothy Dandridge* (1999), which made the industry stand up and take notice. But long before that, this striking beauty was first runner-up in the 1986 Miss USA pageant. A few years later, Berry got her shot at stardom as Emily Franklin on the short-lived television series *Living Dolls* in 1989. She followed that with appearances on *Amen*, *A Different World*, and *They Came From Outer Space* before landing her first movie role in *Jungle Fever* (1991), Spike Lee's critically acclaimed tale of interracial romance.

George Clooney

Most fans know that this handsome hunk helped make the TV medical drama *ER* a mega-hit before jumping into motion pictures. However, *ER* wasn't Clooney's first television series—he also had recurring roles on *The Facts of Life*, *Roseanne*, and *Sisters*. His many hit movies include *The Perfect Storm* (2000), *Michael Clayton* (2007), and *Ocean's Eleven* (2001) and its sequels. Clooney's clout as a leading man helped him branch out into directing, earning acclaim for *Confessions of a Dangerous Mind* (2002) and Oscar nominations for *Good Night, and Good Luck* (2005).

Johnny Depp

There has never been a more popular pirate than Depp, who almost single-handedly made Disney's *Pirates of the Caribbean* franchise one of the most profitable in movie history. Depp is renowned for his chameleon-like acting ability and penchant for quirky roles, but many fans may have forgotten that the three-time Academy Award nominee first came to prominence in the late 1980s on the television series *21 Jump Street*.

Depp had secondary roles in a couple of low-budget movies before that, including *A Nightmare on Elm Street* (1984) and *Private Resort* (1985), but it was *21 Jump Street* that jump-started his movie career.

Leonardo DiCaprio

Leonardo DiCaprio is another hotshot who started out with some less-than-titanic TV roles. The first came in 1990 on the series *Parenthood*. After various bit parts, the teenaged DiCaprio played Luke on the hit family sitcom *Growing Pains*. It was that role that finally got him noticed, and after his Oscar-nominated performance in *What's Eating Gilbert Grape* in 1993, DiCaprio's career was flying high.

Clint Eastwood

A four-time Oscar winner, Eastwood has made his mark as both an accomplished actor and a skilled director, and he too made it big on TV before making it bigger on the silver screen. His breakout role came as Rowdy Yates on the popular Western series *Rawhide*, which ran from 1959 to 1966. While on hiatus from *Rawhide*, Eastwood starred in *A Fistful of Dollars*, an Italian Western for a little-known director named Sergio Leone. The film became an unexpected worldwide box-office hit, resulting in two sequels: *For a Few Dollars More* (1965) and *The Good, the Bad, and the Ugly* (1966). After that, Eastwood's star rose even higher with the role of Inspector Harry Callahan in the *Dirty Harry* franchise.

Tom Hanks

Dressing in drag can give a comic actor a career boost, even if he doesn't have the legs for it. And wearing a dress in the early '80s TV series *Bosom Buddies* gave Tom Hanks the legs he needed to kick off a remarkably successful movie career. Hanks's résumé features some of this generation's best-loved motion pictures, including *Sleepless in Seattle* (1993), *Forrest Gump* (1994), *Cast Away* (2000), and *The Da Vinci Code* (2006), just to name a few. For his efforts, Hanks has been nominated for five Best Actor Oscars and has taken home Oscar gold twice, for *Philadelphia* (1993) and *Forrest Gump*.

Ron Howard

Fondly remembered for his wholesome roles as Opie on *The Andy Griffith Show* and Richie Cunningham on *Happy Days*, Howard enjoyed a spectacular career as a television actor before moving on to motion pictures, where he costarred in George Lucas's *American Graffiti* (1973) and John Wayne's last film, *The Shootist* (1976), among others. In recent years, Howard has made an even bigger name for himself as a producer and director with movies such as *Backdraft* (1991), *Apollo 13* (1995), *The Da Vinci Code* (2006), *Frost/Nixon* (2008), and *A Beautiful Mind* (2001), the latter of which won Oscars for Best Director and Best Picture.

Burt Reynolds

The man who made a career out of playing good ol' boys reigned as Hollywood's leading man in the '70s and '80s with starring roles in escapist fare such as *The Longest Yard* (1974), *Smokey and the Bandit* (1977), and *The Cannonball Run* (1981). And in 1998, Reynolds received an Academy Award nomination for Best Supporting Actor for his performance in *Boogie Nights* (1997). But Reynolds got his start with recurring roles on television series such as *Riverboat*, *Gunsmoke*, and *Hawk*.

Will Smith

Action flicks are Smith's forte, but the former rapper got his start on the wildly popular 1990s television comedy *The Fresh Prince of Bel-Air*. Smith has been nominated for an Oscar twice (*Ali*, 2001; *The Pursuit of Happyness*, 2006) and has starred in some of Hollywood's biggest blockbusters, including *Bad Boys* (1995), *Independence Day* (1996), *Men in Black* (1997), and *I Am Legend* (2007).

John Travolta

Before he became a cinematic superstar and a two-time Academy Award nominee, John Travolta was Vinnie Barbarino, one of the Sweathogs on the 1970s TV show *Welcome Back, Kotter*. In 1977, Travolta starred in John Badham's homage to disco, *Saturday Night Fever* (1977), and never looked back. His other hits include *Grease* (1978), *Urban Cowboy* (1980), and *Pulp Fiction* (1994).

Robin Williams

A stand-up comic before he took up acting, Williams first made a name for himself as Mork from Ork in the late '70s/early '80s television series *Mork & Mindy*. His prolific film career includes hits such as *Good Morning, Vietnam* (1987), *Dead Poets Society* (1989), *Patch Adams* (1998), and *Good Will Hunting* (1997), which earned Williams an Oscar for Best Supporting Actor.

Prehistoric Hollywood

☆ ☆ ☆ ☆

If a stroll along Rodeo Drive lined with Beverly Hills housewives isn't enough to convince you, Hollywood was once home to a vast array of Pleistocene ice age creatures. The La Brea Tar Pits, located near the Miracle Mile district of Los Angeles, have yielded the largest repository of fossils from the last ice age, including plants, insects, and mammals.

Despite the name, the La Brea Tar Pits are actually a series of asphalt deposits that bubble up from the ground. Over the centuries, oil has oozed to the surface to form sticky bogs that have trapped all manner of animals, condemning them to premature deaths but preserving their skeletons. Since paleontologists began excavating the tar pits in 1908, remains have been discovered that date back as far as 40,000 years. These include saber-toothed cats, short-faced bears, dire wolves, and even an American lion. In early 2009, as workers began excavating an underground parking garage next to the tar pits, they stumbled upon a stunning collection of fossils, including a nearly intact mammoth dating back to the last ice age.

Curators from the George C. Page Museum, which houses fossils collected from the site, estimate that the mammoth—whom they named Zed—stood ten feet tall at the hip and was between 47 and 49 years old, which is young for a mammoth. Zed's three broken ribs indicate that he'd likely been injured fighting with other male mammoths, a precursor to the backbiting that is so common in Hollywood these days.

The La Brea Tar Pits are no stranger to the limelight, having been featured in a number of movies, including *Last Action Hero* (1993), Steven Spielberg's *1941* (1979), and the disaster movie, *Volcano* (1997), in which a volcanic eruption originates from the largest tar pit and spews hot lava along the streets of Hollywood.

No Matter What the Cost: 10 of the Most Expensive Movies Ever Made

In today's world of blockbuster movies, moviemakers have been known to spare no expense when it comes to their films. Here are ten movies whose combined costs could easily put a dent in the national debt.*

King Kong (2005): (Cost $205 million)

Hot on the heels of his epic and wildly successful *Lord of the Rings* trilogy (itself reportedly a $310 million project combined), director Peter Jackson brought a proven knack for creating frighteningly convincing fantasy beasts to this remake of his own favorite film: 1933's *King Kong*. Known by then for producing and directing large-scale films, Jackson wanted to fit all of the special effects and action sequences he envisioned for both the overwhelming Skull Island location and for 1930s-era New York City into his version of *Kong*. But doing so ballooned *Kong*'s running time—this remake of the 105-minute 1933 film would run more than three hours in its original theatrical cut. In the end, Jackson's take on the classic story would use close to 2,400 CGI shots, while production costs soared to more than $30 million over budget. (Cost to make this movie in 2009: $227 million.)

Terminator 3: Rise of the Machines (2003): (Cost $200 million)

Because it was the third installment in the popular *Terminator* franchise, simply acquiring the rights to make a second sequel cost more than $20 million. Add to that an initial budget of $20 million for costly digital effects as well as Arnold Schwarzenegger's soon-to-be-legendary $30 million salary, and there was no doubt that *Terminator 3* would earn a spot on the Most Expensive list. Arnold himself is rumored to have thrown a million or so of his own money into the mix because he felt the movie would be missing something if one particular scene—in which a crane crashes into a glass building—was left out. But even that scene couldn't help the movie recoup its production budget at U.S. box offices, where *T3* managed to bring in only $150 million, roughly $50 million less than what it cost to make the film. (Cost to make this movie in 2009: $235 million.)

Pirates of the Caribbean: Dead Man's Chest (2006): (Cost $223 million)
Even Walt Disney himself would have been surprised at the amount of cash that *Pirates of the Caribbean: The Curse of the Black Pearl* brought in ($305 million in the U.S. alone). So what better way to ensure the success of the follow-up than to pump millions more into complex special effects, most notably bringing the ghostly part-man, part-sea creature Davey Jones to life? This sequel brought the *Pirates* franchise itself back to life in a big way: *Dead Man's Chest* earned a whopping $420 million stateside. (Cost to make this movie in 2009: $239 million.)

Waterworld (1995): (Cost $175 million)
The butt of many a movie joke, *Waterworld*'s descent into the annals of movie flops wasn't entirely due to a bad script. One of the main reasons *Waterworld* became a money-sucking nightmare was because the entire film was shot on water (near Hawaii), which is incredibly expensive (it reportedly gave a $35 million boost to the state's economy) and set the stage for all sorts of costly delays due to everything from monsoons to seasickness, not to mention the accidental sinking of a floating set rumored to have weighed more than 180 tons. The film also sank at the box office, earning only $88 million in the States, roughly half of the final budget. However, the foreign box-office tally came to almost $176 million, which saved the film from total failure. (Cost to make this movie in 2009: $248 million.)

Spider-Man 3 (2007): (Cost $258 million)
Already two enormously successful movies into the *Spider-Man* franchise, director Sam Raimi pulled out all the stops for the third chapter, upping the ante by adding a pair of new villains—Venom and New Goblin—as well as more elaborate sets and, of course, tons of CGI effects featuring everyone's favorite web slinger. Raimi's Spidey senses must have been tingling away as he watched his film rake in more than $336 million in the U.S. alone. (Cost to make this movie in 2009: $268.7 million.)

Titanic (1997): (Cost $200 million)
While many people blame this movie's titanic-size budget on director James Cameron's unwillingness to compromise on his vision of what the

film should be, *Titanic* will also long be remembered for the creation of some of the most costly and elaborate sets in film history. Two massive water tanks were utilized: a six-million-gallon indoor tank to film the interior sinking scenes and a 17-million-gallon outdoor tank for exterior shots of the ship. There was even a full-scale replica of the exterior of the *Titanic*, which was later torn apart and sold as scrap. Plus, Cameron used special remote control cameras to shoot footage of the actual *Titanic* on the bottom of the ocean. All that hard work paid off when *Titanic* recouped its budget nearly three times over with almost $600 million taken in stateside and $1.24 billion abroad. (Cost to make this movie in 2009: $269 million.)

Superman Returns (2006): (Cost $268.5 million)

Director Bryan Singer swears to this day that his movie didn't cost nearly $270 million to make. That's probably because the film itself was relatively inexpensive to produce. What caused this film's budget to skyrocket was that it was stuck in preproduction for nearly ten years. During that time, it is estimated that more than $50 million was spent on rewriting the script, building sets, and scouting out and holding multiple filming locations, all before a single shot was ever filmed. Although the movie did make a respectable $200 million in the States, it still seemed like a flop considering the final budget. (Cost to make this movie in 2009: $287.6 million.)

Cleopatra (1963): (Cost $44 million)

When 20th Century Fox announced that Elizabeth Taylor and Richard Burton would appear together in *Cleopatra,* everyone knew it was going to be a blockbuster. What they didn't know was how much it was going to cost.

From the start, money started flying out the window due to confusion over creative vision. Director Rouben Mamoulian spent months—and millions of dollars—planning the production, only to be fired without ever filming a single scene. Replacing Mamoulian was director Joseph L. Mankiewicz, who stepped in to helm a project already $5 million over budget. Taylor and Burton would also cost the production massive amounts of money. The pair were frequently absent from the set because of their on-set romance, an affair that wreaked havoc on both of their marriages. The personal turmoil offscreen sometimes brought production to a standstill. But by far, the largest amount of money was lost on location shooting. Originally, filming began in Rome. Then the production was moved to London, which meant that many of the sets had to be rebuilt. When shooting moved back to Rome, sets had to be reconstructed once again.

When all was said and done, *Cleopatra* barely broke even at the box office, earning nearly $58 million in the U.S. and another $14 million overseas. (Cost to make this movie in 2009: $310.5 million.)

Pirates of the Caribbean: At World's End (2007): (Cost $300 million)

In the third installment in the *Pirates* saga, director Gore Verbinski pulled out all the stops, choosing exotic (and expensive) locations such as St. Vincent, Hawaii, and the Bahamas. Giant water tanks were also constructed for the filming of a now-famous scene in which the *Black Pearl* flips underwater.

But when it came to box-office earnings, the third time wasn't the charm for the *Pirates* franchise. While *At World's End* managed to bring in $309 million in the U.S., it fell far short of the $423 million U.S. gross that the second installment had made. (Cost to make this movie in 2009: $312 million.)

War and Peace (1967): (Cost $100 million+)

So how does a movie released in the Soviet Union more than 40 years ago beat out all of Hollywood's recent big-budget blockbusters? Well, for starters, *War and Peace*, 1968's Oscar winner for Best Foreign Language Film, which took more than seven years to create, had to be released in four installments in certain markets because it was more than seven hours long. Also, at the time, *War and Peace* featured the largest cast of actors and extras ever assembled for a single film— between 120,000 and 150,000 of them. In fact, the film's Battle of Borodino scene is still listed in the *Guinness Book of World Records* as the largest battle scene ever filmed.

No box-office figures are available for *War and Peace* because, at the time of the film's release, the Soviet Union tracked the number of admissions, not how much each patron paid. However, it is estimated that in the Soviet Union alone, more than 135 million people saw the film in the first two years of its release. (Cost to make this movie in 2009: $664.6 million.)

*In order to keep things fair, the cost to make each movie is given in U.S. dollars and has been adjusted to reflect dollar amounts in 2009.

The Sex-sational Trial of Errol Flynn

☆ ☆ ☆ ☆

*When a handsome leading man was charged with rape, his
status in Hollywood was in doubt. But rather than signaling
his end in the business, his popularity soared ever higher.*

The saying "In like Flynn" means little these days, but during the
1940s, it was used to compliment one who was doing exceedingly
well. More to the point, it usually referred to sexual conquests made
by a lucky "man about town."

The saying originated with Hollywood heartthrob Errol Flynn
(1909–1959), the swashbuckling star of *Captain Blood* (1935) and
The Adventures of Robin Hood (1938). A "man's man" in the most
cocksure sense, Flynn was known for his barroom brawls and trysts
both on camera and off, which became part of his star image. He
wore this colorful mantle like a badge of honor, but he did hit a rough
patch in life, when he was charged with two counts of statutory rape.

Swashbuckling Seductor

The alleged crimes took place during the summer of 1942. In one
instance, 17-year-old Betty Hansen claimed that Flynn had seduced
her after she became ill from overimbibing at a Hollywood party.
In the other, 15-year-old Peggy Satterlee insisted that Flynn took
advantage of her on his yacht, *The Sirocco,* during a trip to Catalina
Island. Both women claimed that he referred to them by the nick-
names "S.Q.Q." (San Quentin Quail) and "J.B." (Jail Bait), thereby
suggesting that Flynn knew that they were under age. Flynn was
arrested that fall and charged with two counts of rape. Proclaiming
his innocence, he hired high-powered attorney Jerry Giesler, who
called the women's motives and pasts into question and stacked the
jury with nine females in the hopes that Flynn's considerable charm
might win them over. The move would prove prophetic.

Women of Questionable Character

When the defense presented its case, Giesler went directly for
the jugular. His cross-examination revealed that both women had

engaged in sexual relations *before* the alleged incidents with Flynn and that Satterlee had even had an abortion. Even more damning, Satterlee admitted to frequently lying about her age and was inconsistent in a number of her answers. Suddenly, the veneer of innocence that the women had hoped to project was stripped away.

There was also Satterlee's claim that Flynn had taken her below deck to gaze at the moon through a porthole. Giesler challenged the expert testimony of an astronomer hired by the prosecution, getting the man to admit that, given the boat's apparent course, such a view was physically impossible through the porthole in Flynn's cabin.

The Verdict
By the time Flynn took the stand, the members of the all-female jury were half won over by his charm. By the time he finished arguing his innocence, their minds were made up. The effect was not at all surprising for a man whom actress and eight-time costar Olivia de Havilland once described as "…the handsomest, most charming, most magnetic, most virile young man in the entire world."

When a verdict of "not guilty" was read, women in the courtroom applauded and wept. Afterward, the jury forewoman noted: "We felt there had been other men in the girls' lives. Frankly, the cards were on the table and we couldn't believe the girls' stories."

Continued Fortune in a Man's World
Cleared of all charges, Errol Flynn continued to make movies, resumed his carousing ways, and grew even more popular in the public eye. Many felt that, despite the verdict, Flynn had indeed had sexual relations with the young women, but most were willing to forgive the transgression because the liaisons seemed consensual and the allegations of rape looked like little more than a frame job.

Young men would regard the amorous actor as an ideal to emulate, and women would continue to swoon as always. But years of hard living eventually took their toll on Flynn. By the time he reached middle age, his looks had all but vanished. At the premature age of 50, Flynn suffered a massive heart attack and died. Death only served to cement Flynn's legendary status amongst Hollywood's great actors and its rapscallions alike.

Fast Facts: Disney

- *Everyone's favorite rodent, Mickey Mouse was introduced in the cartoon short* Steamboat Willie *(1928), which was released just after the sync-sound revolution. The cartoon's use of synchronized music and sound effects helped make it a critical success.*

- *Disney's* Snow White and the Seven Dwarfs *(1937) was the first full-length animated feature produced in the United States. The movie debuted two decades after Argentina created the first-ever full-length animated movie,* El Apóstol.

- *Walt Disney called his nine animators the "Nine Old Men," though many were quite young when they started working for Disney Studios. All nine remained with Disney from* Snow White and the Seven Dwarfs *through* The Rescuers *(1977). The influence of the Nine Old Men—Ollie Johnston, Milt Kahl, Les Clark, Frank Thomas, Wolfgang Reitherman, John Lounsbery, Eric Larson, Ward Kimball, and Mark Davis—on commercial Hollywood animation cannot be underestimated.*

- *Singer Ricky Martin voiced the main character in the Spanish version of Disney's* Hercules *(1997). Tate Donovan did the voice in the original English flick.*

- Alice in Wonderland *(1951) was based on two of Lewis Carroll's books:* Alice's Adventures in Wonderland *and* Through the Looking Glass. *But the animated adaptation had one character that Carroll didn't create: the doorknob.*

- Beauty and the Beast *(1991) holds the honor of being the first full-length animated feature to receive a Best Picture Oscar nomination. It ended up losing to* The Silence of the Lambs, *but it still made history: The movie took home the Golden Globe for Best Picture, becoming the first animated movie to do so.*

- Dumbo *is the only Disney title character who never speaks in his movie.*

- *The last film that bore the personal stamp of Walt Disney himself was* The Jungle Book *(1967).*

- *Although Kathleen Turner voiced all of Jessica Rabbit's speaking parts in* Who Framed Roger Rabbit *(1988), she was never credited. Actress Amy Irving did the character's singing.*

- *Dan Castellaneta—best known as the voice of Homer Simpson— stepped in to voice the genie in* The Return of Jafar *(1994), the sequel to* Aladdin *(1992), after Robin Williams turned down the chance to reprise his role. Williams later came back for a third film, the direct-to-video* Aladdin and the King of Thieves *(1995). Castellaneta had already voiced the film, but Disney discarded his voice track when Williams agreed to take the role. Castellaneta did not lose out entirely, however, because he voiced the genie for Disney's* Aladdin *cartoon television series.*

- The Little Mermaid *(1989) was the last animated Disney film to use hand-painted cels shot on analog film. Artists created more than a million drawings for the movie.*

- *The idea for* The Little Mermaid *was actually born in the 1930s. Disney art director Kay Nielsen created pastel and watercolor sketches for the project, but it never got off the ground during her tenure. Nielsen's drawings were pulled from Disney's archives and were used by the modern-day artists working on the movie. Nielsen was credited for "visual development" for her contribution, six decades after she actually did the work.*

- *Animators studied the movement of professional skateboarder Tony Hawk while making* Tarzan *(1999). The way Tarzan slid down a log was based on Hawk's movements while riding his board.*

- *Pumbaa, the warthog from* The Lion King, *is thought to be the first character to pass gas in an animated Disney movie.*

Tim Burton and Johnny Depp

☆ ☆ ☆ ☆

*Pair one of Hollywood's quirkiest actors with one of its quirkiest
directors, and you'd expect to end up with some strange films.
But Johnny Depp and Tim Burton seem to create a unique kind of
cinematic magic together that has produced half a dozen memorable
characters, all who struggle to find their place in the world.*

Misunderstood

Tim Burton often talks of the alienation he felt growing up in a
sterile suburb with peers who had little sympathy for his macabre,
creative personality and how he immersed himself in gothic horror
films to escape, particularly favoring those of Vincent Price. So it's
no surprise that themes of isolation, alienation, and creative refuge
permeate most of his films, from *Pee-Wee's Big Adventure* (1985)
to *Big Fish* (2003). But these themes are probably best conveyed
through the films he's made with his most frequent collaborator,
Johnny Depp. Together they've created six distinctive films featuring
main characters who are outsiders stumbling their way through
a world they don't understand that doesn't understand them. In
return, they create their own alternate world that is outside the
bounds of the conventional normal world.

An Unlikely Duo or a Perfect Match?

Their first effort, *Edward Scissorhands* (1990), allowed Burton the
thrill of working with his childhood idol Vincent Price, who played
a small role as a reclusive scientist who builds a young man but dies
before he can give him hands. Instead, the pale, wild-haired young
fellow played by Depp has a preposterous array of foot-long shears
in place of fingers. Though at first he's able to use his creative side
to become the darling of the neighboring cookie-cutter subdivision,
he eventually finds that the outside world will never accept him
because of his differences. Depp, who had relatively few lines in
the film, did a remarkable job of expressing the innocent Edward's
many emotions through jerky mannerisms and unrestrained facial
expressions.

The duo's next collaboration, *Ed Wood* (1994), was a biopic of the famously bad independent filmmaker from the 1950s. The daring black-and-white film, which was hailed by critics but largely avoided by audiences, again depicted a character with a unique worldview who lives his life fully out of step with his surroundings. Their third and fifth collaborations, *Sleepy Hollow* (1999) and the animated feature *Corpse Bride* (2005), share a supernatural theme and present protagonists who find their rational, familiar existence turned upside down by encounters from beyond the grave. Though the theme of alienation is less pronounced in these two films, both still focus on main characters who are forced to come to terms with a world they suddenly don't understand.

Like *Sleepy Hollow,* their other two collaborations were adaptations of stories first told in other mediums. *Charlie and the Chocolate Factory* (2005) is a remake of a 1971 film based on the beloved children's novel by Roald Dahl. Many fans of the original were skeptical that Burton and Depp would do anything but detract from the signature performance of Gene Wilder as reclusive candy maker Willie Wonka, but their strategy of keeping truer to Dahl's original characterization paid off; the film stayed in theaters for five months and grossed more than $200 million. Their 2007 adaptation of Steven Sondheim's murderous musical *Sweeney Todd* had Depp portraying a crazed barber who sliced his way through 19th-century London in retribution for the family that was unjustly taken from him. Darker and more cynical than their earlier works, the film again showed audiences the heavy toll levied against those whose worldview places them outside the embrace of society.

Burton and Depp Filmography:
Edward Scissorhands (1990)
Ed Wood (1994)
Sleepy Hollow (1999)
Charlie and the Chocolate Factory (2005)
Corpse Bride (2005)
Sweeney Todd: The Demon Barber of Fleet Street (2007)
Alice in Wonderland (2010)

Memorable Sales of Movie Memorabilia

Hollywood is full of history, and plenty of people want to own a piece of it. So how much would you pay for a famous prop from your favorite film? Here are some of the most noteworthy sales of movie memorabilia.

Costly Cane: The bamboo cane Charlie Chaplin used in his 1936 flick *Modern Times* managed to hook in $91,800 at a 2004 memorabilia auction.

A Piece of Charlie: Chaplin's cane wasn't the only thing on the auction block. Two fake mustaches he wore in *The Great Dictator* (1940) drew $23,000 and $34,300 at the same sale.

Pricey Piano: The piano played in the Paris scenes of *Casablanca* sold to the tune of $154,000 in 1988. Donald Trump tried to get the instrument, but a Japanese trading company outbid him.

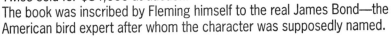

Bond Book: In 2008, an autographed edition of Ian Fleming's *You Only Live Twice* sold for $84,000 at auction. The book was inscribed by Fleming himself to the real James Bond—the American bird expert after whom the character was supposedly named.

Bond Buggy: James Bond is known for his cool cars, so it may be no surprise that Planet Hollywood was willing to shell out $45,900 in 2004 for a moon buggy used in *Diamonds Are Forever* (1971).

Bigger Bond Purchase: Forty-six grand is nothing compared to what the 1965 Aston Martin DB5 driven by Sean Connery in *Goldfinger* (1964) garnered. The gadget-filled vehicle sold to an anonymous bidder for just over $2 million in 2006. The word is rich. Very rich.

Snazzy Sled: The famous sled from Orson Welles's *Citizen Kane* (1941) is now in the hands of Steven Spielberg, who bought the prop for $60,500 via a long-distance phone bid back in 1982.

Conceptual Kane: Some papers described as "concept art" for the mansion in *Citizen Kane* (1941) sold for $16,100 at a 2003 auction.

Spinner Sale: The flying "Spinner" vehicle from *Blade Runner* (1982) spun its way up to the price of $63,250 when it was on the auction block in 2003.

Expensive Leather: In 2008, Hugh Jackman's black leather Wolverine battle suit from *X-Men* (2000) proved worthy of his "sexiest man alive" title. The get-up grabbed $90,000 from a fan.

Raiders Ride: An imitation German car used in the *Indiana Jones* film *Raiders of the Lost Ark* (1981) fetched an impressive $72,000 in 2008.

Jones's Jacket: At a 2005 auction, the leather jacket Harrison Ford wore in the third *Indiana Jones* installment sold for $94,400.

Whoa, Wilson: The friendly volleyball that kept Tom Hanks company in *Cast Away* (2000) cost quite a bit. One of the three balls used in the film scored a whopping $18,400 in a 2001 online auction, and it now sits in the office of Ken May, CEO of Fed Ex/Kinko's.

Invisible Suit: The "invisible suit" worn by Claude Rains in the 1933 horror film *The Invisible Man* went for a very visible $34,000 when it sold in 2003.

Fancy Hat: An original helmet worn by C-3PO in *Return of the Jedi* (1983) capped off a 2008 memorabilia auction with a price tag of $120,000.

Light Saber Liquidation: Luke Skywalker slashed his way past C-3PO's mark with the light saber he used in the original *Star Wars* (1977) and in *The Empire Strikes Back* (1980). In 2005, the prop sold for $240,000.

Darth Vader Disappointment: Turns out the bad guy couldn't top the Jedi at auction. In 2003, Darth Vader's original Lord of the Sith helmet sold for $80,500—merely a third of the final bid for Skywalker's light saber.

Small Sub: In 2003, a miniature version of the *Seaview* submarine from *Voyage to the Bottom of the Sea* (1961) went for $54,625.

Flash Merchandise: A rare poster from the 1936 film *Flash Gordon* brought in $43,125 at auction in 2003.

Loud Outfit: In 2001, the flashy yellow suit worn by Jim Carrey in *The Mask* (1994) went for $16,001 in an online auction by New Line Cinema.

Classy Tie: A tie of Cary Grant's—which was reportedly quite worn and moth-eaten—still managed to sell for $700 in a 2001 Sotheby's auction.

Sandler's Socks: It seems Adam Sandler's socks from *Little Nicky* (2000) didn't share the smell of success. They sold for a mere $250 on eBay in 2001.

Pistol Purchase: The pistol used by Bruce Willis in *The Fifth Element* (1997) managed to pull in $12,650 at an auction in 2003.

Governator's Goods: In 2003, the shotgun used by Arnold Schwarzenegger in *Terminator 2: Judgment Day* (1991) brought in a final selling price of $10,350. However, the jacket he wore in the first *Terminator* (1984) film sold for $41,300.

Forbidden Costume: In 2003, a costume worn by a crew member of the spaceship in the 1956 film *Forbidden Planet* went for the not-so-modest price of $10,925.

Godfather Garb: The famous hat worn by Al Pacino in *The Godfather* (1972) sold for a cool $16,100. An original copy of the script, which was annotated by Marlon Brando, went for $312,800 in 2003—a record-breaking amount for a single movie script.

Humphrey's Hat: A hat described as Humphrey Bogart's "signature fedora" sold for a mere $6,325 in 2003.

A Director's Sweater: Actor-turned-director Ron Howard saw his *Happy Days* sweater sell for $8,050 at a 2003 auction.

Disco Suit: The white polyester suit that John Travolta made famous in *Saturday Night Fever* (1977) sold for $2,000 in 1978. The buyer? Movie critic Gene Siskel. In 1994, the suit was resold for $145,000 at a Christie's auction.

Special Slippers: A rare pair of Dorothy's ruby slippers from *The Wizard of Oz* (1939) were snatched up at a Christie's auction in 2000 for $666,000. The slippers are one of only four pairs known to exist. Another pair is on display at the Smithsonian.

Mel Blanc: That's All Folks!

☆ ☆ ☆ ☆

For decades, he delighted audiences with an assortment of voices
that gave life to an illustrious collection of cartoon characters.
The screen was Mel Blanc's canvas, his voice was his brush,
and his legacy is the many characters he helped create.

Mel Blanc's extraordinary career spanned more than 50 years and
included voice work in almost every entertainment medium, such as
radio, TV, film, and records. Blessed with an uncanny ear, an elastic
esophagus, and an exquisite comedic sense, Blanc provided the
voices for nearly 90 percent of the animated characters in Warner
Bros.'s menagerie of wild and wacky creatures, such as Daffy Duck,
Bugs Bunny, Elmer Fudd, Yosemite Sam, Tweety Bird, Sylvester the
Cat, Porky Pig, and Foghorn Leghorn. He also supplied the mutters,
bleeps, and blips for the largely mute members of the Looney Tunes
troupe, such as Wile E. Coyote. Even the Tasmanian Devil, a
snorting whirling dervish who never utters a single recognizable
word, was one of Blanc's most famous and beloved characters—a
testament to his skills as an actor and a vocal interpreter.

Blanc also supplied the voices of Barney Rubble and Dino the
dinosaur on *The Flintstones*, the first prime-time animated TV series.

In 1961, when he was involved in a horrendous auto accident in
which he broke nearly every bone in his body, the resilient rhetori-
cian missed only five episodes of *The Flintstones*. He even had
recording equipment set up in his hospital room so that he could
keep working. He continued to practice his art in a variety of cartoons, commercials, and television shows throughout the 1960s and
'70s. One of his last major projects was a tour de force performance
in *Who Framed Roger Rabbit* (1988), in which he voiced Bugs
Bunny, Daffy Duck, Tweety Bird, Sylvester the Cat, and Porky Pig.
The last character to feature Blanc's tonsil talents was Mr. Spacely in
Jetsons: The Movie (1990), which was released a year after his
passing in 1989. Before he died, Blanc trained a number of actors to
take his place after he was gone, including his son Noel. Fittingly,
Blanc's tombstone inscription reads, "That's All Folks!"

Film Noir Classics: Shadows and Light

The light from a streetlamp peeks through a window shade, illuminating a detective's dingy office. The detective pours a drink. A mysterious woman suddenly appears in the doorway. "Got a light?" she asks.... This setup is the essence of film noir, a genre that's all about shady characters and moral ambiguity. Here are a few must-see film noir classics.

The Maltese Falcon (1941)
John Huston's *The Maltese Falcon* may be the defining film noir picture—and, some believe, one of the best films ever put to celluloid. Based on Dashiell Hammett's novel of the same name, the movie stars Humphrey Bogart as Sam Spade, the quintessential noir detective, a man who's in it up to his eyeballs with lustful, greedy, and downright dirty underworld characters. Stolen treasure, a femme fatale, and great villains (including a creepy Peter Lorre) add up to a gripping story and indomitable noir magic.

Double Indemnity (1944)
Film noir movies often tell their story through the eyes of the protagonist, who is somehow involved in the plot's major crime. This is true of *Double Indemnity*, a film inspired by a James M. Cain novel. Billy Wilder directs Fred MacMurray and a luminous Barbara Stanwyck in this story about—you guessed it—murder and deception. *Double Indemnity*'s cinematography is indicative of the genre's visual style: The *chiaroscuro* effect, in which the subject is shrouded in deep shadows by the low-key and high-contrast lighting, symbolizes themes of eroded morality and political corruption woven throughout all films in the genre.

Laura (1944)
The American Film Institute ranks *Laura* as the fourth best film in the mystery genre. Director Otto Preminger turns in a great noir pic starring Gene Tierney as the murdered (or is she?) actress that bewitches Detective McPherson. Nominated for several Oscars, *Laura* is a suspenseful and satisfying film.

Murder, My Sweet (1944)
The cynical view of society taken on in *Murder, My Sweet* (based on Raymond Chandler's book *Farewell, My Lovely*) is a hallmark of the film noir genre. Everyone's cagey and corrupt, and anyone who isn't is in big

trouble. Blackmailers run amok as tough-as-nails private eye, Philip Marlowe, takes on the job of finding the missing Velma Valento at the request of her brutish former boyfriend. Instead, Marlowe discovers an ever-widening web of crime and cover-ups. The film is a classic example of the genre, one that influenced similar films in the years to come.

The Killers (1946)
One of the most intriguing aspects of this picture is the dialogue—it comes courtesy of Ernest Hemingway's short story of the same name. Newcomer Burt Lancaster and a radiant Ava Gardner turn in star-making performances in this story about the murder of a boxer. An insurance investigator makes it his job to find out why. Hemingway said that *The Killers* was the one film adaptation of his work that he actually enjoyed.

The Postman Always Rings Twice (1946)
Poor Frank and Cora. Two star-crossed lovers devise a way to be together, despite the odds (Cora's husband, for one.) Their plan involves murder—and they succeed. After that, it's all intrigue and detective work by the local gumshoes. Is justice done? Do the lovers end up together? Grab a whiskey on the rocks and find out in this noir film based on James M. Cain's book of the same name. Look for Lana Turner in a role that showed critics she was more than just a pinup girl.

Out of the Past (1947)
Think you can run away from your past? Not in a film noir flick. Robert Mitchum stars as a former detective now working as a gas-station operator. One day, a man from his past shows up to let him know that scores need to be settled and that old love affairs never really die. When the characters in this movie aren't double-crossing each other, they're lying. When they're not lying, they're snooping—or cheating. This film's duplicitous characters make it a superb example of film noir.

Touch of Evil (1958)
Touch of Evil is well known to Orson Welles fans. Welles was always slated to appear in the movie, but after a series of misunderstandings, he ended up directing, too. Charlton Heston plays a Mexican (yes, Mexican) newlywed, and Janet Leigh is his beautiful bride. The pair run afoul of a corrupt police detective (Welles) who works on instinct to nail the criminals, then fabricates his own evidence to bring them down. Welles's reworking of the script and directorial techniques, especially in the opening shot, make this film a classic. Zsa Zsa Gabor and Marlene Dietrich have supporting roles.

Scaring the Pants Off the Audience

☆ ☆ ☆ ☆

Joy buzzers hidden under theater seats; insurance policies to ensure against "death by fright"; glowing skeletons hovering over the heads of audience members—these are just a few of the gimmicks that legendary movie producer and director William Castle unleashed on audiences in the 1950s and '60s.

Death by Fright and Flying Skeletons

Castle's first gimmick was born out of necessity. Having sunk everything he owned into the making of *Macabre* (1958), Castle was worried that the movie would flop, so he decided he needed a unique way to get people into the theaters. In a stroke of genius, Castle invented Death by Fright Insurance. As people purchased tickets for *Macabre,* they were handed a certificate that claimed to be a $1,000 life insurance policy from Lloyd's of London, which could be redeemed should the filmgoer die of fright during the movie. Castle also hired women to pose as nurses and even parked hearses outside the venues. *Macabre* was a modest hit, and Castle was convinced that he was on to something.

So when the Vincent Price thriller *House on Haunted Hill* was released the next year, Castle claimed that it had been filmed using a process called *Emergo,* which caused the ghosts and ghouls in the movie to come off the screen and into the audience. Toward the end of the movie, a walking skeleton emerges from a vat of acid to "exact its revenge." At that precise moment, theater workers released a glowing skeleton that flew on wires above the heads of audience members. Arrrgh!

"The Tingler is Loose in THIS Theater!"

Hot on the heels of the success of Emergo, Castle came up with a new gimmick for the release of *The Tingler* in 1960. According to Castle, the movie was filmed in *Percepto,* a unique process that allowed moviegoers to "feel every shocking sensation" of the film. Trailers for *The Tingler* carried a guarantee that "The Tingler will break loose in the theater while YOU are in the audience!"

The movie itself centered on a bizarre centipedelike creature—the Tingler—which supposedly lives in the human spinal cord. During the movie, the screen went dark and the characters yelled, "Watch out! The Tingler is loose in THIS theater!" That's when Percepto kicked in, with an image of the Tingler projected onto the screen as though it were crawling on the projector. Prior to the start of the movie, theater employees had rigged several seats with buzzers. Once activated, the buzzers gave those lucky (or unlucky) viewers a mild zap, although many people claimed that it only made them laugh. Either way, once word got out about the buzzers, children tried to be the first inside the theater so they could crawl under the seats to see which of them were "wired."

The Magic of Illusion-O

In 1960, prior to the release of *13 Ghosts*, Castle said that the movie was filmed in *Illusion-O,* which allowed patrons to see ghosts hidden in the movie. As people entered the theater, they were given a "ghost viewer/remover," which was a piece of cardboard with strips of red and blue cellophane. If you wanted to see the ghosts, you looked through the red part of the viewer; if you didn't want to see the ghosts, then you looked through the blue part.

Since the viewers had a red side and a blue side similar to 3-D glasses, many believed the film was shot in 3-D. In reality, the film was shot in black and white with blue tints added to the scenes with the "ghosts," which made them visible when people looked through the red portion of the viewer.

Deciding the Fate of Mr. Sardonicus

For *Mr. Sardonicus* (1961), Castle decided to let his audience decide how the movie would end. As patrons entered the theater, they were all given pieces of cardboard bearing a drawing of a hand giving the "thumbs-up" signal. The film's main character, Mr. Sardonicus, does some dastardly deeds, but by the end, the movie appears to be heading toward a storybook ending. That's when Castle appeared on-screen to explain that the cards were part of the "punishment poll." Castle told the audience that if they felt Mr. Sardonicus deserved to be happy, they should hold their cards with the thumbs-up sign high in the air. If, however, the audience believed Mr. Sardonicus should be punished for his evil deeds, they were to hold their cards up with the thumb facing down. After these instructions, Castle pretended to count the votes, then he let the audience know the results, and the appropriate ending was played.

Castle believed that audiences would almost always vote for the punishment ending and therefore made that the original ending. He was right. The happy ending was never played, not even once.

A Turning Point

Most people believe that *Zotz!* (1962) signaled the beginning of the end for Castle's gimmicks. In the movie, Tom Poston plays a bumbling professor who finds a mysterious gold coin. If he exclaims "Zotz!" while holding the coin, mayhem ensues. Those purchasing tickets were each given a magic Zotz coin, which was nothing more than a piece of gold-colored plastic.

Number, Please

Castle wanted to promote *I Saw What You Did* (1965) with giant plastic telephones because the film centered on a pair of girls who accidentally prank-call a killer. But before the film was released, the telephone company received so many complaints about prank calls that they forbade Castle from promoting his film with phones or even mentioning the role telephones played in the movie. Instead, Castle decided to install seat belts on some of the seats in the back rows—the "shock sections" of the theater—to keep moviegoers from flying out of their seats from shock.

One Last Gimmick

Castle continued to try small gimmicks here and there for the next decade, but his final film to use a gimmick as a promotional tool came in 1975 with the release of his film *Bug*. The film itself was a throwback to the monster-type films that were so popular in the 1950s and '60s. For the film, Castle announced that because there were so many dangerous stunts performed, he had to take out a $1 million life insurance policy on the movie's star. Who was the star of the film? Hercules the cockroach.

Actors, Actresses, and Directors

Anagrams are new words or phrases made by rearranging the letters of the original word or phrase. Check out the new phrases made by rearranging the letters of the names of these Hollywood stars.

Gillian Anderson	Darling alien son
Christian Bale	Bat lair niches
Drew Barrymore	Merry wardrobe
Kim Basinger	Brisk enigma
Pierce Brosnan	Carbine person
Nicolas Cage	Laconic sage
George Clooney	Ego, cool, energy
Sean Connery	On any screen
Russell Crowe	Swell courser
Willem Dafoe	Media fellow
Robert De Niro	Inert brooder
Leonardo DiCaprio	A periodical donor
Ralph Fiennes	Fine shrapnel
Ashton Kutcher	Hot hunk recast
Leonard Nimoy	My alien donor
Natalie Portman	Planet animator
Martin Scorsese	Stress or cinema
William Shatner	Win? Hell, I'm a star!
Sylvester Stallone	Tell Sly: Veteran S.O.S.
Oliver Stone	No overt lies
Meryl Streep	Slyer temper
Donald Sutherland	Haunted landlords

Psycho

☆ ☆ ☆ ☆

Hitchcock's shocking masterpiece was a cinematic
gamble...but it paid off in spades.

Alfred Hitchcock is the undisputed "Master of Suspense" with more than 50 classic thrillers to his credit. But to most contemporary horror hounds, *Psycho* (1960) is the British-born director's most shocking and memorable film.

Psycho is remarkable for many reasons, such as the fact that it kills its heroine midway through the story; hints at (but doesn't actually show) extreme acts of bloody violence; and addresses a variety of adult themes fairly unheard-of for commercial films in 1960.

From Book to Film

Psycho was based on horror writer Robert Bloch's novel of the same name, which was loosely based on real-life murderer Ed Gein, a Wisconsin farmer who robbed graves to fashion masks and clothing out of human skin. Hitchcock acquired the rights to the novel for $9,000 and hired Joseph Stefano (one of the creators of the classic 1960s television show *The Outer Limits*) to write the screenplay.

Because of the story's more horrific aspects, Paramount Pictures was extremely reluctant to finance the movie's production, forcing Hitchcock to scramble for funding through his own production company, Shamley Productions. To cut costs, he filmed *Psycho* primarily with the same crew he used to shoot his popular television series, *Alfred Hitchcock Presents.* He also saved money by filming in black and white, and he deferred his director's fee in exchange for a percentage of the film's ownership. As a result, Hitchcock was able to make *Psycho* for just $800,000.

Death in the Shower

Psycho contains several startling sequences, none more shocking than the shower scene in which Marion Crane (Janet Leigh) is viciously knifed to death by an assailant whom the viewer assumes is Norman Bates's insane mother. The murder lasts just 45 seconds on-screen, but the sequence took seven days to film and consists of more than 70 separate shots. Hitchcock's command of montage editing suggests a violent act that was not actually there in the individual shots. The illusion is that the viewer sees a violent, gory murder, but in reality, the knife and the victim's body are rarely in the same shot. The "blood" that is seen running down the drain was actually chocolate syrup, which showed up well in black and white.

In her book *Behind the Scenes of Psycho: The Classic Thriller,* Janet Leigh dispels several myths about the film, such as the claim that Hitchcock doused her with cold water to make her scream. She also notes that she wore flesh-colored moleskin to cover certain areas of her body but was otherwise naked.

Mixed Reviews
Psycho premiered in New York City on June 16, 1960, then gradually opened across the United States. Hitchcock went to great lengths to encourage moviegoers not to reveal the movie's surprise ending to their friends and asked theater owners to deny admission once the film had started.

While it lacks the graphic violence of today's films, *Psycho* was considered extremely controversial in 1960, and it sparked a heated national debate regarding movie violence. Reviews were mixed. Many reviewers in Great Britain vilified the movie, with more than one calling it the worst film of Hitchcock's career. However, Bosley Crowther of *The New York Times* praised the film and defended it against critics who thought it should be censored or banned outright.

Today, of course, *Psycho* is considered a cinematic classic because of its virtuoso editing and its provocative subtext, which suggests that Norman Bates isn't the only one who's a bit crazy. Most characters in the film have crossed a moral or ethical line for reasons they think are justified, just like Norman thinks he's justified in his actions. The key to the film is Norman's provocative line, "We all go a little mad some time, haven't you," which makes the viewer complicit in guilt. This proved extremely disturbing to audiences and critics at the time, but it's also a signature Hitchcock move. In recognition of its cultural and historical significance, *Psycho* was selected for preservation in the National Film Registry in 1992.

They Also Served: Hollywood's Real Heroes

On the silver screen, they often seem invincible—able to leap tall buildings in a single bound, fearlessly enter a burning building to save the damsel in distress, or calmly capture the bad guy. But for those actors who served in the armed forces and defended their country against all odds, the bullets were real, the action unscripted, and the danger unimaginable. For these heroes, art really did imitate life.

Eddie Albert

Eddie Albert, the star of the sitcom *Green Acres*, had a successful Hollywood career that lasted six decades. But few know that he was also a bona fide World War II hero. On November 21, 1943, while serving in the Marines in the South Pacific, Albert took command of several landing craft and raced to the rescue of 13 wounded marines trapped on an exposed reef at Betio Island. With the tide coming in and under enemy fire, Albert successfully retrieved them all.

Humphrey Bogart

Humphrey Bogart enlisted in the navy in 1918, but the war ended before he saw any combat. He completed his training at the Naval Reserve Station in Pelham Park, New York, and was assigned to the USS *Leviathan*, the navy's largest American troopship, and then the USS *Santa Olivia*. Bogart made several transatlantic trips, helping ferry American troops back home. During World War II, he joined the Coast Guard Auxiliary and regularly reported for duty when he was in California.

Michael Caine

Michael Caine was drafted into the British Army in May 1951 and was initially stationed in Germany as a member of the peacekeeper forces in the occupation army. He later became a rifleman in the Royal Fusiliers and was sent to Korea during the height of the Korean War, seeing extensive battle action at the Sami Chon River. Shortly after arriving in Korea, he contracted malaria, a disease that continued to affect him long after his release from the army in 1953.

R. Lee Ermey
Best remembered for his roles in *Full Metal Jacket* (1987) and *Mississippi Burning* (1988), R. Lee Ermey served in the Marine Corps for 11 years, rising to the rank of staff sergeant. He served 14 months in Vietnam and did two tours of duty in Okinawa.

Dennis Franz
Born, raised, and educated in and around Chicago, Dennis Franz (*Die Hard 2*, 1990; *American Buffalo*, 1996; *NYPD Blue*) was drafted into the U.S. Army after graduating from Southern Illinois University and spent 11 months in an airborne division reconnaissance unit during the Vietnam War. During his tour of duty, Franz was awarded 17 accommodations, including the National Defense Medal, the Vietnam Cross of Gallantry–Individual Medal, the Vietnam Service Medal, and the Parachute Badge.

James Garner
In 1944, at age 16, James Garner left home, lied about his age, and joined the Merchant Marines. Later, he enlisted in the army and served in the Korean War. During his 14 months of service overseas, Garner was wounded twice. He earned his first Purple Heart after sustaining face and hand wounds from shrapnel from a mortar fired by North Korean troops. He was later wounded by his own troops during an exchange of gunfire with the enemy, but it wasn't until 1983—32 years later—that he finally received a second Purple Heart.

Tim McCoy
The film industry was still in its early days when World War I erupted, so very few Hollywood heroes served in the conflict. Tim McCoy was one of those few. He was also a real cowboy and a noted expert on the history of the Old West, particularly Native Americans. During the 1920s, he made more than two dozen movies, including *War Paint* (1926) and *Frontiersman* (1927). He also served in World War II, winning a bevy of medals including a Bronze Star.

Audie Murphy
The most notable performance in the line of duty goes to Audie Murphy, World War II's most decorated soldier with more than 30 medals on his chest, including the Medal of Honor and French Croix de Guerre with Silver Star. Murphy returned to America a national hero and went on to star in more than 40 major motion pictures, including *The Red Badge of*

Courage (1951) and *To Hell and Back* (1955), which was based on his autobiography of the same name.

Lee Powell

The first actor to portray The Lone Ranger on the silver screen, Powell was the only "name" actor who died overseas during World War II. Powell enlisted in the Marines in 1942 and was assigned to the 2nd Battalion at Camp Elliott, California. After shipping overseas, he saw sustained action at Tarawa and Saipan and was promoted to sergeant. After fighting in a battle on Tinian in the Marianas Islands, he became ill after drinking some home-brewed methyl alcohol and died after a brief stay in the hospital.

Harold Russell

As a sergeant in a demolition squad at Camp Mackall, North Carolina, Harold Russell was handling a half-pound chunk of TNT when a defective fuse detonated the explosive. He lost both hands in the accident, becoming one of approximately 1,200 double amputee victims of World War II. He later starred as a disabled veteran in the 1946 film *The Best Years of Our Lives*, a performance which earned him an Oscar for Best Supporting Actor and an Honorary Oscar for his courage and dedication. He is the only person to receive two Academy Awards for the same performance.

Jimmy Stewart

Jimmy Stewart joined the Army Air Corps as a private in 1941, studied painstakingly to become a military pilot, and served stateside for two years as a training instructor until his request for active duty was granted in 1943. Stewart flew a B-24, an aircraft known as The Liberator, for the remainder of the war, partaking in 20 dangerous combat missions as a command pilot, wing commander, or squadron commander. He was awarded the Distinguished Flying Cross with two Oak Leaf Clusters, the Air Medal with three Oak Leaf Clusters, and the French Croix de Guerre with Palm. By the end of the war, Stewart had risen to the rank of colonel. Throughout his film career, he continued to be a member of the U.S. Air Force Reserves and was promoted to brigadier general in 1959.

Lewis Stone

Lewis Stone, who saw his first combat action during the Spanish-American War in 1898, had appeared in only a handful of movies before rejoining the U.S. Army in 1916. He returned from overseas to appear in more than 140 additional films, including *The Prisoner of Zenda* (1922) and *Grand Hotel* (1932).

6 Vampire Movies that Really Sucked

Vampires have been a filmmaker favorite for decades, but throwing Dracula onto the big screen is no guarantee of a big hit. Here are six flicks that succeeded at every vampire's favorite activity: sucking.

The Devil Bat (1940)
This film combined Bela Lugosi with a magical aftershave that encouraged gigantic bats to attack anyone wearing it. Oh, and its tagline was: "Sharp Fanged Blood Sucking DEATH Dives from MIDNIGHT SKIES!" Enough said.

Samson vs. the Vampire Women (1963)
Giving *The Devil Bat* a run for its money, *Samson vs. the Vampire Women* told the story of a father who hired a professional wrestler to keep vampires away from his daughter. Why, you ask? Because the vampires wanted to kidnap her, then force her to marry the devil. Seriously…we couldn't make this stuff up if we tried.

Planet of the Vampires (1965)
Ads for *Planet of the Vampires* declared: "This was the day the universe trembled before the demon forces of the killer planet!" This Italian flick focused on two spaceships that crashed on a far away planet filled with undead folks. Sounds like a blast!

Billy the Kid vs. Dracula (1966)
If there are two things that just don't mix, it's vampires and the Wild West. So it should come as no surprise that this thriller—in which Dracula dons a cowboy hat and dukes it out with Billy the Kid—is not considered a classic.

Dracula Blows His Cool (1982)
This movie tells the story of a famous ancestor of Dracula who scores a gig as a fashion photographer. With the oh-so-catchy tagline of "You'll die laughing," we can't imagine why this one never reached blockbuster status.

Vampires on Bikini Beach (1988)
Some supermodels found themselves fighting off vampires while on a photo shoot in this blood-sucking adventure. The girls just happen to be in bikinis for most of the movie, too—pure coincidence, for sure.

Stars Behind Bars!

Most actors have done their time working their way up the ladder through roles in B-movies, television, or theater. But a surprising number of actors have literally done time—as in prison time. Here's a sample:

Lillo Brancato

Brancato played Robert De Niro's son in *A Bronx Tale* (1993) and a bumbling mobster on *The Sopranos.* But drug addiction took its toll on his career. In December 2005, Brancato and a friend broke into an apartment looking for drugs. In the process, an off-duty policeman was shot and killed. Brancato was charged with second-degree murder and attempted burglary. He was acquitted on the murder charges in 2008 but served time for attempted burglary.

Rory Calhoun

A popular leading man who appeared in numerous Westerns, Calhoun was a petty criminal as a teenager and served three years in a federal reformatory for car theft. Reformed by a priest, he was a blue-collar worker until a chance meeting with star Alan Ladd led to a career in the movies, including two Marilyn Monroe films: *How to Marry a Millionaire* (1953) and *River of No Return* (1954).

Errol Flynn

One of the most popular leading men in Hollywood history, Errol Flynn frequently found himself in trouble with the law. His various stints behind bars included two weeks in a New Guinea jail for hitting an Asian man who addressed him without the prefix "Mr." and several days in lock-up for striking a customs officer in the tiny African country of Djibouti.

Stacy Keach

In the mid-1980s, the star of the acclaimed Western *The Long Riders* (1980) served six months in prison for smuggling cocaine into England.

Paul Kelly

Paul Kelly played lead roles in many B-films, mostly crime melodramas. In the late 1920s, he killed his best friend, actor Ray Raymond, in a fistfight over Raymond's wife, actress Dorothy MacKaye. He served two years for manslaughter, then went on to a successful film and stage career, receiving a Tony Award in 1948 for his role in *Command Decision.*

Robert Mitchum

As a teenager in the 1930s, Mitchum was arrested for vagrancy in Georgia and was sentenced to a week's work on a chain gang, but he escaped the first chance he got. In California, in 1948, the movie tough guy served 50 days in jail for marijuana possession.

Tom Neal

A leading man in the 1940s and '50s, Neal was convicted of involuntary manslaughter for the murder of his third wife, who was shot in the head in 1965. He served seven years at the California Institution for Men in Chino.

Tommy Rettig

As a child actor, Rettig gained lasting fame as Lassie's master in the popular 1950s TV series. But in 1972, he was arrested for growing marijuana, and in the mid-1970s, he was sentenced to five and a half years in prison for smuggling cocaine into the U.S. The charges were dropped after an appeal, as was another drug charge five years later.

O. J. Simpson

A football Hall of Famer whose movies include *Capricorn One* (1978) and *The Naked Gun* (1988), Simpson was acquitted of the murder of his ex-wife, Nicole Brown, in 1995. In December 2008, the football superstar was handed a sentence of 9 to 33 years in prison for armed robbery and kidnapping as a result of a botched attempt to get back items Simpson claimed a sports memorabilia dealer had stolen from him.

Christian Slater

In 1989, Slater was involved in a drunken car chase that ended when he crashed into a telephone pole and kicked a policeman while trying to escape. He was charged with evading police, driving under the influence, assault with a deadly weapon (his boots), and driving with a suspended license. In 1994, Slater was arrested for trying to bring a gun onto a plane. In 1997, he was sentenced to 90 days in jail for cocaine abuse, battery, and assault with a deadly weapon.

Mae West

In 1926, Mae West, one of Hollywood's most iconic sex symbols, was sentenced to ten days in jail when her Broadway show, *Sex*, was declared obscene.

Fred and Ginger

☆ ☆ ☆ ☆

Fred Astaire and Ginger Rogers seemed to have little in common—he a genteel, slightly shy charmer, and she a quick-witted, slightly brash girl-next-door. But when they hit the dance floor, the chemistry between them was as impossible to deny as it was difficult to explain, and they remain one of the most famous on-screen pairings in history.

Fred Astaire and Ginger Rogers followed rather similar paths in their early years that would eventually lead them to costar in a series of romantic musicals that epitomized the Hollywood glamour of the 1930s. As a child, Astaire and his sister Adele worked the vaudeville circuit as a dance act, tapping and sashaying their way through increasingly larger venues until they became the toast of Broadway. Rogers got into vaudeville as a teen, after filling in as a dancer one night in an Eddie Foy musical revue. Later, she won a dance contest in Fort Worth, Texas. She too made her way to Broadway, where she met Astaire for the first time. In 1930, she was appearing in George Gershwin's *Girl Crazy* while Astaire was performing with his sister at another theater. He dropped by the Gershwin show during rehearsals and reportedly helped Rogers work out the choreography for a dance to "Embraceable You." The pair went on one date but didn't really connect on a personal level. Then, in 1931, Rogers went to Hollywood where she quickly became popular in supporting roles. Astaire remained in New York until his sister decided to retire, then he too went to the West Coast in pursuit of a movie career.

Fred and Ginger Go to Hollywood
Both performers ended up under contract at struggling RKO Studios and were paired up for the 1933 film *Flying Down to Rio*. In the film, they performed a single number, which introduced a dance called the Carioca, and, in the process, they stole the show from stars Dolores Del Rio and Gene Raymond. Astaire and Rogers made eight more films together during the next six years, earning $30 million for RKO and creating some of the most memorable moments in movie history

with their magically romantic dance numbers, including "The Continental" from *The Gay Divorcee* (1934), "The Piccolino" from *Top Hat* (1935), and the "Waltz in Swing Time" from *Swing Time* (1936). The films centered around conventional boy-meets-girl plotlines and were remarkably chaste, but the moment the music started, the star couple transported themselves to an otherworldly realm of beauty and charm, taking their audience along for the ride.

A Magical Pairing

Then as now, Astaire was considered one of the world's greatest dancers for the imagination and distinctively casual grace he brought to his routines. Rogers worked hard to keep up with his moves, but she made her own unique contribution by displaying her considerable acting skills even as they glided around sweeping balconies and art deco penthouses. Through her subtle facial expressions, she gave the impression that dancing with Fred Astaire was the most blissful thing a woman could ever do.

The pair went their separate ways in 1939 and enjoyed lengthy and successful solo careers. Rogers would go on to win an Academy Award in the drama *Kitty Foyle* (1940), and Astaire would continue to add to his glories on the dance floor and become a major star at prestigious MGM. But neither would again perform with as perfect a partner until they reunited for their last film, the 1949 MGM musical *The Barkleys of Broadway*.

Fred and Ginger Filmography:
Flying Down to Rio (1933)
The Gay Divorcee (1934)
Roberta (1935)
Top Hat (1935)
Follow the Fleet (1936)
Swing Time (1936)
Shall We Dance (1937)
Carefree (1938)
*The Story of Vernon and Irene
    Castle* (1939)
The Barkleys of Broadway (1949)

Pop Quiz: Famous Movie Quotes

When a line from a movie is really, really good, it's immediately absorbed into popular vernacular. Think about it: You've probably said, "May the Force be with you" a few times, right? See if you can match these famous quotes with their respective movies.

1. "Face it, girls, I'm older and I have more insurance."

2. "He-e-e-e-re's Johnnie!"

3. "Here's lookin' at you, kid."

4. "I can't believe I gave my panties to a geek."

5. "I drink your milkshake!"

6. "I have always depended on the kindness of strangers."

7. "I'll have what she's having."

8. "I love the smell of napalm in the morning . . . smells like victory."

9. "Mrs. Robinson, you're trying to seduce me."

10. "Nobody puts Baby in the corner."

11. "One morning I shot an elephant in my pajamas. How he got in my pajamas I don't know."

12. "Roads? Where we're going we don't need roads."

13. "Shaken, not stirred."

14. "What we've got here is failure to communicate."

15. "We didn't need dialogue. We had faces then."

16. "You can't handle the truth!"

17. "You had me at 'Hello.'"

18. "You're tearing me apart! . . . You . . . you say one thing, he says another, and everyone changes back again!"

19. "You talkin' to me?"

20. "You've gotta ask yourself one question: 'Do I feel lucky?' Well do ya, punk?"

Answer Choices:

A. *A Few Good Men* (1992)

B. *Animal Crackers* (1930)

C. *Apocalypse Now* (1979)

D. *A Streetcar Named Desire* (1951)

E. *Back to the Future* (1985)

F. *Casablanca* (1942)

G. *Cool Hand Luke* (1967)

H. *Dirty Dancing* (1987)

I. *Dirty Harry* (1971)

J. *Fried Green Tomatoes* (1991)

K. *Goldfinger* (1964)

L. *The Graduate* (1967)

M. *Jerry Maguire* (1996)

N. *Rebel Without a Cause* (1955)

O. *The Shining* (1980)

P. *Sixteen Candles* (1984)

Q. *Sunset Boulevard* (1950)

R. *Taxi Driver* (1976)

S. *There Will Be Blood* (2007)

T. *When Harry Met Sally* (1989)

The Fabulous Chateau Marmont

☆ ☆ ☆ ☆

*For stars looking to escape the stranglehold of celebrity, the
Chateau Marmont has become the hotel of choice. From
Clark Gable to Lindsay Lohan, the castlelike hotel perched
high above Sunset Boulevard has sheltered them all.*

An Unlikely Beginning

When attorney Fred Horowitz began construction of an apartment
building in 1927, he couldn't have known that the stylish structure,
modeled after a castle in France's Loire Valley, would someday become
the haven for reclusive stars. But that's precisely what happened.

In February 1929, the Chateau Marmont Apartments opened for
business, but with the stock market crash and the Great Depression
only months away, the timing couldn't have been worse. The operation floundered until 1931 when it was turned into a hotel—a move
that proved fortuitous beyond the builder's wildest dreams.

A Starring Role

The identity of the Chateau's first celebrity renter may be lost to time,
but history shows that the hotel quickly gained favor with Hollywood's
beautiful people. Greta "I want to be alone" Garbo came to the hotel
expressly for such privacy, as did fellow screen legends Clark Gable,
Jean Harlow, Errol Flynn, Carole Lombard, William Holden, and
countless others. In short order, a clientele of Hollywood elites, who
were bent on privacy, adopted the hotel as their own.

What Happens at the Chateau . . .

But not all came to the Chateau to hide. In fact, many came to raise
Cain. It was a bonus that this too could be accomplished discreetly
at the hotel. "If you must get into trouble, do it at the Chateau
Marmont," Columbia Pictures founder Harry Cohn cautioned young
male stars William Holden and Glenn Ford. In an era when a scandal could mean a one-way ticket to Palookaville, the moviemaker's
advice made great sense. It was advice that had already been
heeded by the likes of Jean Harlow, who lived with Hal Rosson

at the Chateau Marmont without benefit of marriage. The general public had no idea that the two had been living it up in sin for a year before they were married.

Demonstrating that bad boys will generally act in kind, movie magnate Howard Hughes would often spy on beautiful women at the hotel's pool. He accomplished this from his attic room aided by a pair of prism binoculars. Decades later, Jim Morrison, lead singer of The Doors, injured his back while attempting to swing from a drainpipe into his room at the Chateau. Another crazy moment saw members from the rock band Led Zeppelin tearing through the hotel's lobby on motorcycles, causing much damage in the process.

But such antics amounted to small potatoes when compared with comedian John Belushi's sad stay at the hotel. On March 5, 1982, after an extended drug and alcohol binge, the beloved star of *Animal House* (1978) and *Saturday Night Live* died in his room from an overdose of cocaine and heroin. The heartbreaking story proved too large for even the Chateau Marmont to suppress.

An Oldie but a Goodie

These days, the grand hotel draws celebrities in droves with no sign of slowing down. A visit might uncover such shining lights as Jude Law, Christina Ricci, Toby McGuire, Winona Ryder, and scores of others. Some, including Ryder, drop in for good times at the hotel's watering hole, Bar Marmont. Others, like publicity-shy Robert De Niro, come to escape public scrutiny. "I would rather sleep in a bathroom than any other hotel," quipped director Billy Wilder after being put up on a cot near the ladies' washroom because all the rooms were full. Where the fabulous Chateau Marmont is concerned, such dogged loyalty has clearly withstood the test of time.

Created in Canada

Canada has contributed more to American culture than just rye whiskey, ice hockey, and back bacon. If you check the passports of these stars of the silver screen, you'll discover that they too came from north of the 49th parallel.

Dan Aykroyd

Born in Ottawa, Ontario, in 1952, Aykroyd is best known for memorable roles in *The Blues Brothers* (1980), *Trading Places* (1983), and *Ghostbusters* (1984). Aykroyd proved he is a diverse character actor by tackling dramatic roles in *My Girl* (1991) and *Driving Miss Daisy* (1989), the latter of which earned him an Oscar nomination for Best Supporting Actor.

Neve Campbell

Born in 1973, in Guelph, Ontario, Campbell studied ballet before moving to Hollywood to star in the TV series *Party of Five* in 1994. The star of such box-office hits as *Scream* (1996), *The Craft* (1996), and *Wild Things* (1998), Campbell attained critical praise when she coproduced, cowrote, and starred in Robert Altman's *The Company* (2003), an engaging examination of the world of professional ballet.

John Candy

Often typecast as the lovable fat guy, this Toronto native honed his skills at Chicago's Second City before landing a role on the landmark TV series *SCTV*. Candy excelled as a comic actor in 1980s classics such as *Splash* (1984), *The Great Outdoors* (1986), and *Uncle Buck* (1989), but he was just beginning to show promise as a character actor in films such as *Planes, Trains and Automobiles* (1987) and *JFK* (1991) when he died of a heart attack at age 43 while filming *Wagons East* in 1994.

Jim Carrey

The first actor to command—and receive—a $20 million salary (for *The Cable Guy* in 1996), Jim Carrey's comedies get the box office buzzing, but his dramatic work in films such as *The Truman Show* (1998) and *Man on the Moon* (1999) has earned him Golden Globe accolades. Born in Newmarket, Ontario, in 1962, Carrey captivated audiences with his rubber-faced expressions in *Ace Ventura: Pet Detective* (1994), *The Mask* (1994), and *Dumb and Dumber* (1994).

Michael J. Fox

Activist, actor, and author Michael J. Fox was born in Edmonton, Alberta, in 1961, and moved to Hollywood at the age of 18. After a series of TV roles, particularly his breakout role on *Family Ties,* Fox shot to Hollywood fame by appearing in the *Back to the Future* trilogy starting in 1985. He went on to strike box-office gold in films such as *Casualties of War* (1989), *Doc Hollywood* (1991), and *The American President* (1995). He acts infrequently since being diagnosed with Parkinson's disease in 1991.

Eric McCormack

Another talented Toronto native, Eric McCormack was trained at the Ryerson Theater School and the Banff Center for the Arts. He spent five years as a Shakespearean actor at the Stratford Festival before taking his chances in more commercial fare on Canadian television. After moving to L.A. and guest-starring on a variety of shows, McCormack landed the plum role of Will Truman on *Will & Grace* in 1998. Though the series ended in 2006, he remains a popular television actor.

Mike Myers

The creator of compelling characters such as goofy Wayne Campbell (*Wayne's World,* 1992), master spy Austin Powers, and world dominator Dr. Evil, Myers was a regular on *Saturday Night Live* for six seasons. Born in Toronto, in 1963, Myers also provided the voice for the animated character Shrek in a series of box-office blasts produced by DreamWorks.

Ellen Page

Born in 1987, in Halifax, Nova Scotia, Page became the fourth-youngest actress in history to receive a Best Actress Oscar nod when she was cited for her work in *Juno* (2007). Since moving to Hollywood to star in the 2005 feature *Hard Candy,* Page has appeared in a handful of films, including *X-Men: The Last Stand* (2006) and *Smart People* (2008).

Mary Pickford

Known as "America's Sweetheart," Mary Pickford was actually born in Toronto, in 1892. She was best known for her signature curls and tomboy personality as well as her roles in *Rebecca of Sunnybrook Farm* (1917) and *Coquette* (1929), the latter for which she won a Best Actress Oscar. Along with Charlie Chaplin, Douglas Fairbanks, and D. W. Griffith, this silent-screen pioneer helped found the creative film studio United Artists.

Leslie Nielsen

In his six decades as a Hollywood actor, Nielsen's career has gone through several phases, and the longevity of this native of Regina, Saskatchewan, is a testament to his talent. The sci-fi classic *Forbidden Planet* (1956) ranks among the best work of his early career as a leading man. He also starred on several popular TV series, including *Peyton Place* and *The Bold Ones: The Protectors*. Later in life, when many actors think about retiring, Nielsen became a comedic actor in *The Naked Gun* film series, a spoof of police flicks.

Christopher Plummer

Best known for playing Captain Von Trapp in *The Sound of Music* (1965), Plummer was born in Toronto in 1929. Also known for his deft and highly regarded work in films such as *The Silent Partner* (1978), *A Beautiful Mind* (2001), and *Inside Man* (2006), Plummer is regarded as one of the finest actors of his generation never to be nominated for an Academy Award.

Seth Rogen

Renowned for his abilities as a writer, comedian, actor, and producer, Rogen was born in Vancouver, British Columbia, in 1982. After beginning his career as a stand-up comedian, he moved to Los Angeles to star in the short-lived television series *Freaks and Geeks*. TV's loss was the big screen's gain, as Rogen has helped create a bevy of box-office bonanzas, including *The 40-Year-Old Virgin* (2005), *Knocked Up* (2007), and *Pineapple Express* (2008).

Martin Short

Martin Short was born in Hamilton, Ontario, in 1950 and has delighted film fans with his manic mannerisms in *¡Three Amigos!* (1986), *Father of the Bride* (1991), and *The Spiderwick Chronicles* (2008).

Donald Sutherland

The star of such critically acclaimed films as *The Dirty Dozen* (1967), *M*A*S*H* (1970), *Klute* (1971), and *Ordinary People* (1980), Donald Sutherland was born in Saint John, New Brunswick, in 1935 and migrated to Hollywood in the early 1960s after studying drama in London. Noted for his portrayal of offbeat and off-kilter characters, Sutherland holds a degree in engineering from the University of Toronto.

Behind the Scenes of
Back to the Future

☆ ☆ ☆ ☆

The Back to the Future *films are cinematic classics, but
the time-traveling trilogy had to overcome countless
challenges in its quest to capture audiences worldwide.*

The Beginning

If Robert Zemeckis really could go back in time, he'd probably
avoid a lot of the headaches that came with creating the *Back to the
Future* films. The movies that brought us Doc Brown and Marty
McFly faced more than their share of issues—and the problems
started before the first part had even been cast.

Zemeckis and cowriter and producer Bob Gale struggled to get
the idea for *Back to the Future* off the ground. The two were turned
down by every studio they approached and for nearly every reason
imaginable. For example, Disney thought the plot and its Freudian
undertones were too risqué. Other studios said the family-friendly
jokes weren't risqué enough.

Zemeckis has said that the commercial failure of his 1980 film
Used Cars made selling the *Back to the Future* script even more
difficult. It wasn't until 1984, with the success of his film *Romancing
the Stone,* that studios were willing to revisit the concept and take a
gamble on his proposal.

The Leading Man

Once *Back to the Future* finally got the green light from Steven
Spielberg's Amblin Entertainment, Zemeckis and Gale discovered
that they couldn't get the leading man they wanted. Michael J. Fox
was their ideal guy for Marty McFly, but his work with the TV series
Family Ties conflicted with the movie's production schedule, so they
cast Eric Stoltz in the role instead.

Within weeks, though, it became clear that something wasn't
right. Even though they'd shot numerous scenes with Stoltz, Zemeckis and Gale convinced the studio to let them recast the part. With

some careful negotiations, they were able to secure Fox for the role and resume filming.

Fox may have been perfect for Marty, but he brought with him his own set of challenges. Because Fox was still starring on *Family Ties*, Zemeckis and his crew had to work around his hectic schedule and film most of his scenes overnight. At times, production workers went to great lengths to accomplish this, dividing scenes into a number of shots and then filming Fox's shots separately and lighting locations to create the illusion of daylight while shooting at night.

The Title

Even with all of the pieces in place, Zemeckis and Gale found themselves fighting to keep their film's title. The head of Universal Studios told the two that no one would want to see a movie with the word *future* in the title and suggested that they call it *Spaceman from Pluto* instead. The ill-fated inspiration came from the scene in which Marty poses as an alien to convince his teenage father to ask Marty's future mother to the dance.

Executive producer Steven Spielberg solved the title trouble by sending a memo back to the Universal exec in which he thanked him for the "joke" and acted as if everyone thought the idea was a hoax. The exec, seemingly wanting to save face, never brought it up again.

Back to the Future's mix of adolescent humor and nostalgia for the 1950s was a surefire formula for a hit, and the film became the highest-grossing film of the year, raking in $208 million. But the success was bittersweet for Fox: He went from television actor to movie star, but, unfortunately, he was typecast in high-concept comedies as the young man on the cusp of manhood, as in *The Secret of My Success* (1987). When Fox tried to transition to dramas, his association with adolescent comedies combined with his short stature and youthful face doomed him to failure in more serious fare.

The Sequel

Contrary to popular belief, Zemeckis and Gale never intended for *Back to the Future* to be a series—they barely thought the first movie would get made! And even though the first film ends with Marty and Jennifer going to the future with Doc to see about their children, it was only meant for laughs, not to set the stage for a sequel.

In fact, the two say they wrote themselves into a corner by having Jennifer get into the car with Doc and Marty. Having her knocked out within the first moments of *Back to the Future Part II* was the only way they could come up with that made her presence work and still allowed for the story they wanted to tell.

The Missing Actor

Crispin Glover, who portrayed George McFly in the original *Back to the Future* film, created plenty of challenges for the creative team. Now widely known for his oft-eccentric behavior, Glover wanted to portray George in some unusual ways. In the DVD commentary, Zemeckis and Gale said they had to bend over backwards to get him to wear some of the wardrobe they'd selected for the character and to follow the direction they'd laid out for the part.

The biggest hurdle of all, though, came with the start of the second installment. According to Zemeckis and Gale, Glover made unreasonable demands when negotiating his return to the role. When he wouldn't budge, the filmmakers had no choice but to move forward on the film without him.

With the absence of such a recognizable character, the pair had to take steps to ensure that the movie still made sense. That's why George was dead for part of the movie and was wearing a futuristic upside-down back brace in the segments when he did appear. Zemeckis and Gale figured audiences would be less likely to notice the change in actors with the added distraction.

The second film did, however, use some archived footage of Glover in scenes meant to depict the past. Glover ended up suing Spielberg and received a settlement for the unauthorized use of his likeness.

The success of Part II led to *Back to the Future Part III,* in which Doc and Marty wind up in the Wild West. In the end, of course, the numerous challenges didn't keep the *Back to the Future* trilogy from soaring to success. Overall, Marty McFly's catchphrase may be the best way to sum up the adventure: "Whoa...that was heavy."

Hollywood Celebs on Marriage

Movie stars are not generally known for reaching their golden wedding anniversaries (or even silver, for that matter). Perhaps that explains some of these more cynical takes on marriage from Hollywood's elite.

"They say marriages are made in heaven. But so [are] thunder and lightning."
—*Clint Eastwood*

"Behind every successful man is a woman; behind her is his wife."
—*Groucho Marx*

"I'm the only man in the world whose marriage license reads: 'To Whom It May Concern.'"
—*Mickey Rooney (who's been married eight times)*

"I planned on having one husband and seven children, but it turned out the other way around."
—*Lana Turner*

"Sex was for men, and marriage, like lifeboats, was for women and children."
—*Carrie Fisher*

"Marriage is a custom brought about by women who then proceed to live off men and destroy them, completely enveloping the man in a destructive cocoon or eating him away like a poisonous fungus on a tree."
—*Richard Harris*

"The trouble with some women is that they get all excited about nothing—and then marry him."
—*Cher*

"Do you know what it means to come home at night to a woman who'll give you a little love, a little affection, a little tenderness? It means you're in the wrong house, that's what it means."
—*George Burns*

"If you want to sacrifice the admiration of many men for the criticism of one, go ahead, get married."
—*Katharine Hepburn*

"When an actor marries an actress they both fight for the mirror."

—*Burt Reynolds*

"I was married by a judge. I should have asked for a jury."

—*Groucho Marx*

"Marriage is too interesting an experiment to be tried only once."

—*Eva Gabor (who was married five times)*

"I think prenups are very important. I have one and I'm not married!
I have one with anyone I go to dinner with."

—*George Clooney*

"Marriage is a great institution, but I'm not ready for an institution yet."

—*Mae West*

"Marriage is really tough because you have to deal with feelings . . . and
lawyers."

—*Richard Pryor*

"There is one thing I would break up over and that is if she caught me
with another woman. I wouldn't stand for that."

—*Steve Martin*

"Always get married early in the morning. That way, if it doesn't work
out, you haven't wasted a whole day."

—*Mickey Rooney*

"My wife and I were happy for 20 years. Then we met."

—*Rodney Dangerfield*

"Whatever you may look like, marry a man your own age—as your
beauty fades, so will his eyesight."

—*Phyllis Diller*

"The husband who wants a happy marriage should learn to keep his
mouth shut and his checkbook open."

—*Groucho Marx*

"If you never want to see a man again, say, 'I love you, I want to marry
you, I want to have children . . .'; they leave skid marks."

—*Rita Rudner*

"Ah, yes, divorce . . . from the Latin word meaning 'to rip out a man's
genitals through his wallet.'"

—*Robin Williams*

Strange Stories from On the Set

Hang around a movie buff long enough and you're sure to hear about strange things that happened on the set while famous movies were being filmed. These are the kind of stories that leave you wondering, "Could that really be true?" Well, curious reader, read on and you might be surprised at what you learn!

Indiana Jones and the Scene-Stopping Stomach Virus

Believe it or not, one of the most famous scenes in *Raiders of the Lost Ark* (1981)—when Indy decides to simply shoot a sword-wielding enemy rather than fight him—was not originally in the script. Rather, the scene was improvised by Harrison Ford himself. Why? Well, the script called for Indy and the swordsman to engage in a massive fight that would have required several shots and hours of shooting. But Ford, who had come down with a rather nasty case of dysentery, was weak and in pain, making it too difficult for him to do the extensive swordplay that the script called for. So he asked director Steven Spielberg, "Can't I just shoot the guy?" His wish was granted.

Bob Geldof Hits *The Wall*

In a scene from the cult classic *Pink Floyd: The Wall* (1982), actor and musician Bob Geldof, playing the role of Pink, is called upon to trash his hotel room. As cameras rolled, Geldof started breaking everything in sight. But when he pulled down the venetian blinds, he inadvertently cut his left hand. Undeterred, Geldof simply wrapped some cloth around his bloody hand and allowed cameras to keep rolling. Though the entire scene was later edited down, scenes showing Geldof cutting his hand, as well as the bloody cloth on his hand, were left in.

Willy Wonka's Somersault

The famous scene in the original *Willy Wonka & the Chocolate Factory* (1971), in which Mr. Wonka greets the lucky winners with a somersault, wasn't in the original script. When first offered the role, actor Gene Wilder said he would do it under one condition: He wanted to do a somersault after faking a limp when he was first introduced. Wilder believed that the act would show audiences that Willy Wonka was capable of all sorts of surprises and that anything could happen. The director agreed, and the now-famous scene was added.

James Dean Takes Method Acting One Step Further

He only made three movies before his life was tragically cut short, but James Dean was known for giving all he had in every scene. Case in point, in *Rebel Without a Cause* (1955), during the scene in which Dean's character, Jim Stark, angrily pounds on a desk in a police station, Dean got so into character that, according to costar Jim Backus, he broke two bones in his hand. The scene was left in the finished film, so when viewers see Dean writhing in pain with tears in his eyes, those emotions are the real deal.

Martin Sheen's Rampage

The scene that opened Francis Ford Coppola's *Apocalypse Now* (1979) didn't look like much on paper. It simply called for actor Martin Sheen to mime a bit of drunken despair in a hotel room, over which his voiceover would eventually be added. But Sheen, a method-style actor, decided that he wanted to explore the dark side of the character from the inside out, so prior to shooting he got intoxicated and then worked himself up into an intense emotional state. Once cameras started rolling, Sheen launched into the unscripted, improvised breakdown of his character, which included accidentally smashing his right fist through a real glass mirror. Despite pleas from the frightened crew, Coppola, who remains an advocate of the method and character improvisations, ordered them to keep filming. The final product was edited down and used in the finished film and has since become one of the legendary performances from the Film School Generation of actors.

Spider's Fake Gunshot Wounds

While filming the scene in *GoodFellas* (1990) in which Michael Imperioli's character, Spider, is shot to death while carrying a drink to Joe Pesci's character, Tommy, Imperioli cut his hand on a glass and had to be taken to the hospital. Seeing the fake gunshot wounds all over Imperioli, emergency room attendees immediately began preparing to operate. When they were told the wounds were fake, they were so outraged that they ordered Imperioli back into the waiting room, where he sat for three hours before being seen.

Blowing a "Razz"-berry

☆ ☆ ☆ ☆

Since 1981, the Golden Raspberry Awards, or Razzies,
have been presented annually in Hollywood to
"honor" the year's worst achievements in film.

The Razzies are voted upon by the Golden Raspberry Award
Foundation, which, unlike the Academy of Motion Picture Arts
and Sciences, is open to members of the public. A Razzie Award
consists of a plastic raspberry painted gold atop a reel of Super
8 film. Razzies are presented in categories such as Worst Picture,
Worst Director, Worst Actor, Worst Actress, Worst Screenplay, and
Worst Screen Couple. When Ben Affleck was presented with the
Worst Actor Razzie on *Larry King Live* in 2003 for his performances
in *Gigli, Daredevil,* and *Paycheck,* he accidentally broke the award,
which is valued at a whopping $4.97. Razzies founder John Wilson
recovered it, sold it on eBay, and raised enough money to pay for
the theater rental for the following year's ceremony.

"I'd Like to Thank the Academy…"

Although many superstars have won Razzie awards, only a few have
actually accepted the award in person. Halle Berry collected her
Worst Actress Razzie at the 2004 ceremony for her performance
in *Catwoman* and mocked the Oscar acceptance speech she gave
when she won for *Monster's Ball* (2001). The audience greeted her
description of *Catwoman* as a "god-awful movie" with laughter and
enthusiastic applause.

Director Paul Verhoeven attended the awards ceremony to
accept the Worst Picture and Worst Director Razzies for his box-
office dud *Showgirls* (1995). Screenwriter Brian Helgeland became
only the fourth person to voluntarily accept his Golden Raspberry
Award and the first person to win both a Razzie and an Oscar in the
same year. His Worst Screenplay Razzie for the Kevin Costner flop
The Postman (1997) countered his Academy Award for Best
Adapted Screenplay for *L.A. Confidential* (1997). Rumor has it that
Helgeland likes to display both awards side-by-side on his mantle.

The Razzies' Biggest Winners... or Losers

- Two movies have won seven Razzie Awards: *Showgirls* (1995) and *Battlefield Earth* (2000). But *I Know Who Killed Me* (2007) set a new Razzie record by winning eight of the not-so-coveted awards.

- *Gigli* (2003) was the first and, so far, the only movie to win Razzies in each of the top five categories: Worst Picture, Worst Director, Worst Actor, Worst Actress, and Worst Screenplay.

- Sylvester Stallone has been the recipient of the most Razzie Awards, with 30 nominations and 10 wins, including Worst Actor of the Decade for his performances in *Rhinestone* (1984), *Rambo: First Blood Part II* (1985), *Rocky IV* (1985), *Cobra* (1986), *Over the Top* (1987), *Rambo III* (1988), *Lock-Up* (1989), and *Tango & Cash* (1989).

- Madonna leads the way for female Razzie winners with five wins plus a Worst Actress of the Century award.

- In 2004, Ben Stiller was nominated as Worst Actor for a record five different movies: *Along Came Polly, Dodgeball, Starsky & Hutch, Envy,* and *Anchorman,* but Ben Affleck won for *Surviving Christmas* and *Jersey Girl.*

- Winning three Razzies for *Norbit* (2007), Eddie Murphy became the first person to win a Golden Raspberry Award for both male and female performances in the same film.

- The only non-Hollywood people to win Razzies are President George W. Bush, Defense Secretary Donald Rumsfeld, and Secretary of State Condoleezza Rice, who all appeared in Michael Moore's 2004 documentary *Fahrenheit 9/11.*

- Eight actors have won both Razzies and Oscars during their careers (although not for the same performance): Marlon Brando, Charlton Heston, Faye Dunaway, Laurence Olivier, Roberto Benigni, Halle Berry, Liza Minnelli, and Nicole Kidman.

- Tom Cruise and Katie Holmes were the Golden Raspberry Award winners in a one-off category for their performance in 2005 as the Most Tiresome Tabloid Target. Not surprisingly, neither actor attended the ceremony to collect the award.

Hollywood's Great Romances

With a success rate hovering just above rock bottom, Hollywood hookups are notoriously short-lived. But every rule has its exceptions. Somehow, some way, these committed celebrities managed to weather the storm.

Paul Newman and Joanne Woodward

Long considered the gold standard of Hollywood pairings, Newman and Woodward met in New York in 1953. But when they fell for each other on the set of *The Long, Hot Summer* (1958), neither could have known that their relationship would stand the test of time. Sadly, that included Newman's wife Jackie Witte, who gallantly stepped aside and gave him a divorce. With love in their eyes and hope in their hearts, Newman and Woodward tied the knot on January 29, 1958. After 50 loving years of marriage to Woodward, Newman died on September 26, 2008. When they vowed to stay together "till death do us part," these two really meant it.

Jimmy Stewart and Gloria Hatrick McLean

Known for such heartwarming movies as *It's a Wonderful Life* (1946) and *The Shop Around the Corner* (1940), Jimmy Stewart often portrayed the down-to-earth, straight-shooting everyman. In a bona fide case of life imitating art (or vice versa), Jimmy Stewart was very much like his on-screen persona. After marrying Gloria Hatrick McLean in 1949, he adopted her sons Ronald and Michael for good measure. The loving pair added a set of twin girls (Judy and Kelly) to the family and remained happily married until Gloria's death in 1994. Stewart's success at staying hitched when so many other celebrities had joined the alimony pool may be explained by his attitude. "I'm the inarticulate man who tries," said Stewart about his knack for landing on his feet. "I don't really have all the answers, but for some reason, somehow, I make it."

Fred MacMurray and June Haver

MacMurray was one of Hollywood's most versatile stars during the industry's Golden Age, appearing as the down-to-earth leading man who could still crack jokes when the script called for it. He was cast in musicals, comedies, dramas, and even against type as the cynical insurance man in Billy Wilder's film noir *Double Indemnity* (1944). June Haver was the blonde musical star who worked in Betty Grable's shadow at 20th Century Fox. Known as the "sweetest star in Hollywood," Haver had been a performer since childhood but was looking for something more in her life. Both MacMurray and Haver had lost their spouses prematurely and were working through their grief when they met in 1954 at a party thrown by John Wayne. After that night, the two were never separated, marrying in June of that year. Haver gave up her career, content to let her husband be the actor in the family, and the two were separated only by MacMurray's death in 1991.

Ossie Davis and Ruby Dee
African American actors Ossie Davis and Ruby Dee worked in theater, on television, and in film during a time when people of color found it difficult to land roles with depth and dignity. The two met in 1946 when Ossie made his Broadway debut in *Jeb Turner,* and Dee had a small part in the cast. They married two years later.

Davis excelled in films such as *Shock Treatment* (1964) and *The Scalphunters* (1968), while Dee was featured in *Take a Giant Step* (1961) and on television in the highly acclaimed miniseries *Roots: The Next Generation* (1979). Spike Lee also paid homage to their legacy by casting them both in *Do the Right Thing* (1989). Both were honored in their later years with the National Medal of Arts from the NEA in 1995 and the Kennedy Center Honors in 2004. Davis's death in 2005 seemed the only possible thing that could separate this devoted pair.

Patrick Swayze and Lisa Niemi
Patrick Swayze met Lisa Niemi in 1971, when she was a 15-year-old student at his mother's dance school in Houston, Texas. They were married in 1975. An aspiring actress/dancer, Niemi put her career aside for Swayze's and moved with him to New York City, where he trained at the Harkness Ballet School and the Joffrey Ballet School. But Swayze's dancing career was cut short by an old football injury to his knee. He changed course to become an actor, catching his big break when Francis Ford Coppola cast him as part of the ensemble of young male actors in *The Outsiders* (1983). Swayze's star rose steadily throughout the 1980s and early 1990s, peaking with *Dirty Dancing* (1987), *Ghost* (1990), and *Point Break* (1991). Niemi always supported her husband quietly from the sidelines, and, in March 2008, when Swayze announced

that he had pancreatic cancer, she stepped up to care for him. Their last project together was the memoir *The Time of My Life*, which was published in September 2009, two weeks after Swayze passed away.

Goldie Hawn and Kurt Russell
A hip Hollywood pair that has chosen to laugh in the face of convention and stay together despite the odds, Hawn and Russell met while filming *Swing Shift* (1982) and immediately went bonkers for each other. The couple has managed to keep the flame burning ever since. Accomplishing this feat without the benefit (pitfalls?) of marriage may be the key to their success. Although Russell and Hawn have both been married before, neither seems in a rush to reprise that role.

Tom Hanks and Rita Wilson
Despite Hollywood's many temptations and myriad opportunities, Tom Hanks has remained a one-woman sort of fellow. His first marriage (to actress Samantha Lewes) lasted more than nine years, and his 1988 marriage to Rita Wilson is still going strong. With customary humility, Hanks spelled out the reason for his current success. "I'm a lucky man. She could have done better, but, you know, every now and again, you win the lottery."

Will Smith and Jada Pinkett
Will Smith first met Jada Pinkett in 1990, when she tried out for the role of his girlfriend on the hit TV series *The Fresh Prince of Bel-Air*. She didn't get the part, but the two kept in touch and were platonic friends while Smith was married to his first wife, Sheree Zampino. After the marriage broke up in 1995, Smith and Pinkett spent more time together and discovered there was more to their relationship. They married in December 1997 and reportedly get on like two peas in a pod.

David Arquette and Courteney Cox
One of Hollywood's quirkiest couples, the offbeat and zany Arquette (*Scream*, 1996; *The Grey Zone*, 2001) and the unpretentious beauty Cox, best known as Monica Geller on the long-running hit TV series *Friends*, are proof that opposites attract. After meeting on the set of *Scream*, the unlikely twosome were married in 1999. In true Hollywood spirit, the union has produced a production company, as well as a daughter (Coco Riley), born in 2004. A decade of marriage may not sound particularly long, but in Hollywood, years of matrimony are akin to "dog" years. If held to this standard, the Arquettes are well past their golden anniversary. Good show!

Holiday Classics

The holidays mean different things to different people, but in America you can be pretty sure that at some point the holidays will involve big meals, gift wrap, and holiday-themed movies. Such films have become as much a part of the season as visits to the mall to see Santa. And yeah, sometimes these movies can get a little sentimental, but 'tis the season!

Christmas in Connecticut (1945)

Barbara Stanwyck stars in this delightful romantic comedy about a magazine columnist with a reputation as an expert home-maker and cook who lives on the perfect Connecticut farm with the ideal family. In reality, she is a single city girl who can neither cook nor take care of a household. When her editor sends a recuperating soldier to stay with her at Christmas, she must find a farm and act like the happy homemaker she pretends to be. This lighthearted Christmas tale eschews the heavy sentiment of most classic films in favor of charm and romance.

It's a Wonderful Life (1946)

How could any holiday movie list not include this one? Now hailed as a masterpiece, this black-and-white Jimmy Stewart classic is the film by which all other holiday movies are measured. A heartwarming tale of redemption and gratitude, Frank Capra's story is likely to get you every time. Watch for timeless lines like, "Every time a bell rings, an angel gets its wings" and "I'll give you the moon, Mary!"

Miracle on 34th Street (1947)

Many holiday movies are hits with audiences but fall flat with critics and awards committees. Not *Miracle on 34th Street,* an eminently satisfying holiday picture that garnered four Academy Award nominations and three wins. A movie essentially about the existence of Santa Claus, this story has been remade in several television and celluloid versions, but the 1947 edition, which stars a young Natalie Wood, is considered the best.

The Bishop's Wife (1947)
Cary Grant stars as Dudley the angel in this sophisticated film about a pastor who has lost his way and the wife he neglects. David Niven and Loretta Young star as the earthly couple whose lives are improved by the presence of Dudley. Sentimental but not sappy, the film offers plenty of Christmas cheer but also subtly suggests the importance of sacrificing for a greater purpose, which is the true meaning of Christmas.

White Christmas (1954)
This Christmas classic features the music of Irving Berlin and spotlights musical stars Bing Crosby and Danny Kaye as a top song-and-dance act, who first meet as soldiers during World War II. After achieving stardom in nightclubs and on Broadway, the duo is introduced to a pair of beautiful sisters (played by Rosemary Clooney and Vera Ellen) who—as luck would have it—can sing and dance, too! When the group travels to Vermont for a special show, romantic mix-ups and renewed acquaintances bring out warmhearted humor, all set to a timeless soundtrack.

Babes in Toyland (1961)
This musical fantasy starring Annette Funicello (from the original Mickey Mouse Club) and Ray Bolger (from *The Wizard of Oz*) turned out to be one of Disney's most popular movies, at least during its initial release. Based on a 1903 operetta by Victor Herbert, characters in the film include Mother Goose favorites like Tom the Piper and Little Bo Peep, and they are played by a host of popular Disney actors, including Ed Wynn, Tommy Kirk, and Gene Sheldon.

A Christmas Story (1983)
In recent years, cable network TBS has aired *A Christmas Story* for 24 hours straight, starting on Christmas Eve—that's how much people cherish this beloved holiday film. There's not a single misstep in this touching, sidesplittingly funny tale about a nine-year-old boy named Ralphie who wishes desperately for a special Christmas gift. Set in the 1950s, the scenes of Christmases past will warm your heart while you're wiping your eyes from laughing so hard at the misadventures of the movie's young protagonist. And remember: "You'll shoot your eye out!"

Scrooged (1988)
Still riding on the mega-success of *Ghostbusters* (1984), actor Bill Murray headlined another film with ghostly costars. A modern take on Charles Dickens's *A Christmas Carol*, *Scrooged* contains similar plot points and

themes of heartlessness and redemption with modern-day updates. The ghosts of Christmases past, present, and future are all on the goofy side in this comedy, and Murray's Scrooge character is as witty as he is bitter. The film is famous for Murray's completely ad-libbed conclusion. A must-see for Murray fans and those who love Christmas flicks.

Christmas Vacation (1989)
Chevy Chase is one funny guy, but when he's playing tirelessly optimistic everyman Clark Griswold, he's at his best. One in a series of National Lampoon movies starring Chase, this holiday installment is a fan favorite. For the Griswold family this Christmas, everything goes from bad, to really bad, to ridiculously horrible . . . to great. The characters are lovable even when they're despicable—especially Randy Quaid as Cousin Eddie—and the pratfalls will make you laugh even while you're wincing. A holiday movie must for sure.

Home Alone (1990)
Child actor Macaulay Culkin became an instant superstar when *Home Alone* hit theaters: The movie grossed $17 million in its first weekend and is still among the highest-grossing movies ever. Culkin plays Kevin, a child accidentally left behind when his family goes to Paris for Christmas. It's up to Kevin to defend the house when two wacky burglars try to rob the place. *Home Alone* isn't strictly a holiday movie, but the film has many touching Christmas-themed moments that warm the heart.

The Nightmare Before Christmas (1993)
A feast for the eyes, Tim Burton's freaky *Nightmare* will delight the kids and the kid in you, too. Using stop-motion animation, this modern classic tells the story of Jack Skellington, the "Pumpkin King" of Halloween Town, and how he tries to bring Christmas into his world of ghosts, witches, and goblins. Funny, weird, and definitely touching, *Nightmare* sounds a lot scarier than it is. Listen for a great score by Danny Elfman and check out the retooled soundtrack released in 2006.

Elf (2003)
Comedian Will Ferrell turns in perhaps his most popular role of all time as Buddy the Elf, a human adopted in infancy by Santa's elves. Now fully grown, Buddy realizes that he's not a real elf and decides to find his real father—a heartless New York executive on the "naughty list." Achingly charming but never saccharine, *Elf* was an instant hit with audiences, grossing more than $220 million worldwide.

William Desmond Taylor

☆ ☆ ☆ ☆

The murder of actor/director William Desmond Taylor was like something out of an Agatha Christie novel, complete with a handsome, debonair victim and multiple suspects, each with a motive. But unlike Christie's novels, in which the murderer was always unmasked, Taylor's death remains unsolved nearly 90 years later.

On the evening of February 1, 1922, Taylor was shot in the back by an unknown assailant; his body was discovered the next morning by a servant, Henry Peavey. News of Taylor's demise spread quickly, and several individuals, including officials from Paramount Studios, where Taylor was employed, raced to the dead man's home to clear it of anything incriminating, such as illegal liquor, evidence of drug use, illicit correspondence, and signs of sexual indiscretion. However, no one called the police until later in the morning.

Numerous Suspects

Soon an eclectic array of potential suspects came to light, including Taylor's criminally inclined former butler, Edward F. Sands, who had gone missing before the murder; popular movie comedienne Mabel Normand, whom Taylor had entertained the evening of his death; actress Mary Miles Minter, who had a passionate crush on the handsome director who was 28 years her senior; and Charlotte Shelby, Minter's mother, who often wielded a gun to protect her daughter's tarnished honor.

Taylor's murder was the last thing Hollywood needed at the time, coming as it did on the heels of rape allegations against popular film comedian Fatty Arbuckle. Scandals brought undue attention on Hollywood, and the Arbuckle story had taken its toll. Officials at Paramount tried to keep a lid on the Taylor story, but the tabloid press had a field day. A variety of personal foibles were made public in the weeks that followed, and both Normand and Minter saw their careers come to a screeching halt as a result. Taylor's own indiscretions were also revealed, such as the fact that he kept a special souvenir, usually lingerie, from every woman he bedded.

Little Evidence

Police interviewed many of Taylor's friends and colleagues, including all potential suspects. However, there was no evidence to incriminate anyone specifically, and no one was formally charged.

Investigators and amateur sleuths pursued the case for years. Sands was long a prime suspect, based on his criminal past and his estrangement from the victim. But it was later revealed that on the day of the murder, Sands had signed in for work at a lumberyard in Oakland, California—some 400 miles away—and thus could not have committed the crime. Coming in second was Shelby, whose temper and threats were legendary. Shelby's own acting career had fizzled out early, and all of her hopes for stardom were pinned on her daughter. She threatened many men who tried to woo Mary.

In the mid-1990s, another possible suspect surfaced—a long-forgotten silent-film actress named Margaret Gibson. According to Bruce Long, author of *William Desmond Taylor: A Dossier,* Gibson confessed to a friend on her deathbed in 1964 that years before she had killed a man named William Desmond Taylor. However, the woman to whom Gibson cleared her conscience didn't know who Taylor was and thought nothing more about it.

The Mystery Continues

Could Margaret Gibson (aka Pat Lewis) be Taylor's murderer? She had acted with Taylor in Hollywood in the early 1910s, and she may even have been one of his many sexual conquests. She also had a criminal past, including charges of blackmail, drug use, and prostitution, so it's entirely conceivable that she was a member of a group trying to extort money from the director, a popular theory among investigators. But according to an earlier book, *A Cast of Killers* by Sidney D. Kirkpatrick, veteran Hollywood director King Vidor had investigated the murder as material for a film script and through his research believed Shelby was the murderer. But out of respect for Minter, he never did anything about it.

Ultimately, however, we may never know for certain who killed William Desmond Taylor, or why. The case has long grown cold, and anyone with specific knowledge of the murder is likely dead. Unlike a Hollywood thriller, in which the killer is revealed at the end, Taylor's death is a macabre puzzle that likely will never be solved.

Films Based on Fact When, In Fact, Those Facts Were Fiction

Directors and writers frequently take creative license when adapting a real-life story or historical event for the big screen. The filmmakers are after a universal truth, not a literal one, so audiences tend to allow for a few distorted or left-out facts. But when the facts that form the foundation of the film are false, perhaps that creative license should be revoked. Below are some examples of films that were seemingly based on real events but altered some major facts.

Birdman of Alcatraz (1962)
Going by the title alone, one might assume that convict Robert Stroud (played by Burt Lancaster in the film) earned his famous nickname by raising and breeding canaries inside the walls of Alcatraz. However, prison records show that all of Stroud's aviary activity actually took place at Leavenworth Federal Penitentiary in Kansas when he was imprisoned there from 1912 to 1942. When Stroud was transferred to Alcatraz, he was not permitted to continue his work with birds.

The Texas Chain Saw Massacre (1974)
The opening sequence of the film purports that the story about to be shown on-screen is based on real events that happened on August 18, 1973. However, the actual movie wrapped filming on August 14, 1973, four days before the supposed events even occurred. The movie was actually based loosely on the murders committed by Wisconsin serial killer Ed Gein between 1947 and 1957.

Midnight Express (1978)
In this flick, American Billy Hayes gains his freedom from a Turkish prison by impaling the head guard on a clothes rack, stealing his keys and uniform, and escaping. In real life, the head guard that tortured and threatened Hayes during his stay in prison was actually killed in a café outside the prison by another former inmate.

The Untouchables (1987)
In a key plot point of the movie, Al Capone crony Frank Nitti kills two members of Treasury agent Eliot Ness's team before being killed himself

when Ness pushes him off the courthouse roof during Capone's trial. In reality, Nitti never killed any Treasury agents and didn't meet his demise by being tossed from a roof. In fact, there is no evidence to suggest that any of Ness's men died. Nitti was imprisoned with Capone in 1931 and committed suicide in 1943.

Braveheart (1995)
In Mel Gibson's Academy Award-winning film, the decisive battle between the followers of Scottish resistance leader William Wallace and the English forces led by John de Warenne is fought on a wide, open plain. But history tells us that the bloody barrage that saw the Scottish troops decisively defeat the English actually took place on and near Stirling Bridge where it crosses the River Forth.

Remember the Titans (2000)
In this motivational tale, Gerry Bertier, the defensive leader of the T. C. Williams high school football team, is paralyzed in a car accident before the championship game, and his injury inspires the team to persevere and eventually win the state championship. Bertier really was severely injured in an automobile accident, but the injury didn't occur until after the season ended. He actually played in the championship game and helped the team win the Virginia state title.

A Beautiful Mind (2001)
In Ron Howard's stirring film, mathematician John Nash (played by Russell Crowe) gives a moving acceptance speech after winning the Nobel Prize in Economics. Truth be told, Nash actually received the Nobel Memorial Prize for Economics, which was not one of the prizes originally established by Alfred Nobel in 1895. Instead, it is named in honor of him and is endowed by a bank. Nobel prizes are only awarded for Chemistry, Physiology or Medicine, Literature, and Peace—and Nash did not speak at the ceremony.

21 (2008)
In this film, an MIT professor named Mickey Rosa teaches a group of predominantly white students to count cards at casino blackjack tables and use the technique to win millions. However, while the basic facts are accurate, the students who were involved in the cheating scheme were not white; they were Asian American, and there was no professor. Three university graduates formed the team and helped teach them the methods they used.

Joan Crawford

☆ ☆ ☆ ☆

Movie megastar or box-office poison? Loving mother or wire hanger-hating madwoman? During the course of her long career in Hollywood, Joan Crawford amazed and confused millions of people as they sought to understand her and figure out who she really was.

Reaching for Stardom

On March 23, 1905, Lucille Fay LeSueur was born in San Antonio, Texas. In her late teens, she joined a traveling theatrical company, and by age 20, she was performing in a chorus line on Broadway.

In 1925, Lucille was contracted by MGM to appear as an extra in six films, receiving her first credit on *Pretty Ladies* (1925). MGM then picked up her option, though studio execs, including Louis B. Mayer, insisted on a name change. In one of the most famous publicity stunts in Hollywood history, MGM held a contest for fans to select a suitable name for her. The starlet made her debut as Joan Crawford in *Old Clothes* (1925). Crawford did everything the studio asked of her, and more—from appearing in unworthy films to making herself available for all photo opportunities. All of this led MGM screenwriter Frederica Sagor Maas to utter the now-famous words: "No one decided to make Joan Crawford a star. Joan Crawford became a star because Joan Crawford decided to become a star."

Douglas Fairbanks Jr. and the Clark Gable Affair

After a short courtship, Crawford married Douglas Fairbanks Jr. on June 3, 1929. Trouble started brewing when Crawford began filming *Laughing Sinners* (1931), and then *Possessed* (1931), with Clark Gable. Rumors quickly began to circulate that Crawford and Gable were having an affair, and the couple was anything but discreet with their behavior. Studio execs demanded that the pair curtail the affair, which they did, more or less. But the chemistry between the two was palpable, so the studio cast them in eight films together.

In May 1933, Crawford filed for divorce from Fairbanks, and less than two years later, she married actor Franchot Tone, with whom she appeared in seven films. But the studio made much of Crawford's level of stardom compared to Tone's, which created a lot of tension in the marriage, and the couple filed for divorce in 1939. That same year, Crawford appeared as the villainess in the film *The Women*. She campaigned for the role, and studio execs finally gave it to her, though they disliked the fact that she was playing a hard-edged, unrepentant home wrecker.

Box-Office Poison

In 1932, when the *Motion Picture Herald* released its poll of the top ten moneymaking movie stars, Joan Crawford topped the list. In fact, she held down the top slot in the poll for the next four years. But by 1937, Crawford had not only fallen from the top spot, she didn't even make the top ten. Perhaps that's why the following year, the *Independent Film Journal* referred to her as "box-office poison," though she was in good company because Katharine Hepburn, Greta Garbo, and Marlene Dietrich were also labeled as such by trade magazines in the late 1930s.

Adopting Children

In 1940, although unmarried at the time, Crawford adopted a daughter, Christina. Then, after Crawford married her third husband, Phillip Terry, in July 1942, they adopted another child, Christopher. But when Christopher's birth mother found out who had adopted her child, she petitioned the court and was awarded custody. Crawford was outraged and immediately took steps to adopt another boy, whom she named Phillip Terry Jr. When Terry and Crawford divorced in 1946, the eccentric actress received full custody of the two children and legally changed Phillip Jr.'s name to Christopher Crawford. The following year, Crawford adopted two more girls whom she named Cindy and Cathy.

Crawford continued to accept whatever movie roles were offered to her, but they were coming less frequently. In 1943, when her contract with MGM was terminated by mutual consent, Crawford moved to Warner Bros., who gave her more control over her material and directors. Despite the fact that she won a Best Actress Oscar for her role in *Mildred Pierce* (1945) and appeared in a handful of solid dramas, Crawford left Warner Bros. in 1952.

Al Steele and the Pepsi-Cola Company

In May 1955, Crawford married her fourth and final husband, Alfred Steele, the president of Pepsi-Cola. Soon after, Crawford made herself an unofficial spokesperson for Pepsi and began traveling extensively to promote the beverage. When Steele died unexpectedly of a heart attack in 1959, Crawford took his spot on the Board of Directors, even though she had no background in running a business.

In 1961, Crawford was offered a starring role in *What Ever Happened to Baby Jane?* (1962). She played Blanche Hudson, a former A-list actress who had become confined to a wheelchair; Bette Davis portrayed Blanche's sadistic sister. The two actresses were reputedly engaged in a bizarre feud that may have stemmed from the 1930s, when both were interested in Franchot Tone. Legend has it that Crawford complained that Davis intentionally kicked her during a scene. Seeking revenge, Crawford allegedly strapped weights to her body for the scene in which Davis was required to lift her.

Feigning Illness?

When director Robert Aldrich cast Crawford and Davis in *Hush . . . Hush, Sweet Charlotte* (1964), everyone warned him that he was asking for trouble—and he got it. According to some reports, the two stars were constantly bickering and would often go out of their way to anger each other. Davis seemed to take great pride in trying to get Crawford to snap and appeared to have succeeded when Joan claimed to have fallen ill and left the set. Aldrich begged Crawford to come back, and she did, but when she again claimed she was ill, Aldrich demanded that she be examined by a company physician. Crawford refused and several days later checked into a hospital with an "undisclosed illness." Believing Crawford was faking, Aldrich promptly fired her, scrapped all of the existing footage she appeared in, and replaced her with Olivia de Havilland. Crawford reportedly cried for 39 hours straight after hearing of her replacement.

Turning to Television

With movie scripts no longer coming her way, Crawford turned to the world of television. In 1968, Crawford's daughter Christina, who was also an actress, took medical leave from *The Secret Storm,* the soap opera on which she was a regular. Somehow, Joan convinced producers that she should fill in until Christina returned, despite their 30-year age difference. But during taping, Crawford repeatedly muffed her lines, which caused her to get so angry that she lost it altogether and was reportedly sent home and told not to return.

Joan had several other appearances on TV shows and starred in one final movie, *Trog* (1970), but she was never able to recapture the level of stardom that she once had. Still, by 1972, with her final acting appearance on the TV series *The Sixth Sense*, Crawford's career had spanned an amazing 45 years.

Seclusion and Death

In 1973, when Crawford was told that her services were no longer needed at Pepsi-Cola, she began to withdraw from society. When she saw some unflattering photos of herself at her last known public appearance on September 23, 1974, she is said to have remarked, "If that's how I look, then they won't see me anymore." With that, Joan Crawford was rarely seen again until her death on May 10, 1977.

When Crawford's will was read, her two youngest children, Cathy and Cindy, each received roughly $78,000. As for Christina and Christopher, Crawford's will simply stated that "for reasons which are well known to them," they were to receive nothing.

Mommie Dearest

Roughly 18 months after Crawford's death, Christina published *Mommie Dearest*, a book that candidly discussed Joan's (alleged) erratic behavior. (The book was later made into a movie of the same name, starring Faye Dunaway as Crawford.) Christina described how her mother choked her, drank excessively, obsessed over her appearance, and had a revolving door of lovers. But far and away, the most infamous scene in the book (and movie) was the one in which Joan found wire hangers in Christina's closet, which sent Joan into a rage, during which she screamed "No wire hangers! No more wire hangers ever!"

Christina maintains that everything was described in the book exactly as it happened. Crawford's other children and her friends claim that they never saw any of the strange behavior related in the book. True or not, the book has overshadowed Crawford's decades-long career and her glamorous image.

Hope and Crosby

☆ ☆ ☆ ☆

*Bing Crosby and Bob Hope were both capable performers
in any number of areas—comedy, drama, song, and dance.
And they excelled in virtually every medium of popular
entertainment, from theater, radio, and music to film, television,
and live performance. But when Paramount Pictures teamed
them with Dorothy Lamour in a series of comic adventure
movies starting in 1940, the pair cemented their status as
superstars and helped shape the landscape of comedic films.*

Bob Hope and Bing Crosby had been
close friends since 1932, when they
worked together at the legendary
Paramount doing an old vaudeville
routine in a New York variety
show. Later they teamed up
on Hope's popular NBC
radio program that first
aired in 1937, developing a
natural banter based on perfect
comic timing. Later, in Hollywood, the two would often display their
shtick at various industry events or at Crosby's Del Mar Turf Club.
A Paramount executive who saw their routine began searching for a
vehicle to showcase their repartee. A script that had been sitting on
the shelf for some time was rewritten for them as *Road to Singapore*
and became Paramount's biggest moneymaker of 1940.

Two Buddies Hit the Road... and the Silver Screen

Hope and Crosby made six more movies following the strict formula
of *Road to Singapore*. In these *Road* pictures, the pair always played
world-traveling second-rate entertainers and con men who stumbled
from one misadventure to another. Dorothy Lamour was the exotic
love interest the two friends competed over in most of the films,
with Crosby usually winning out. While the two male leads ended
up doing good in the end by foiling some villain's plan, there was

usually some moral ambiguity to the characters along the way. They typically got themselves into trouble by pursuing wealth or romance through a dishonest scheme, and neither was above selling out the other to save his own skin. In their third outing, *Road to Morocco* (1942), Crosby actually sells Hope's character into slavery just to put some cash in his empty pocket.

Winging It

Typically, the final cut of a *Road* picture barely resembled the original script. Hope and Crosby each had their own team of writers who worked independently to produce material for each star. Then the actors would work in their own lines with the cameras rolling, giving each other opportunities to ad-lib in response. This daring, creative approach gave their banter a spontaneous, natural style that became their trademark.

The other truly innovative aspect of the Hope-Crosby films was the actors' regular habit of "breaking the fourth wall" by talking directly to the audience, a notoriously difficult gag to pull off. Hope in particular was noted for doing this in extreme ways. In one film, as Crosby is about to launch into song, Hope turns to the camera and tells the audience that it would be a good time for them to go get popcorn. In another, the pair find themselves stranded in a lifeboat and Hope goes into a faux dramatic death scene. When Crosby interrupts to point out an approaching rescue ship, Hope fully breaks character and berates his partner for ruining his chance at an Oscar. The films also contain many references to current events and other popular performers, making them seem a bit dated, but they remain influential entries in the buddy film genre even today.

Hope and Crosby Filmography:
Road to Singapore (1940)
Road to Zanzibar (1941)
Road to Morocco (1942)
Road to Utopia (1946)
Road to Rio (1947)
Road to Bali (1952)
The Road to Hong Kong (1962)

Movie Junkie

Perhaps it's because it hits close to home, but Hollywood has long held a fascination with movies about drug and alcohol abuse, though for years, feature films about drug addiction were forbidden under the Motion Picture Production Code. While some of the stories on this list are bleaker than others and some choose to moralize while others reserve judgment, they all work as cautionary tales.

Reefer Madness (1936)

This propaganda film was created to scare the public straight about the dangers of marijuana use. It has become a camp classic—but unfortunately for its creators, not because it worked very well. The plot is simple: Viewers follow "Bill" as he goes insane from smoking pot. Murder and death ensue, but the whole thing strikes most viewers as dated and a little silly, due to the heavy-handed approach the filmmakers took in warning people about "reefer madness." Because of its educational purpose, the film was not under the jurisdiction of the Production Code.

The Man with the Golden Arm (1955)

The Production Code, Hollywood's censorship machine during the Golden Age, did not allow on-screen depictions of drug use, even if the film was critical of drugs. This drama, based on Nelson Algren's bestseller, was the film that changed that ruling in the Code. Otto Preminger's tight direction, Sam Leavitt's gritty cinematography, and Frank Sinatra's realistic portrayal of musician and addict Frankie Machine offered a down and dirty look at addiction that is still gripping. Elmer Bernstein's jazzy score added to the film's contemporary, urban milieu.

Valley of the Dolls (1967)

Fame! Fortune! Addiction to pills! This film is also a bit of a camp classic, likely due to its hammy dialogue and melodramatic story line. Ambitious divas-in-training find scandal and self-destruction on the road to stardom in Hollywood. The "dolls" of the title refer to the barbiturates that the young actresses take by the handful. Look for Patty Duke in a role far removed from her earlier work as a role model for adolescent girls.

The Panic in Needle Park (1971)
Al Pacino is said to have nailed down the role of Don Corleone in *The Godfather* (1972) after Coppola saw him in this gritty tale of heroin addiction in New York City. It's believed that *Panic* was the first major film to show junkie characters actually injecting the drugs to which they are so addicted. The screenplay was written by renowned husband-and-wife superstar writers John Gregory Dunne and Joan Didion.

Clean and Sober (1988)
There is hope! Michael Keaton stars in this redemption tale of an alcoholic who struggles to find a new way of life while in rehab. He battles setbacks, eats humble pie, and fights his demons—a typical day in the life of a recovering addict. Look for Morgan Freeman and Kathy Bates in supporting roles in a movie that resists the urge to moralize.

Drugstore Cowboy (1989)
A band of addicts/pharmacy thieves wreak havoc as they hit hospitals and drugstores for their next fix of prescription pain medicine. Director Gus Van Sant made his name with this gritty film starring Matt Dillon. Look for a cameo by the late writer William S. Burroughs as a narcotics-abusing "priest."

Leaving Las Vegas (1995)
Alcohol is the drug of choice in this Oscar-winning film starring Nicolas Cage and Elisabeth Shue as two people in love at the bottom. Cage's character is a totally out-of-control alcoholic who comes to Las Vegas for one reason and one reason only: to drink himself to death. He ends up falling in love, but take a cue from the title and don't expect a happy ending—you're going to need a box of tissues handy for this one.

Trainspotting (1996)
Travel to Scotland for a tale of unrelenting heroin abuse by a group of friends in Edinburgh! See a man dive into a toilet! Watch as he withstands the horrors of withdrawal! *Trainspotting* put director Danny Boyle on the map, along with his leading man—an emaciated Ewan McGregor—and gave the world an all-too-true portrait of drug abuse in the slums of the UK. Beware: The imagery in this film is not for those with weak stomachs.

Half Baked (1998)
If you're looking for high art—pun intended—you probably shouldn't look here, but for a few giggle-inducing gags and some amusing cameos

(including Willie Nelson and Snoop Dog), *Half Baked* might suit you. Comedian Dave Chappelle headlines this goofy "cannabis comedy," which he also cowrote.

Requiem for a Dream (2000)
Hailed by some critics and fans to be *the* definitive "drug movie" and a masterpiece of a film, period, *Requiem* recounts a slow, excruciating descent into hell. "Hell" is addiction, and the story follows three different addicts as they fall deeper and deeper into the horrors of their disease. Oscars were won, people were shocked. In editing the film, director Darren Aronofsky spliced together more than 2,000 cuts, giving it a spastic, frenetic feel, not unlike being in the throes of addiction. Like all the movies on this list, this film should be viewed by young people only in the presence of responsible adults. While *Requiem* provides a certain kind of antidrug abuse message, the amputations, criminal behavior, and graphic sexual situations will be too much for some young folks.

Traffic (2000)
Directed by Steven Soderbergh, *Traffic* tells a fast-paced, dramatic, and multifaceted story of the drug trade, from poppy fields to Mexican drug cartels, from DEA raids in slums to the dorm rooms of wealthy college kids. A star-studded cast, which includes Benicio Del Toro, Michael Douglas, and Catherine Zeta-Jones, appears in this award-winning tale of drugs, deception, and destruction.

Love Liza (2002)
Just when you thought Hollywood films had covered every conceivable kind of drug addict.... In *Love Liza*, Philip Seymour Hoffman plays a character devastated after his wife commits suicide. Less about drugs than it is about dysfunctional mourning, this film makes our list due to the addiction Hoffman's character suffers from—he's a gasoline sniffer.

Spun (2002)
The moral of this story is pretty clear: Never, ever, ever take methamphetamine. Filmed and edited in a way that mimics the perspective of a meth addict (with hallucinatory images, bizarre situations, and sped-up sequences followed by those in slow motion), *Spun* follows a few days in the lives of speed users. A few humorous moments occur, but for the most part, this movie, featuring Jason Schwartzman, Mickey Rourke, and Brittany Murphy, is an exercise in the futility and madness of drug abuse.

Pop Quiz: Grauman's Chinese Theatre

Grauman's Chinese Theatre is a Hollywood landmark famous for its forecourt where many stars have left a little of themselves behind.

1. Who were the first three stars to leave their handprints outside the theater?

2. Who added the message "You made my day" to his handprints?

3. Grauman's Chinese Theatre is the most sought-after theater in Hollywood for studio premieres. What was the first film to premiere there?

4. Over the years, some Hollywood stars have left some unusual impressions in the cement. Who left an imprint of his fist?

5. In 1943, which actress left an imprint of her "million dollar legs"?

6. Two stars have left imprints of their footprints in bare feet instead of wearing shoes. Harpo Marx was the first. Who was the second, on April 13, 1999?

7. *Harry Potter* stars Daniel Radcliffe, Emma Watson, and Rupert Grint left their hand- and footprints outside the theater in 2007. What else did each of them leave an imprint of?

8. Three famous horses have left hoofprints in the cement. Can you name them?

9. Surprisingly, the prints in the cement are not limited to humans and animals. In 1977, three movie characters were immortalized in the forecourt. Two of them were not organic beings. Can you name them?

10. Which comedian left an imprint of his cigar along with the message "Going in style"?

Answer Key: 1. Mary Pickford, Douglas Fairbanks, and Norma Talmadge on April 30, 1927; 2. Clint Eastwood; 3. Cecil B. DeMille's *The King of Kings* on May 18, 1927; 4. John Wayne; 5. Betty Grable; 6. Sean Connery; 7. Their magic wands; 8. Tony Mix's horse Tony, Roy Rogers's Trigger, and Gene Autry's Champion; 9. Three characters from *Star Wars* were honored: Darth Vader, R2-D2, and C-3PO; 10. George Burns

279

The Curse of Superman

☆ ☆ ☆ ☆

Superman may be indestructible, but the same can't be said of the men who played him on television and in the movies. In fact, several actors who have portrayed the "Man of Steel" have died tragically.

George Reeves

The first Superman actor to fall victim to tragedy was George Reeves, who played the "Man of Steel" and his mild-mannered alter ego, Clark Kent, in the popular TV series *Adventures of Superman* for six seasons in the 1950s. Prior to that, Reeves had small roles in several motion pictures, including *Gone with the Wind* (1939), *Samson and Delilah* (1949), and *Rancho Notorious* (1952).

His role as Superman made Reeves a household name and an idol to millions of children, so his death from a single gunshot wound to the head on June 16, 1959, was devastating news nationwide.

Reeves's death was initially labeled a suicide, but almost immediately, there was speculation among friends and colleagues that he had been murdered. It was not an unlikely scenario. Reeves was a notorious ladies' man who had a reputation for having affairs with the wives and girlfriends of important men, including, it was rumored, studio executives and mobsters. In the weeks prior to his death, Reeves had reportedly received several death threats and had survived three suspicious automobile accidents, including one that resulted when the brake fluid was mysteriously drained from his car.

Several investigators have researched George Reeves's bizarre death over the years and found numerous inconsistencies in the police reports, but what really happened to the small-screen superhero that fateful night may never be known. In 1961, Reeves's body was exhumed and cremated, eliminating any possibility of a new autopsy.

Lee Quigley: Superbaby

Two individuals who portrayed the "Man of Steel" on the big screen also met an untimely demise. The first was Lee Quigley, who, at age seven months, portrayed baby Kal-El, an infant Superman in the 1978 film. Despite his early break in show business, Quigley had a troubled childhood and, in 1991, died at age 14 from intentionally inhaling solvent fumes.

Christopher Reeve: *The* Man of Steel

More widely reported was the death of actor Christopher Reeve, who played Superman in the 1978 film and its three sequels. A relatively unknown actor when he landed the role, Reeve had appeared in the submarine action flick *Gray Lady Down* (1978) and on the soap opera *Love of Life.* He saw Superman as a way to advance his career and wisely so—the character made him a household name.

Reeve's career took flight after *Superman,* and his subsequent films included *Somewhere in Time* (1980), *Deathtrap* (1982), and *The Remains of the Day* (1993). But in May 1995, disaster struck when, during an equestrian competition, Reeve was thrown from his horse. The fall broke his neck and left him a quadriplegic. But despite his disability, the actor persevered. Reeve subsequently became an advocate for spinal cord research and eventually was able to return to acting and directing.

However, despite the best medical care money could buy, Reeve was felled by a simple bed sore, a common complication among people with paralysis and something the actor had experienced many times before. This time, however, the wound became severely infected, and on October 9, 2004, Reeve went into cardiac arrest after receiving a dose of an antibiotic. He fell into a coma and was rushed to the hospital, where he died the next day at age 52.

For most actors who have portrayed a well-known fictional character in the movies, the biggest curse is being typecast. But for George Reeves and Christopher Reeve, the curse of Superman was much more. The character brought both actors international acclaim but also proved that wearing a bright red S on your chest doesn't make you indestructible or invincible.

Have I Seen that Scene Before?

If you've ever watched a movie and thought a particular scene looked familiar, you might be correct. Many movies "borrow" scenes and elements from earlier films as a sort of homage. While there are parodies and spoofs—what is Austin Powers *but a take on* James Bond*—other films are more sly. Think of it as a way for the writers and directors to acknowledge their influences through allusion.*

Stairways Not to Heaven
In Brian De Palma's gangster saga *The Untouchables* (1987), the train station shootout takes place on a stairway. This scene was inspired by the Odessa steps sequence in *Battleship Potemkin* (1925), which was directed by Sergei Eisenstein. Ironically, De Palma wanted the shootout to be on a period train, but cost concerns made this impossible. Instead, it was decided that the scene would pay homage to the earlier film through the use of the baby carriage falling precariously down the stairs. And, if you have a keen eye, you'll notice several sailors caught in the crossfire, which is also a nod to the Russian film.

Gold and Oil
James Bond seems to face many villains with unique plans for world domination, but these foes often employ strangely similar methods. One of the most memorable images of the 007 classic *Goldfinger* (1964) was actress Shirley Eaton covered in gold paint from head to toe. *Quantum of Solace* (2008) features a scene with Gemma Arterton as Strawberry Fields, who meets a similarly gruesome end, but this time the erstwhile Bond girl was covered in thick black oil. Bond may always get the girls, but the girls seem to get it in the end.

Bridges Too Far
Picture this: A hero in an exotic land is chased across a long rope bridge, only to find himself trapped. Sounds like the climax of *Indiana Jones and the Temple of Doom* (1984), but actually, Tommy Lee Jones found himself in a similar predicament a year earlier in *Nate and Hayes*. But in fairness, *The Man Who Would Be King* (1975) offered up a scene with Sean Connery trying to get out while the getting's good. And of course, all these may have been inspired by *Perils of Nyoka* (1942), a Republic serial that also featured a hero in trouble on a bridge.

City Shootout

Quentin Tarantino's *Reservoir Dogs* (1992) paved the way for the writer/director to make *Pulp Fiction* (1994). However, *Reservoir Dogs*, a story about jewel thieves, is itself guilty of a heist. Tarantino made no secret of the fact that he was inspired by Hong Kong action cinema, but *Reservoir Dogs* features a remarkable number of moments lifted from the Ringo Lam-directed *City on Fire* (1987), starring Chow Yun-Fat. Not only do both stories feature an undercover cop in a gang in which the criminals don't know each other, but there is also a similar "Mexican standoff" climax just before the credits roll.

When Is a Western a Western?

A Fistful of Dollars (1964), starring Clint Eastwood, put a new spin on the traditional Western. Shot in Spain—yet considered a "Spaghetti Western" because it was directed by Sergio Leone and produced by an Italian film studio—this movie was actually a remake of Akira Kurosawa's 1961 film *Yojimbo* (*The Bodyguard*), which itself was a samurai flick influenced by Hollywood films, including Westerns. *Yojimbo* was remade again by Walter Hill as the gangster film *Last Man Standing* (1996), which starred Bruce Willis.

The Hidden Inspiration

Ever wonder why George Lucas included R2-D2 and C-3PO as comic relief in the original *Star Wars* (1977)? Well, take a gander at Akira Kurosawa's 1958 epic *The Hidden Fortress*. It features a very similar duo of secondary characters arguing as they attempt to escape the main enemy's army. Throw in a princess-saving plot, and you get the idea that heroic stories don't only happen in a galaxy far, far away.

Name-dropping

In *Batman Returns* (1992), Christopher Walken plays corrupt business mogul Max Shreck. This is director Tim Burton's homage to German Expressionist actor Max Schreck, who portrayed the vampire in F. W. Murnau's original *Nosferatu* (1922).

Monster Mash

The sight of pitchfork-wielding townspeople bent on burning the monster and putting an end to Dr. Frankenstein's experiments is a cinematic device that has been parodied and spoofed many times. But the original sequence from *Frankenstein* (1931) was re-created almost shot for shot—and in black and white—for the beginning of *Van Helsing* (2004).

Blacklisted!

☆ ☆ ☆ ☆

During the Red Scare, hundreds of film and television careers were destroyed by a vindictive hunt for Communists in Hollywood.

In September 1947, Dalton Trumbo was at the height of his career as a screenwriter. He was highly acclaimed, well paid, and still basking in the accolades he received for his work on two patriotic war films: *A Guy Named Joe* (1943) and *Thirty Seconds Over Tokyo* (1944). That month, an FBI agent delivered Trumbo a subpoena from the House Un-American Activities Committee (HUAC), a special investigative committee of the U.S. House of Representatives. Trumbo, along with 42 other film industry professionals—actors, directors, producers, and writers—were named as key witnesses in HUAC's probe into Communist subversion in Hollywood. The good times were about to end for Dalton Trumbo.

The Hunt for Reds in October

HUAC was created in 1937 to "investigate disloyal or subversive activities in America," such as the Ku Klux Klan and organizations sympathetic to Nazi Germany. HUAC also worked diligently to ferret out American Communist Party (ACP) members and supporters in the U.S. government and media. HUAC cooled its heels during World War II, when the Soviet Union was an ally, but ramped up its pursuits with the postwar onset of the Second Red Scare, which later gave rise to a similar but totally unrelated Red-baiting phenomenon: Joseph McCarthy and the notorious Senate Committee hearings of the 1950s. But in 1947, HUAC had turned its attention to Hollywood.

Citing Soviet-sympathetic war films such as *Mission to Moscow* (1943) and *Song of Russia* (1944), HUAC announced formal hearings to determine if Hollywood filmmakers were undermining U.S. security and freedom by covertly planting Communist propaganda in American films. Those subpoenaed by HUAC were expected to provide details of Communist activity in Hollywood and, more importantly, name names.

On October 20, 1947, the hearings opened with testimony from several "friendly" witnesses. One of them was Walt Disney, who readily fingered several individuals as Communists, claiming that they incited labor unrest in Hollywood. Ronald Reagan, then-president of the Screen Actors Guild, also testified and claimed that Communist intrigue was rampant in Tinseltown.

The Hollywood Ten

Disney and Reagan were followed by ten individuals (including Trumbo, Samuel Ornitz, and John Howard Lawson—screenwriters who were also members of the Writers Guild of America, which Lawson founded) who refused to cooperate with an investigation that they considered a modern-day witch hunt. These "unfriendly" witnesses condemned the hearings as unconstitutional and invoked their Fifth Amendment rights when asked about their involvement with Communist organizations.

For their defiance, the Hollywood Ten, as they were dubbed, were cited for contempt of Congress on November 24. They were also fired by their respective studios and the Motion Picture Producers and Distributors of America barred them from working in Hollywood until they were acquitted or purged of contempt and declared under oath that they were not Communists. The ten remained unrepentant, and in early 1948, they were convicted of contempt. In 1950, after failed appeals, they began serving six-month to one-year prison sentences. Trumbo and his cohorts also became charter members of the now-notorious Hollywood blacklist.

The List that Ate Hollywood

During the next several years, the blacklist grew into a monster that devoured Hollywood careers—a monster that was willingly fed by numerous anticommunist organizations. In 1949, the American Legion presented Hollywood execs with a list of 300 film industry members that they suspected of Communist affiliation. Fearing Legion-organized film boycotts, the studios adopted it as their de facto blacklist. In 1950, a pamphlet known as *Red Channels* pegged 151 TV and radio professionals as Communist sympathizers. Those named were blacklisted from their respective industries to avoid boycotts of products sponsored by the shows.

From 1951 to 1952, HUAC launched more hearings in which witnesses sold out others to save their own careers. Among them was director Edward Dmytryk, a guilt-ridden member of the Hollywood Ten, who betrayed 26 colleagues in exchange for an early jail release and the resumption of his directing career.

HUAC reports produced another blacklist of 212 Hollywood professionals who soon lost their jobs. Most were writers who were relatively unknown outside Hollywood. But several prominent actors, producers, and directors landed on the list, including Charlie Chaplin, Lee Grant, Zero Mostel, Orson Bean, and Larry Parks.

Many on the list also had earlier screen credits omitted. Unable to earn a living, dozens of blacklisted professionals left Hollywood (and even America) to continue their careers elsewhere. Approximately 90 percent of those blacklisted never worked in Hollywood again.

Breaking the Blacklist

Open resistance to the blacklist began to emerge in 1956, when TV and radio personality John Henry Faulk sued the group Aware Inc. after its erroneous labeling of him as a Communist supporter kept him from getting a job at a radio station. Faulk's court victory in 1962 put an end to the blacklist altogether. Soon afterward, several television productions began hiring and crediting blacklisted artists.

Even before then, there were signs that the blacklist was losing strength. In 1960, director Otto Preminger named Dalton Trumbo as the screenwriter for his upcoming film *Exodus.* That same year, Universal Pictures announced that Trumbo would be similarly credited on *Spartacus,* having been hired two years before by the film's executive producer and star, Kirk Douglas. Dalton Trumbo's 13-year nightmare was coming to an end.

Few knew it then, but Trumbo had already trumped the black-list. During the 1950s, some blacklisted artists, including Trumbo, worked under different names. Trumbo wrote *Roman Holiday* (1953) under the alias Ian McLellan Hunter. He also penned *The Brave One* (1956) using the name Robert Rich as his "front." Both efforts earned Oscars for Best Writing, which meant golden redemption for Dalton Trumbo.

How to Rent Your Home as a Movie Set

Q: What kinds of homes are movie companies looking for?

A: Location scouts look for all types of property, from multimillion-dollar mansions to seedy one-room apartments and everything in between; it all depends on the scene being shot. About 70 to 80 percent of all location filming in southern California takes place in private residences, so there is no shortage of demand. But even if you don't live in the Los Angeles area, your home could still have a future in show business. You can apply directly to location scouts, and most states have local film commissions.

Q: How do I get started?

A: Take a lot of photos of your house, both the interior and exterior. Take pictures of every room, including unique details, and make a lot of copies. Send them to any location scouts you find listed in film-industry directories. Also send them to your state film commission and ask to fill out a list agreement.

Q: What should you expect when a film crew uses your home?

A: If you're a neat freak or hate the thought of 50 strangers traipsing across your living room carpet, then renting your home as a movie set is definitely not for you. It can be disconcerting for any homeowner to watch as set decorators completely transform a home. They might cover your walls with ratty wallpaper, replace your furniture with dusty props, or even splatter the floor with fake blood. Professional film crews always clean up after shooting has finished, and you may even benefit from a new paint job or restored woodwork. Still, you'll want to ensure that you get everything—especially any specific concerns—in writing.

Q: How much can you expect to earn?

A: The IRS allows you to rent out your home tax-free for up to 14 days per year. Hollywood studios will pay from $1,000 to $5,000 (or more) per day to rent a home on top of putting the owners up in a hotel if the shoot makes it impossible for them to stay there. They'll also pay for the cost of boarding any pets. Fees are always negotiable, but don't make unreasonable demands or the location scouts will simply find somewhere less expensive, like your neighbor's house, perhaps.

The Great White North Stands In for the Big Apple

With seductive tax breaks, top-quality technical staff, and beneficial exchange rates, Canada beckons Hollywood producers in search of film locations. As such, the city of Toronto, with its towering skyscrapers, ethnic neighborhoods, and cosmopolitan appeal, is a frequent stand-in for New York City. Such was the case with the following films.

Moonstruck (1987)
Canadian Norman Jewison directed this romantic comedy about the complexity of relationships, the lure of the full moon, and an opera-loving baker who falls in love with his brother's fiancée. Jewison used Toronto's rich assortment of ethnic neighborhoods for various New York street scenes in this Academy Award-winner starring Nicolas Cage and Cher.

Don't Say a Word (2001)
This psychological crime thriller, which stars starring Michael Douglas, Sean Bean, and Brittany Murphy, involves a father who must rescue his kidnapped daughter by unlocking the mind of a mental patient who knows too much about a ten-year-old crime. The movie gained fame among set designers for rebuilding an unused portion of the Toronto subway system to re-create New York's Canal Street station.

Down to Earth (2001)
This clever remake of *Here Comes Mr. Jordan* (1941) and *Heaven Can Wait* (1978) stars Chris Rock as a stand-up comedian who is called to heaven before his time. The film used popular Toronto nightlife niches such as the Pantages Theatre, Yuk Yuk's Comedy Club, and the Silver Dollar Room to simulate New York lounges of libation.

Serendipity (2001)
This charming romantic comedy starring John Cusack and Kate Beckinsale tackles the possibility that chance and coincidence can work together to help two soulmates find each other. The film utilized well-known Toronto locations such as the Royal York Hotel and the neighborhood known as High Park. The Holt-Renfrew department store on Bloor Street stood in for Bloomingdale's.

Death to Smoochy (2002)

Directed by Danny DeVito, this comedy stars Robin Williams and Edward Norton as battling children's TV hosts. The film used Toronto locations such as Union Station, Maple Leaf Gardens, and the CBC Broadcasting Center to re-create the Big Apple.

Cold Creek Manor (2003)

This creepy thriller about a dream home that turns into a nightmare stars Dennis Quaid, Sharon Stone, and Christopher Plummer. Filmed entirely in Canada, the city scenes were shot along the pastoral elegance of Adelaide Street, the gritty, industrial section of Parliament Street, and the store-studded splendor of Yonge Street in downtown Toronto.

How to Lose a Guy in 10 Days (2003)

This sharp comedy concerns the devious relationship between a frustrated magazine journalist and an advertising executive. Directed by Donald Petrie and starring Kate Hudson and Matthew McConaughey, the movie was filmed in part in New York but also in and around Toronto's Air Canada Centre, Bloor Street Cinema, and the Rosewater Supper Club.

New York Minute (2004)

This comedy about the New York misadventures of two twins with opposing personalities stars Mary-Kate and Ashley Olsen. The film prominently features the renowned Royal York Hotel, wide and spacious University Avenue, and the Lower Bay street subway station, which was originally refurbished for the movie *Don't Say a Word* (2001).

Cinderella Man (2005)

Director Ron Howard's depression-era biopic about boxer James J. Braddock's courageous comeback from financial doom stars Academy Award winners Russell Crowe and Renée Zellweger. The outside of The Bay, a downtown Toronto department store, was redressed to look like Madison Square Garden, while the legendary Maple Leaf Gardens was used for the fight sequences.

Get Rich or Die Tryin' (2005)

This biographical drama about and starring rapper Curtis "50 Cent" Jackson tells the story of the New York-born artist's rise from the son of a drug-dealing mother to a rich and respected rapper. The film inventively used Humber River Regional Hospital, Givens Shaw Public School, and The Big Bop nightclub to stand in as locations from Jackson's youth.

The Best Years of Our Lives

☆ ☆ ☆ ☆

Director William Wyler's The Best Years of Our Lives *(1946)
is a World War II movie without the war. Rather than
focusing on what America's fighting forces went through on
the battlefront, this film deals with what they faced when
they returned home and assimilated back into society—a
truly novel approach for the era in which it was made.*

A War Movie Like No Other

Inspired by a 1944 pictorial in *Time* magazine and a novella by
MacKinlay Kantor, *The Best Years of Our Lives* is the story of the
challenges faced by three servicemen as they leave the war behind
and try to pick up the pieces of their civilian lives. Army sergeant Al
Stephenson (Fredric March) barely knows the wife (Myrna Loy) he
left at home years earlier. Fred Derry (Dana Andrews) is a dashing
Air Force bombardier who is involved with two women: his party-
loving wife (Virginia Mayo) and Stephenson's daughter, Peggy
(Teresa Wright). And Homer Parrish (Harold Russell) is a sailor
and former football hero who returns to his high school sweetheart
fearful of her reaction to the hooks he wears in place of the hands
he lost in a fire.

The title *The Best Years of Our Lives* is somewhat ironic. Some
soldiers considered their "best years" to be those spent in the military
because they traveled the world and learned new skills. But after they
returned home, they had to settle for dead-end jobs, like Fred. Other
soldiers felt that the war had robbed them of their "best years"
because they came home scarred or disabled, like Al and Homer.
Either way, returning home was not always a joyous occasion.

A Unique Perspective

Released in 1946, just a year after the war's end and during a period
in which thousands of battle-weary servicemen were returning home
to an uncertain future, *The Best Years of Our Lives* portrayed an
aspect of the war that no other movie had dared address before, and
it did so with realism and compassion.

Clocking in at 172 minutes, the movie takes its time developing its main characters and the issues they face as they abandon their uniforms for civilian clothes. Viewers come to know them and their families intimately and, in doing so, understand their individual hopes and fears. In lieu of traditional movie action, we're treated to a realistic story without easy answers that certainly hit home for millions of postwar moviegoers. The film's realism is enhanced by legendary cinematographer Gregg Toland's deep-focus photography.

The performances in *The Best Years of Our Lives* are skillful and deeply nuanced. However, special mention must be made of Harold Russell, a veteran who really did lose his hands in the war and who had been fitted with prosthetic hooks. In Kantor's original story, Homer was a spastic. However, director William Wyler knew that no actor could convey such a condition with realism, so he briefly considered eliminating the character from the script—until he heard about Russell, whose prosthetic hands fit the bill perfectly. Wyler arranged to meet Russell, and the director was so impressed with the GI's attitude that he changed the character of Homer to accommodate Russell's disability.

A Surprise Hit

The Best Years of Our Lives proved to be a spectacular success. Filmed on a budget of around $2 million, it grossed more than $11 million in the United States during its initial run, which, by some accounts, made it the biggest box-office draw since *Gone with the Wind* in 1939.

More impressively, the film garnered seven Academy Awards: Best Picture; Best Director; Best Actor (Fredric March); Best Actor in a Supporting Role (Harold Russell); Best Film Editing; Best Music, Scoring of a Dramatic or Comedy Picture; and Best Writing, Screenplay (Robert E. Sherwood). Russell also received an honorary Oscar for "bringing hope and courage to his fellow veterans through his appearance in *The Best Years of Our Lives*." This made Russell the only actor ever to win two Academy Awards for the same role. However, he would not appear before the camera again until he made *Inside Moves* in 1980.

Fast Facts: Main Men

- *Humphrey Bogart is buried with a small, gold whistle. It was placed there by his wife Lauren Bacall in remembrance of her famous line to him in* To Have and Have Not *(1944): "You know how to whistle, don't you, Steve? You just put your lips together and blow." The two met on the set of that film, and Bogart gave the whistle to Bacall before they married.*

- *Cary Grant got his stage name from executives at Paramount Studios. They apparently thought the name Cary Grant would resonate with the public, though they first tried to get their new discovery to accept the name Cary Lockwood.*

- *Jimmy Stewart held a degree in architecture from Princeton University. He graduated in 1932, three years before his first credited film appearance.*

- *Jack Nicholson began his Hollywood career as a messenger boy for MGM. After he finished high school in the mid-1950s, he worked in the studio's cartoon department and mailroom.*

- *Paul Newman graduated from Ohio's Kenyon College in 1949. He worked in his family's sporting goods store, then sold copies of* Encyclopaedia Britannica *to pay for his tuition at the Yale Drama School.*

- *Robert Redford almost snagged the lead role of Ben Braddock in* The Graduate *(1967). But director Mike Nichols thought it would be unrealistic that Redford would have such a hard time getting the girl.*

- *James Dean died in a car crash shortly after getting a speeding ticket. While filming* Giant, *Dean appeared in a PSA for auto safety, ironically ending with the line: "The life you save may be … mine."*

- *Filmmakers had to get creative when working with Marlon Brando, who rarely memorized his lines. Cue cards were often employed, and in* Superman *(1978), Brando's lines were supposedly written on the baby Kal-El's diaper.*

- In 1964, Sidney Poitier became the first African American man to win an Academy Award, when he received the honor for his role in Lilies of the Field (1963). He later became the first black actor to leave his hand- and footprints at Grauman's Chinese Theatre.

- While under contract to MGM, Clark Gable balked at playing gangsters and villains. Studio head Louis B. Mayer decided to punish him by lending him to the much smaller Columbia Pictures to play the lead in a wacky little comedy called It Happened One Night (1934). Gable won an Oscar for the role.

- During the late 1960s, Harrison Ford worked as a carpenter in Los Angeles. He was apparently known as one of the finest cabinetmakers in the city, and he still does carpentry as a hobby.

- Clint Eastwood wrote the scores for some of his films, including Million Dollar Baby (2004) and Changeling (2008). Occasionally, his musician son, Kyle, scores his films, keeping it all in the family.

- Dustin Hoffman and Paul McCartney were having dinner together when Hoffman recounted the story of Pablo Picasso's last words: "Drink to me, drink to my health. You know I can't drink any more." As the story goes, McCartney picked up a guitar and started playing, and the song "Picasso's Last Words" was born.

- George Clooney's first steady acting job was on a mid-1980s medical sitcom called E/R, which also starred Elliott Gould and Jason Alexander. A decade later, he landed the role of Dr. Doug Ross in the hit medical drama ER. He's the only actor to star in two separate fictional series with the same name.

- Brad Pitt played plenty of sports in high school: He was on the golf, tennis, and swimming teams at Kickapoo High in Springfield, Missouri. He also belonged to the Forensics Club and the Key Club, a service organization for high school students.

Slasher Films

☆ ☆ ☆ ☆

It's easy for most of us to rattle off the iconic killers who rule the cinematic landscape of slasher films—Freddy, Jason, Michael Myers, Leatherface. But their reigns of terror were actually made possible by another movie maniac you've probably never heard of.

We all know the basic scenario that inevitably plays out in the standard slasher film: An unstoppable killer stalks a group of teens or young adults in a remote setting, using various sharp or pointy objects to dispatch them in workmanlike fashion until one would-be victim manages to do him in (until the next sequel, anyway). From the late 1970s through the 1980s, Hollywood made enormous profits by churning out dozens of these teen screamers. The films never used big-name actors and rarely deviated from the formula. All it seemed to take to draw in audiences was a killer who brought a modicum of creativity to his work and amassed a respectable body count.

As disturbing and provocative as these films were, they had a tendancy to offer a surprisingly conventional moral subtext. The killers usually suffered some cruel injustice in their formative years, and their murder sprees were often motivated by a quest for justice, as misdirected and twisted as it might seem. More importantly, the victims commonly engaged in some kind of socially unacceptable behavior—promiscuity, drug use, the betrayal of a friend—right before meeting their gruesome fates. The lone survivor, often a female (known as "the last girl" in horror terminology), would always be guiltless of any such transgressions.

Michael Myers Breaks Through

Although some early examples of the genre by independent film-makers—such as Tobe Hooper's *The Texas Chain Saw Massacre* (1974) and Bob Clark's *Black Christmas* (1974)—became well known in the early 1970s, film historians generally cite *Halloween* (1978) as the first mainstream slasher film. Directed by a young John Carpenter, *Halloween* featured capable actors—including Jamie Lee Curtis in her big-screen debut—and focused more on suspense than on the killings. The film was widely hailed as a modern horror masterpiece and is still remembered for its disturbing opening scene, in which the camera offers the killer's perspective as he commits his first murder. As a result, the viewer sees things through the eyes of a psychopathic killer. Critics at the time thought the technique was too disturbing because it forced audience members to identify with a psychopath who equates sex with violence. However, its success led to an onslaught of low-budget knockoffs, most notably the *Friday the 13th* series.

The popularity of these films eventually waned, though the late 1990s saw a resurgence of the genre with the *Scream* franchise, which freshened up the genre by featuring recognizable stars and having the characters make references to classic slasher films. More recently, series such as *Hostel* and *Saw* found a niche by delving into new levels of cruelty and violence, though they don't follow the traditional slasher premise. These movies established a new subgenre sometimes referred to as gornography, or torture porn. These cousins to the slasher movie feature villains who don't just kill their victims but torture them in remarkably horrific and protracted ways.

Fuad Who?

Ironically, the explicit gore that seems to be so innovative in these recent torture films actually harkens back to cinema's true original slasher—Fuad Ramses. Never heard of him? You're not alone. But *Blood Feast*, the 1963 film that featured him, made movie history by graphically depicting dismembered corpses and bloody entrails for the first time. Fuad, you see, was bent on performing a cannibalistic ritual that would resurrect an ancient Egyptian goddess. Right before the viewers' eyes, he kills a succession of young women and savagely harvests their body parts—chopping off limbs, gouging out brains, even tearing out a tongue with his bare hands. Produced on a budget of $25,000 by sexploitation pioneers Herschell Gordon Lewis and Dave Friedman, the poorly made film raked in $4 million and paved the way for all the slasher and gore films that would follow.

Hollywood on Ice

In Hollywood, the love of ice is usually confined to cocktail glasses. Yet some of the silver screen's stateliest stars have donned the blades and skated to box-office glory.

The Game That Kills (1937)
Rita Hayworth stars as the coach's daughter in this film that features gangsters, gamblers, goons, gals, and good guys. It's a mystery about a pro hockey player who is killed during a game. His brother is convinced it wasn't an accident and sets out to prove it.

Idol of the Crowds (1937)
The Duke straps on skates in this tall tale of a retired hockey player who returns to the game to make some money so he can improve and expand his chicken farm. It's worth the price of admission to see how they disguise John Wayne's complete lack of balance and skating skill.

Love Story (1970)
Hockey provides a backdrop that is often lost amid the tears that this film elicits. As a member of the Harvard Crimson hockey team, Ryan O'Neal's character falls in love Ali MacGraw, a wisecracking music student from the other side of the tracks. Academy Award-winning actor Ray Milland is quietly effective in the role of the disapproving father.

Slap Shot (1977)
George Roy Hill, the Academy Award-winning director of *The Sting* (1973), manages to muscle productive performances out of Paul Newman, Strother Martin, Michael Ontkean, and Lindsay Crouse in this madcap on-ice romp about a failing hockey team in a fledgling minor league.

Youngblood (1986)
Rob Lowe leaves the safety net of the Brat Pack to star with former NHL renegade Eric Nesterenko in this tale of an American hockey star who goes to Canada to see how the game is really played and learns some hard lessons. Keanu Reeves and Patrick Swayze are also featured.

The Cutting Edge (1992)
A spoiled figure skater can't find a doubles partner that she gets along with, so her trainer hires a former hockey player to fill the bill. Moira

Kelly and D. B. Sweeney star as the battling couple who fall in love on the ice, winning an Olympic medal in the process. Director Paul Michael Glaser (Starsky from *Starsky and Hutch*) elevates the material by focusing on his stars' chemistry.

The Mighty Ducks (1992)
Emilio Estevez stars as a hotshot lawyer who's cooled down by a drunk driving conviction and forced to coach a ragtag peewee hockey team as punishment for his crime. The movie was such a box-office hit that Disney decided to make a pair of sequels, buy an NHL team, and name the fledgling franchise after the flick (The Mighty Ducks of Anaheim).

Mystery, Alaska (1999)
Russell Crowe, Burt Reynolds, Hank Azaria, Mary McCormack, and writer/producer David E. Kelley join forces in this whimsical tale about a senior hockey team from a small Alaska community that challenges the New York Rangers to a grudge match in the great outdoors.

Miracle (2004)
Kurt Russell stars as U.S. Olympic hockey coach Herb Brooks in this portrayal of America's improbable victory over the highly favored Russian team at the 1980 Winter Olympics in Lake Placid, New York. Most of the actors who portrayed the real-life heroes were former hockey players with little or no acting experience.

Blades of Glory (2007)
In this over-the-top comedy, Will Ferrell and Jon Heder star as figure skaters who are banned from competition after a horrendous fistfight on the ice. When they realize that they are banned from competing as singles but not from *the pairs* competition, they swallow their pride, suppress their anger, and team up to get back on the ice.

The Love Guru (2008)
It was a bomb at the box office, but Mike Myers's misguided movie was actually a labor of love dedicated to his hometown Toronto Maple Leafs. In the last few decades, the real-life legion of lovable losers has offered much more comedic relief with their play on the ice than any Tinseltown treatment could produce.

Western Costume

☆ ☆ ☆ ☆

Where does a filmmaker go when a movie that's set in Victorian England, the antebellum South, or the battlefields of World War I requires authentic clothing for 500 extras? Western Costume is one of the few companies in the world that can provide it all.

One of the oldest film-related businesses in Hollywood, Western Costume was founded by Lou Burns in 1912. A former Indian trader, Burns had amassed a large collection of Native American clothing and artifacts before settling in Los Angeles. He approached William S. Hart, a pioneering actor and director of cowboy films, to point out how inaccurate the Native American clothing was in most films. Hart hired Burns as an advisor and supplier on his productions, and Western Costume was born.

The company quickly expanded to offer authentic outfits from any era or culture. It was involved in such important silent films as *The Birth of a Nation* (1915), *The Sheik* (1921), and *The Gold Rush* (1925). When sound was introduced to the movies, Western Costume provided outfits for the first film with spoken dialogue, *The Jazz Singer* (1927). The advent of color films brought a new emphasis on opulent wardrobes, and Western Costume stepped up to provide memorable period clothing for *Gone with the Wind* (1939) and *The King and I* (1956); the company also created what may be the most famous article of clothing ever to appear in a film— the ruby slippers Dorothy wore in *The Wizard of Oz* (1939). The list of classics that the company has outfitted seems endless—*West Side Story* (1961), *The Godfather* (1972), *Young Frankenstein* (1974), *Jurassic Park* (1993), *L.A. Confidential* (1997), and *Gangs of New York* (2002), to name a few.

Western Costumes is not open to the public most of they year, but if you happen to be in Hollywood during the month of October, the company does open its doors for Halloween rentals, allowing you to choose from actual costumes worn by stars in films such as *Ben-Hur* (1959), *Grease* (1978), and *The Untouchables* (1987).

Orson Welles

☆ ☆ ☆ ☆

Orson Welles was the type of director who always chose quality over quantity. While many of his contemporaries made far more motion pictures during their careers, every movie in which Welles was involved revealed the depth of his genius.

Jack-of-all-Trades

Orson Welles was born in Kenosha, Wisconsin, on May 6, 1915. His parents separated when he was six, and he lived with his mother, a skilled pianist, until her death two years later. After that, he lived with his father, an inventor and manufacturer, until his father died in 1930. Maurice Bernstein, a devoted friend of Welles's mother, became his guardian and enrolled him in the Todd School in Woodstock, Illinois, where he got his first taste of the theater. At an age when most children can't even spell Shakespeare, Orson could quote extensively from the Bard's plays and was even staging his own dramas. Welles graduated in 1931 and headed to Ireland on his own.

Welles made his stage debut at the Gate Theatre in Dublin in 1931, and he performed in numerous Shakespearean plays in the years that followed. In 1937, he and producer John Houseman formed the Mercury Theatre in New York City, which became known for its daring and innovative productions of the classics. A year later, he panicked the nation with a radio broadcast of H. G. Wells's *War of the Worlds,* which was structured like a series of news flashes interrupting a musical concert hour. Folks really thought Martians were invading New Jersey!

By this time, Welles had made a name for himself in both the theater and in radio. With each medium, he was known for experimenting with existing forms and narrative conventions so that his work was fresh and innovative. Given his triumphs in theater and notoriety in radio, it was not surprising that in 1940, Hollywood came calling with hopes that Welles could match that success in the film industry. Orson Welles was about to embark on a new artistic adventure—and he was only 25 years old! Newspaper columnists and press agents began calling him the "Boy Wonder" or "Boy Genius."

A Consummate Filmmaker

Welles moved to Hollywood in 1940, working under contract for RKO Pictures. It was an unprecedented contract for the time because Welles was allowed to star in, direct, write, or coproduce his films, or any combination thereof. This granted him a level of creative control that no other Hollywood director had at the time, and others resented him for it.

His first film was *Citizen Kane* (1941), which was loosely based on the life of newspaper magnate William Randolph Hearst. Almost everything about the movie— which Welles wrote, directed, and starred in—was revolutionary, from the deep-focus cinematography (in which the foreground, middle ground, and background of many scenes are all in focus) to his use of expressionist, high-contrast lighting and innovative sound effects to enhance dramatic mood. Response to *Citizen Kane* was tepid at the time of its release, but the film is now considered Welles's masterpiece and one of the greatest movies ever made.

Welles followed *Citizen Kane* with an adaptation of the popular Booth Tarkington novel *The Magnificent Ambersons* (1942). But the failure of *Kane* and RKO's dislike of Welles's vision of *Ambersons* resulted in his dismissal from the studio. Thus began his career-long difficulty with making films the way he wanted them made. In many ways, *Citizen Kane* was the highlight of his directorial career because he never again had the creative control he enjoyed on that film. Few industry insiders offered support, and there were many snide remarks both on and off the record at the expense of the "Boy Genius." Welles directed and starred in his next three films, *The Stranger* (1946), *The Lady from Shanghai* (1947), and *Macbeth* (1948), while scrounging for acting work at other studios. Welles's deep booming voice and his talent as an actor helped him earn a living, and he costarred in many other popular movies throughout his career, including *The Third Man* (1949), *The Long, Hot Summer* (1958), *A Man for All Seasons* (1966), and *Catch-22* (1970). On the stage, he appeared in a London production of *Othello* in 1951 and a New York production of *King Lear* in 1956.

Career in Decline

In the early 1950s, Welles moved to Europe, where he produced, directed, and starred in movie adaptations of *Othello* (1952) and *Mr. Arkadin* (1955). During this time, Welles's films weren't as well received as his earlier works, and his next American film, *Touch of Evil* (1958), which he directed and starred in, all but ended his illustrious directorial career.

Based on the novel *Badge of Evil* by Whit Masterson, *Touch of Evil* featured Charlton Heston as a Mexican police detective who becomes entangled in the criminal underworld of a corrupt Mexican border town. Upon completion, the movie was taken from Welles and reedited by the studio without his input. The resulting film was weakened by studio interference, but the visual style, innovative camerawork, and performances by Welles and costar Marlene Dietrich made the movie a favorite for generations of film enthusiasts. Disgusted by the studio's interference, Welles returned to Europe. In 1998—nearly four decades after its initial release—*Touch of Evil* was restored using a 50-page memo written by Welles and was rereleased in theaters so that the world could finally see the movie—considered by many critics to be Welles's second greatest film—the way the influential director had intended.

Talk-Show Favorite

Sadly, Welles became almost a caricature of himself in his later years, appearing frequently on late-night talk shows, shilling for a well-known wine company, and endorsing other products on television commercials in the United States and abroad.

None of that, however, can detract from the tremendous influence Orson Welles and his movies have had on Hollywood and the filmmakers who came after him. His motion pictures continue to stand as a testament to his skill and creativity, both in front of the camera and behind it.

Tracy and Hepburn

☆ ☆ ☆ ☆

Spencer Tracy and Katharine Hepburn are best remembered for their series of romantic comedies that rested on sharp-witted banter between the two stars. But their decades-long love affair was also one of the biggest open secrets in Hollywood.

Spencer Tracy and Katharine Hepburn both struggled to develop their careers during a difficult first decade in the film industry in the 1930s. Hepburn had enjoyed some significant early successes, such as the 1933 films *Morning Glory* and *Little Women,* but a string of lackluster roles and her headstrong nature and independent inclinations (the woman wore *pants,* for goodness sake!) gave her the reputation of being box-office poison until she found her niche with the smash hit *The Philadelphia Story* (1940). Tracy, too, had struggled to establish himself as leading-man material throughout the early '30s and frustrated studio execs with both his ego and his bouts of drinking. He finally began to gain the respect of audiences and his colleagues after his triumphs in *Captains Courageous* (1937) and *Boys Town* (1938).

A Turning Point

When Tracy and Hepburn met for the first time while filming *Woman of the Year* (1942), both were poised to either reach the pinnacle of Hollywood stardom or slip back to the ranks of second-tier celebrities. Fortunately for them—and for movie lovers everywhere—their perfect pairing in this and the eight subsequent battle-of-the-sexes comedies they would go on to film helped solidify their star images and ensure their places in Hollywood history.

The contrast of Tracy's gruff working-class sensibility and Hepburn's haughty educated persona made them one of the big screen's most volatile couples. In films such as *Without Love* (1945), *State of the Union* (1948), *Adam's Rib* (1949), and *Pat and Mike* (1952), they exchanged brilliantly witty barbs over politics, business, and the roles of men and women in modern society as they coyly courted each other in cat-and-mouse fashion. For Hepburn, the roles softened her reputation as a brash, headstrong woman by bringing credence to her progressive viewpoints while at the same time showing that an independent woman could still find love with a traditional man. Tracy, on the other hand, expanded his stout, fatherly image to become a credible, even desirable, romantic figure.

Offscreen Passion

The pair fell deeply in love on the set of their first film and embarked on a complicated but heartfelt 25-year-long affair that did much to fuel their on-screen chemistry. Tracy had been married since 1923 and, as a devout Catholic, would not consider divorce. Though known as a philanderer long before meeting Hepburn, he was apparently wracked by guilt over his unfaithfulness and often took it out on her in public. In seeming contrast to her outspoken reputation, Hepburn put up with the abuses simply because she was in love and, as she described it, that meant putting Tracy's needs before her own. While the circumstances of their relationship were unseemly and at times even unhealthy, many of their colleagues in the industry were moved by the obvious devotion and sacrifice that characterized the couple. Tracy remained married but continued his involvement with Hepburn until his death in 1967. Theirs was a match that only could have been made in Hollywood.

Tracy and Hepburn Filmography:
Woman of the Year (1942)
Keeper of the Flame (1942)
Without Love (1945)
The Sea of Grass (1947)
State of the Union (1948)
Adam's Rib (1949)
Pat and Mike (1952)
Desk Set (1957)
Guess Who's Coming to Dinner (1967)

From Soap Suds to the Silver Screen

Though much maligned by elitist critics, the soap opera genre represents a unique narrative form with both strengths and weaknesses, just like any other mode of storytelling. Soaps typically shoot around 100 pages of dialogue per day, and it's a challenge to keep a character fresh for months or years at a time. These are just a couple of reasons why soaps are a training ground for young actors. Many popular movie stars got their starts on the soaps. Here are some of the most notable.

Kevin Bacon
This prolific actor had a small role in *Animal House* (1978) before his 1979 TV debut on *Search for Tomorrow*. Then, from 1980 to 1981, he played a troubled teen on *Guiding Light*. Since then, Bacon has been involved in so many entertainment projects that there's even a game called "Six Degrees of Kevin Bacon," in which almost everyone in Hollywood is somehow linked to him. These days, in addition to acting, Kevin and his brother make music and tour as The Bacon Brothers.

Alec Baldwin
Film and television actor Alec Baldwin (*Glengarry Glen Ross*, 1992; *Malice*, 1993; *Pearl Harbor*, 2001; *The Good Shepherd*, 2006) made an impression on viewers as the strikingly handsome young Billy Allison Aldrich on *The Doctors* from 1980 to 1982.

Taye Diggs
Taye Diggs, star of movies (*How Stella Got Her Groove Back*, 1998), stage (*Rent*), and television (*Private Practice*), lit up the small screen as a talent scout named Adrian "Sugar" Hill on *Guiding Light* in 1997.

Tommy Lee Jones
From 1971 to 1975, this future Oscar winner played a bad seed on *One Life to Live*. As Dr. Mark Toland, Jones portrayed a moody man married to a frigid wife. The combination played out as a recipe for disaster, until finally, he was murdered by a woman while he was running from the law.

Demi Moore
In 1982, long before she starred in *Ghost* (1990), *A Few Good Men* (1992), and *G.I. Jane* (1997), Demi Moore beat out hundreds of

contenders for the role of Jackie Templeton on *General Hospital*. She was an instant sensation as a sassy reporter who went to great lengths to get a scoop.

Julianne Moore
A frequent gimmick on soap operas is for an actor to play twins—typically with opposite personalities. In the mid-1980s, Julianne Moore (*Magnolia*, 1999; *The Hours*, 2002) starred as Frannie and Sabrina on *As the World Turns*. Sabrina had been adopted by a wealthy couple and raised in England, while Frannie was the daughter of an all-American middle-class family.

Ryan Phillippe
Before tackling serious dramas such as *Flags of Our Fathers* (2006) and *Stop-Loss* (2008), Ryan Phillippe handled the controversial role of Billy Douglas, a gay teenager, on *One Life to Live* from 1992 to 1993. Soaps often feature a plot with a social message, and Billy's story line made a strong statement against hate crimes.

Meg Ryan
Before she was the queen of romantic comedies, Meg Ryan was tangled up in a love triangle on *As the World Turns*. From 1982 to 1984, the spunky actress portrayed good girl Betsy Stewart, who was in love with blue-collar Steve Andropoulos. Her stepfather didn't approve, so Betsy married unscrupulous Craig Montgomery instead. But true love prevailed when Betsy left Craig and married Steve in May 1984. Ryan's movie career took off after she left the show, and her memorable role in *When Harry Met Sally* (1989) solidified her place as a leading lady.

Amber Tamblyn
From 1995 to 2001, Amber Tamblyn played Emily Quartermaine, the kindhearted teenage daughter of Port Charles's wealthiest family on *General Hospital*. She later starred in the hit prime-time series *Joan of Arcadia* and the popular film series based on Ann Brashares's best-selling young-adult novel *The Sisterhood of the Traveling Pants* (2005).

Kathleen Turner
Kathleen Turner sizzled in *Body Heat* (1981)—her big screen debut—but fans of the daytime drama *The Doctors* already knew her as Nola. From 1978 to 1979, Kathleen played trampy Nola Dancy, a girl from the wrong side of the tracks who married someone from the right side.

Pop Quiz: More Famous Movie Quotes

So you think you know your movie quotes? See if you can match these famous quotes with their respective films.

1. "And I guess that was your accomplice in the wood chipper."

2. "Dad always used to say the only causes worth fighting for were the lost causes."

3. "Don't worship me until I've earned it."

4. "Excuse me while I whip this out."

5. "Get your stinkin' paws off me, you damn dirty ape!"

6. "I coulda been a contender."

7. "I'll be back."

8. "I'll never let anyone put me in a cage!"

9. "I'm not bad. I'm just drawn that way."

10. "I'm the king of the world!"

11. "I see dead people."

12. "I wanted to meet interesting and stimulating people of an ancient culture, and kill them."

13. "Look, you shoot off a guy's head with his pants down, believe me, Texas is not the place you wanna get caught."

14. "Open the pod bay doors, HAL."

15. "Schwing!"

16. "She's my sister *and* my daughter!"

17. "That's what I love about these high school girls, man: I get older, they stay the same age."

18. "To infinity and beyond!"

19. "You shall not pass!"

Answer Choices:

A. *Blazing Saddles* (1974)

B. *Breakfast at Tiffany's* (1961)

C. *Chinatown* (1974)

D. *Dazed and Confused* (1993)

E. *Fargo* (1996)

F. *Full Metal Jacket* (1987)

G. *The Lord of the Rings: The Fellowship of the Ring* (2001)

H. *Mr. Smith Goes to Washington* (1939)

I. *On the Waterfront* (1954)

J. *Planet of the Apes* (1968)

K. *The Sixth Sense* (1999)

L. *The Terminator* (1984)

M. *Terms of Endearment* (1983)

N. *Thelma & Louise* (1991)

O. *Titanic* (1997)

P. *Toy Story* (1995)

Q. *2001: A Space Odyssey* (1968)

R. *Wayne's World* (1992)

S. *Who Framed Roger Rabbit* (1988)

Rudolph Valentino

☆ ☆ ☆ ☆

Hollywood is chock-full of male sex symbols. However, none of today's pretty boys holds a candle to the great Rudolph Valentino. When the iconic Italian actor died unexpectedly in 1926 at age 31, many of his female fans were despondent to the point of suicide.

In 1895, Rodolfo Pietro Filiberto Raffaele Guglielmi di Valentina d'Antonguolla was born in Castellaneta, Italy, to Marie Berthe Gabrielle Barbin and Giovanni Antonio Giuseppe Fidele Guglielmi, a veterinarian who died of malaria when Rodolfo was 11. According to news reports at the time of Valentino's death, as a child, he was spoiled by his mother and was somewhat of a delinquent. Eager to leave his village, he set sail for America in 1913, where he worked odd jobs until landing a gig dancing at Maxim's, a nightclub for the wealthy in New York City, where he specialized in the tango. That led to a national dance tour, which eventually took him to Hollywood, where his dashing good looks and exotic persona propelled him to superstardom.

Hitting the Big Time

Indeed, Valentino quickly became one of the most popular actors of Hollywood's silent era, appearing in classics such as *The Sheik* (1921), *Blood and Sand* (1922), and *The Son of the Sheik* (1926), which turned out to be his last film. At the height of his career, Valentino was pulling in a whopping $7,500 per week!

Valentino's tragic end came while he was promoting *The Son of the Sheik.* He took ill on August 15, 1926, and was rushed to Polyclinic Hospital in New York City, where he was diagnosed with a ruptured appendix and gastric ulcers. Doctors performed surgery, but the actor's condition only worsened. He died on August 23 of peritonitis and a ruptured ulcer, complicated by septic pneumonia and septic endocarditis.

The public's outpouring of grief over Valentino's death was unlike anything seen before. Police had to cordon off the hospital to keep the growing throngs of female fans at bay. Legend has it that two women attempted suicide outside the hospital, while in London, actress Peggy Scott actually drank poison while gazing at photographs of the actor. An estimated 80,000 to 100,000 people passed through his open-casket viewing in New York City. Actress Pola Negri, who claimed she was engaged to Valentino, sent a floral arrangement that included 4,000 roses.

An Outpouring of Grief

When Valentino's body was transported to Hollywood, thousands of people watched the funeral train pass by. An invitation-only service was held at the Church of the Good Shepherd in Los Angeles, while a crowd estimated at 7,000 showed up at Hollywood Memorial Park, where the actor was entombed. Charlie Chaplin was a pallbearer, Lon Chaney and John Gilbert were ushers, and Cecil B. DeMille, Douglas Fairbanks, and Samuel Goldwyn were honorary pallbearers. Bushels of flowers were dropped from an airplane as Valentino's casket was carried to the vault in the Cathedral Mausoleum.

Valentino's burial there was supposed to be temporary while an elaborate mausoleum was constructed, complete with life-size statues of the actor in his most famous movie roles. But the Valentino estate simply didn't have the funds for such a memorial, and his resting place in the Cathedral Mausoleum became permanent.

Interestingly, Valentino's plot was owned by June Mathis, who is often credited with discovering the actor. Mathis died of a heart attack a year after Valentino, and his body was transferred to the vault intended for Mathis's husband, where it remains.

The Lady in Black

The bizarre theatrics surrounding Valentino's death didn't end after he was laid to rest. Since 1927, an annual memorial service has been held on the anniversary of his death. Over the years, the service has often been attended by the Lady in Black. Around 1930, a woman dressed all in black, her face hidden behind a veil, brought flowers to the actor's crypt; she continued the tradition for decades. Several rumors arose regarding the mystery woman's identity, including one that suggested she had been a gravely ill girl who had once been visited by Valentino.

Alas, the truth is a lot more complicated and cynical. In fact, there have been multiple ladies in black, some of them planted by

Paramount Pictures to continue Valentino's legend long after his death. The first was probably Ditra Helena Medford, also known as Ditra Flame, a former vaudeville performer who, in 1940, came forward as the Lady in Black. Flame was the head of the Valentino Memorial Guild, a fan organization, and she claimed she had been coming to Valentino's crypt incognito as the Lady in Black for years. She stepped up in 1940 in order to stake her claim as the original because she felt imposters were invading her territory. In the early 1950s, her appearances at the crypt irked the Valentino family, and there was much controversy over whether such theatrics were proper. In 1954, when the newspapers were much less respectful of Flame's devotion than they had been, she stopped going to the crypt on the anniversary of Valentino's death. She returned in the mid-1960s but dressed in street clothes like the other memorial attendees. In 1977, she changed her mind and began attending the memorial services as the Lady in Black once again.

In 1938, Paramount Pictures hired a woman to be a Lady in Black to coincide with the rerelease of *The Sheik* that year. Sometimes more than one Lady in Black showed up in the same year on the anniversary of Valentino's death, exploiting the theatricality of the whole phenomenon.

Other Ladies in Black included Marion Benda, a chorus girl who had been Valentino's date on the night he fell ill. Emotionally unstable, she actually believed Valentino had married and impregnated her. For a while, Benda and Ditra Flame fought it out in the press over who was the real deal, but Benda's outrageous lies and deteriorating mental condition gave Ditra's story the edge. Then there was Estrellita del Regil, a peculiar fan who claimed her mother had been the original Lady in Black and that she had become one to honor a family tradition. Other family members disputed this, but del Regil kept her vigil from 1976 to 1993.

And in 2002, 76 years after Valentino's death, a new Lady in Black emerged; Karie Bible has "taken the veil," so to speak, as a way to preserve Hollywood history.

Rudolph Valentino was the original Latin Lover, a role he played on-screen and off. And though his films are seldom shown today, dedicated fans continue to pay their respects and visit his final resting place.

Oscar: The Scoop on the Statue

The gold-plated statue that symbolizes silver screen success has had a rich and varied history, so much so that it deserves its own Tinseltown tribute. Here are a few tasty tidbits that honor Hollywood's holy grail.

- The silver screen status symbol was first dubbed "Oscar" in 1934 when Margaret Herrick, the Academy's librarian, remarked that the statue bore a striking resemblance to her uncle, Oscar Pierce. The gilded prize officially became known as Oscar in 1939.

- From 1942 until 1944, Uncle Oscar was plastered—literally. Because of a shortage of metal during World War II, the icon was molded from mortar instead of being gilded with gold. Later, the recipients were allowed to exchange their awards for gold-plated ones.

- The first Academy Award winner who refused to accept an Oscar was writer Dudley Nichols, who turned down his statue for the 1935 film *The Informer* because the Writers Guild was on strike at the time.

- Three-time Academy Award recipient Jack Nicholson reportedly uses one of his screen sculptures as a hat stand, while Oscar-winning couple Susan Sarandon and Tim Robbins allegedly display their pair of statues in the washroom.

- In 2000, 55 Oscar statues were stolen from a loading dock by a pair of pilfering employees. Fifty-two of the busts were found by a man rummaging through a downtown garbage bin. In a twist only Hollywood could have scripted, the stepbrother of the hero who found the missing merchandise was charged in the theft. Later in 2000, another statue turned up in the possession of lawyer Stephen Yagman. The 54th missing Oscar was discovered in 2003 when law enforcement agents raided a home in a drug bust. One of the legendary statues remains at-large.

- The saga of the stolen statue has also plagued actors William Hurt and Whoopi Goldberg. Hurt's prize was ripped off in 2005 while he was relocating. Whoopi's was clipped when she sent it back to the Academy to be cleaned. Goldberg's gilded guy was also discovered in a downtown trash bin in 2002. Hurt's prize is still on the loose.

Foodie Films

What could be better than sitting down to a movie with a big bucket of popcorn? How about sitting down to a movie with a buttery lobster, a juicy steak, or a piping hot wedge of lasagna? In every culture, food plays a significant role, so more than a few films over the years have focused on epicurean delights. Here are a few that are sure to get your stomach growling.

Babette's Feast (1987)
Based on a story by Danish writer Isak Dineson, this French–Danish movie won the Oscar for Best Foreign Language Film. Two beautiful young sisters, who have been forbidden to marry by their strict, religious father, grow old and increasingly bitter. They hire a needy French woman named Babette to cook and clean for them, but when Babette wins the Parisian lottery, she decides to leave town. Before she goes, she cooks a sumptuous French meal for the sisters and their nearly forgotten suitors. The images of Babette's dinner are downright delectable, and the movie delicately stirs themes of love, faith, and patience into each bite.

Fried Green Tomatoes (1991)
A movie about friendship, inspiration, and tasty home cookin', *Fried Green Tomatoes* gets labeled as a "chick flick" but truly has something for everyone. Based on the popular novel by Fannie Flagg, the movie follows a forty-something woman (Kathy Bates) as she tries to get her husband's attention. She meets an elderly woman (Jessica Tandy) in need of a friend and listens to her tale of friendship, mystery, and intrigue. In turn, the muddled middle-ager is inspired to seize the day and tend to what's truly important in life. You'll have to watch the film to learn the integral part the title dish plays in the stories of several generations of strong Southern women.

Like Water for Chocolate (1993)
It's Mexico. It's hot. It's 1910, and Tita is bound by tradition not to marry while she cares for her elderly mother, but of course, Tita falls in love with Pedro. To be close to Tita, Pedro marries her sister (gee, thanks honey), but of course, Tita and Pedro can't contain their passion for each other. In the film, which was adapted from a novel by Laura Esquivel and directed by her husband, Alfonso Arau, Tita shows her

feelings through her cooking and the result is ... well, *hot*. You can't miss the steamy, though sometimes heavy-handed, love scenes. Be warned: You'll probably have a craving for either hanky-panky, guacamole, or chocolate by the time the credits roll.

Big Night (1996)
Written by actor Stanley Tucci and codirected by Tucci and actor Campbell Scott, *Big Night* follows the trials, tribulations, and tiramisus of a pair of Italian brothers who are trying to make their New Jersey restaurant a success in the 1950s. The story is based on Tucci's own experiences and examines the conflict between art and commerce. A rival restaurant nearby offers bigger portions of inferior food and terrible Chianti but continues to thrive, while the brothers' smaller restaurant struggles. A plan is hatched for a "big night" to honor singer Louis Prima at the restaurant, and the characters scramble to make everything perfect. The movie is stocked with great scenes around the table and in the kitchen and offers laughs, some Old World nostalgia, and a whole lotta pasta!

Chocolat (2000)
Nominated for five Academy Awards, this sensuous film is packed with exceptional actors and a lot of cocoa powder. Juliette Binoche plays Vianne, a chocolatier who opens up shop in a sleepy French village to find that her product inspires latent passions in the villagers. Not everyone is pleased about this, especially the town's stuffy mayor, played brilliantly by Alfred Molina. When heartthrob Johnny Depp comes to town, he and Vianne find their hearts melting like a couple of bonbons. The movie is languid and lighthearted—perfect for an after-dinner treat.

Ratatouille (2007)
The combination of food and rodents doesn't readily appeal to most, but somehow it works in Pixar's *Ratatouille*. This animated feature follows the adventures of Remy, a rat with culinary skills that lead him all the way to the kitchen of a famed Parisian restaurant. Director Brad Bird (*The Incredibles*, 2004) keeps *Ratatouille* sizzling with dazzling animation, hilarious details, and more than a few heartwarming moments. And we promise: No rodents were harmed during the making of this film.

Love on the Set:
The Bergman-Rossellini Scandal

☆ ☆ ☆ ☆

It didn't take much to rock the staid conventions of society in the 1950s. A director and his leading lady found that out the hard way.

It began with a fan letter sent in 1949. "I saw your films . . . and enjoyed them very much," the letter began. It was addressed to Italian filmmaker Roberto Rossellini and was written by none other than actress Ingrid Bergman, who wrote it after seeing his movie *Open City* (1945). Bergman's letter also suggested that he direct her in a film. Their resulting collaboration was 1950's *Stromboli,* but the movie was eclipsed by the controversy that swirled around the couple when word got out that the married Bergman was having a baby by Rossellini, who was also married. The ensuing scandal engulfed Bergman in a scarlet torrent of hatred so vitriolic that she would find herself branded on the floor of the U.S. Senate as "a horrible example of womanhood and a powerful influence for evil."

A Hollywood Success Story

Since taking America by storm in *Intermezzo: A Love Story* (1939), the talented Swedish-born Bergman had costarred with Humphrey Bogart in *Casablanca* (1942), been menaced by Charles Boyer in *Gaslight* (1944), and been romanced on-screen by Cary Grant, Gary Cooper, and Gregory Peck. Audiences loved her in strong but pious roles such as the nun in *The Bells of St. Mary's* (1945). In fact, Bergman had been Hollywood's top box-office female draw three years in a row. To the public, the beautiful actress with the sunny smile had it all: a fabulous career, an adoring husband, and a devoted daughter. But privately, Bergman's marriage had entered rocky shoals, and she was looking for new acting challenges after the failure of her pet film project, *Joan of Arc* (1948). Consequently, the idea of working with Rossellini—a director being hailed for his mastery of what would come to be called Italian neorealist cinema—was appealing. Bergman later admitted, "I think that deep down I was in love with Roberto from the moment I saw *Open City.*"

On Location

Stromboli was filmed on location in Italy, and rumors of an affair between Bergman and Rossellini soon reached America. During filming, Bergman received a letter from Joseph Breen, head of America's stentorian Production Code office—which enforced morality in motion pictures—asking her to deny rumors of the affair. Instead, on December 13, 1949, the woman who had played a nun and other saintly figures admitted she was carrying Rossellini's love child. A firestorm of negative publicity followed the announcement.

Bergman was reproached by Roman Catholic priests and received thousands of letters denouncing her—she was even warned not to return to America. On February 2, 1950, Bergman and Rossellini's son, Robertino, or Robin, was born. Less than two weeks later, *Stromboli* was released in the United States to disastrous reviews and very little business.

The Storm Grows

The scandal reached critical mass (and the height of lunacy) on March 14, when Senator Edwin C. Johnson railed against Bergman on the Senate floor. Johnson proposed a bill that would protect America from the scourge that film stars of questionable "moral turpitude," such as Bergman, threatened. He suggested future misconduct could be avoided if actors were required to be licensed, with the license being revoked for salacious behavior. Though this idea was met with derision, Bergman's career in Hollywood was all but dead.

After divorcing their spouses, Bergman and Rossellini wed in Mexico on May 24, 1950. The couple continued to make films together in Italy and had twin girls Isabella (who went on to her own film stardom) and Isotta Ingrid in 1952. By the time Bergman was hired to star in *Anastasia* in 1956, America was ready to forgive her, and the actress was rewarded with both the New York Film Critics Award and her second Best Actress Oscar. By that point, her marriage to Rossellini—tested by financial problems and the director's affair while making a film in India—was nearing an end.

Bergman would go on to another marriage and further acclaim in her career, but she was always quick to point to the importance of her relationship with Rossellini, and the two remained devoted. Bergman died of breast cancer in 1982 on her 67th birthday.

Hollywood's Urban Legends

If ever there was a breeding ground for urban legends, it would be in the Hollywood Hills. Simply put, people love to hear all sorts of gossip about stars and movies... the weirder the better. Here are some of the strangest urban legends to come out of Hollywood.

Humphrey Bogart was the Gerber Baby

Everyone knows the famous black-and-white drawing of the baby that graces Gerber baby food products. Well, there's an urban legend that the baby is none other than actor Humphrey Bogart. This legend probably took off due to the fact that Bogart's mother, Maud, was a commercial illustrator who actually did sell drawings of her son to advertising agencies. In fact, she did allow one of her drawings of Humphrey to be used in a baby food advertisement—for Mellin's Baby Food. However, Gerber did not start producing baby food until 1928, and by that time, Bogart was 29 years old, making it unlikely—but not impossible—that Bogart could be the Gerber baby. We now know that Ann Turner Cook was the lucky model in 1928. She was drawn by artist Dorothy Hope Smith, who submitted the drawing to Gerber.

Disney on Ice

In life, Walt Disney warmed the hearts of millions. In death, Disney is rumored to have had himself frozen until such a time that scientists could warm him up and bring him back to life. What sounds like something out of a sci-fi movie may have been rooted in the fact that Walt Disney liked to keep his personal life private, so when he died, specifics about his burial were kept under wraps, leading to all sorts of speculation. Rumors were further fueled when Disney was buried in Forest Lawn Cemetery in Glendale, California, which does not publicly list who is interred there. But Walt Disney's unfrozen remains are indeed there, in the Freedom Mausoleum, along with those of several family members.

Three Men and a Baby... and a Ghost!

There's a scene in the movie *Three Men and a Baby* (1987) in which Ted Danson's character, Jack, and his mother are walking through Jack's house while the mother is holding the baby. As they walk in front of a window, the ghostly image of a boy is seen standing in the background. When the characters walk by the window a second time, the boy has been replaced by what appears to be a shotgun. Legend has it that the ghost belongs to a boy who accidentally shot himself to death with a shotgun in the house where the movie was filmed.

Of course, the truth is a little less spooky. What many people mistake for the boy's apparition is nothing more than a cardboard cutout of Danson, which was supposed to be part of a sub-plot involving Jack's appearance in a dog food commercial. And those scenes weren't filmed in a house, either. They all took place on a studio set in Toronto.

Munchkin Suicide in *The Wizard of Oz*

In *The Wizard of Oz* (1939), shortly after Dorothy and the Scarecrow convince the Tin Man to join their posse, they begin singing and skipping down the Yellow Brick Road. As they round the bend in the road and dance off the screen, a strange, dark shape can be seen moving in a bizarre fashion to the left of the road. It is said that one of the Munchkins, heartbroken over a failed love affair, chose to take his own life as the cameras rolled. It makes for a creepy story, but there's no truth to it. What people are actually seeing is nothing more than an exotic bird flapping its wings. Prior to filming, the director decided that adding strange, exotic birds to the scene would add a bit more color, so he rented several such birds from the Los Angeles Zoo and allowed them to roam freely about the set.

Bill Cosby vs. *The Little Rascals*

During the late 1950s and '60s, the *Our Gang* comedy shorts from the 1930s and '40s were rerun on television under the name *The Little Rascals*. Though broadcast under a new name for a new generation, the shorts were the same old movies from back in the day. Nothing was updated, including the racist stereotypes imparted upon black cast members Matthew "Stymie" Beard and Buckwheat. During the 1970s, when *The Little Rascals* had all but disappeared from the tube, rumors circulated that comedian Bill Cosby, a positive African American role model, had purchased the rights to the *Our Gang* series so they would never be made public again. However, there was no truth to the rumor. The truth is much less salacious—the outdated content of the *Our Gang* series simply did not appeal to audiences at the time.

A Law for the Future Uncle Fester

As the bizarre and bald member of The Addams Family *TV series (1964–1966), the frighteningly adorable Uncle Fester charmed fans young and old. This was nothing new; actor Jackie Coogan had been wowing audiences since childhood.*

Born John Leslie Coogan, little Jackie was the son of vaudevillians, who, like many, spent their careers on the road, families in tow, traveling the different theater circuits, much like musical acts do today. Many vaudevillian families incorporated their children into their acts, with little thought to their suitability for such a life or their long-term educations. Charlie Chaplin caught Jackie's act in Los Angeles and was so impressed that he cast the boy in a comedy short called *A Day's Pleasure* (1919). This association with Chaplin led to his first feature role in the classic *The Kid* (1921).

Appearing in popular silent films such as *The Kid* and *Oliver Twist* (1922) cemented the child actor's status. The cute kid with the pageboy haircut raked in a whopping $4 million before his 18th birthday, making him one of Hollywood's highest paid performers of the time. Clearly, the only thing small about Coogan was his stature.

Despite ruling the popularity roost, Coogan found his financial state far from secure. His parents had complete control of his holdings, but tragically for Jackie, his parents didn't have his best interests in mind. Through a combination of greed and ineptness, the dastardly duo drove Jackie Coogan Productions straight into the ground. After a 1935 accident claimed the life of his father, a grown-up Coogan realized what had happened, but the damage had already been done. After suing the family company to reclaim his earnings in 1938, Coogan would recoup just $126,000. The sum represented one-half of the floundering firm's remaining value.

Coogan's predicament made headlines and caused people to question how such a travesty could happen. To spare other child actors a similar plight, in 1939, the State of California enacted the California Child Actor's Bill (aka the Coogan Act), which directs a portion of a child actor's earnings into a trust fund. The sweeping law came too late for a young Jackie Coogan, but at least the child star's loss had not been in vain.

The Wit and Wisdom of Alfred Hitchcock

Most film fans think of Alfred Hitchcock as a cinematic genius whose understanding of filmmaking techniques has rarely been surpassed, but he was also a savvy manipulator of the media. Hitch liked to provoke attention with his observations on the mystery genre and the macabre, which added to his image as "The Master of Suspense." In more serious contexts, he made insightful comments about the medium of film that directors are still learning from today. Here are a few of his droll quips:

- "What is drama but life with the dull bits cut out?"

- "There is no terror in a bang, only in the anticipation of it."

- "Our evil and our good are getting closer together today."

- "People always think villains are extraordinary, but in my experience they are usually rather ordinary and boring...."

- "I never look through the camera; I think only of that white screen that has to be filled up the way you fill up a canvas. That's why I draw rough setups for the cameraman."

- "As far as I'm concerned, the film has been made on paper, that's the most important and fascinating stage.... I wish I didn't have to go into a studio."

- When a parent complained to the director that his daughter refused to take a shower after seeing *Psycho* (1960), Hitchcock replied, "Have her dry cleaned."

- "In films, murders are always very clean. I show how difficult it is and what a messy thing it is to kill a man."

- "Television has brought back murder into the home—where it belongs."

- "I never said all actors are cattle, what I said was all actors should be treated like cattle."

- "When an actor comes to me and wants to discuss his character, I say, 'It's in the script.' If he says, 'But what's my motivation?,' I say, 'Your salary.'"

Doug Jones: Acting Incognito

☆ ☆ ☆ ☆

Odds are very good you've seen actor Doug Jones in one of the dozens of films he's made, perhaps even in a featured role. But the chances are equally good that if you were introduced to him, you'd swear you'd never seen him before.

Fast-Food Start

Actor Doug Jones has appeared in more than 40 films and many TV shows, but even the most avid film buff could likely pass him on the street or sit down next to him on the bus without recognizing him. While he has often played minor characters that are identified in the credits with rather anonymous descriptions such as "Thin Infected Man" or "Sewer Imp," Jones has also appeared in featured roles in well-known films including the *Hellboy* series, *Pan's Labyrinth* (2006), and *Fantastic Four: Rise of the Silver Surfer* (2007). How can an actor who has played leading characters in world-famous films remain unrecognized? Because most of the time, Jones portrays nonhuman characters and wears heavy makeup and prosthetics.

Jones first became interested in acting while attending college in the Midwest where he grew up. He moved to Hollywood in 1985, shortly after graduation, hoping to break into the business. He appeared in a number of music videos and television commercials, and it was one of those TV spots that introduced him to the world of prosthetics. He made a series of commercials for McDonald's as "Mac Tonight," a piano-playing crooner with a giant crescent-moon-shaped head (to the folks at McDonald's that seemed like a logical way to hawk burgers). Eventually, both Jones and the Hollywood industry recognized that he had a unique combination of skills that made him perfect for this kind of work. He stands a lanky 6′4″ and has had formal training as a mime and a contortionist. And if that wasn't enough, he is loose-jointed in both legs. He began taking makeup-laden roles such as the likable zombie Billy Butcherson in the Disney Halloween comedy *Hocus Pocus* (1993), a giant mutant insect in the sci-fi thriller *Mimic* (1997), and a yeti in the live-action/animation romp *Monkeybone* (2001). Before long, Jones had become a go-to performer for filmmakers needing to cast roles with unusual physical requirements. But it was his work with director Guillermo del Toro that first began to bring Jones recognition outside the industry.

Headline Roles

The pair had met each other on the set of *Mimic*, which del Toro directed, and hit it off at a lunch during which the director eagerly quizzed Jones on his experience playing nonhuman roles. Years later, during preproduction for the comic-book film *Hellboy* (2004), del Toro was reviewing character sketches with his staff when one of them pointed to the rendering of a lanky, fishlike creature named Abe Sapien and said it reminded him of Doug Jones. The director agreed and gave his old colleague the high-profile role as the psychic sidekick to the title character. Jones gained wide recognition for his expressive physical portrayal of the sensitive character, despite the fact that the voice was dubbed by David Hyde Pierce of *Frasier* fame. When del Toro began work on his masterful fable *Pan's Labyrinth* (2006), he cast Jones as the mythical title character who guides a young girl on her journey through a fairy-tale world. Jones also took on the role of the menacing Pale Man for the film, which won an Oscar for makeup. In 2007, he earned a plum role in the *Fantastic Four* sequel as the Silver Surfer, though the character was voiced by Laurence Fishburne. Although the film garnered mixed critical reviews, Jones's amazing physical portrayal of the other-worldly being earned him universal acclaim.

- *Jones landed a more traditional role in* My Name Is Jerry *(2009), an indie comedy about a down-on-his-luck door-to-door salesman who can barely utter, "My name is Jerry," before doors slam in his face. Jerry is also a father to a teenager and has a love interest, allowing Jones to express emotions generally not part of his shtick.*

Horse-ing Around

For decades, directors have been moved to make movies about horses. In fact, the subgenre of films about the majestic animals offers dozens of horse-centric movies to choose from. Most of the films have similar themes: nobility in the face of cruelty, loyalty between animal and human, and strength in times of adversity. So curl up with some oats, and check out some of the most famous horse movies in the stable.

Black Beauty (1921, 1933, 1946, 1971, and 1994)

Anna Sewell's 1877 novel, narrated from the point of view of a horse, has been adapted for the silver screen at least five times. In addition to the films, several TV versions have been made, too. A favorite amongst fans seems to be the 1946 black-and-white film version starring Mona Freeman, but with so many adaptations to choose from, you can see the touching story of Beauty in a variety of styles from different eras.

My Friend Flicka (1943)

If you want the full story of the horse named Flicka, you should probably read the 1941 book by author Mary O'Hara. The film version tones down the story for younger audiences, but the basics are the same: A young boy, played by the talented Roddy McDowall, befriends a horse and the pair experience many joys, trials, and tribulations, which bring them closer together. A television series based on the story aired in the late 1950s, and you can still catch it in reruns from time to time.

National Velvet (1944)

Before she was Cleopatra, Elizabeth Taylor was Velvet Brown, a young girl whose love for a horse named "The Pie" keeps it out of the glue factory. After Velvet saves the horse, she trains it to compete in the Grand National horse race, with the help of an embittered ex-jockey, played by Mickey Rooney. When the jockey hired to ride her beloved horse shows his lack of faith in the animal, Velvet decides to disguise herself as a boy and ride him herself. In 1978, a less beloved sequel, *International Velvet*, was released.

The Black Stallion (1979)

This film, produced by Francis Ford Coppola, is the classic "boy and his horse" story. A boy and an Arabian stallion are shipwrecked together on an island. The two keep their distance for a while, but a friendship blossoms—cue swelling music and stirring scenes of galloping on the beach. When the two are rescued, "The Black" is entered into a nail-bitingly close race. The boy is coached by a former jockey, played by Mickey Rooney in a nod to his role in *National Velvet*. Beautifully directed by Carroll Ballard, who was adept at handling nature-driven stories, *The Black Stallion* is high drama fit for the whole family.

The Horse Whisperer (1998)

This film, starring Robert Redford, Kristin Scott-Thomas, and a young Scarlett Johannson, tells the tale of a traumatized young girl and her equally troubled horse. A trainer seems to magically heal the horse, which helps to heal the girl. Featuring sweeping shots of the wide-open Montana landscape, a romantic spark between the trainer and the girl's mother, and lots of tear-jerking moments, *The Horse Whisperer* got mixed reviews, but it is a well-crafted adult drama directed by Redford.

Seabiscuit (2003)

During the Great Depression, stories about underdogs (or underhorses, for that matter) were eaten up by a public needing a shot of hope. Enter Seabiscuit, an undervalued, undersized thoroughbred whom no one thought could win any races. Seabiscuit proved them all wrong. His story was first turned into a best-selling book by Laura Hillenbrand before it became an acclaimed film starring Jeff Bridges, William H. Macy, and Tobey Maguire.

Hidalgo (2004)

Based on the life of Frank Hopkins, a cowboy who rode with Buffalo Bill's Wild West Show, *Hidalgo* tells the story of a man, his horse (that's Hidalgo), and a race that no one believed he could win. Set against the backdrop of the Arabian desert, *Hidalgo* follows Hopkins, played by a rugged Viggo Mortensen, as he dodges those who would have him lose the centuries-old Ocean of Fire race across the desert. A little love interest and a lot of white-knuckle moments with a steed that just won't quit make this movie a must-see for horse lovers.

Development Hell

☆ ☆ ☆ ☆

Hollywood studios buy the rights to dozens of novels, video games, comics, and original screenplays every year. But before a movie is made, it goes through a process known as "development," which includes all stages from the conception of the story through the first versions of the script to the signing of contracts. This can be a tortuous and often unending process for screenwriters and filmmakers, whose projects get stuck in development so long that their artistic vision is changed beyond all recognition. Some projects remain in this "Development Hell" for decades before production begins, while many others never emerge. It seems that in Development Hell, no one can hear the writers scream.

Everyone Has an Opinion...

And nowhere is this truer than in Hollywood. As different directors and production execs are attached to a project, they invariably bring their own opinions about how the script should be changed. When a studio or production company believes a project is no longer timely or viable, it goes into "turnaround," meaning that the studio sells off the rights to the story in return for all or some of the development costs incurred to that point. This process can be repeated over and over for months, years, or even decades.

Watchmen—More than 20 Years in Development

In 1987, 20th Century Fox purchased the movie rights to Alan Moore's celebrated graphic novel *Watchmen.* For 20 years, the project languished in Development Hell before a big-screen adaptation finally hit theaters in 2009. Fox developed the script until the mid-1990s when it was picked up by Warner Bros. Famed action producer Joel Silver (*The Matrix*, 1999) and director Terry Gilliam (*12 Monkeys*, 1995) worked on the project, but in the end, Silver was unable to raise the capital for the $100 million budget, and Gilliam decided that *Watchmen* would be better as a miniseries.

In 2001, the project reemerged at Universal Studios. Screen-writer David Hayter (*X-Men*, 2000) was hired to pen a new draft, but Universal wouldn't let him direct, so the project went into turnaround yet again. Paramount picked it up in 2004 and hired director Darren Aronofsky (*Requiem for a Dream*, 2000). When he dropped out to shoot *The Fountain* (2006), the studio turned to Paul Greengrass (*The Bourne Supremacy*, 2004). This time the movie progressed as far as screen-testing actors, but an escalating budget and a change of studio heads at Paramount curtailed the project once more. In 2005, the project was back at Warner Bros. with Zack Snyder (*Dawn of the Dead*, 2004) as director. After Alex Tse reworked Hayter's script, the movie finally went into production and shooting began in 2007.

A Confederacy of Dunces

No, this isn't a reference to the Hollywood studio system but rather to John Kennedy Toole's Pulitzer Prize-winning comic novel. In 1980, the movie rights to the book were picked up by 20th Century Fox. But a series of events have kept the project in Development Hell ever since. First, many consider it nearly impossible to translate the humor of *Dunces* to film because it primarily stems from the eccentric musings of the central character, Ignatius J. Reilly. In 1982, John Belushi had agreed to play Ignatius, with Richard Pryor costarring. But Belushi died of an accidental overdose before he could seal the deal.

John Candy and later Chris Farley were also considered for the lead role before their untimely deaths. By 2003, the project had been picked up by Oscar-winning director/producer Steven Soderbergh (*Traffic*, 2000). The script was rewritten, and Will Ferrell agreed to play Ignatius. However, difficulties later emerged over the publishing rights and filming was initially pushed back to 2007 before being scrapped altogether. British writer/comedian Stephen Fry has written a version of the script, but as yet, the project remains locked in Development Hell at Paramount.

More in Development Hell

A movie adaptation of the DC Comics creation *Wonder Woman* has been in Development Hell for years. And in the mid-1990s, Hollywood began developing a movie version of the popular 1970s TV show *The Six Million Dollar Man*. If *Watchmen* is any guide, expect it to reach theaters sometime around 2018.

Fast Facts: Movie Props

- *The record for the greatest number of props used in a single movie belongs to* Gone with the Wind *(1939), which boasted more than 1,250,000 items.*

- *The telephone that Harpo Marx ate in* The Cocoanuts *(1929) was made of chocolate, and the bottle of ink he drank was cola. Similarly, the old shoe Charlie Chaplin ate in* The Gold Rush *(1925) was made of licorice.*

- *The gun used by Johnny Mack Brown in the 1930 version of* Billy the Kid *was William "Billy the Kid" Bonney's actual firearm. And Wild Bill Hickok's pocket Derringer was used as a prop in the 1924 Western* The Iron Horse.

- *The golden spike that united the Union Pacific and Central Pacific Railroads at Promontory Point, Utah, in 1869, was used to reenact that remarkable event in the 1939 flick* Union Pacific.

- *For the 1916 war drama* The Crisis, *the U.S. government loaned filmmakers the dispatch box (a box for holding official papers and transporting them from place to place) used by Abraham Lincoln during his presidency.*

- *The severed horse's head that made such an impact in* The Godfather *(1972) was real. It came from a butcher's shop.*

- *Jimmy Stewart kept every hat he wore in a movie starting with his debut in* The Murder Man *in 1935.*

- *The simple, tattered hat worn by Henry Fonda in* On Golden Pond *(1981) was once owned by Spencer Tracy, who had received it as a gift from the great director John Ford. It was given to Fonda as a gift by his costar, Katharine Hepburn, during their first day on the set.*

- *The armor worn by Geraldine Farrar in the 1916 movie* Joan the Woman *was crafted of pure silver. This wasn't because of extravagance, but for necessity—prior to the widespread use of aluminum, silver was the lightest durable metal available.*

- *In Legal Eagles (1986), starring Robert Redford, $10 million worth of original paintings and sculptures were used as props. Among them were works by Roy Lichtenstein and Pablo Picasso.*

- *One of the most expensive props ever featured in a movie was the full-size replica of a Spanish galleon constructed for Roman Polanski's Pirates (1986). It cost more than $10 million to make.*

- *Custard pies were a staple of early slapstick comedies, but directors found that real custard pies fell apart when tossed. A California pastry shop solved the dilemma by creating pies with double-thick crusts and a filling of flour, water, and whipped cream. Today, shaving cream is also used.*

- *Milk was added to the water used to create the raindrops in Singin' in the Rain (1952) so they would show up better on film.*

- *The swarm of locusts in The Good Earth (1937) was created by filming coffee grounds settling in water, then reversing the film.*

- *Perhaps the most amazing effect of all, though, is the parting of the Red Sea in Cecil B. DeMille's The Ten Commandments (1923). This effect was created by pouring water over two giant blocks of clear gelatin, then reversing the film.*

- *In The Maltese Falcon, the aforementioned bird symbolizes "the stuff that dreams are made of." Supposedly, two heavy lead falcons were made for the film, each weighing more than 40 pounds. Sources claim that the second was made because the first was dented when it was dropped on the film's star, Humphrey Bogart.*

Marilyn Monroe

☆ ☆ ☆ ☆

Marilyn Monroe was—and still is—one of the sexiest women ever to grace the silver screen. But, like so many of her fellow movie stars, Monroe's deeply troubled personal life often overshadowed her professional achievements. This was especially true when the world learned of her tragic death on August 5, 1962, at age 36.

Troubled Beginnings

Marilyn Monroe was born Norma Jean Baker on June 1, 1926. Her life was troubled almost from the start; her mother was institutionalized with mental problems, and the man she was told was her father, Edward Mortensen, was killed in a motorcycle accident when she was three. As a result, Norma Jean spent most of her childhood in foster care.

Norma Jean married at 16, then found success as a model, which eventually led to a name change and a brief contract with 20th Century Fox. Her first credited role came in *Dangerous Years* (1947). It was a critical flop, and studio head Darryl F. Zanuck didn't know what to do with this breathy starlet, so her contract was not renewed. However, she later returned and made most of her films for Fox.

Monroe's chaotic personal life made constant news. She married baseball legend Joe DiMaggio in 1954, but their union was tumultuous, and they divorced nine months later. In 1956, she married playwright Arthur Miller, who was nearly 11 years her senior; the marriage lasted until 1961. There are rumors that Monroe was also involved with President John F. Kennedy and his brother Robert as well.

A Hollywood Starlet's Tragic End

In her final months, Monroe was living in a house in the Brentwood section of Los Angeles. On the evening of August 4, she was visited by her psychiatrist, Dr. Ralph Greenson, then she made several phone calls from her bedroom, including one to actor Peter Lawford, a Kennedy family confidante.

Late that night, Monroe's housekeeper, Eunice Murray, noticed a light coming from under the actress's bedroom door, which she thought was odd. When Monroe didn't respond to her knocks, Murray went around to the side of the house and peered through the bedroom window. Monroe looked peculiar, Murray later told police, so she called Greenson, who broke into Monroe's bedroom and found her on the bed unconscious. Greenson then called Monroe's personal physician, Dr. Hyman Engelberg, who pronounced the actress dead. It was then that the police were notified.

Los Angeles Police Sgt. Jack Clemmons was the first on the scene. He said he found Monroe naked and facedown on her bed with an empty bottle of sleeping pills nearby. A variety of other pill bottles littered the nightstand.

Monroe's body was taken to Westwood Village Mortuary then transferred to the county morgue, and her house was sealed and placed under guard. Los Angeles Deputy Medical Examiner Dr. Thomas T. Noguchi performed Monroe's autopsy and concluded in his official report that the actress had died from an overdose of Nembutol (a sleeping pill) and chloral hydrate (a mild sedative) and ruled that it was a "probable suicide."

Suicide, Murder, or Accidental Overdose?

Over the years, conspiracy theorists have had a field day with Monroe's death because of numerous inconsistencies between Noguchi's autopsy report and the evidence at the scene, as well as in the stories of those who were at the scene. Some conspiracy theorists believe that Monroe was murdered and that her death was made to look like a suicide. By whom remains a mystery, though the most prevalent theory—unproved by anyone—is that the Kennedy family had her killed to avoid a scandal. However, given Monroe's habit of taking more medication than doctors prescribed, because she thought she had a high tolerance for it, accidental overdose cannot be ruled out.

Today, Marilyn Monroe remains as popular as ever. Her image graces a wide variety of products worldwide, and the resulting royalties generate nearly a million dollars per year. Even in death, Hollywood's most famous blonde goddess continues to bask in the bright spotlight of fame.

The Dummy Did It

Many of Hollywood's most oddball flicks seem to feature ventriloquists and their wooden sidekicks. It's a subgenre of filmmaking that contains more movies than you might think. Here are some of the best:

The Unholy Three (1925)
In this silent thriller, Lon Chaney plays a sideshow ventriloquist named Echo who teams up with a strong man and a dwarf to rob people by selling them talking parrots. Of course, the parrots talk only when Echo, in disguise as an old lady, is around to make them talk via ventriloquism. When customers complain that their birds won't speak, Echo and his diminutive colleague, who is disguised as a toddler, drop by their homes, which they case for future robberies. A silent movie about ventriloquism might seem odd, but Chaney, whose makeup mastery is one of the highlights of the movie, manages to make it work.

The Great Gabbo (1929)
In this early talkie, German director-turned-actor Erich von Stroheim portrays The Great Gabbo, a ventriloquist who slowly goes insane and starts to channel his innermost desires through his dummy, Otto. Trivia buffs will be interested to learn that this obscure little film was actually referenced in an episode of *The Simpsons.*

The Unholy Three (1930)
This remake of the 1925 silent film of the same name was Lon Chaney's first—and last—talkie (he died a couple of months after its release). The story is essentially the same as the original, with Chaney again playing sideshow ventriloquist/master criminal Echo, who joins forces with some of his carny colleagues for a series of Park Avenue heists. Harry Earles reprises his role as Tweedledee, the dwarf with crime in his heart.

Charlie McCarthy, Detective (1939)
Edgar Bergen and his dummy, Charlie McCarthy, were one of the most popular radio and motion picture ventriloquist acts of the 1930s and '40s. In this flick, the duo investigate the mysterious death of a newspaper editor with ties to the mob. Bergen and Charlie appeared in numerous movies over the years, including *You Can't Cheat an Honest Man* (1939) starring W. C. Fields.

Dead of Night (1945)

This critically acclaimed British film is actually an anthology of super-natural horror vignettes. Its concluding segment is about a ventriloquist, played by Michael Redgrave, who is driven insane when his dummy appears to come to life.

Devil Doll (1964)

Also from England, this horror flick concerns a ventriloquist/hypnotist named The Great Vorelli, who enlists his very animated dummy, Hugo, to help him get rid of his clingy mistress, Magda.

Magic (1978)

Long before he terrified audiences as Hannibal Lecter in *The Silence of the Lambs* (1991), Anthony Hopkins made audiences squirm as an unbalanced ventriloquist named Corky, who is psychologically tormented by his dummy, Fats. Richard Attenborough directed and William Goldman wrote the screenplay based on his best-selling novel of the same title.

Pin (1988)

This psychological thriller features a life-size medical mannequin instead of a traditional ventriloquist's dummy, but it frightens just the same. Terry O'Quinn plays Dr. Linden, a father who finds that he can teach his children about the body most effectively through the dummy, which he calls Pin, short for Pinocchio. When Dr. Linden dies, his disturbed son, Leon (David Hewlett), adopts Pin as part of the family with horrifying consequences.

Dummy (2002)

Academy Award-winner Adrien Brody stars as Steven, a man who has great difficulty expressing himself until he takes up ventriloquism. By speaking through his dummy, Steven learns to overcome his crippling social phobias and discovers that he finally has the fortitude to pursue the girl of his dreams. Illeana Douglas and Milla Jovovich costar.

Dead Silence (2007)

James Wan and Leigh Whannell, the duo behind the popular *Saw* horror franchise, teamed up to make this entertaining flick about a small town haunted by a group of dolls owned by a ventriloquist named Mary Shaw. Shaw had been murdered years earlier by townsfolk who believed she was responsible for the death of a young boy. Though the dolls were buried with Mary, they start appearing before the individuals responsible for her death, foreshadowing their own grisly doom.

Dorothy Meets the Dark Side

☆ ☆ ☆ ☆

"Somewhere Over the Rainbow" isn't the only memorable song tied to the 1939 classic The Wizard of Oz. *Many believe this beloved film has an unusual secondary soundtrack—Pink Floyd's classic 1973 album* The Dark Side of the Moon.

The Dark Side of the Rainbow

Judy Garland and Roger Waters may not seem like a match made in heaven, but thanks to one of pop culture's stranger urban legends, the leading lady from *The Wizard of Oz* may be forever linked to the lead songwriter from Pink Floyd.

The reason: Plenty of people insist that Pink Floyd's *The Dark Side of the Moon* was crafted with Garland and her Oz-destined gang in mind. Pop in the movie and play the music simultaneously, and you'll see a slew of curious connections.

In the phenomenon known as "The Dark Side of the Rainbow," fans cite more than 100 things that seem to sync up when the film and album are played simultaneously. To experience it for yourself, queue up the movie and the album, and as soon as the MGM lion roars for the 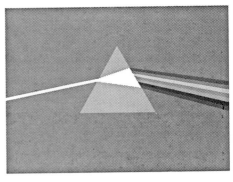 third time at the beginning of the film, hit "play" to start *The Dark Side of the Moon* and witness the magic.

Some of the more noteworthy match-ups are as follows:

- Dorothy balances on a fence at Uncle Henry's farm as the lyrics "balanced on the biggest wave" are heard during the song "Breathe."

- Dorothy falls off the fence and is rescued as the chaotic intro to "On the Run" begins.

- Dorothy's neighbor, the wicked Miss Gulch, rides her bicycle as the alarming sound of bells rings out during the intro to "Time."

- Dorothy runs away from home as the line "No one told you when to run" from "Time" is heard.

- The tornado appears in the sky as the song "The Great Gig in the Sky" plays. Some say the song's slide guitar swells with the tornado and that the operatic vocals vary in intensity to match Dorothy's experiences.

- The song "Us and Them" plays as Dorothy meets the Wicked Witch of the West. The word *black* echoes as the witch first appears. The phrase *black and blue* is sung as the two talk. Dorothy wears a blue outfit in the scene; the witch is dressed in black.

- The lyrics "who knows which is which"—from "Us and Them"— play as the Wicked Witch of the West sees the remains of her sister, the Wicked Witch of the East.

- The song "Brain Damage" plays as the Scarecrow sings "If I Only Had a Brain."

- It's worth noting that *The Dark Side of the Moon* is only 43 minutes long, while the run time of *The Wizard of Oz* is more than 100 minutes. Some say the experience ends when the album ends; others suggest you should play the album again to witness more synchronized moments.

Origins and Validity

"The Dark Side of the Rainbow" phenomenon first gained attention in the mid-1990s, though it's not clear who originally discovered it. A radio disc jockey is credited with bringing the concept to the mainstream by discussing it on the air in 1997. MTV News soon followed up with a story of its own, cementing the odd experiment's place in movie and music history.

The members of Pink Floyd have long denied any deliberate synchronization, calling the idea "absolute nonsense." An engineer who worked on *The Dark Side of the Moon* has also pointed out that VHS technology didn't even exist when the album was recorded in the early 1970s, so the band would have had a tough time watching the movie during their recording sessions.

The Jazz Singer

☆ ☆ ☆ ☆

Midway through The Jazz Singer *(1927), Al Jolson
extols the audience: "Wait a minute! Wait a minute!
You ain't heard nothin' yet!" And indeed they hadn't.
With those words, Jolson gave moviegoers something
few had ever experienced—synchronized speech.*

Based on Samson Raphaelson's 1921 short story "The Day of Atone-
ment," *The Jazz Singer* is about the son of a cantor who defies his
father and runs away from home to become a singer. Interestingly,
Al Jolson was not the first choice to play Jakie Rabinowitz, aka Jack
Robin; both Eddie Cantor and George Jessel turned down the role
before the producers approached Jolson.

Many people wrongly assume that *The Jazz Singer* was Hollywood's first sound movie. In fact, several short motion pictures with
synchronized sound had entertained audiences previously. And the
feature-length *Don Juan* (1926) featured a synchronized musical
score and sound effects. *The Jazz Singer* is historic primarily for its
use of spoken dialogue.

It's important to note, however, that *The Jazz Singer* is only
25 percent "talkie." The rest of the synchronized sound is primarily
musical numbers and accompaniment. But even that small percentage was enough to make audiences clamor for more, and the following year, Warner Bros. released its first all-talking movie, the
gangster flick *Lights of New York* (1928).

Thanks in part to its novelty and to the "realism" that spoken
dialogue added to the viewing experience, *The Jazz Singer* was a
box-office smash, grossing more than $3.5 million during its initial
release, which lasted well over a year. The film's success had such a
profound effect that it brought an almost immediate end to silent
movies. Within four years, nearly every Hollywood film was a talkie.

Motion picture technology has enjoyed a remarkable evolution
during the years, but synchronized sound—which made people
return to see *The Jazz Singer* again and again—remains one of the
medium's most important innovations.

Pop Quiz: Capra's Shining Stars

Frank Capra was one of the most successful and popular directors of Golden Age Hollywood. Modern fans know his enduring classics such as Mr. Smith Goes to Washington *(1939) and* It's a Wonderful Life *(1946), both starring Jimmy Stewart. But he made dozens of films with other big-name performers. Can you match up the actors listed below with the Capra films they starred in?*

Answer Choices: Lionel Barrymore; Claudette Colbert; Gary Cooper; Cary Grant; Frank Sinatra; Barbara Stanwyck

1. This actor was at the peak of his acting career when he starred in *A Hole in the Head* (1959). He played lovable loser Tony Manetta, who struggles to raise a son on his own, keep a free-spirited girlfriend, and chase his dream of becoming a wheeler-dealer in Miami.

2. Known for his rugged good looks, this star played Longfellow Deeds in *Mr. Deeds Goes to Town* (1936). Deeds is a simple small-town fellow who inherits a fortune from a distant relative and gets caught up with fast talkers in New York City.

3. In an attention-getting early role, this actress crafted a notable performance in *The Bitter Tea of General Yen* (1933), a controversial drama about the fiancée of an American missionary who reluctantly develops a relationship with an enigmatic Chinese warlord.

4. This actor played the dastardly Mr. Potter in *It's a Wonderful Life,* but a decade earlier, he costarred with a young Jimmy Stewart as the patriarch of an eccentric family in *You Can't Take It with You* (1938).

5. This actor is known for his suave, sophisticated image, but in an early role, he portrayed a flustered young newlywed who discovers that his beloved maiden aunts have been poisoning men and hiding the bodies in their cellar in the outlandish comedy *Arsenic and Old Lace* (1944).

6. *It Happened One Night* (1934) was an Oscar-winning smash that proved to be a breakthrough for both Capra and this gifted actress, who plays a spoiled heiress running away from her interfering father.

Answer Key: 1. Frank Sinatra; 2. Gary Cooper; 3. Barbara Stanwyck; 4. Lionel Barrymore; 5. Cary Grant; 6. Claudette Colbert

Protecting the Past

☆ ☆ ☆ ☆

The National Film Preservation Board works to save classic movies.

Motion pictures aren't forever. In fact, fewer than 20 percent of the feature films made in the 1920s survive in complete form, and the percentage drops to just 10 percent for movies made in the 1910s.

That's a lot of lost movies, and the number increases every year. In 1988, in an effort to save cinema's cherished heritage, Congress established the National Film Preservation Board and in 1996, created the federally chartered National Film Preservation Foundation to find, restore, and preserve motion pictures of all types. Organizations represented on the National Film Preservation Board include the Academy of Motion Picture Arts and Sciences, Motion Picture Association of America, Directors Guild of America, Writers Guild of America, American Film Institute, and American members of the International Federation of Film Archives.

The Foundation's Role

The National Film Preservation Foundation awards grants and raises private funds to help American film archives preserve movies and make them available to the public. The Foundation places special emphasis on what it calls "orphan films," those that do not have owners, such as studios, to pay for their restoration and preservation. The most at-risk films are newsreels, silent films, experimental movies, documentaries, films without copyright protection, and important amateur footage, such as the Zapruder film of John F. Kennedy's assassination.

Film preservation is a race against time. Many of the earliest motion pictures were lost because they were made with volatile nitrate stock, which disintegrates with age. As a result, many had become gelatinous masses when their film canisters were opened decades later. Sadly, the so-called "safety film" onto which many older movies were transferred had problems of its own, including an irreversible film decay called "vinegar syndrome." In addition, many Technicolor movies made during the 1950s and '60s are fading fast.

Many of today's movies are projected digitally and released on DVD within months of their theatrical release, so their preservation is not an issue; theoretically, as they are transferred from one new electronic medium to the next, they will continue to look as crisp and vibrant as the day they were "born." But storing digital data is costly, and digital technology changes so rapidly that equipment used to store and view films today may be obsolete tomorrow.

But saving older movies—even those made as recently as the 1950s and '60s—is a much more immediate concern and an expensive and very time-consuming endeavor. In many cases, movies must be pieced together from prints found around the world. And sometimes, they must be meticulously restored frame by frame.

A National Treasure

Every year, the Library of Congress selects 25 movies for addition into the National Film Registry. More than 500 movies are now included in the collection, ranging from *Blacksmith Scene,* a film from 1893, to the Coen Brothers' dark comedy *Fargo* (1996). The collection is far-ranging in type and subject matter and includes many well-known cinematic classics as well as a large number of films that hold little public interest but have great historical significance. Among them: *Dickson Experimental Sound Film* (1894–1895); *President McKinley Inauguration Footage* (1901); *San Francisco Earthquake and Fire, April 18, 1906* (1906); *Jeffries–Johnson World's Championship Boxing Contest* (1910); and *From the Manger to the Cross* (1912).

The Registry discourages copyright owners of classic movies from altering the films by cutting, colorization, or other means. If a film on the Registry is altered by the copyright holder, the DVD or video packaging must feature a warning that informs consumers that the movie has been altered. Much of the manipulation of older films by copyright owners has stopped, partly due to the efforts of the Registry.

Motion pictures are sometimes taken for granted as a mere diversion, but their decay is inevitable unless they are properly preserved. Thanks to the efforts of the National Film Preservation Board and the Library of Congress, more movies that might have been lost will now be around for the world to enjoy forever.

Lana Turner and the Death of a Gangster

☆ ☆ ☆ ☆

On the evening of April 4, 1958, Beverly Hills police arrived at the home of actress Lana Turner to discover the dead body of her one-time boyfriend Johnny Stompanato, a violent gangster with underworld ties. He had been stabbed to death, but the exact circumstances of his demise were muddied by the sensational reporting of the tabloid press.

Sweater Girl

Lana Turner's first credited film role came in 1937 with *They Won't Forget,* which earned her the moniker "Sweater Girl," thanks to the tight-fitting sweater her character wore. Turner went on to star in hits such as *Honky Tonk* (1941), *The Postman Always Rings Twice* (1946), and *Peyton Place* (1957).

Hanging with the Wrong Crowd

Offscreen, Turner was renowned for her many love affairs. During her lifetime, she amassed eight marriages to seven different husbands. It was shortly after the breakup of her fifth marriage to actor Lex Barker in 1957 that Turner met Johnny Stompanato. When she discovered that his name was not John Steele (as he had told her) and that he had ties to underworld figures such as Mickey Cohen, she realized the negative publicity that those ties could bring to her career, so she tried to end the relationship. But Stompanato incessantly pursued her, and the pair engaged in a number of violent incidents, which came to a head on the night of April 4.

Turner's 14-year-old daughter, Cheryl Crane, rushed to her mother's defense after hearing Stompanato threaten to "cut" Turner. Fearing for her mother's life, the girl grabbed a kitchen knife, then ran upstairs to Turner's bedroom. According to Crane's account, Turner opened the door and Cheryl saw Stompanato with his arms raised in the air in a fury. Cheryl then rushed past Turner and stabbed Stompanato, killing him. Turner called her mother, who brought their personal physician to the house, but it was too late. By the time the police were called, much time had passed and evidence had been moved around. According to the Beverly Hills police chief, who was the first officer to arrive, Turner immediately asked if she could take the rap for her daughter.

At the crime scene, the body appeared to have been moved and the fingerprints on the murder weapon were so smudged that they could not be identified. The case sparked a media sensation, especially among the tabloid press, which turned against Turner, essentially accusing her of killing Stompanato and asking her daughter to cover for her. Mickey Cohen, who paid for Stompanato's funeral, publicly called for the arrests of Turner and Crane. For years, ugly rumors surrounding the case persisted.

"The Performance of a Lifetime"?

During the inquest, the press described Turner's testimony as "the performance of a lifetime." But police and authorities knew from the beginning that Turner did not do it. At the inquest, it took just 20 minutes for the jury to return a verdict of justifiable homicide, so the D.A. decided not to bring the case to trial. However, Turner was convicted of being an unfit mother, and Crane was remanded to her grandmother's care until she turned 18, further tainting Turner's image. There was an aura of "guilt" around Turner for years, though she was never seriously considered a suspect in the actual murder.

As fate would have it, Turner's film *Peyton Place*, which features a courtroom scene about a murder committed by a teenager, was still in theaters at the time of the inquest. Ticket sales skyrocketed as a result of the sensational publicity, and Turner parlayed the success of the film into better screen roles, including her part in a remake of *Imitation of Life* (1959), which would become one of her most successful films. She appeared in romantic melodramas until the mid-1960s, when age began to affect her career. In the '70s and '80s, she made the transition to television, appearing on shows such as *The Survivors, The Love Boat,* and *Falcon Crest.*

Fast Facts: The Godfather

- *Marlon Brando wasn't the only guy up for the role of Don Vito Corleone. Paramount Pictures actually wanted Ernest Borgnine. Trade magazines also claimed at the time that George C. Scott and Laurence Olivier were considered for the role, and Burt Lancaster is said to have wanted the part as well.*

- *During a screen test, Brando actually stuffed his cheeks with cotton or tissues to make his character look "like a bulldog."*

- *To achieve the look of an older, jowly man, Brando wore a dental device during his scenes. The piece is now displayed at the American Museum of the Moving Image in Queens, New York.*

- *Producer Robert Evans wasn't pleased with director Francis Ford Coppola's preliminary work, and from the beginning, he and Coppola had butted heads. Evans talked about having Elia Kazan on standby in case he decided to fire Coppola. Kazan was considered because he had worked previously with Brando on* A Streetcar Named Desire *(1951) and* On the Waterfront *(1954), and, therefore, might have been able to handle the actor's temperament better than Coppola.*

- *Pacino has said that studio execs weren't impressed with his early scenes and that they considered firing him. But the scene in which his character shoots Sollozzo and McCluskey in the restaurant convinced the studio to keep him onboard.*

- *Martin Sheen, Warren Beatty, Jack Nicholson, Dustin Hoffman, Ryan O'Neal, and James Caan all read for the role of Michael Corleone.*

- *Brando never learned the majority of his lines. Instead, he read from cue cards while filming. This is typical of the way Brando worked as an actor because he liked to improvise the exact wording of his lines as a way of internalizing his characters.*

- *Sylvester Stallone tried out for the part of Paulie, which went to John Martino.*

- *Did you know that* The Godfather *spawned a board game? It hit store shelves in the early 1970s.*

- *In one of the most famous programming events in television history,* The Godfather Saga *was broadcast in November 1977. The four-night, nine-hour broadcast was edited by Coppola and film editor Walter Murch, and it integrated footage from both* The Godfather *and* The Godfather: Part II *(1974) in chronological order.* The Godfather Saga *contained additional footage not included in either* Godfather *theatrical release, bridging the two stories and fleshing out certain subplots.*

- TV Guide's *"50 Greatest Movies on TV and Video" ranked* The Godfather: Part II *at No. 1 and the original at No. 7.*

- *The cat Brando holds in the opening scene of* The Godfather *wasn't part of the script. Coppola found the stray wandering around the Paramount lot and, knowing the actor's talent with props, he plopped it in Brando's lap just before shooting the scene.*

- *The score for* The Godfather *created a minor scandal in Hollywood. Composer Nino Rota was nominated for an Oscar, but then someone realized that he had simply taken his music from* Fortunella *(1958) and changed it around a bit. Subsequently, Rota's Oscar nomination was withdrawn.*

- *Paramount considered shooting* The Godfather *in Kansas City, Missouri, because executives had experienced problems with the unions on previous occasions when shooting in New York City.*

- *You won't find his name in the credits, but George Lucas worked on a montage of crime scene photos and newspaper headlines for* The Godfather.

- *The actors playing Brando's sons in the movie ranged from 6 to 16 years younger than him in real life.*

Divorce Lawyer to the Stars

☆ ☆ ☆ ☆

During the 1970s and '80s, Marvin Mitchelson was the divorce lawyer to have when a Hollywood relationship went stale. With Mitchelson doing the bidding, a star knew he or she had gotten the very best. But when he sat across the table, woeful be the person who had to square off against him.

A Shark Prowls Hollywood

When the love bug bites in Hollywood, excesses of most every form generally follow. From luxurious diamond rings to lavish wedding ceremonies, it seems nothing is too expensive to express the feelings of the love-struck. The Hollywood jet set lives for such ostentatious moments, especially if the paparazzi and gossip columnists are on hand to record the pageantry. But fairy-tale endings rarely occur in Hollywood. And when the rich and famous of Tinseltown fall *out* of love—a turn of events about as frequent as the flow of bad scripts—assets once flaunted suddenly need to be divided. This is where super-lawyer Marvin Mitchelson (1928–2004) famously stepped in to make his mark. Like a hired gun in a high noon shootout, Mitchelson put the fear of God into his opponents as he reassured his clients that their salvation was firmly in his hands.

Going for the Jugular

Mitchelson first came to prominence for his role in *Douglas v. California* (1963), a landmark Supreme Court decision that provided free legal access for the indigent involved in the appeals process. As groundbreaking as his arguments were, the case produced less than a blip on the Hollywood radar. After all, Hollywood doesn't know much about indigence.

The case that really put Mitchelson on the Tinseltown map was a civil suit featuring Michelle Triola, the former live-in lover of Hollywood tough-guy actor Lee Marvin, who was best known for his portrayal of twin gunfighters in *Cat Ballou* (1965) and Major Reisman in *The Dirty Dozen* (1967). Although the two had never married during their six-year romance, forward-thinking Mitchelson argued that his client should receive *palimony* (a word he coined by combining *pal* with *alimony*) because Triola had given up her career as a singer to support Marvin. Because California doesn't recognize common-law marriage, it was an interesting tactic. The case resulted in a cash award for Triola, but the decision was ultimately overturned. Nevertheless, Mitchelson had come to the fore as a super-bold divorce attorney who was willing to change accepted precepts if necessary.

Love Me, Love Me Not

The list of celebs represented by Mitchelson reads like a celebrity Hall of Fame. Sylvester Stallone, Zsa Zsa Gabor, Robert De Niro, Hugh Hefner, Quincy Jones, and many others sided up with the legal beagle in an effort to stop the bleeding when their unions turned sour. In 1964, the lawyer represented Pamela Mason, wife of actor James Mason. With the steely nerve of a seasoned pro, Mitchelson maneuvered the actor into a $1 million settlement—an astonishing amount for the time. On the other side of the coin, in 1987, Mitchelson saved Joan Collins a whopping sum in a pre-nuptial case involving ex-husband Peter Holm. Mitchelson's reputation as a winner was so strong that he actually settled a custody case on behalf of Anna Kashfi—ex-wife of Marlon Brando—in the actor's living room.

To the Victor Go the Spoils

With each win boosting his bottom line, Mitchelson lived as large as those that he represented. His assets included the requisite Hollywood mansion, a fleet of luxury cars, and a seemingly endless supply of cash. But with these trappings came a downside. In Mitchelson's later years, he ran into difficulties with drug abuse, tax evasion, and malpractice suits and eventually wound up bankrupt. He served a two-year stint in federal prison for his tax problems, and upon his release, he worked for other lawyers until his license was restored in 2000. But through it all, his devoted wife, Marcella, stood dutifully by his side. In what could be described as the ultimate irony, their 45-year union proved that a happy marriage *could* stand the test of time—even in Hollywood, the unofficial capital of divorce.

Cary Grant's Acid Test

✩ ✩ ✩ ✩

In the 1950s and '60s, Cary Grant was one of Hollywood's top box-office draws, starring in popular movies such as An Affair to Remember *(1957) and* Charade *(1963). In sharp contrast to the debonair persona he cultivated on-screen, Grant also participated in an experimental psychotherapy program in which he underwent more than a hundred trips on the hallucinogenic drug LSD.*

It's not easy to picture Hollywood's quintessential leading man as an acid eater. On-screen, Cary Grant's matinee idol looks and sophisticated charm made him one of the most popular stars ever. He was ranked No. 2 on the American Film Institute's list of Greatest Screen Legends and was a favorite of Alfred Hitchcock, appearing in some of the acclaimed director's best films, including *Suspicion* (1941), *Notorious* (1946), *To Catch a Thief* (1955), and *North by Northwest* (1959). And author Ian Fleming partially modeled his James Bond character on the British-born Grant.

Offscreen, however, Grant was somewhat insecure and suffered a turbulent personal life that saw him married five times. In fact, it was Grant's third wife, Betsy Drake, who, around 1956, first introduced him to doctors prescribing the experimental drug lysergic acid diethylamide, better known as LSD. By the late 1950s, Grant was a regular patient of Los Angeles psychiatrists Dr. Mortimer Hartman and Dr. Arthur Chandler, who supervised the actor's frequent acid trips.

He Turned On, Tuned In, But Didn't Drop Out

Prior to 1966, LSD was available legally in the United States as an experimental psychiatric drug. Researchers like Hartman, Chandler, and Dr. Oscar Janiger, cousin of the famed Beat poet Allen Ginsberg, recruited hundreds of L.A. residents as human volunteers to gauge the therapeutic potential of LSD in treating neuroses in people who are unresponsive to conventional therapies. Before the drug became associated with the hippie movement and before Timothy Leary's endorsement that urged users to "turn on, tune in, and drop out" became a counterculture slogan, the use of psychedelics in scientific research drew little attention from the public or media.

Although Cary Grant's acid trips took place outside of the usual clinical environment, Dr. Hartman or Dr. Chandler always designated a monitor to constantly observe him, ready to talk him down should he experience a bad trip.

Grant publicly discussed the therapeutic value of LSD. He likened the hallucinations he experienced during those LSD trips to the act of dreaming and felt the drug helped him come to terms with his star image and reconcile his past, particularly unresolved conflicts with his parents. He also credited LSD therapy with helping him gain control over his drinking.

LSD and Alcohol

Dr. Albert Hofmann first formulated LSD by accident in 1938 at a Swiss pharmaceutical company. Five years later, he accidentally discovered its effects when he undertook the world's inaugural acid trip. The CIA and U.S. military later tried using the drug's disorienting effects as a nonlethal warfare tactic before researchers began to explore the drug's psychiatric potential. Cary Grant was not the only Hollywood celebrity to participate in these studies. Other volunteers included actors Jack Nicholson, James Coburn, and Dennis Hopper, author Aldous Huxley, and musician/conductor Andre Previn.

While Cary Grant spoke positively about his LSD use, he also recognized the inherent dangers of the drug. "I found it a very enlightening experience," he once said. "But it's like alcohol in one respect: A shot of brandy can save your life, but a bottle of brandy can kill you. And that's what happened when a lot of young people started taking LSD, which is why it became necessary to make it illegal."

---

* As a teenager, Cary Grant joined the Bob Pender comedy troupe, where he learned to dance, perform acrobatics, stilt-walk, and pantomime. The experience gave him a lifelong agility, physical grace, and poise that suited his star image.

The Many Faces of Frankenstein

Frankenstein has shown up in films featuring everything from a space robot to a beast made from the body parts of prostitutes. (Yes, really.) Here are some of his most unusual appearances.

I Was a Teenage Frankenstein (1957)
Professor Frankenstein, a university science teacher, uses the bodies of deceased athletes to build his own monster companion, but the hastily assembled fellow turns out to be not-so-friendly. In fact, he heads right over to the campus and starts killing people!

Frankenstein 1970 (1958)
In this futuristic film (futuristic to audiences in 1958, anyway), Frankenstein struggles with tough times. He decides to sell his family's story to a television production company, then he uses the money to build a massive monster that lives off his deceased butler's brain.

Frankenstein Meets the Space Monster (1965)
A NASA-built robot goes haywire after being shot by Martians, who are on their way to Earth to kidnap women for breeding.

Frankenstein '80 (1972)
Another flick with a futuristic title, *Frankenstein '80* tells the tale of a sex-starved monster that roams the streets to find lovely ladies. The tagline, "He had a bone to pick," says it all.

Frankenstein Island (1981)
Some hot-air balloonists crash-land on a quiet island and find a descendent of Dr. Frankenstein living with mutants and bikini-wearing Amazonian warrior women.

Frankenhooker (1990)
A former med student's fiancée dies in a lawnmower accident. He saves her head, then combines it with body parts taken from prostitutes. She then goes on a killing spree. Did he really think that would end well?

Favorite Comedies

Anagrams are new words or phrases made by rearranging the letters of the original word or phrase. Check out the new phrases made by rearranging the letters of these Hollywood films.

The American President	A predicament's therein
Bad News Bears	Babe's wardens
The Blues Brothers	The robbers hustle
Catch Me If You Can	A chief contumacy
Charlie's Angels	Heeling rascals
Coming to America	A cinematic groom
Death to Smoochy	A comedy hotshot
Ferris Bueller's Day Off	Ferrari fell, boy fussed
Forrest Gump	Forgets rump
Kindergarten Cop	Rocked parenting
The Man with Two Brains	Wow, ban the S. Martin hit
Mean Girls	Maligners
Miss Congeniality	Misogynistic elan
Ocean's Thirteen	Hesitant encore
Ocean's Twelve	Leave cons wet
Office Space	A scoff piece
Patch Adams	Madcap hats
The Producers	He's corrupted
Shaun of the Dead	Headhunted oafs
Small Time Crooks	Scammers took ill
The Truman Show	No truth, we sham
Waking Ned Devine	Even dead winking

Biblical Films: The Sword and the Sandal

Hollywood has a history of adapting best-selling books for the silver screen and turning those written wonders into box-office bonanzas. So it's not surprising that the Bible—the top selling tome of all time—would lead all contenders in big-screen adaptations. Here are some films that tackle the testaments to create an epic blend of sword and sandal.

The King of Kings (1927)
This silent film classic by legendary director Cecil B. DeMille recounts the last weeks of Jesus' life through the eyes of Mary Magdalene and Judas. Renowned for its use of the two-color Technicolor process in the closing sequences to depict Christ's resurrection, the film features intertitles that were excerpted in part from the Scriptures.

The Robe (1953)
The first film released in CinemaScope, a wide-screen format, this film examines the problems and guilt faced by the Roman tribune (Richard Burton) who commands the military unit that supervises the crucifixion of Christ. The robe in question is the garment Jesus wore upon his entry into Jerusalem, which falls into the possession of Burton's character.

The Ten Commandments (1956)
Another biblical offering from the astute eye of Cecil B. DeMille, this remake of his own 1923 silent master-piece was the last film he directed. Based on the life of Moses, the film is best remembered for its legend-ary parting of the Red Sea and the stoic, stern-jawed performance of Charlton Heston as Moses.

Ben-Hur (1959)
This adaptation, which won 11 Oscars, was actually the third remake of Lew Wallace's novel. Famous for its spectacular and pivotal chariot race scene, the film invokes the spirit of Christ and his teachings without using him as a central on-screen character.

Barabbas (1962)
This film, based on a biblical figure introduced in the Gospel of Mark whose life is spared while Jesus' is condemned, is a parable about the

moral dilemmas presented by choice and chance. The film featured a revolutionary soundtrack using minimal orchestration and a convincing performance by Anthony Quinn as the title character.

The Greatest Story Ever Told (1965)
This star-studded depiction of Christ's life was noteworthy for featuring Swedish actor Max von Sydow in the pivotal role of Jesus. Von Sydow was ably supported by a bevy of Hollywood names, including major stars such as Martin Landau, Charlton Heston, and Sidney Poitier. John Wayne, Ed Wynn, and Angela Lansbury appear in brief cameos in a bit of stunt casting that was the film's claim to fame.

Jesus Christ Superstar (1973)
Norman Jewison's film version of Andrew Lloyd Webber's ground-shaking rock opera was dismissed by critics upon its release, but it remains a faithful, emotional, and clever take on an oft-told story. Using barren sets and a modern approach, the film features a selection of time-tested tunes and a pair of virtuoso performances by Ted Neeley as Jesus and Carl Anderson as Judas.

Jesus of Nazareth (1977)
Franco Zeffirelli directed this six-hour epic that follows Christ through his birth, death, and resurrection. Based on the writings of the four gospels of the New Testament, the movie, which was filmed entirely in Tunisia and Morocco, stars some of the biggest names in cinema at the time, including Laurence Olivier, James Earl Jones, Peter Ustinov, Anthony Quinn, and Anne Bancroft.

The Last Temptation of Christ (1988)
Martin Scorsese's portrayal of Jesus as a mortal human being, fraught with fear and distracted by doubt, continues to stir debate to this day. Regardless of the fervor it caused, the film is a worthy study of Christ as a man who questions both his moral fortitude and his ability to carry the cross for humankind.

The Passion of the Christ (2004)
Mel Gibson's violent yet largely traditional take on the final hours of Jesus' life aroused passionate debate about accuracy, anti-Semitism, and the depiction of violence. It also smashed box-office records, registering more than $370 million in ticket sales in the United States alone to become the top-grossing R-rated movie in history up to that time.

Trouble for the Prince of Noir

☆ ☆ ☆ ☆

Robert Mitchum was the original offscreen bad boy—before James
Dean ever appeared on the scene. He defined cool before Hollywood
knew the hip meaning of the word. He was rugged, handsome, and
jaunty. A hobo turned actor, he was the antithesis of the typical
movie hero—and he was on his way to becoming a star, primarily in
film noir. Then it happened: A drug bust with a buxom blonde, and
Mitchum was in the headlines in a way he never intended.
Ironically, this incident accelerated his stardom.

In August 1948, Hollywood tabloids were embla-
zoned with headlines proclaiming the scandalous
drug bust (for possession of marijuana)
of actor Robert Mitchum, who was
in the company of 20-year-old aspiring
actress Lila Leeds. This was the era of the
marijuana frenzy: The government was
at war with cannabis users, and propaganda, entrapment, blatant lies, and
excessive punishments were just a few of the weapons they used.
Mitchum was the perfect whipping boy. The actor was no stranger
to pot and hashish, having experimented with both as a teenage
hobo riding the rails. He was also a fugitive from the law, having
escaped from a Georgia chain gang after being arrested for vagrancy
in Savannah at age 16. Despite hiring Jerry Giesler, Hollywood's hottest defense attorney, Mitchum was found guilty and was sentenced
to 60 days on a prison farm. His "I don't give a damn" smirk when
his sentence was pronounced would define the attitude of the drug
culture that burst upon the scene as the '40s came to a close.

A Career Ruined?

When Mitchum was sentenced, he was earning $3,000 a week—a
princely sum at the time. He was married to his childhood sweetheart, Dorothy Spence, and was in the midst of a seven-year contract with RKO studios. When the tabloids ran a picture of inmate

91234 swabbing the jail corridors in prison attire, Mitchum antici-pated it would be "the bitter end" of his career and his marriage. In reality, the publicity had the opposite effect. With the exception of becoming a small embarrassment to the studio and causing the cancellation of a speech Mitchum was scheduled to deliver to a youth group, the actor's offscreen bad-boy persona had little nega-tive effect on his career or personal life. If anything, it only added to his counterculture, tough-guy, antihero image.

Great PR

While Mitchum served his 60-day sentence on the honor farm (which he described as "Palm Springs without the riff-raff"), RKO released the already-completed film *Rachel and the Stranger* (1948). Not only did movie audiences stand and cheer when Mitchum appeared on the screen, the low-budget movie also became the studio's most successful film of the year.

In 1950, another judge reviewed Mitchum's conviction and reversed the earlier court decision because the arrest smelled of entrapment: Leeds's Laurel Canyon bungalow had been bugged by two overly ambitious narcotics agents. The judge changed Mitchum's plea to not guilty and expunged the conviction from his records—not that Mitchum appeared to care one way or the other. By then, he was a bona fide Hollywood star.

A Long and Successful Livelihood

Mitchum enjoyed an illustrious career, making more than 70 films, some to critical acclaim. He also enjoyed success as a songwriter and singer, with three songs hitting the best-seller charts. His marriage remained intact for 57 years, possibly a Hollywood record. He earned a star on the Hollywood Walk of Fame along with several other prestigious industry awards. Not a bad lifetime of achievements for a pot-smoking vagabond fugitive from a chain gang. Often seen with a cigarette dangling from his sensual lips, Mitchum died of lung cancer and emphysema on July 1, 1997, at his home in Santa Barbara, California. He was 79 years old.

Hollywood Heroes

Hollywood celebrities tend to make the tabloid pages for all the wrong reasons. Every now and then, though, they find themselves in the headlines for heroic deeds rather than scandalous behavior.

Mark Harmon

The actor, best known for his roles on *St. Elsewhere* and *NCIS*, became a real-life hero in 1996 when two teenage boys crashed their Jeep near his Brentwood home. Harmon's wife, actress Pam Dawber, was the first on the scene, so when she saw the car in flames, she yelled for her husband to bring a sledgehammer. Harmon smashed a window, wrestled one of the boys from his seat belt, and then pulled him to safety. The boy was on fire so the actor rolled him on the ground to extinguish the flames. A fire department spokesman praised Harmon for his heroics, stating, "These boys certainly owe their lives to the quick and selfless action of Mr. Harmon."

Harrison Ford

This movie star doesn't confine his heroics to the big screen when he's playing Han Solo or Indiana Jones. Ford has twice turned real-life hero to rescue stranded hikers in his Bell 407 helicopter. In July 2000, the accomplished pilot picked up the distress call from two female hikers on Table Mountain in Idaho. One was overcome with altitude sickness after a five-hour climb, so Ford flew in to airlift her to the hospital. The woman didn't recognize her famous rescuer until after she'd vomited in his hat.

A year later, Ford's flying skills were called upon again in the rescue of a 13-year-old Boy Scout who went missing in Yellowstone National Park. After scouring the area for two hours, Ford spotted the boy and swooped down to rescue him. He even shared a joke with the boy, who had managed to survive overnight wearing only a T-shirt and shorts. "Boy, you sure must have earned a merit badge for this one," said the actor.

Cuba Gooding Jr.

On the night of Memorial Day 2007, Cuba Gooding Jr. went to pick up dinner for his family from Roscoe's House of Chicken 'n' Waffles in Hollywood. When the Oscar-winning actor saw a young man collapse, bleeding from a gunshot wound, he ran to help. He called into the restaurant for towels and managed to stem the bleeding. The *Jerry Maguire* (1996) star hailed a passing police car and cradled the injured man until an ambulance arrived at the scene.

Gerard Butler

Before he became famous as the heroic lead in *300,* the 2007 movie adaptation of Frank Miller's graphic novel, Gerard Butler was honored for his real-life heroism. The Scottish actor received a Certificate of Bravery from the Royal Humane Society of Scotland in 1997 after he risked his life to pull a drowning boy from the River Tay, the longest river in Scotland. Butler was enjoying a picnic nearby when he saw the child drowning and immediately dived in to rescue him.

Tom Cruise

Tom Cruise has a history of coming to the aid of folks in trouble, though the tabloid press seems to focus more on his couch-jumping and religious beliefs than his good deeds. In 2006, he and his wife, Katie Holmes, assisted a young couple who had been in a car accident. Ten years earlier, Cruise rescued a young woman who had been hit by a car. He called an ambulance for her, then paid her emergency room bill. However charitable these acts were, they pale in comparison to an incident in London in 1998. While out walking, Cruise came across a woman being mugged. The woman was sitting in her Porsche when a man opened the car door and began grabbing the jewelry from her hands and arms. The woman screamed, and Cruise ran to her aid, chasing off the mugger in mid-theft. Reportedly, he prevented the loss of at least some of the jewelry the woman was wearing—worth between $120,000 and $150,000.

Todd Bridges

After his role as Willis Jackson on the popular sitcom *Diff'rent Strokes* came to an end in 1986, actor Todd Bridges tended to make headlines for all the wrong reasons. He endured a much-publicized battle with cocaine addiction and, in 1990, even stood trial for the attempted murder of a drug dealer. In 2001, however, Bridges made headlines for rescuing a paraplegic woman from drowning in Lake Balboa in Los Angeles. The 50-year-old woman was fishing while buckled into her motorized wheel-chair. When the chair accidentally rolled into the lake and fell on its side, her head was trapped underwater. Bridges and his brother James ran to the woman's aid and managed to pull her to safety.

Martin and Lewis

☆ ☆ ☆ ☆

*In 1946, a suave, handsome, and enviably charismatic crooner
teamed up with a manic, insecure, aspiring funnyman. To the
surprise of everyone, they became one of the most phenomenally
successful comic pairings in Hollywood history.*

In early 1946, Dean Martin was a modestly
successful singer who made regular appearances on the radio and in East Coast nightclubs. At the same time, Jerry Lewis was
a 19-year-old comic struggling to secure
himself a spot on that same nightclub
circuit. That year, they were introduced
by a mutual friend and struck up a
casual friendship. Later in 1946, they
found themselves on the same bill at the
Havana–Madrid in Manhattan.

   On occasion, after the evening's string
of performances ended, the two would get
some extra stage time with a largely
improvised act in which Lewis inter-
rupted the suave crooner's songs with his
crazy antics. That summer, the pair again found themselves working
at the same venue, this time the 500 Club in Atlantic City. They
both felt that their earlier collaboration had shown promise, so they
joined forces for their stint at the 500. Lewis wrote a few bits to
bring some structure to the act, but for the most part, they simply
started off with Lewis coming out as a busboy who caused a ruckus
in the middle of a song by Martin and then just let the performance
go where it would. The act was a smash, and within a few months
they were a successful team pulling down $5,000 a week.

What Made It Work

The Martin and Lewis act relied on the contrast between the two
as the source of its humor. Lewis acted as an outrageously juvenile

man-child with a screechy voice and a bumbling physical presence. Martin, on the other hand, was drop-dead gorgeous with a seductively sleepy baritone and an unflappably confident persona. The juxtaposition was comedic dynamite, and audiences couldn't get enough. Almost overnight, they became the hottest live act in the country, which brought them lucrative television, radio, and film contracts.

Their first Hollywood film together, *My Friend Irma* (1949), was a working-girl romantic comedy that was based on a long-running radio show. Though Martin and Lewis played secondary characters, their comic interplay was among the strong picture's highlights, and they were soon headlining a string of highly successful movies. They made an incredible 16 films together in seven years, following the same formula in each—Lewis mugged as an inept, immature bumbler, and his devoted best friend Martin smoothed over his inevitable troubles while winning the heart of a beautiful girl.

What Made It Fail

As the two sat side-by-side at the pinnacle of the entertainment industry, it was almost inevitable that jealousy would undermine the relationship. The press and public tended to fawn over Lewis's comic antics while giving little recognition to the critical role that straightman Martin played in creating that humor. The act broke up in 1956, and the two men didn't speak to each other again until Frank Sinatra surprised Lewis by bringing his old partner out in front of the cameras on Lewis's Muscular Dystrophy Telethon in 1976 for an emotional reunion.

Martin and Lewis Filmography:

My Friend Irma (1949)	*The Caddy* (1953)
My Friend Irma Goes West (1950)	*Money from Home* (1953)
At War with the Army (1950)	*Living It Up* (1954)
That's My Boy (1951)	*3 Ring Circus* (1954)
Sailor Beware (1952)	*You're Never Too Young* (1955)
Jumping Jacks (1952)	*Artists and Models* (1955)
The Stooge (1952)	*Pardners* (1956)
Scared Stiff (1953)	*Hollywood or Bust* (1956)

Sci-Fi Flicks that Leaped from the Printed Page

Most movie fans may not know it, but quite a few classic science-fiction flicks have deep literary roots. In some cases, the source material is well known: The Time Machine, The War of the Worlds, and The Invisible Man by H. G. Wells, for instance, or Jules Verne's Twenty Thousand Leagues Under the Sea. But many other movies are based on books or short stories so obscure that only the geekiest sci-fi fans are aware of them. Here are a few examples:

Farewell to the Master by Harry Bates

Considered by many critics to be one of the best science-fiction stories ever written, this tale of a visit from a technologically advanced alien being and his robot guardian hit the big screen in 1951 under the title *The Day the Earth Stood Still,* starring Michael Rennie as the extra-terrestrial Klaatu. Keanu Reeves starred in a 2008 remake of the film.

Flowers for Algernon by Daniel Keyes

This poignant story of a developmentally challenged young man whose intelligence is temporarily boosted through a scientific breakthrough made a star out of Cliff Robertson, who played the lead character in the 1968 screen adaptation, *Charly.*

Who Goes There? by John W. Campbell (aka Don A. Stuart)

This chilling short story about a shape-shifting alien who terrorizes the crew of a remote Arctic outpost has been adapted twice for the big screen—once in 1951 as *The Thing from Another World* and again in 1982 as simply *The Thing.* The 1982 version, which starred Kurt Russell and was directed by John Carpenter, adheres more closely to the original text.

The Sentinel by Arthur C. Clarke

Film fans know this short story better by the title *2001: A Space Odyssey* (1968), which was directed by Stanley Kubrick. However, *The Sentinel* provides only a basic framework for the movie; don't expect a lot of mind-blowing psychedelic space travel in the book.

Do Androids Dream of Electric Sheep? by Philip K. Dick

This compelling story of humanlike "replicants" and the cop who hunts them down when they go bad was made into the much-heralded Ridley Scott flick *Blade Runner* (1982), which starred Harrison Ford.

We Can Remember It for You Wholesale by Philip K. Dick

If you're an Arnold Schwarzenegger fan, you probably know this story better as *Total Recall* (1990). In this film, Schwarzenegger plays a man who doesn't know whether his memories of a trip to Mars are real or not. Author Philip K. Dick has become well known among screenwriters in recent years, and many of his stories have received the Hollywood treatment.

The Racer by Ib Melchior

Before Sylvester Stallone hit it big as underdog pugilist Rocky Balboa, he costarred with David Carradine in the film version of this futuristic thriller retitled for the big screen as *Death Race 2000* (1975). A 2008 remake of the movie, simply titled *Death Race*, starred Jason Statham.

Eight O'Clock in the Morning by Ray Faraday Nelson

This sly story of alien infiltration and subliminal manipulation became a showcase for wrestler "Rowdy" Roddy Piper when director John Carpenter brought it to the silver screen in 1988 under the title *They Live*.

The Cosmic Frame by Paul W. Fairman

This short story, first published in 1955, deals with what happens to a young couple after they accidentally run over an alien. It was adapted—rather loosely—as the low-budget 1957 Edward Cahn flick *Invasion of the Saucer Men*.

The Fly by George Langelaan

Two movie adaptations have been made of this short story, which was originally published in the June 1957 issue of *Playboy* magazine. The first film, which was released in 1958, starred Vincent Price, but the remake, directed by David Cronenberg and released in 1986, was a much more graphic version that starred Jeff Goldblum in the title role.

Jean Harlow

☆ ☆ ☆ ☆

*The Hollywood sky is filled with stars, and for a few fleeting
years, none burned brighter than Jean Harlow. Sadly, the
blonde bombshell's tragic death at age 26 ended a remarkable
career that likely would have lasted for decades.*

On March 3, 1911, Harlean Carpenter was born in Kansas City,
Missouri. Her father was a dentist and her mother was a housewife
with aspirations of stardom. Harlean grew into a pretty teenager
who eloped with her wealthy boyfriend, Charles McGrew, when she
was just 16. They settled in Beverly Hills, but Harlean quickly grew
bored with her husband's drinking and what she saw as the tedious
lifestyle of the wealthy, so they divorced soon afterward.

Big Break

On a bet, Harlean visited Hollywood's Central Casting, using her
mother's maiden name, Jean Harlow, instead of her own. Casting
directors were instantly smitten by her beauty, and Harlow soon
found herself working in small roles, including a scene in the Laurel
and Hardy silent short *Double Whoopee* (1929), in which she loses
her skirt in a car door.

At age 18, Harlow hit the big time in the Howard Hughes epic
Hell's Angels (1930). Hughes loaned her out several times, most
notably to Frank Capra for *Platinum Blonde* (1931). After that, she
quickly became known in fanzines as the "Platinum Blonde" or the
"Blonde Bombshell." She then appeared in several well-received
films, including *Dinner at Eight* (1933), starring Wallace Beery; *Red
Dust* (1932), with frequent costar Clark Gable; *Bombshell* (1933);
and *China Seas* (1935).

Tragedy and Scandal

In 1932, Harlow married screenwriter and director Paul Bern. Sadly,
Bern died under unusual circumstances just a few months later, his
naked body discovered on the dressing room floor of the couple's
Easton Drive home with a bullet in his brain. (Harlow had been

visiting her mother the evening before and was not present when Bern died.) Bern's death was ruled a suicide, though some investigators have speculated that he was murdered based on the fact that many of MGM's top brass arrived on the scene at least two hours before the police were notified. What damning evidence, some wondered, were they trying to cover up?

Harlow survived the scandal that briefly surrounded Bern's death and went on to make one hit after another for MGM, including *Libeled Lady* (1936), which received an Academy Award nomination for Best Picture and rave reviews for the fair-haired actress. Indeed, Harlow's career was at its peak in 1937, though her personal life was in turmoil. She was involved in a failed relationship with actor William Powell, whom she desperately wanted to marry, and she experienced increasingly poor health for much of the spring.

A Star Burns Out

On May 29, Harlow collapsed on the set of *Saratoga* (1937). She returned home that afternoon and summoned her doctor. Harlow was initially diagnosed with the flu, but her health continued to deteriorate. Eventually, she became too weak to be transported to the hospital, and for several days her mother would permit only Powell to visit her.

Harlow rallied briefly, and on June 4, her mother told the press that she was on the mend. Unfortunately, Harlow was suffering from a major illness that has been difficult to pin down. She was rushed to Good Samaritan Hospital, where she slipped into a coma and died on the morning of June 7. Some say she died of an acute gall bladder infection and kidney failure, while others claim it was uremic poisoning.

News of Harlow's sudden death rocked the entertainment community. Her funeral was held at the Wee Kirk of the Heather Church in Forest Lawn Memorial Garden in Glendale, California, where actors Nelson Eddy and Jeannette MacDonald sang Harlow's favorite song, "Ah! Sweet Mystery of Life." Fans mobbed the ceremony, stealing flowers from the wreaths as keepsakes, and the funeral devolved into an embarrassing media circus.

Harlow was interred at Forest Lawn, right next to MGM exec Irving Thalberg, one of the men who helped make her a star.

The Making of *King Kong*

☆ ☆ ☆ ☆

*Very few movies have had the kind of cultural impact enjoyed by
King Kong (1933). Its iconic imagery is familiar to almost everyone,
and it remains a critical favorite more than 75 years after its
premiere. In fact, the American Film Institute included* King Kong
on its list of the Ten Best Fantasy Films of all time.

A King Is Born

When *King Kong* premiered in March
1933, audiences were awestruck by the
work of talented special effects techni-
cians who brought the film's giant
dinosaurs to life and gave the massive
gorilla Kong a personality that moviegoers could relate to.

The driving force behind *King Kong*
was Merian C. Cooper, who came up
with the concept of a primitive gorilla
trapped in the concrete jungle of New York City. For his film,
Cooper had planned on using real gorillas and lizards—that is until
he met Willis O'Brien, a stop-motion animator who was using the
process to create lifelike dinosaurs for a movie called *Creation.*

When the expensive production of *Creation* was canceled,
O'Brien approached Cooper about using stop-motion animation in
his gorilla movie. Cooper brought the idea to David O. Selznick, the
vice president in charge of production at RKO Pictures, who shared
Cooper's enthusiasm for the project. He authorized a special effects
test reel, which convinced the brass at RKO that *King Kong* could
be just the thing to pull the studio out of debt.

Produced from a script by James Ashmore Creelman and Ruth
Rose, *King Kong* was a groundbreaking movie for its time. O'Brien
and his crew vastly improved the stop-motion animation process,
giving Kong facial expressions and convincing reactions to the action
around him. As a result, both Kong and the film's dinosaurs look
amazingly lifelike.

A Miniature Marvel

Though King Kong appears to be as much as 50 feet tall in the movie, the real Kong measured just 18 inches. Marcel Delgado crafted the model as an articulated metal skeleton and covered this armature with foam rubber, latex, and rabbit fur. For close-ups and scenes in which Kong holds Fay Wray, full-size arm, hand, and head models were made. A full-size leg was created for scenes in which Kong steps on natives as he rampages through the island village. (Contrary to claims made years later, the original King Kong was never portrayed by a man in a gorilla suit.) The movie also required the creation of various articulated dinosaurs and other creatures, all of which, like Kong, were brought to life by stop-motion animation.

Many of the movie's key scenes required the use of rear-screen projection, which allowed actors Fay Wray and Bruce Cabot to appear seamlessly in scenes with, and react to, Kong and the other terrifying denizens of Skull Island. RKO shared a special Academy Award with Fox Film Corp. and Warner Bros. for developing a more reliable rear-screen projection system during the production of *King Kong*.

Hollywood's First Scream Queen

Fay Wray was already an established actress when she appeared in *King Kong*. She spends much of the movie screaming as Kong carries her through the jungle and protects her from various dangers—though all of her screams were recorded after filming was completed.

Most of *King Kong* was filmed in or around the RKO studio and back lot in Culver City, California. The huge wall and gate that protects the natives of Skull Island from Kong was reportedly first used in Cecil B. DeMille's 1927 production *The King of Kings*. The producers of *King Kong* also economized by using jungle sets from *The Most Dangerous Game,* which was being filmed at RKO at the same time as *King Kong.* Some of the same mattes, such as the giant log across the ravine, can be clearly identified in both films.

King Kong cost around $670,000 to make and was a tremendous success. It grossed more than $1.7 million during its initial release and had a role in saving RKO from financial ruin. A sequel, *The Son of Kong,* was immediately put into production and released in December 1933. However, its smaller budget and rushed production schedule were evident, and it didn't fare nearly as well as the original.

Questionable Kongs

The giant gorilla character Kong did not appear in the movies again until 1962, when Japan's Toho Studios pitted him against Godzilla in a movie that annoyed fans of the original, even though Kong took the prize for toe-to-toe combat. An updated version of *King Kong* starring Jessica Lange was produced in 1976 by Dino DeLaurentiis, who decided to go with legendary makeup artist Rick Baker in a gorilla suit for the portrayal of Kong, instead of using stop-motion animation. Even though the remake earned an Oscar for special effects, fans of the original were outraged and the movie was vilified by critics. In 2005, Peter Jackson, an avowed *King Kong* fan, released his own affectionate remake of the original, relying on state-of-the-art computer effects to bring Kong, the horrifying creatures of Skull Island, and 1930s-era New York City to the big screen. Despite a host of enthusiastic critical raves, ticket sales for this 187-minute take on *Kong* were mediocre at best (it cost $207 million to produce but collected just $218 million in America), making it a major disappointment at U.S. box offices. The picture did far better business abroad.

In addition to its two official remakes and related sequels, *King Kong* has spawned scores of "big monkey" movies over the decades, including the 1949 classic *Mighty Joe Young*, with effects by Willis O'Brien and his protégé, Ray Harryhausen. King Kong has also appeared in television commercials and in print advertising, comic books, and elsewhere.

Beauty may have killed the beast in the movie, but the big gorilla's status as a groundbreaking cinematic icon will live forever.

- *Merian C. Cooper's original idea for* King Kong *was inspired in part by the story of how Komodo dragons—first brought to New York's Bronx Zoo in 1926 by adventurer W. Douglas Burden—died quickly in captivity. Not only did Cooper envision a battle between a live, captured African gorilla and a Komodo dragon for his film project, he also borrowed the K in Komodo for the name of his leading ape, Kong.*

Pop Quiz: Oscar-Winning Leading Ladies

Each of these leading ladies won an Oscar for Best Actress in a Leading Role. Can you match the winner with the film in which she starred?

1. Julie Andrews	A. *The Accused* (1988)
2. Ingrid Bergman	B. *Annie Hall* (1977)
3. Halle Berry	C. *Blue Sky* (1994)
4. Marion Cotillard	D. *Coal Miner's Daughter* (1980)
5. Louise Fletcher	E. *Coquette* (1929)
6. Jodie Foster	F. *The Divorcee* (1930)
7. Audrey Hepburn	G. *Gaslight* (1944)
8. Katharine Hepburn	H. *Hud* (1963)
9. Diane Keaton	I. *Johnny Belinda* (1948)
10. Jessica Lange	J. *Kitty Foyle* (1940)
11. Vivien Leigh	K. *La Vie en Rose* (2007)
12. Patricia Neal	L. *Mary Poppins* (1964)
13. Gwyneth Paltrow	M. *Monster's Ball* (2001)
14. Mary Pickford	N. *Morning Glory* (1933)
15. Ginger Rogers	O. *One Flew over the Cuckoo's Nest* (1975)
16. Norma Shearer	P. *Roman Holiday* (1953)
17. Sissy Spacek	Q. *Shakespeare in Love* (1998)
18. Elizabeth Taylor	R. *A Streetcar Named Desire* (1951)
19. Joanne Woodward	S. *The Three Faces of Eve* (1957)
20. Jane Wyman	T. *Who's Afraid of Virginia Woolf?* (1966)

Answer Key: 1. L; 2. G; 3. M; 4. K; 5. O; 6. A; 7. P; 8. N; 9. B; 10. C; 11. R; 12. H; 13. Q; 14. E; 15. J; 16. F; 17. D; 18. T; 19. S; 20. I

Modern Documentaries that Hit It Big

Documentaries don't have much of a chance in the current marketplace. Distributors are reluctant to handle scholarly pics that they feel are best suited to cable TV, while theaters assume most moviegoers will choose an action-packed blockbuster, a raucous comedy, or the newest animated dazzler. Some documentaries have surprised industry pundits by breaking through these barriers to captivate audiences of all ages. Here are a few that defied the odds.

Rattle and Hum (1988)

In October 1988, Irish rockers U2—whom *Time* magazine had dubbed "Rock's Hottest Ticket"—released an album and a film, both titled *Rattle and Hum*, which featured a mix of new songs, covers, and live recordings that were meant to pay tribute to the band's love for America and its legendary rock musicians. Filmed while U2 crisscrossed the United States on The Joshua Tree tour, this "rockumentary" mixes band interviews, concert footage, recording sessions at the famed Sun Studio in Memphis, and other candid footage, including a side trip to Graceland as the Irish lads pay homage to the King of Rock 'n' Roll, Elvis Presley. Some critics praised the film, while others denounced it as pretentious and misguided. But fans loved it and took it for what it was meant to be—a behind-the-scenes look at U2 as they embraced America.

Roger & Me (1989)

According to Box Office Mojo, three of the six top-grossing documentaries of all time were made by filmmaker/rabble-rouser Michael Moore: *Bowling for Columbine* (2002), *Fahrenheit 9/11* (2004), and *Sicko* (2007). But *Roger & Me* started it all and opened up the public's eyes to a different kind of documentary—one that relies less on academic narration and instead focuses more on colorful commentaries, clever editing, and controversial subject matter. *Roger & Me* follows Moore on his quest to interview Roger B. Smith, who was the CEO of General Motors at the time. As the film progresses, Moore uncovers the fallout caused by a plant closure in his hometown of Flint, Michigan—but he never does get his interview with the elusive leader of a corporate giant, who doesn't seem to want to comment on the company's responsibility to the American worker. *Roger & Me* introduced Moore to American audiences, and the modern documentary has never been the same since.

Super Size Me (2004)

In 2003, newbie filmmaker Morgan Spurlock underwent an experiment that, to some, might have sounded like fun. He decided to eat a steady diet of McDonald's for 30 straight days to expose the evils of the kind of diet that many Americans view as normal. The resulting documentary, aptly titled *Super Size Me*, explores the frightening consequences of the fast-food diet on Spurlock's body (skyrocketing cholesterol, rapid weight gain, loss of sexual appetite, etc.) and also exposes the somewhat scurrilous methods that the fast-food industry uses to worm its way into the mouths and wallets of consumers. The film was an overnight sensation and was nominated for an Oscar, and Spurlock—who had previously been rejected five times by the University of Southern California's lauded film school—won the Best Director award at the 2004 Sundance Film Festival.

March of the Penguins (2005)

Who knew penguins could be so dramatic and captivating? This 2005 documentary, which grossed an astonishing $77 million at the box office on its initial U.S. theatrical release, focuses on a colony of Emperor penguins as they march *single file* over 70 miles in arctic temperatures to breed in a specific spot. The team of filmmakers behind this award-winning documentary blends scientific information with breathtaking, never-before-seen footage of penguins in their brutalizing Antarctic world. Narrated by Morgan Freeman, this wildlife stunner is the second-highest grossing documentary of all time. Go Penguins!

An Inconvenient Truth (2006)

The fifth-highest grossing documentary of all time and winner of the 2006 Oscar for Best Documentary, *An Inconvenient Truth* isn't what you might call a "feel good" picture. Narrated by dedicated environmentalist and former Vice President Al Gore, the film shows audiences around the world what Gore has been lecturing about for years: Mother Earth is in trouble, it's largely our fault, and we need to do something about it— NOW! The documentary drew large audiences due in part to Gore's relaxed-but-resolved demeanor as he presented fact after disturbing fact about global warming and the state of the planet. *An Inconvenient Truth* is part lecture, part science class, part horror flick, and part inspirational message, but one thing is clear: The film was right on time.

The Historic (and Haunted) Roosevelt Hotel

☆ ☆ ☆ ☆

Situated at 7000 Hollywood Boulevard, the 12-story Roosevelt Hotel is an integral part of Hollywood's history. For more than 80 years, this hotel has served as a temporary home away from home for some of the world's biggest celebrities, who love to soak in the atmosphere. In fact, many of the stars who visit the Roosevelt enjoy themselves so much that they frequently return . . . even in death.

Now Open for Business

The Roosevelt, named after President Theodore Roosevelt, was the brainchild of a group that included actor Douglas Fairbanks and was designed to function as a haven for actors who lived on the East Coast but found themselves in Hollywood making movies. When the doors swung open for business on May 15, 1927, nearly $3 million had been spent building the 400-room hotel. The design captured the flavor of southern California with its Spanish colonial style.

It didn't take long for the who's who of Hollywood to start visiting the Roosevelt, using it for industry functions and doing business in its sunken lobby or elegant Library Bar. The era's biggest stars, including Mary Pickford, Gloria Swanson, Greta Garbo, Charlie Chaplin, and Will Rogers, were present at the hotel's inaugural ball. The Roosevelt was even the site of the very first Academy Awards ceremony, which was held in the hotel's Blossom Room on May 16, 1929. The ceremony included several activities, but the actual awards presentation was the shortest in Academy Awards history, lasting approximately five minutes with a grand total of 15 awards handed out.

Over the years, more and more stars made the Roosevelt their hotel of choice, including Clark Gable, Errol Flynn, Hugh Hefner, Frank Sinatra, Elizabeth Taylor, Judy Garland, and Al Jolson. In addition, a variety of lesser-known but important personnel, from musicians to voice instructors to writers, stayed for extended periods of time on the studios' tabs while working on various movies.

But the years began to take their toll on the Roosevelt, and by the 1980s, the building had fallen into such disrepair that it came close to being demolished. A major hotel chain saved it from the wrecking ball and began making extensive renovations. They worked hard to reflect the Roosevelt's original charm and color schemes, focusing a lot of attention on the sunken Spanish-style lobby adorned with rounded Moorish windows and a bubbling fountain. The renovators discovered the lobby's huge, original, wrought-iron chandelier in pieces in the basement and spent six months putting it back together. It has been said that all of the banging during the renovation was enough to wake the dead—literally.

You're Never Alone at the Roosevelt

The first documented encounter with a ghost at the Roosevelt came in December 1985. The hotel was scheduled to reopen a month later, so employees were frantically working to complete the renovation. Employee Alan Russell was working in the Blossom Room when he felt a cold spot. Alarmed, he called some of his coworkers over and they felt it too, although they couldn't find a rational explanation as to why that one area would be cold.

Since then, guests and employees alike have reported seeing a man in dark clothing standing in precisely the same spot where Russell felt the cold spot. Who this man is remains a mystery.

Shortly after the newly renovated Roosevelt opened for business, the front desk started getting calls from confused guests who reported hearing disembodied voices coming from empty hallways. At other times, guests would call to complain about a loud conversation coming from the room next door, only to be told that the room was empty and locked up tight.

The ghosts of the Roosevelt might have started out being heard rather than seen, but that was to change, too. Guests and employees have also reported seeing dark figures roaming the hallways late at night. In one instance, the ghost of a man dressed all in white was seen walking through the walls of the hotel.

Over time, the ninth floor of the hotel became a haven for much of the paranormal activity. Things were said to have gotten to the point that some Roosevelt employees refused to go up to the floor alone at night.

In 1992, in an attempt to find some answers, psychic Peter James was invited to the Roosevelt. As he wandered the halls of the hotel, James claimed to have encountered several famous ghosts. He felt Humphrey Bogart's spirit near the elevators and bumped into Carmen Miranda's specter while walking down the hallway on the third floor. James stated that when he ventured down to the Blossom Room, the ghosts of Edward Arnold and Betty Grable were present.

The Roosevelt's Most Famous Ghost

Peter James also encountered one of the Roosevelt's most famous spectral residents—Marilyn Monroe. In life, Monroe frequented the Roosevelt and even had one of her very first photo shoots in the hotel's pool area. So while it's not surprising that Monroe's ghost would choose to hang around the hotel, it chose an unusual place to haunt. Her ghost is sometimes seen reflected in a mirror that hung in the room where she often stayed.

Weary of the stories of ghostly images appearing in the mirror, hotel management removed the mirror from the room and placed it in the manager's office. Apparently, Monroe's ghost made the move, too. One day, employee Susan Leonard was cleaning in the office when she looked into the mirror and saw a blonde woman standing behind her. When Leonard turned around, the woman had vanished.

Today, the mirror resides on the first floor near the elevators. And yes, Marilyn's ghost still makes an occasional appearance.

A Ghost with a Thing for the Ladies

The other famous ghost said to haunt the Roosevelt is that of Montgomery Clift. Specifically, Clift's ghost hangs out in Room 928, the room he called home for several months during the filming of *From Here to Eternity* (1953).

While Clift's ghost is traditionally only heard or felt, every once in a while he decides to reach out and touch someone. One evening in the 1990s, a young wife was reading in bed. When she felt her husband touch her on the shoulder, she rolled over to ask him what he wanted but found him fast asleep. It proves that just when you think you've eluded the ghosts of the Roosevelt and made it safely up to your room, you still might be in for a spooky surprise.

The Curse of Atuk

☆ ☆ ☆ ☆

Curses are a well-established part of Hollywood lore. There are all sorts of rumors about cursed actors, cursed sets, and cursed movies, and believe it or not, there is even supposed to be a cursed script.

In 1963, author Mordecai Richler penned the novel *The Incomparable Atuk*, which tells the story of an Eskimo named Atuk who tries to adapt to life in Toronto. Several years later, United Artists bought the movie rights to the book, and screenwriter Tod Carroll adapted it for the big screen, shortening the title to *Atuk*.

Legend has it that Carroll wrote the screenplay with comedian John Belushi in mind for the role of Atuk. Apparently, Belushi was very interested in the role, until his untimely death on March 5, 1982.

After Belushi's death, United Artists began looking for another comedian to portray the hefty Atuk. In 1988, they reportedly signed loudmouthed comedian Sam Kinison, who filmed one scene with director Allan Metter before walking off the set and quitting. United Artists filed a lawsuit against Kinison for $5.6 million, which almost ruined him. But the alleged curse was not quite finished with the doomed comedian. Kinison was killed in April 1992 when the car he was driving was struck by a drunk driver. Another curse victim?

Comedian John Candy was next in line for the role, but a fatal heart attack on March 4, 1994, put an end to that.

A few years later, the script was reportedly given to *SNL* star Chris Farley. Like those before him, Farley was contemplating taking the part when he died—in an eerily similar fashion to his idol, John Belushi—from an accidental drug overdose on December 18, 1997.

Farley allegedly showed the script to Phil Hartman, who was interested in a supporting role. A few months after Farley's death, the script took its last victim to date when Hartman was shot to death by his wife on May 28, 1998.

So where's the script now? As of this writing, United Artists still owns the rights, but there are no plans under way to turn *Atuk* into a movie. Of course, with its dark and twisted track record, producers would be hard-pressed to find an actor brave enough to accept the title role.

Great Movie Gimmicks

In an attempt to fill seats and boost profits, producers have introduced some mighty strange lures through the years. From mild to wild, each "grabber" was designed to enhance the movie-viewing experience as it boosted the bottom line. Sometimes, the gimmicks even worked.

3-D Movies

Although 3-D movies were being experimented with as far back as the 1890s and technical break-throughs continue to this day, the most extensive fad in 3-D, or stereo-scopic filmmaking, occurred in the 1950s.
The technology's high-water mark arrived with *House of Wax* (1953), starring Vincent Price. The movie featured what has become the holy grail of 3-D scenes: a wisecracking carnival barker hitting paddleballs directly into the faces of a stunned audience. The 3-D effect was so pronounced during this memorable scene that people flinched and recoiled, doing their best to avoid being "hit" by the optical illusion. Although 3-D movies can be genuinely fun to watch, some viewers experience queasiness while wearing the goofy cardboard glasses. Today's digital technology has allowed some 3-D movies to work without the flimsy glasses, and 3-D films are staging a comeback.

Smell-O-Vision

Smell-O-Vision was the brainchild of Mike Todd Jr., son of the famed Hollywood producer best known for the epic *Around the World in Eighty Days* (1956) and for his brief marriage to Elizabeth Taylor. The idea for Smell-O-Vision was simple. After setting up a network of scent-carrying tubes beneath theater seats, a worker would manually release scent vials at crucial moments during a film. For instance, when the crack of a gun was heard, a gunpowder scent might be released. When a couple came together in a romantic embrace, the scent of flowers would waft through the air. A small army of scents stood at the ready to mimic life and improve a film's realism, but therein lay an inherent flaw. It was soon discovered that a smorgasbord of dissimilar odors was not necessarily a pleasant thing, particularly when they intermingled in the still air of a confined movie theater. Only one film, the aptly titled *Scent of Mystery*

(1960), was made using the system. Todd reportedly ended up losing his entire investment and eventually left the film business. A similar idea (Odorama) arrived with the 1981 film *Polyester*. In this incarnation, scratch-and-sniff cards were used to augment key scenes in the movie. But like Smell-O-Vision before it, the idea proved to be a genuine stinker.

Free Vomit Bags

To the uninitiated, this might sound like a genuinely bad idea, but in fact, it was pure movie genius. The bags were distributed for *Mark of the Devil* (1970), a film whose original German title translates to *Witches Tortured Till They Bleed*. The pitch, of course, was that the flick was so very shocking that it could easily produce retching. "This vomit bag and the price of one admission will enable you to see...the first film rated V for violence...." teased the blood-red writing on the side of each bag. Far from being dissuaded by such a distasteful thought, gore fans and horror aficionados rushed to buy tickets. By the standard of today's shock films, the movie might seem rather tame, but a much-hyped scene depicting a woman's tongue being severed is said to have put many a vomit bag to the test.

Sensurround

Those attending a showing of *Earthquake* (1974) got more than they bargained for, particularly if they neglected to read signs hawking "Sensurround." This special effects system developed by Universal promised to bring the real sound and feel of an earthquake to viewers. To say that it succeeded would be an understatement. During the film, a low-frequency rumble was produced by a bank of strategically placed loud-speakers. This created a booming sensation that was felt as much as heard during critical portions of the movie. For some patrons, the sensation was a genuine kick. For others, it was downright troubling, both physically and mentally. The system was used to enhance three other movies (*Midway*, 1976; *Rollercoaster*, 1977; and the theatrical print of the made-for-TV film *Battlestar Gallactica*, 1978) before being retired in 1978. It was just as well. In multiplex cinemas where Sensurround had been featured, patrons attending adjacent movies often complained about carryover noise. But that was nothing compared to what occurred at Grauman's Chinese Theatre in Hollywood. During their showing of *Earthquake*, errant pieces of plaster allegedly dropped from the ceiling, putting the safety of movie patrons in jeopardy. In a case of technology run amok, Sensurround made the moviegoing experience just a bit too realistic.

The Great Train Robbery

☆ ☆ ☆ ☆

*At the turn of the 20th century, short film clips were displayed
in parlors, known as nickelodeons, on individual viewers
called Kinetoscopes and Vitascopes. Customers stood in line
to be thrilled by such seemingly mundane scenes as a train
pulling into a station or a man and a woman kissing.*

Prolific inventor Thomas Edison
produced these clips in a studio
in the exotic moviemaking locale of
West Orange, New Jersey. Edison's
camera operator, Edwin S. Porter, had a greater vision for movies.
Believing the clips could tell complete stories, he produced and
directed America's first "feature film"—1903's *The Great Train
Robbery*—although it was only 12 minutes in length.

A Flurry of Firsts

Porter was a pioneer in location shooting, and he was the first to
have one location stand in for another, using the northern New
Jersey woods as a substitute for the Wild West. He was also the first
to use a method of dynamic editing called crosscutting, in which
the viewer's attention is focused on two separate but simultaneous
scenes of action. In addition, Porter found a way to move the bulky
camera so that it was mobile rather than stationary.

More importantly, his film had a beginning, a middle, and an
end. Bandits stop a train, rob its passengers, and make their escape
on horseback. A posse gives chase and guns down the bandits.
Porter based the story on an 1896 stage play of the same name and
the real-life adventures of outlaws Butch Cassidy and the Sundance
Kid, who robbed a Wyoming train in 1899.

The director obviously knew the potential impact that moving
pictures could have—he finished *The Great Train Robbery* with a
scene of an outlaw firing his pistol right into the camera, causing
startled viewers to duck and recoil in surprise.

It wouldn't be the last time that happened in the movies.

Tinseltown's Tattlers:
From Parsons to Perez

Gossip—a nonstop whirr that feeds and exploits the movie machine—has been a part of the film industry since its inception.

Louella Parsons

Louella Parsons, the original diva of Hollywood dish, got her start as a journalist in Chicago in the early 1910s. At the *Chicago Record–Herald,* she wrote about the city's movie industry from an insider's perspective because she also worked for Essanay Studios as a scenario editor. Her column is considered by many to be the film industry's first celebrity gossip column. Eventually, she made her way to New York where she immersed herself in the city's film circles. She landed a job for the *New York Morning Telegraph,* then in 1923, she began working for publishing magnate William Randolph Hearst's *New York American.* She may have remained in the Big Apple indefinitely, if not for Hearst's love interests.

When Hearst fell head over heels for stage actress Marion Davies, the two began a decades-long affair but were unable to marry because his wife refused to grant him a divorce. Davies had already made her first film, *Runaway Romany* (1917), before she met Hearst. Davies was a natural comedienne with a radiant charisma, and movie producers wanted to exploit her flare for comedy. But after she became involved with Hearst, he was determined to make her a serious dramatic actress. He set up Cosmopolitan Pictures to produce Davies's serious films, which were released through and distributed by other studios. No stranger to the powers of propaganda, Hearst enlisted the help of Louella Parsons to give Davies attention in her column, though some claim it was Parsons's idea to make the boss's girlfriend look good. In exchange for promoting Marion Davies and dismissing or criticizing her rivals, Parsons was given a more generous contract. In 1925, when Parsons was diagnosed with tuberculosis, doctors advised her to move west to a drier climate, so she moved to Los Angeles. By that time, Hearst and Davies were already in Hollywood, where Davies was enjoying a successful career, returning to comedies at the end of the silent era.

Hearst gave Parsons a job at his Los Angeles paper, and her column soon took off. The studios took notice of her popularity and did everything they could to curry her favor. Gifts poured into her office. Invitations to Hollywood parties filled her mailbox. Doing everything they could to control the images of their stars, studio publicists provided Louella Parsons with insider tidbits in exchange for well-placed publicity and for keeping unflattering details out of her column.

By the 1930s, no Hollywood marriage, birth, or divorce escaped Parsons's notice or opinion. She expanded beyond her column to host a weekly radio show that reached a national audience, which only increased her fame and power. And as long as the studios fed her exclusives, her opinions remained positive. But if she felt slighted or neglected, the sting of her column could ruin a career. For instance, she was so angered that Orson Welles based the title character in *Citizen Kane* (1941) on her beloved boss William Randolph Hearst that, for several months, she made it a point to ignore most of the actors who appeared in the film. Her animosity toward Welles lasted for years.

Hedda Hopper

Parsons was the reigning "Queen of Hollywood" until the late '30s when former actress Hedda Hopper, who became famous for her outlandish hats, posed the first real threat to her rule. A modestly successful silent film star, Hopper was on the lookout for a new career. She tried politics and even ran for the Los Angeles city council but lost. In 1938, she turned to "journalism" and launched a gossip column in the *Los Angeles Times*. Her personal Hollywood connections allowed her to bypass and even criticize the studio publicity machine. At first, Parsons did not take Hopper seriously, but when Hopper's longtime friendships with casts and crew started to pay off with exclusives, Parsons was enraged. By the 1940s, their rivalry was notorious, and it only intensified when Hopper launched a radio gossip show of her own. Now there were two "Queens of Hollywood," and publicists had to work hard to avoid appearing to favor one over the other. Ultimately, it was the collapse of the studio system that weakened both writers' power. By the late 1950s, Louella Parsons and Hedda Hopper were still writing, but both were focused more on the threat of liberal Communist infiltration than on Hollywood scandals. Both columnists believed that they were helping national security in their efforts to rat out Communists.

Perez Hilton

By the 1970s, the line between "gossip" and "news" had begun to blur. Recognizing the popularity of celebrity stories, magazine publishers started delivering in a format that made it difficult to pinpoint where the news ended and gossip began. With the launch of *People* magazine in 1974, the judgmental tone of Hollywood's former gossips became a thing of the past. Magazines welcomed cheerful human interest profiles delivered straight from celebrity publicists. That is, until the rise of the Internet.

In 2004, Mario Lavandeira, an out-of-work actor, started a celebrity blog as a hobby. Soon, his unfiltered entries, often crass and always opinionated, began to attract a following that snowballed into an explosion. His Web site, PerezHilton.com (a play on his idol, Paris Hilton) is now a major online site, supposedly receiving nearly nine million hits a day. Following in the tradition of Louella Parsons and Hedda Hopper, Hilton now has a radio show and has become a Hollywood celebrity in his own right. Between appearances on *The View* and MTV, he manages to attend the best Hollywood parties.

With an army of paparazzi recording every detail of a star's life, it is increasingly difficult for anyone, no matter how famous, to control his or her own image. Perez Hilton boasts that he has created "Hollywood's most hated Web site." In fact, as of late 2009, he was fending off multiple lawsuits. In the end, it doesn't matter if one loves or hates him. As long as millions of people keep reading his blog, Perez Hilton truly is Hollywood's reigning "Gossip Queen."

"Two of the cruelest, most primitive punishments our town deals out to those who fall from favor are the empty mailbox and the silent telephone."

—Hedda Hopper

Fast Facts: Titanic

- *All in all, there were about 1,000 extras used in* Titanic *(1997). But if you were lucky enough to be hired as a "core extra" on the film (there were 150 of them), you were given reading material about the etiquette and tastes of the era so you would know how the wealthy talked, walked, and conducted themselves in 1912.*

- Titanic *was the first film with a budget of $200 million. RMS* Titanic *itself would have cost about $120–$150 million to build in 1997.*

- *Director James Cameron makes a couple of appearances in his movie: first, as a gray-bearded reveler during the party below deck and later as a passenger waiting for a lifeboat.*

- *On September 27, 1995, while shooting the* Titanic *wreckage scenes in the North Atlantic, Cameron and the crew had a wreath-dropping ceremony to commemorate the victims of the sinking.*

- *The filmmakers had only one chance to get the shot of the grand staircase room flooding because once it was flooded, it would be ruined, obviously. However, other parts of the ship, such as corridors, were constructed so they could be re-flooded for multiple shots.*

- *So far, only three films have won 11 Academy Awards:* Titanic *(1997),* Ben-Hur *(1959), and* The Lord of the Rings: The Return of the King *(2003).*

- *Gwyneth Paltrow, Claire Danes, and Gabrielle Anwar auditioned for the role of Rose.*

- *The water, though it looks frigid, was heated to about 80 degrees. Therefore, all the breath you see coming from the mouths of passengers was added later via computer.*

- *Reba McEntire auditioned for the role of the "Unsinkable" Molly Brown, and she did well. But Cameron had his heart set on Oscar-winner Kathy Bates for the small but showy role.*

- *Celtic New Age singer Enya declined to do the score for the film.*

- *Reportedly, director James Cameron offered to give up his share of the gross (10 percent of the studio's initial gross) when fears about the budget had the studio worried. But studio execs refused because they believed the film wouldn't make money anyway.*

- Titanic *holds the record for the biggest moneymaker in cinematic history. In North America alone, it grossed more than $600 million. Worldwide, it made more than $1.8 billion, making it the first film to earn more than $1 billion in its initial box-office release.*

- Titanic *was No. 1 at the U.S. box office for a record 15 straight weeks.*

- *In the film, a 17-year-old female character is the last person rescued. In actuality, crew member Charles Joughin was supposedly the last survivor pulled from the freezing waters.*

- *Director James Cameron drew all the pictures of Rose—in fact, it's Cameron's hand seen in close-up while Jack is sketching.*

- *Both Rupert Everett and Rob Lowe were considered for the role of Cal.*

- *The average cost of a day's shooting for* Titanic *was between $225,000 and $250,000. Two complicated scenes, the dome implosion and the South Hampton dock, cost about $500,000 per day.*

- Titanic *began shooting on September 18, 1996, and finished on March 22, 1997, making it a 163-day shoot.*

- *On the last day of shooting in Halifax, where the contemporary scenes involving treasure hunter Brock Lovett were shot, a prankster on the set spiked the cast and crew's clam chowder dinner with PCP, which caused 56 people to end up in the emergency room.*

Sci-Fi Settings

While science-fiction movies are often set in regions of space entirely alien to our own, a simple fact is consistent with them all—no matter the setting, every one is filmed right here on Earth. The stories and locations may be out of this world, but here are some real places that stood in for a galaxy far, far away.

Ape World

Although Charlton Heston's character returned home at the end of *Planet of the Apes* (1968), he didn't actually make it to the East Coast of the United States. The crash scene at the beginning of the movie was filmed in Glen Canyon, Utah, while the Statue of Liberty scenes, along with much of the rest of the film, were shot in Malibu, California.

More Monkeys

In Tim Burton's 2001 remake of *Planet of the Apes*, astronaut Mark Wahlberg crash-lands in an unknown time and place that looks remarkably like Hawaii. Actually, it was Hawaii...some of it anyhow. Additional footage was shot at California's Trona Pinnacles and at Lake Powell, which straddles the Utah–Arizona border.

One for the Conspiracy Theorists

Capricorn One (1977) took its story from the conspiracy theory that the 1969 *Apollo* mission to the moon had been faked by NASA and the U.S. government. In Hollywood's version, three astronauts become pawns of the space program when their mission to Mars is canceled due to faulty equipment and lack of funds. They are ordered to fake it in the desert, which was actually Red Rock Canyon State Park in California. This is a clever twist on the use of locations because *Capricorn One*'s fictional American public is fooled into believing they are seeing Mars, just as real-life moviegoers suspend their disbelief regarding locations when they watch sci-fi movies.

Tatooine, Home Planet of Luke Skywalker

Luke Skywalker may have been a poor moisture farmer from a truly backwater planet, but it was actually the upscale Sidi Driss Hotel in Tunisia that served as the backdrop for his boyhood home on the planet Tatooine in the original *Star Wars* (1977), as well as the later prequels. Other North African locations, including Chott el Djerid, were also used, and Death Valley National Park in California doubled for the planet as well.

The Ewoks' Forests of Endor

Whether you love 'em or hate 'em, the Ewoks of Endor did save the day for the Rebel Alliance at the end of *Return of the Jedi* (1983), and the tall trees of the Redwood National and State Parks in northern California served as stand-ins for those of the forest moon.

Chill Out on Ice Planet Hoth

Luke Skywalker and the Rebel Alliance cooled off on the frozen world of Hoth before fighting off an invasion by the Empire's giant AT-AT walkers. The real Hoth locations—Finse and the nearby Hardangerjøkulen, the fifth largest glacier in mainland Norway—were actually part of the Nazi occupation of the Scandinavian nation during World War II.

Dune's Planet Arrakis

The desert world known as Dune in the 1984 film was actually the Samalayuca Dunes in the Mexican state of Chihuahua. Located near the Texas border, they are among the largest and deepest sand dunes in North America, but don't expect to find any giant sand worms there.

Mars Invasion

In one of a few recent films about the colonization of Mars, Val Kilmer led a mission to the *Red Planet* (2000), but instead of training for interplanetary travel, he merely had to travel to Coober Pedy in South Australia, while Gary Sinise's *Mission to Mars* (2000) took its cast on a journey to Jordan.

A World of Aliens

James Cameron's 1986 blockbuster *Aliens* was set on a planet known as LV-426, but most of the film was actually shot at Pinewood Studios in Buckinghamshire, England. The climactic scenes at the atmosphere-processing station were filmed in London at the Acton Lane Power Station. No aliens were harmed during the production of the film.

Total Arnold

A favorite among Arnold Schwarzenegger fans, *Total Recall* (1990) sends Arnold to Mars, but California's future "Governator" didn't have to venture too far from home—most of the film was shot in Mexico.

Hoop Dreams

No sport combines athletic grace, physical dexterity, and visibly stunning displays of prowess and power quite like the game of basketball. It is also a pursuit in which success is not always determined by sheer size and strength. Here are a few films that properly portray basketball as the stuff of dreams.

Hoosiers (1986)

Inspired by the Cinderella story of Milan High School—a school that, despite having only 73 male students, won the Indiana State Championship in 1954—this film accurately captures the spirit and substance of small-town dreams and big-time success. Buoyed by realistic dialogue and attention to detail, this endearing drama, starring Gene Hackman, Dennis Hopper, and Barbara Hershey, is considered one of the best basketball movies ever made.

White Men Can't Jump (1992)

This refreshing comedic exercise uses basketball to tear down racial and cultural stereotypes while building up the importance of friendship, tough choices, and the ability to hit nothing but net from way downtown. Wesley Snipes and Woody Harrelson star as ball-toting hustlers who learn hard lessons on the hard pavement of the inner-city courts.

Hoop Dreams (1994)

This unflinching and carefully focused documentary follows the lives and dreams of William Gates and Arthur Agee, two high school stars with NBA aspirations. Uncompromising in its portrayal and outlook, the film is a harsh criticism of American social systems that can't adequately deal with poverty or fairly treat its victims. But the underlying message is that failure can be its own reward and that making an effort is as important as achieving a goal.

Space Jam (1996)

A loving tribute to the majestic magnificence of Michael Jordan and the wacky weirdness of cartoon characters such as Bugs Bunny and Daffy Duck, this animated family film is pure entertainment. The plot follows Jordan, who is sucked into Looney Tune Land to help the classic Warner Bros. characters in a space-age basketball game against alien invaders.

Other sports legends, such as Charles Barkley, Larry Bird, and Patrick Ewing, make cameo appearances.

He Got Game (1998)

Basketball serves as a metaphor for examining the tenuous one-on-one relationship between an imprisoned father (Denzel Washington) and his son (NBA All-Star Ray Allen). Director Spike Lee carefully crafts a well-paced story and extracts a believable, often brilliant, performance out of Allen, who handles the complexities of the role with the same dexterity that he often flashes on the hard court.

Love & Basketball (2000)

The title says it all. This engaging and emotional tale tells the story of a pair of star-crossed lovers (Omar Epps and Sanaa Lathan) whose bittersweet romance is complicated by daunting dreams, hopeful aspirations, and hard choices. Throw in some brilliant basketball, and you have a winning recipe that cooks courtside.

O (2001)

Call it "The Bard Under the Boards." This compelling, intricate overhaul of Shakespeare's *Othello* examines the relationship between an African American basketball star—the only black student in an all-white prep school—and his girlfriend, who is also the dean's daughter. As in the classic play, this updated tale is fraught with jealousy, doubt, and revenge, all of which collide in a chilling climax.

Coach Carter (2005)

This film is based on the true story of high school basketball coach Ken Carter, who made headlines in 1999 for benching key members of his undefeated team because of poor grades. By daring to challenge his players to achieve academically as well as athletically, Carter convinces his charges that the pursuit of knowledge is life's only worthy pursuit.

Glory Road (2006)

Glory Road is the poignant and penetrating portrayal of Coach Don Haskins, who had to make tough decisions by looking beyond the color of his players' skin to see their talent inside. That conviction allowed the 1966 Texas Western College Miners to become the first team with an all-black starting lineup to capture the NCAA national championship.

Woody Allen: The Gifted Neurotic

☆ ☆ ☆ ☆

In 1951, a skinny Jewish kid from Brooklyn began a career in entertainment that would eventually make him one of Hollywood's biggest stars. His contributions as an actor, producer, and director have made Allen Stewart Konigsberg a household name—although you probably know him better as Woody Allen.

Write On, Kid

As a teenager, Allen began selling jokes to newspaper columnists and stand-up comics who liked his clever, "woe-is-me" style. When Allen left home, he enrolled at NYU to study film but eventually dropped out of the program. There didn't seem to be much point in spending all his time studying when he was able to make good money writing bits for humorist Herb Shriner and, before long, comedy sketches for *The Ed Sullivan Show, The Tonight Show,* and the short-lived but critically acclaimed *Caesar's Hour.*

By the time he reached his twenties, Allen was also writing stage plays, some of which later became films. He also began crafting material for himself, and in the early 1960s, he became a stand-up comedian, presenting himself as a neurotic, self-obsessed therapy junkie with a voracious sexual appetite—a character that wasn't much different from Allen himself. It worked, and he landed gigs on television and in prominent nightclubs and, by 1969, he'd been featured on the cover of *Life* magazine.

Roll Camera

It seemed a natural progression for Allen to work in film, so he tried his hand as a screenwriter and actor. But his first screenwriting job, *What's New Pussycat?* (1965), left a bad taste in his mouth; between directorial cuts, the divalike demands of actor Warren Beatty (who eventually quit the film because of "artistic differences"), and fights with meddling producers, moviemaking didn't seem like anything Allen wanted to be a part of—unless he could be in charge.

Once the rookie filmmaker got ahold of the reins, however, Hollywood was his oyster. The first project that gave him complete artistic control was a critical success: American International Pictures purchased the rights to a low-budget Japanese spy film and asked Allen to write the dialogue for the English dub. *What's Up, Tiger Lily?* (1966) was a spy spoof laden with one-liners and self-conscious parody. A string of successful, uniquely Woody Allen pictures began in 1969 with *Take the Money and Run* and continued throughout the early 1970s with hits such as *Bananas* (1971), *Everything You Always Wanted to Know About Sex* (*But Were Afraid to Ask*) (1972), and *Sleeper* (1973).

Allen had made a name for himself, but his tour de force came in 1977 with *Annie Hall*, which won the Oscar for Best Picture. The movie, Allen's deliberate twist on the romantic comedy genre, chronicles the rise and fall of the sweet, funny, and poignant relationship between Alvie (played by Allen) and Annie (Diane Keaton). Keaton won a Best Actress Oscar for the role and started a fashion trend with the floppy hats and men's trousers she wore in the film.

Prolific, Terrific (and Not-So-Terrific)

After the riotous success of *Annie Hall,* Allen produced the Ingmar Bergman-inspired drama *Interiors* (1978) and then *Manhattan* (1979), another picture starring himself and Diane Keaton, as well as a young Mariel Hemingway. The film, Allen's so-called "love letter to New York," was well received. Woody Allen was officially a sophisticated, significant auteur, clearly influenced by Bergman and Federico Fellini. That's what the critics said, anyway—most people just went to his films to be entertained.

And they were entertained throughout the 1980s, though the stories Allen told increasingly combined both comic and tragic themes, as in *Stardust Memories* (1980), *Broadway Danny Rose* (1984), *Hannah and Her Sisters* (1986), *Crimes and Misdemeanors* (1989), and *The Purple Rose of Cairo* (1985), the last of which stars Allen's then-partner actress Mia Farrow and is considered one of his best films. Allen's work grew increasingly autobiographical, and he became more interested in parodying and deconstructing film conventions and genres.

The 1990s brought more success for Allen, including hits such as *Shadows and Fog* (1991), *Husbands and Wives* (1992), *Bullets Over Broadway* (1994), and *Mighty Aphrodite* (1995). The Academy was generous with Oscar nominations (and a few wins) for Allen and the actresses who appeared in his films, and Woody continued to have his pick of Hollywood's finest actors for his projects. Part of his appeal to actors is his reputation, and part of it is his low-key directorial style that allows actors to discover their characters and interpret them.

The Soon-Yi Thing

Since 1980, Allen had been in a serious relationship with actress Mia Farrow, who starred in many of his films. The two never married, but they adopted two children together and had a son of their own. Farrow also brought several children to the relationship, including some from her previous marriage to Andre Previn, though Allen never formally adopted them. In 1992, when Farrow found nude photographs of her 21-year-old adopted daughter, Soon-Yi Previn, in Allen's possession, she separated from him at once. Allen and Soon-Yi revealed that they were in a relationship (despite a 35-year age difference). They were married in 1997 and have two children together.

Woody Returns

At the turn of the 21st century, the director's popularity—and, some would say, his comic style and attention to detail—waned. Was it because of the Soon-Yi scandal? Perhaps. Films such as *The Curse of the Jade Scorpion* (2001), *Hollywood Ending* (2002), and *Melinda and Melinda* (2004) were critical and commercial disappointments.

Then, in 2005, Allen directed *Match Point,* a drama that adapted the moral themes of Dostoevsky to a modern setting. *Match Point* was a success at the box office and with critics, too. The film grossed $23 million in its initial release—more than any Allen film of the previous 20 years—and earned even more abroad. Allen's next success came in 2008 with *Vicky Cristina Barcelona,* a sensual comedy starring Scarlett Johansson (a recent favorite of Allen's) and Penelope Cruz, who won an Oscar for Best Supporting Actress.

Now in his 70s, Woody Allen doesn't seem to be slowing down. His talent for wearing numerous hats within the motion picture industry has left an indelible mark on the art form.

Popcorn and the Cinema

☆ ☆ ☆ ☆

Popcorn could be called the smell of the cinema, but the buttery treat wasn't always favored in movie houses. In fact, theater owners initially resisted the idea of letting the salty stuff inside their doors.

Popcorn Resistance

Popcorn's romance with the box office started in the 1920s, but in those days, the corn was popping *outside* of theaters, especially in large urban areas. Back then, vendors set up carts outside movie houses and sold the snack to crowds on their way in.

The 1920s was the era of the picture palace, when huge theaters were constructed with elaborate decor designed for comfort, class, and escapism. Greasy popcorn didn't fit with that image. Historians say it wasn't until the Great Depression that theater owners realized that the snack could bring in added profits. That realization was the beginning of the movie industry's most famous partnership.

The Rise and the Pop

By the 1930s, with the rise of the electric popping machine, popcorn in theaters was commonplace. Prior to that, popcorn poppers sent nasty burning smells into the air, but with the olfactory offense eliminated, the path was clear for nonstop popping.

Popcorn was inexpensive to make, which helped it rise in popularity during the Depression. Theater owners could price a bag at an affordable ten cents and still manage to make money from the sales. Popcorn demand skyrocketed as the '30s progressed, and when World War II began, the government's rationing of sugar made popcorn a favored alternative to sweeter snacks.

Popcorn Today

These days, movie theaters rely heavily on snacks to make a profit. It is estimated that concessions account for nearly half of the revenue at some theaters. The selections have expanded, but popcorn continues to make up a significant part of the equation—and it's one crunch you can count on hearing for years to come.

To Live and Die in L.A.

Hollywood is a place where stars are made. It can also be the place where celebrities meet a tragic end. Here are some stars who have had their dreams—and lives—come to an end in the City of Angels.

John Belushi

Actor and comedian John Belushi, most famous for his work on *Saturday Night Live* and in the movies *Animal House* (1978) and *The Blues Brothers* (1980), died of an overdose at the Chateau Marmont hotel on Sunset Boulevard. On the night of March 4, 1982, after partying at clubs along the Sunset Strip, Belushi and friends returned to Bungalow No. 3 at the Chateau. When the party disbanded, Belushi had celebrity groupie Cathy Evelyn Smith shoot him up with a speedball, a mix of cocaine and heroin. The next morning, Belushi's personal trainer found him lying on the bed in the bungalow. At age 33, Belushi was dead. Smith eventually served 18 months for manslaughter.

William Frawley

Most know William Frawley as cranky Fred Mertz from everyone's favorite sitcom *I Love Lucy*. But before playing Fred, Frawley was a respected character actor (*Miracle on 34th Street*, 1947; *The Babe Ruth Story*, 1948; *The Lemon Drop Kid*, 1951). After *I Love Lucy*, he enjoyed a turn as Uncle Bub on the hit TV show *My Three Sons*. Sadly, as Frawley was strolling in Hollywood in 1966, he collapsed from a massive heart attack. A kind passerby dragged him into the Knickerbocker Hotel, but he was already gone. Coincidentally, he was just half a block away from his star on the Hollywood Walk of Fame.

William Holden

Legendary actor William Holden appeared in classic movies such as *Sunset Boulevard* (1950), *Bridge on the River Kwai* (1957), and *The Wild Bunch* (1969). He was known as a very private person and a bit of a drinker, both of which contributed to the circumstances of his death. On November 16, 1981, the building manager of the Shorecliff Towers in Santa Monica discovered Holden's body in his fourth floor apartment. Holden had slipped on a throw rug and lacerated his head on a table. Forensic evidence indicated that the 63-year-old actor had bled to death some four days before his body was found.

Haing S. Ngor
Winner of the Best Supporting Actor Oscar for *The Killing Fields* (1984), actor Haing S. Ngor had survived Pol Pot's brutal Khmer Rouge dictatorship in Cambodia only to lose his life on the streets of Los Angeles. On February 25, 1996, as he returned to his home on North Beaudry Avenue between Chinatown and Dodger Stadium, Ngor was gunned down in his driveway during a robbery attempt by a street gang. Ngor may have been killed because he refused to relinquish a gold locket containing a picture of his late wife, who had died under the Khmer Rouge regime.

Notorious B.I.G.
In the early hours of March 9, 1997, influential rap artist Christopher Wallace, also known as Biggie Smalls or Notorious B.I.G., was gunned down by a drive-by shooter outside the Petersen Automotive Museum on Wilshire Boulevard. Wallace was at the museum to attend the after-party for *Vibe* magazine's Soul Train Music Awards. At around 12:30 A.M., Wallace left the event with his entourage. When his vehicle stopped at a red light just 50 yards from the museum, a black Chevy Impala pulled alongside, and the driver fired numerous rounds from a 9mm pistol, hitting the 24-year-old rap star in the chest. His murder remains unsolved, although plenty of conspiracy theories surround his death.

Ramon Novarro
Dark, exotic, and handsome, Ramon Novarro was groomed to fill Valentino's sheik costume after the untimely death of the screen icon, but the coming of sound shifted audiences' tastes from exotic types to down-to-earth heroes with the touch of the common man. Novarro was all but forgotten until Halloween night in 1968, when two young thieves broke into his mansion on Laurel Canyon Drive, tortured the 69-year-old former star, and then beat him to death. Small wonder that his ghost still roams the house.

River Phoenix
At about 1 A.M. on October 31, 1993, the young star of *Stand By Me* (1986) and *My Own Private Idaho* (1991) collapsed and died of drug-induced heart failure outside Johnny Depp's Sunset Boulevard nightclub, The Viper Room. River's younger brother, Joaquin Phoenix, dialed 911 as River suffered convulsions on the sidewalk and then lay motionless. Toxicological tests revealed that the 23-year-old not only had deadly levels of cocaine and herion in his system but also traces of Valium, marijuana, and cold medicine.

Cross-Dressing Characters

An actor is only as good as his (or her) role, especially when that role requires playing the opposite sex. Hollywood is chock-full of movies in which men have played women and vice versa. Here are just a few:

- Charlie Chaplin played a woman in three films: *A Busy Day* (1914), *The Masquerader* (1914), and *A Woman* (1915).

- Wallace Beery appeared in drag as a Swedish housekeeper in a series of comedies produced in the 1910s, including *Sweedie the Swatter* (1914), *Sweedie Springs a Surprise* (1914), and *Sweedie and Her Dog* (1915).

- Sydney Howard played a gym teacher who masquerades as the headmistress of a school to break up a college romance in the 1934 comedy *Girls Please!*

- Tony Curtis and Jack Lemmon both donned dresses in an effort to hide from gangsters in Billy Wilder's classic comedy *Some Like It Hot* (1959).

- Dustin Hoffman played an actor who dons a dress to pass as an actress who joins the cast of a soap opera in *Tootsie* (1982).

- Julie Andrews portrayed a woman playing a man playing a woman in the Blake Edwards comedy *Victor Victoria* (1982).

- Linda Hunt received an Academy Award for her portrayal of news cameraman Billy Kwan in *The Year of Living Dangerously* (1982).

- Dom DeLuise hammed it up as Aunt Kate in the horror spoof *Haunted Honeymoon* (1986).

- Debra Winger played archangel Emmett in *Made in Heaven* (1987).

- Robin Williams played a father who dresses in drag to portray the title role in *Mrs. Doubtfire* (1993).

- Tyler Perry portrayed a gun-toting, smart-mouthed senior citizen named Madea in *Diary of a Mad Black Woman* (2005).

- John Travolta was completely transformed into the hefty but fashionable Edna Turnblad in the movie version of the musical *Hairspray* (2007).

Pop Quiz: The Name Game—Part 2

Name changes are almost mandatory in Hollywood, and it's easy to see why. Tom Cruise sounds worlds sexier than Thomas Cruise Mapother IV. How well can you match these celebs with their birth names?

Stage Name	Birth Name
1. Charles Bronson	A. Krishna Bhanji
2. Mel Brooks	B. Nathan Birnbaum
3. George Burns	C. Eric Marlon Bishop
4. Nicolas Cage	D. Charles Bunchinski
5. Sandra Dee	E. Nicholas Kim Coppola
6. Troy Donahue	F. Carlos Irwin Estevez
7. Jamie Foxx	G. Demetria Gene Guynes
8. Whoopi Goldberg	H. Natalie Hershlag
9. Boris Karloff	I. Margaret Mary Emily Anne Hyra
10. Ben Kingsley	J. Caryn Elaine Johnson
11. Janet Leigh	K. Merle Johnson Jr.
12. Jayne Mansfield	L. Mel Kaminsky
13. Demi Moore	M. Jeanette Morrison
14. Jack Palance	N. Walter Jack Palahnuik
15. Natalie Portman	O. Vera Jane Palmer
16. Meg Ryan	P. William Henry Pratt
17. Charlie Sheen	Q. Jerome Silberman
18. Gene Wilder	R. Natalia Nikolaevna Zakharenko
19. Natalie Wood	S. Alexandra Zuck

Answer Key: 1. D; 2. L; 3. B; 4. E; 5. S; 6. K; 7. C; 8. J; 9. P; 10. A; 11. M; 12. O; 13. G; 14. N; 15. H; 16. I; 17. F; 18. Q; 19. R.

389

What Really Killed John Wayne?

☆ ☆ ☆ ☆

The Conqueror (1956) wasn't exactly John Wayne's masterpiece. According to "The Duke" himself, the film was actually written with Marlon Brando in mind for the lead role, and this historical drama has been criticized for miscasting Wayne in the part. However, The Conqueror *has been connected to far worse things than box-office failure: Some say the movie is to blame for Wayne's death from stomach cancer two decades after its debut. What's more, Wayne isn't the only person believed to have died as a result of the project.*

Radiation Exposure

The questions surrounding *The Conqueror* come as a result of its filming location: The movie was shot near St. George and Snow Canyon, Utah, an area in the vicinity of a nuclear testing site. In the early 1950s, the U.S. military set off nearly a dozen atomic bombs just miles away from the location, sending clouds of radioactive dust into St. George and Snow Canyon. Work on *The Conqueror* began just two years later, even though the film company and cast knew about the radiation. To make matters worse, after the location work had wrapped, the film's crew transported dirt from the area back to soundstages in Hollywood to help re-create the setting for in-studio shooting. (At the time, the effects of radiation exposure were not as well documented as they are today.)

In the years following the filming of *The Conqueror*, numerous members of the cast and crew developed cancer. Aside from Wayne, at least 45 people from the group died from causes related to the disease, including actress Agnes Moorehead, who died in 1974 from uterine cancer; actress Susan Hayward, who died from brain and skin cancer at age 57 in 1975; and director Dick Powell, who, in 1963, passed away at age 58 from lymphatic cancer. Actors Pedro Armendariz and John Hoyt and both took their own lives after learning of their diagnoses.

An article published in *People* magazine in 1980 stated that 41 percent of those who worked on the movie—91 out of 220 people—later developed cancer. That figure reportedly didn't include the hundreds of Utah-based actors who worked as extras. Still, the numbers far exceeded any statistical normality for a given group of individuals. A scientist with the Pentagon's Defense Nuclear Agency was quoted in the article as saying: "Please, God, don't let us have killed John Wayne."

Broader Findings

While many of the actors were heavy smokers—Wayne included—the strange circumstances surrounding the filming of *The Conqueror* have turned into an underground scandal of sorts. And the general findings from the city of St. George certainly don't help quell the concerns.

In 1997, a study by the National Cancer Institute found that children who lived in the St. George area during the 1950s were exposed to as much as 70 times the amount of radiation than was originally reported because of contaminated milk taken from exposed animals. Consequently, the study reported that the children had elevated risks for cancer development. The report further stated that the government "knew from the beginning that a Western test site would spread contamination across most of the country" and that the exposure could have easily been avoided.

The government eventually passed an act called the Radiation Exposure Compensation Act, which provided $50,000 to people who lived downwind of the nuclear testing site near St. George and had been exposed to radiation. At least 40,000 people are thought to have been exposed in Utah alone. While John Wayne is the most famous of them, the true cause of his cancer may never be definitively known.

• *The actor known as John Wayne was born Marion Morrison. The name John Wayne came about in 1930 in the months before filming began on* The Big Trail. *Twentieth Century Fox wanted a catchier moniker, and the name Anthony Wayne—from the Army general known as "Mad" Anthony—caught their attention. They substituted "John" for "Anthony," and Marion Morrison became John Wayne.*

How to Get a Star on the Hollywood Walk of Fame

They say you'll know you've made it in Hollywood when they give you your very own star on the Hollywood Walk of Fame, which is located along Hollywood Boulevard. But just how do all those celebs go about getting their very own star? Well, read on, because you might be surprised at just how easy it is to get one.

Q: Who can apply for a star?

A: Anyone who makes/made their living in one of five categories: Live Theater/Performance, Motion Pictures, Radio, Recording, and Television.

Q: How does one begin the application process?

A: Complete and mail in a nomination form by the end of May to be eligible for a star in June of the following year. The form must be accompanied by a bio and a photo of the nominee, their qualifications, and a list of their contributions to the community. Also applicants must be sponsored by agents, fan clubs, producers, or local businesses, who provide a letter of agreement.

Q: What criteria must a star applicant meet?

A: For someone to be considered for a star, the applicant must have been involved with the entertainment industry for more than five years and/or have made contributions to the community. Applicants must also agree to attend a dedication ceremony if they are accepted. The Walk of Fame has been criticized for withdrawing an honor if a star refuses to appear in person.

Q: Who decides who gets a star?

A: Each year, the Walk of Fame Committee, which is part of the Hollywood Chamber of Commerce, is responsible for choosing from the submitted applications to select a new group of entertainers to receive stars on the Hollywood Walk of Fame. Once the Committee has made its selections, they still must be approved by the Hollywood Chamber of Commerce's Board of Directors and the City of Los Angeles' Board of Public Works Department.

Q: How many people are awarded a star each year?

A: The committee annually nominates up to 20 people to receive a star.

Q: How many people apply for a star each year?

A: On average, the Committee receives 300 applications per year.

Q: Do you have to be alive to get a star?

A: No. Every year, one star is awarded posthumously. However, friends and family must wait five years after the entertainer's death before submitting an application. The Committee has been criticized for its failure to honor many industry pioneers because they lack a presence among the public and there are no family members to pony up the fee.

Q: How much does each star cost?

A: Each recipient must pay $25,000 to the Walk of Fame Trust upon receiving his or her star.

Q: How do people find out if they've been awarded a star?

A: Each June, the Committee announces who will receive a star the following year.

Q: What are the stars made of?

A: The stars are made of coral terrazzo with brass accents.

Q: Do people get to choose where their star goes?

A: No, the stars are placed in areas as they are awarded. Stars are also faced in alternating opposite directions so that people walking either way on the sidewalk can read them.

Q: How can I get directions to a specific star after it's in place?

A: The Hollywood Chamber of Commerce hosts an online search engine that notes the location of current stars.

Q: Can I attend the presentation ceremony when the stars are unveiled?

A: Yes, the ceremony is open to the general public.

Q: What if an applicant doesn't get picked?

A: Applicants are permitted to reapply as many times as they like.

Hollywood Drops the Ball

It's hard not to like a sports movie, even if you're not into sports. However, when a movie is based on a historic sporting event or a real athlete, sometimes the filmmakers take dramatic license to make a more logical story, to suggest a moral, or even for legal reasons. Here are some all-star sports movies that stand out for fumbling a few details.

Knute Rockne All American (1940)

Remembered for Ronald Reagan's portrayal of George "The Gipper" Gipp and Pat O'Brien's performance as Knute Rockne, this one has plenty of heart, even if some of the facts are a bit clouded, such as Rockne's role in developing the forward pass. Although he may have *popularized* it, it had been used before Knute hit the gridiron. Likewise, Gipp's famous deathbed speech, in which he urges Rockne to "Tell them to win one for the Gipper," was most likely an inspiring fabrication.

Pride of the Yankees (1942)

Long before the TV movie *Brian's Song* made it okay for men to cry during a movie, the story of Lou Gehrig told what it was like to be "the luckiest man on the face of the earth." This film also went to great lengths to get the facts straight, including having right-handed Gary Cooper wear a uniform with the letters reversed to depict the lefty slugger Gehrig and then reversing the film during processing. However, there were notable departures, including the fact that the final speech was heavily rearranged for dramatic effect. In reality, Gehrig ended with the famous line rather than beginning with it.

Chariots of Fire (1981)

This film took the Oscar for Best Picture for its portrayal of the 1924 Summer Olympics in Paris, but it also took liberties with the accuracy of events. In real life, Eric Liddell knew months in advance that the preliminary heats in his main event would be held on a Sunday, and teammate Harold Abrahams competed and *lost* in the 1920 Olympics. Also, the two were not rivals as the film depicts. Instead, the experiences of these two athletes, whose religions defined them, are used to weave a timeless story of religious tolerance and the power of faith.

Eight Men Out (1988)

This film captures the darkest days of baseball (at least until the recent steroid scandals), but there are a few details that are totally off base—such as southpaw pitcher Dickie Kerr being right-handed in the movie. The film recounts the story of the 1919 World Series between the Chicago White Sox and the Cincinnati Reds, after which eight White Sox players were accused of accepting bribes to lose the series. The players were accurately depicted as victims caught between organized gambling syndicates and team owners (and their selfish agendas), but the film does take liberties with some facts. For example, Chick Gandil's pro career did not end because of the scandal. He had already retired before the scandal was exposed because Sox owner Charles Comiskey would not give him a $1,000 raise. At least this one, while making it hard to root, root, root for the home team, shows that the villains weren't just those who took the money.

Rudy (1993)

The true story of Daniel "Rudy" Ruettiger was the first film given permission to shoot on the campus of the University of Notre Dame since *Knute Rockne All American*. And while this true story is proof that dreams do come true in the world of sports, the film's low budget did allow for some inaccuracies to creep in. For example, cars in street scenes were of later models than those of the era in which the film was set, and a New York City scene set in the late 1960s included the World Trade Center towers, which were not completed until the early 1970s. The film also portrays Ruettiger's high school as coed years before it was in real life. One scene that took a great deal of dramatic license sees a player set his shirt on Coach Dan Devine's desk to sacrifice his place on the "dress list." It never happened. In fact, Devine had planned to put Ruettiger in the game all along. But for the sake of a dramatic story line, Devine agreed to be painted as the villain in the film.

Invincible (2006)

It's a fantasy that every Monday morning quarterback dreams about—playing for his favorite professional football team. This film, starring Mark Wahlberg, captured the look and feel of the 1970s authentically enough, but it fumbled badly on a few key points, notably that the real Vince Papale wasn't a complete unknown when he tried out for the Philadelphia Eagles in 1976. In fact, Papale had played for the World Football League's Philadelphia Bell for two seasons before trying out for the Eagles.

Gene Tierney: On a Razor's Edge

☆ ☆ ☆ ☆

Famed for her roles in movies such as Otto Preminger's
Laura *(1944), the screen adaptation of Somerset Maugham's novel*
The Razor's Edge *(1946), and* The Ghost and Mrs. Muir *(1947),*
Gene Tierney was one of the most glamorous stars of the 1940s
and '50s. Offscreen, however, she was plagued by mental health
problems, and she was eventually institutionalized and
underwent years of brutal shock treatment.

Gene Tierney's early life belies her tumultuous later years. Born to
an affluent family, she was educated in private schools on the East
Coast and in Switzerland. As a young woman, she told her family
that she wanted to be an actress, so her father formed Belle-Tier,
a corporation designed to develop and promote her burgeoning
career. And, with her high cheekbones, delicate complexion, and
blue-green eyes, Tierney's good looks were certainly an asset.

In 1939, while playing a supporting role in *The Male Animal,*
she was seen by studio head Darryl F. Zanuck, who signed her to a
long-term contract with 20th Century Fox. Her first film for Fox,
The Return of Frank James, found her in the Old West playing
opposite Henry Fonda. She made for a glamorous, if not realistic,
outlaw's gal. After several years of forgettable roles in routine films,
Tierney landed her signature role—the title character in *Laura*
(1944), a film noir about a girl presumed dead who makes an impact
on the detective assigned to the case. Director Otto Preminger
made good use of Tierney's classic beauty by making a huge portrait
of Laura central to the story line. Even when Laura, the flesh-and-
blood character, was offscreen, the portrait kept her presence and
beauty in the forefront.

The other classic film on which Tierney left her mark was
Leave Her to Heaven (1945), another film noir in which she was cast
as a murderess. In this film, Tierney's sophisticated beauty helped
sell a character who used her looks to hide her inner demons. For
her performance, Tierney received an Academy Award nomination.
Finally, stardom was in her grasp . . . but it didn't last long.

Downward Spiral

Many friends of the actress point to the birth of Tierney's first daughter as the trigger for her mental illness. While filming *Heaven Can Wait* in 1943, the actress became pregnant with husband Oleg Cassini's child. Tragically, she contracted German measles (rubella) during the pregnancy and her daughter Daria was born prematurely. The baby girl was blind, deaf, and weighed only three pounds. When doctors announced that Daria would never progress beyond the mental age of 18 months, Tierney was devastated. She agreed to put Daria into a home that could provide the round-the-clock care she required, and soon after, Tierney and Cassini separated for the first time. Years later, Tierney encountered a fan who recalled meeting the actress in 1943, when the fan had sneaked out of quarantine while sick with German measles. In her autobiography, Tierney stated, "After that I didn't care whether...I was anyone's favorite actress."

Shortly after she and Cassini finally divorced in 1952, Tierney began to exhibit symptoms of mental illness, starting with severe mood swings and progressing to paranoid neurosis. In 1954, while on the set of *The Left Hand of God* with Humphrey Bogart, she struggled to remember her lines and became increasingly confused. Tierney was admitted to at least two institutions, where she was diagnosed with depression, among other problems. During her 18-month stay at one institution, she underwent electric shock treatment. By the time of her release, years of her past had been erased from her memory, but the treatment did little to improve her mental health. In December 1957, Tierney was admitted to a mental hospital, where she was subjected to ice treatments, during which she was wrapped from the neck down in icy wet sheets. This was followed by another brief visit to a sanitarium and more torturous treatment.

After spending most of 1958 and part of 1959 hospitalized, Tierney put her mental troubles behind her and finally found peace when she married Texas oilman Howard Lee in 1960. But by then, Tierney's acting career was drying up. She was offered the lead role in *Return to Peyton Place* (1961), but she turned it down when she found out she was pregnant. She later had a miscarriage. She returned to the screen in 1962 for Preminger's *Advise & Consent* but had only a handful of acting roles after that. A longtime heavy smoker, Tierney died of emphysema in 1991 at age 70.

Pucker Up, Hot Stuff: Great Screen Kisses

Who doesn't love a great kiss? In the movies, a good smooch is made even greater because it's larger than life up there on the big screen. A memorable screen kiss could result from serious star chemistry; it could serve as a major plot point; or it could just be hot for hot's sake. Here are a few of Hollywood's most unforgettable kisses.

May Irwin and John Rice, *The Kiss* (1896)

The first film ever made of a couple kissing certainly merits a place among the most famous movie kisses. Actors May Irwin and John Rice kiss chastely for W.K.L. Dickson (working for Thomas Edison) in a 20-second film aptly titled *The Kiss*. Although the pair was simply reenacting a scene from a play called *The Widow Jones*, many regarded the film as "disgusting" and demanded that it be withdrawn from viewing. Still—perhaps not surprisingly—*The Kiss* became the most popular film produced by Edison's film company that year.

John Barrymore and Company, *Don Juan* (1926)

As he swashbuckles his way through everything in his path, legendary lover Don Juan (played by John Barrymore) makes time for some prodigious kissing in this vintage film. Between hand kisses, kisses up the arms, and locking lips with his two leading ladies—Mary Astor and Helene Costello—as well as various other smoochable women who crossed his path, a whopping 191 kisses were planted by Barrymore in *Don Juan*—a record that has yet to be broken.

Vivien Leigh and Clark Gable, *Gone with the Wind* (1939)

In the final days of the Civil War, dashing Rhett Butler (Gable) saves Scarlett O'Hara (Leigh) from a burning Atlanta. As they part ways in the countryside, with Rhett going off to fight for a losing cause and Scarlett on her way home to Tara, he sweeps the saucy Southern belle into his arms and tells her that he's a soldier who "wants to carry the memory of your kisses into battle with him...you're a woman sending a soldier to his death with a beautiful memory. Scarlett! Kiss me!"

Katharine Hepburn and Jimmy Stewart, *The Philadelphia Story* (1940)

Some of the best movie kisses ever are the ones you totally didn't see coming. In this classic film, Hepburn's character, Tracy, is about to marry a man who obviously doesn't deserve her. The night before the nuptials, Tracy flirts with Mike (Jimmy Stewart). The only way Mike, a reporter, can get her to be quiet is to lay one on her. Well, one or two.

Regis Toomey and Jane Wyman, *You're in the Army Now* (1941)

The longest kiss in film history occurs between dreamy Capt. Joe Radcliffe (Regis Toomey) and kittenish Bliss Dobson (Jane Wyman) in this comedic film. They get to kissin' and don't let each other come up for air for more than three minutes.

Lauren Bacall and Humphrey Bogart, *To Have and Have Not* (1944)

This tale of love and adventure on the island of Martinique is famous for introducing Lauren Bacall to Humphrey Bogart, who became a real-life couple. In a scene charged with electricity, Bacall sits in Bogart's lap and kisses him. When he inquires what that was all about, she coolly tells him, "Been wondering if I would like it." They kiss again, and she remarks, "It's even better when you help."

Burt Lancaster and Deborah Kerr, *From Here to Eternity* (1953)

Two lovers, frolicking in the sea, run out of the surf and tumble onto the beach in a passionate kiss. The movie and the kiss caused a stir with audiences at first because Kerr's character was cheating on her husband when she kissed Lancaster's character. Other people were uncomfortable with the fact that the two were in bathing suits and were *lying down* when they locked lips. Scandalous!

Marlon Brando and Eva Marie Saint, *On the Waterfront* (1954)

Edie Doyle (Eva Marie Saint) is minding her own business in her room when Terry (Brando) bursts in. Terry is tortured by his love for Edie and his guilt over killing her brother. Edie puts that all aside and basically admits that she loves him, too. Terry pins her against the wall, and they take the kiss all the way to the floor.

Lady and the Tramp (1955)

It's a setup that would probably work only in a cartoon, but it's romantic nonetheless. Two dogs are having a cozy spaghetti dinner in the moonlight and happen to be chomping different sides of the same noodle. They chew and chew, not looking at each other, and then, bam! Nose to nose and deeply in love.

Audrey Hepburn and George Peppard, Breakfast at Tiffany's (1961)

The kiss shared between an emotional Holly Golightly and a fed-up but head-over-heels-in-love Paul "Fred" Varjack is significant for its setting: a rainstorm. Kisses in the rain always get a thumbs-up from audiences. Other memorable rainy kisses include an upside-down one in *Spider-Man* (2002) and a love-and-rain-soaked one in *The Notebook* (2004).

Peter Finch and Murray Head, Sunday Bloody Sunday (1971)

Perhaps the first screen kiss between two men in a mainstream commercial film, this one caused quite a stir when audiences first saw it. The scene between the two actors was so shocking to Peter Finch's wife when she saw it at the premiere that she screamed. Finch has said of the risky smooch in the critically acclaimed film, "I did it for England."

Al Pacino and John Cazale, The Godfather: Part II (1974)

After Don Michael Corleone (played by Pacino) figures out that his brother Fredo has betrayed him, Michael embraces his brother and forcefully kisses him on the mouth, saying, "I know it was you, Fredo. You broke my heart, you broke my heart." This was a "kiss of death" because Fredo doesn't last long afterward.

Carrie Fisher and Harrison Ford, The Empire Strikes Back (1980)

The first kiss between Princess Leia and Han Solo was a long time coming, and that made it one of Hollywood's most memorable. Fisher's character says at one point that she'd "rather kiss a wookie" than the handsome pilot played by Ford, but that only added to the audience's anticipation. When the two finally lip-locked, it was well worth the *Star Wars*-size wait.

The First 22 Cartoons to Win an Oscar

Not all Oscar winners are made of flesh and blood; some are made of ink.

1. *Flowers and Trees* (1931/32, Walt Disney, Producer)
2. *The Three Little Pigs* (1932/33, Walt Disney, Producer)
3. *The Tortoise and the Hare* (1934, Walt Disney, Producer)
4. *Three Orphan Kittens* (1935, Walt Disney, Producer)
5. *The Country Cousin* (1936, Walt Disney, Producer)
6. *The Old Mill* (1937, Walt Disney, Producer)
7. *Ferdinand the Bull* (1938, Walt Disney, Producer)
8. *The Ugly Duckling* (1939, Walt Disney, Producer
9. *The Milky Way* (1940, MGM, Rudolph Ising, Producer)
10. *Lend a Paw* (1941, Walt Disney, Producer)
11. *Der Fuehrer's Face* (1942, Walt Disney, Producer)
12. *Yankee Doodle Mouse* (1943, MGM, Frederick Quimby, Producer)
13. *Mouse Trouble* (1944, MGM, Frederick Quimby, Producer)
14. *Quiet Please!* (1945, MGM, Frederick Quimby, Producer)
15. *The Cat Concerto* (1946, MGM, Frederick Quimby, Producer)
16. *Tweetie Pie* (1947, Warner Bros., Edward Selzer, Producer)
17. *The Little Orphan* (1948, MGM, Frederick Quimby, Producer)
18. *For Scent-imental Reasons* (1949, Warner Bros., Edward Selzer, Producer)
19. *Gerald McBoing-Boing* (1950, UPA/Columbia, Stephen Bosustow, Producer)
20. *The Two Mouseketeers* (1951, MGM, Frederick Quimby, Producer)
21. *Johann Mouse* (1952, MGM, Frederick Quimby, Producer)
22. *Toot, Whistle, Plunk and Boom* (1953, Walt Disney, Producer)

Blaxploitation

☆ ☆ ☆ ☆

The genre that gave us *Shaft* (1971), *Super Fly* (1972), and Pam Grier, as well as memorable soundtracks littered with classic soul and funk, is known as *blaxploitation.* This film genre emerged in the early 1970s at a time when exploitation movies—those that sacrificed artistry to focus on gritty and sensational content—were growing in popularity. They usually featured a great deal of graphic imagery, such as sex, exaggerated violence, and gore. Essentially, a blaxploitation picture is an exploitation movie with a black cast who typically find themselves battling "The Man" and other unsympathetic white characters. The protagonist is an assertive, urban black man (or woman) who is tough, sexy, and not intimidated by white authority figures.

The 1971 cult hit *Sweet Sweetback's Baadasssss Song* is often credited with creating the genre. Melvin Van Peebles starred in, wrote, directed, scored, edited, produced, and largely financed the entire film himself. The story centers on a young black man, who was raised by prostitutes. After seeing two white policemen beat a young black revolutionary to death, he kills a couple of corrupt cops, then goes on the run. The movie was visually influenced by European films in its use of unusual camera angles, rapid editing, freeze frames, and superimpositions. And the film's soundtrack featured songs from a previously unknown band called Earth, Wind & Fire.

MGM and other studios noticed the box-office success of the film and followed it with movies such as *Shaft* (1971), starring Richard Roundtree; *The Mack* (1973) with Max Julien and Richard Pryor; and *Super Fly* (1972), which starred Ron O'Neal and featured Curtis Mayfield's soulful soundtrack.

The blaxploitation genre wasn't restricted to male heroes. Movies such as *Cleopatra Jones* (1973) and the Pam Grier vehicle *Foxy Brown* (1974) featured black females who were just as empowered as their male counterparts. The blaxploitation genre's influence is apparent in newer movies—such as Quentin Tarantino's *Jackie Brown* (1997) and the 2009 blaxploitation spoof *Black Dynamite*—and undoubtedly broke barriers for mainstream black actors and filmmakers such as Spike Lee, Forest Whitaker, Samuel L. Jackson, and John Singleton.

Modern Horror Movies

If you love getting the daylights scared out of you, you've got to watch these essential horror movies—but maybe not alone. When you're not covering your eyes in terror, consider the artistry of the genre. In most modern horror flicks, there are many layers being addressed, including social commentary and sidesplitting humor.

Rosemary's Baby (1968)
Have you ever met a kid you thought must have been the spawn of Satan? Well, Rosemary (played by Mia Farrow) actually gives birth to such a child. This Roman Polanski-directed flick focuses more on conveying disturbing feelings than on projecting blood and gore, but if you want to be scared, it'll do the job.

The Exorcist (1973)
When a nice little girl gets possessed by the devil, it's ... well, it's messy. If you grew up Catholic and like to be grossed out, then this modern classic, directed by William Friedkin, is for you (or anyone with a fondness for horror movies done right). Just don't eat too much popcorn while you're watching—you might not keep it down.

The Texas Chain Saw Massacre (1974)
For a movie this scary, director Tobe Hooper used remarkably little blood and gore, but don't worry ... the motives of the grotesque Sawyer family are creepy enough to give you the chills. The word *massacre* is in the title for a reason, so if you're looking for a movie with truly frightening villains and more than a little carnage, look no further.

Carrie (1976)
The girl who everyone makes fun of gets her revenge in this classic Stephen King horror tale. We won't give anything away, but let's just say that Carrie, played by a young Sissy Spacek, has a terrifying power at her command. Director Brian De Palma used gallons upon gallons of fake pig's blood in the making of one unforgettable scene.

Halloween (1978)
Michael Myers—the killer in this often imitated but never duplicated horror favorite—quietly creeps up on the teenagers he slaughters. Terror is deftly conveyed in director John Carpenter's low-budget but

super-effective flick that has had not one, not two, but eight sequels, plus a remake, which spawned its own sequel. Tip: Stick with the original. Jamie Lee Curtis made her big-screen debut in this thriller.

The Amityville Horror (1979)
When the Lutz family moves into a quaint Dutch-Colonial house in Amityville, New York, they have no idea what they're in for. In this horror classic based on a book by Jay Anson (purportedly a "true story"), the haunted house is the main character. Voices, slamming doors, a swarm of flies, and many more scream-inducing events take place from start to finish, even though a priest (played by Rod Steiger) attempts to bless the house in hopes of exorcising the demons. The reason for all this trouble? A family *was* actually murdered in the house in 1974, and some still firmly believe that 112 Ocean Avenue is haunted by their spirits. Maybe, maybe not…but it sure made for a frightening movie.

Friday the 13th (1980)

One of the most profitable slasher films in history, *Friday the 13th* has spawned sequels, novels, comic books, and tons of merchandise. Before all that, there was just the story of how a bunch of doomed teenagers met a hockey-mask-wearing killer named Jason. Spoiler alert: It doesn't go well for the teenagers. Look for a young Kevin Bacon in one of his early roles.

The Shining (1980)
A haunted hotel in the middle of nowhere becomes the home of Jack Nicholson and family for the winter—and that's when the terror begins. Tidal waves of blood, corpses in the shower, ghostly twins who roam the halls, and a total breakdown of Jack's sanity make this Stanley Kubrick film, based on Stephen King's best-selling novel, a must for any horror movie fan.

The Evil Dead (1981)
This fright-filled film, which gave director Sam Raimi his start, has gone beyond "classic" to achieve cult status. When five college students decide to hang out in an abandoned cabin in the woods, they accidentally release evil spirits. From there, it's nonstop horror (and humor, actually) as the teens fall, one by one, at the hands of some pretty angry demons.

Children of the Corn (1984)

When the kids of a small Nebraska town turn on the adults, they're not looking to eat more cookies and play hide-and-seek. Murder and death come to the grown-ups in this film adaptation of a Stephen King short story. Not too many parents named their kids Malachai after this movie came out.

Candyman (1992)

Based on a Clive Barker story, this movie preys on the fears behind urban legends. A girl working on her college thesis decides that there's no harm in conjuring a fake ghost who supposedly haunts a Chicago housing project. Turns out that the "Candyman" isn't so fake after all....

The Blair Witch Project (1999)

This film, shot in a documentary style, caused quite a sensation when it was released. Rumor had it that the shaky footage of doomed teens out in the woods looking for a fabled witch was actually real and that the fate of the kids was no joke. Despite its realism, this film was actually a fictional narrative by indie directors Daniel Myrick and Eduardo Sanchez, but that doesn't dampen its bone-chilling spookiness.

Saw (2004)

If you're looking for major blood and guts in a horror movie, here's your flick. Saw is so disturbing and graphic that it has garnered criticism for being almost pornographic. The "saw" in question is only one of the horrifying instruments used in the film for torture and mayhem. Several sequels have been made, and the franchise has a strong following, though they've never been critically acclaimed.

The Grudge (2004)

An American version of what some have called the scariest movie of all time hit theaters in 2004, starring Sarah Michelle Gellar of the cult TV show Buffy the Vampire Slayer. Based on the Japanese film Ju-On, the plot is simple: When someone dies in the grip of sorrow or rage, they unleash a curse that travels around and kills other people. Though this film tackles subplots and has a nonlinear structure, it's still a horror film—one you might want to watch with the lights on.

Esther Williams:
Glamorous When Wet

☆ ☆ ☆ ☆

Esther Williams was one of the biggest female box-office draws of the 1950s, enchanting America with her big-budget aquatic musicals and her daring on-screen stunts. Despite a wholesome, athletic image, the oft-married actress had a passionate and tempestuous personal life involving a string of Hollywood heartthrobs.

Esther Williams was an accomplished swimmer who earned a spot on the 1940 Olympic team; unfortunately, the games were canceled due to the outbreak of World War II. But it didn't take long for movie producers to notice the striking, athletic beauty. Williams made her film debut in 1942 alongside Mickey Rooney in *Andy Hardy's Double Life*. She wowed audiences with her grace and natural beauty, much to the delight of executives at MGM, who had been courting the statuesque young woman for some time in hopes of featuring her in a series of aquatic films to counter the success that rival 20th Century Fox had enjoyed with ice-skating star Sonja Henie. Within two years, Williams was starring in her first musical—the hugely successful *Bathing Beauty* (1944)—and America had a new darling of the silver screen.

Box-Office Bombshell

Knowing they had a hot property on their hands, MGM spent six figures converting a soundstage into an elaborate aquatic set rigged with fountains, fireworks, and other special effects. For the next 15 years, Williams made use of the set to headline two dozen films—mostly aquatic musicals—and bring in more revenue than any other female film star of the era. She was paired with some of Hollywood's hunkiest leading men, including Peter Lawford, Van Johnson, Jeff Chandler, Fernando Lamas, and Victor Mature, but in every film, Williams remained the main attraction.

In addition to her comely features and strong-willed all-American image, Williams consistently thrilled audiences with her graceful and daring maneuvers in the water. But those thrilling moments did not come without cost. She nearly drowned while filming *Texas Carnival* (1951) and once ended up in a body cast with three broken vertebrae thanks to a heavy tiara that her director insisted she wear while performing a high dive in *Million Dollar Mermaid* (1952). While doing a water-skiing routine for *Easy to Love* (1953), she was almost maimed by a boat propeller, but she did successfully pull off a dangerous jump over a full orchestra on a floating platform. That same film also called for a spectacular 80-foot dive out of a helicopter, but Williams drew the line and insisted on a stunt double—because she was three months pregnant!

By the late 1950s, Williams was reaching the end of her athletic prime, and she attempted to broaden her range in dramas such as *The Unguarded Moment* (1956) and *Raw Wind in Eden* (1958). Though a capable actress, she was not able to pull off the transition. Her film career petered out by the early 1960s, so she retired.

Rocky Romances

Williams was breathtakingly beautiful, and she found herself courted by men of all stripes from the earliest days of her career. Sadly, most of these relationships took a considerable toll on her. Johnny Weissmuller, who was known almost as well for his lascivious behavior as for his world-famous performances as Tarzan, pursued the unwilling starlet relentlessly when they worked together in the Billy Rose Aquacade, a swimming and diving show, in San Francisco. Her first marriage ended badly when her husband objected to her entering the film industry, and her second husband squandered much of the fortune she had earned with MGM. In the 1950s, she indulged in passionate affairs with costars Jeff Chandler and Victor Mature before taking Fernando Lamas as her third husband. Though dedicated and often tender, Lamas was fiercely jealous and vain, which made life difficult for Williams. After his death, she married a French literature professor who supported her post-Hollywood career in swimsuit design. A true show business trouper, Williams never let physical challenges or her rocky personal life interfere with her climb to the top of the Hollywood high dive.

Fast Facts: Academy Awards

- Nearly 6,000 people (mostly actors) vote on the Academy Award winners. All are members of the Academy of Motion Picture Arts and Sciences (AMPAS).

- Fifteen Oscars were awarded in 1929, the first year the ceremony was held. All but one award went to a man—the Best Actress award was the only honor bestowed upon a woman that year. Janet Gaynor took the honor for her roles in 7th Heaven (1927), Sunrise (1927), and Street Angel (1928). After the first year, nominees were selected for only one film.

- In 1934, Bette Davis was nominated for an Oscar through a write-in campaign. She was nominated for Best Actress for her performance in Of Human Bondage (1934). The Academy has since prohibited such write-in votes on final Oscar ballots.

- Accounting firm PricewaterhouseCoopers has been protecting the Oscars' integrity almost since the beginning. The company—then known as Price Waterhouse—signed with the Academy in 1934.

- The winner of the first Oscar ever presented didn't show up to receive his award. Emil Jannings won the Best Actor award in 1929 for his roles in The Way of All Flesh (1927) and The Last Command (1928), but he was in Europe during the ceremony, so he received the statue early.

- The inaugural Academy Awards ceremony took place on May 16, 1929, in the Blossom Room of the Hollywood Roosevelt Hotel. The 270 invited guests, all of whom were members of the industry, each paid $5 to attend.

- You can't buy a ticket to the Academy Awards—it's an invitation-only event.

- *The first Best Supporting Actor and Actress awards were given out in 1937 for films made in 1936. Walter Brennan won the former for his role in* Come and Get It, *while Gale Sondergaard took the Actress honors for her part in* Anthony Adverse.

- *In 2001,* Shrek *won the first-ever Academy Award for Best Animated Feature Film.*

- *The Academy Awards have been delayed three times: The first time came in 1938, when fierce floods hit Los Angeles and caused the ceremony to be postponed for a week. In 1968, the Oscars were pushed back two days following the assassination of Dr. Martin Luther King Jr. And in 1981, producers delayed the Awards by 24 hours after John Hinckley Jr.'s attempt on President Ronald Reagan's life.*

- *Wings (1927) is the only silent film to win the Best Picture award.*

- *Made of gold-plated Britannia metal, Oscar statues are 13.5 inches tall, weigh 8.5 pounds, and have an estimated value of $300. They are manufactured in Chicago, Illinois, using one of only two molds in existence.*

- *During World War II, Oscars were briefly made of plaster because metal was crucial for military use.*

- *The longest-ever Oscar ceremony took place in 2002. It lasted about 4 hours and 20 minutes.*

- *The shortest-ever Oscar ceremony—awards presentation, speeches, and all—lasted only 15 minutes in 1929, the first year for the event.*

- *Irving Berlin is the only person to present an Oscar to himself.*

- *At the 1943 Academy Awards ceremony, Greer Garson made a six-minute acceptance speech for her Best Actress Oscar for her role in* Mrs. Miniver *(1942). Later, the Academy created a 45-second rule to avoid such lengthy speeches.*

Bogie and Bacall

★ ★ ★ ★

*Humphrey Bogart and Lauren Bacall set the screen ablaze in
their first film together and also fell in love on the set. They
made three more films together and enjoyed a storied romance
as Hollywood's golden couple until Bogart's death in 1957.*

Becoming Bogie

Humphrey Bogart spent much of the 1930s in secondary roles
playing gangsters, with an occasional stint as a leading man. But he
achieved superstardom after a series of films in the early 1940s—
High Sierra (1941), *The Maltese Falcon* (1941), and, of course,
Casablanca (1942)—in which he crafted
a distinctive on-screen persona as a
world-weary, tough-as-nails man of
action who nonetheless harbored a
well of sentimentality at his core.

Building a Bacall

Just as Bogart was hitting his
stride, a young model named Betty
Joan Perske was seeking her way
into the film business. Her break
came when the wife of director
Howard Hawks saw her photo on a
magazine cover and convinced her husband to give the strikingly
beautiful 19-year-old a screen test. A short while later, as the story
goes, Hawks told Bogie that the two of them were going to shape
the young starlet into Bogie's perfect on-screen match—a bold
female powerhouse who could handle anything the world threw
at her. At Hawks's request, Perske changed her name to Lauren
Bacall, and the famed director thrust the young ingenue into the
smoldering role of Marie "Slim" Browning opposite Bogart's Harry
"Steve" Morgan in *To Have and Have Not* (1944).

Loosely based on the Ernest Hemingway novel of the same name,
the story plays out in exotic Martinique, where boat captain Morgan

reluctantly agrees to smuggle a pair of French resistance fighters past the Nazis. Though the plot affords plenty of opportunities for heroism and drama, the real action unfolds as Morgan and sassy barroom singer "Slim" fall in love and find respite from the harsh world around them in each others' arms.

Bacall stunned audiences in her film debut, offering a sultry, jaded performance that did exactly what Hawks had intended—set her up as the female counterpart to the silver screen's toughest tough guy. She also won Bogart's heart in the process. He was at the end of a difficult third marriage when filming started, but the two costars were married a year later.

Hollywood's Perfect Couple

Bogie and Bacall's fascinating on-screen chemistry fueled a rabid interest in their personal lives among the public, and the star couple did not disappoint. They showed they were no more likely to back down from a dangerous fight than their cinematic counterparts, speaking out stridently against the scare tactics of the House Un-American Activities Committee, which would later amount to professional suicide for many others in the film industry. Also, like the rugged individuals they played on-screen, they eschewed the high-profile Hollywood nightlife, preferring to host low-key dinner parties at home with a close-knit group of friends.

The couple continued to thrill audiences by making three more films together during the 1940s. In the classic crime drama *Key Largo* (1948), widow Bacall inspires disillusioned war veteran Bogart to stand up for what's right one last time. *The Big Sleep* (1946) and *Dark Passage* (1947) are gritty film noir flicks in which the pair fight their way through a maze of crime and corruption. In a testament to the Hollywood publicity machine of the Golden Age, the tagline for *Dark Passage* perfectly summarizes the public's perception of Bogie and Bacall, both personally and professionally: "TOGETHER… AND TORRID AGAIN!"

Bogart and Bacall Filmography:

To Have and Have Not (1944)	*Dark Passage* (1947)
The Big Sleep (1946)	*Key Largo* (1948)

More Movie Records

*Movies break box-office records all the time—but that's just the tip
of the iceberg when it comes to how films make Hollywood history.
Here are some of the industry's other superlatives.*

Biggest Money-Making Movie Star: Harrison Ford
Indiana Jones himself holds the honor of being Hollywood's biggest box-
office earner in starring roles. Harrison Ford has pulled in more than
$3.5 billion for studios in his various roles over the years, and that's just
in America. Worldwide, Ford's films have made an additional $3.4 billion.
Combined, that's about $7 billion. Guess being buddies with George
Lucas isn't such a bad idea.

Highest-Grossing Actor: Samuel L. Jackson
Harrison Ford may be a star who packs 'em in, but Jackson is a character actor who not only appears in more films but in a wider variety of
films—from blockbusters to indies. That distinction gives him the edge
as the highest-grossing actor to date. As of 2009, his 68 movies had
grossed $7.42 billion dollars.

Most Influential Actress: Lillian Gish
Gish acted in films from 1912 to 1987, beginning her career with D. W.
Griffith. Along with others in the Griffith stable of actors, she helped
develop a style of acting for the camera that differed from the broad
style used on the stage. Gish continued to act through almost every
period of film history: the silent era (1912–1927); the Golden Age
(1930s–1940s); the Transition Period (1950s), the Film School Generation (1960s–1970s), and the first part of the contemporary era (1980s).

Most Leading Roles in Movies: John Wayne
No one has outshot The Duke when it comes to sheer number of leading
roles. Though the figures are sometimes disputed, many sources say that
Wayne starred in a whopping 142 movies during his acting career.

Most Frequently Portrayed Monster: Dracula
According to *Guinness World Records*, Dracula is the most frequently
portrayed horror character in the movies, with around 160 portrayals to
date. The combination of seduction and menace that generally accom-
panies the vampire tale is obviously too powerful for viewers to resist.

Most Acting Credits: Mel Blanc

He may not have been on the movie posters, but Mel Blanc gets top billing in the category of overall acting credits. Blanc—best known for voicing Bugs Bunny, Barney Rubble, and dozens of other famous characters—worked in so many films, shows, radio programs, and cartoons that it is next to impossible to nail down an exact number of acting credits, but it's estimated that he had his name attached to more than 700 films. And that doesn't even take into account his extensive television work.

Most Profanity in a Movie: *South Park: Bigger, Longer, and Uncut*

Leave it to the kids from *South Park* to snag the distinction of having the most profanity in a single film. According to the Internet Movie Database, *South Park: Bigger, Longer, and Uncut* (1999) proudly squeezed 399 naughty words into its 81 minutes. (More than a third of them were the f-word.) If that's not enough—and it most certainly is—the movie also offered a couple hundred "offensive gestures" to boot.

Most Expensive Movie Stunt: *Cliffhanger*

A jump between two speeding planes lands *Cliffhanger* (1993) the record for the most expensive stunt in a movie. Stuntman Simon Crane leaped from one plane to the other at an altitude of 15,000 feet. The stunt cost $1 million to pull off, and it was done in one take. Such death-defying feats may never be surpassed because contemporary movies rely heavily on computer-generated images, the knowledge of which takes some of the thrill out of action films.

Most Expensive Movie Explosion: *Pearl Harbor*

The 2001 war epic *Pearl Harbor* waged a battle of its own to make the movie's most massive explosion happen. It took 14 cameras to capture the explosion of six ships in the way director Michael Bay envisioned. According to the Internet Movie Database, Bay and his crew set up 700 sticks of dynamite, 2,000 feet of cord, and 4,000 gallons of gasoline on the 600-foot ships. Add that to the 100 extras in the harbor and the six planes flying overhead, and you've got yourself a $5.5 million explosion. The blasts, which lasted only seven seconds in the film, took seven months to pull off.

Midnight Cowboy Takes the Gold

☆ ☆ ☆ ☆

In Hollywood, the late 1960s saw a loosening of conservative values, as evidenced by memorable films such as Alice's Restaurant, Easy Rider, *and* Bob & Carol & Ted & Alice, *all of which were released in 1969. Also released that year was* Midnight Cowboy—*the only X-rated motion picture to win an Academy Award for Best Picture.*

Based on the book by James Leo Herlihy and directed by John Schlesinger, *Midnight Cowboy* tells the story of Joe Buck (Jon Voight), a handsome but naive young Texan who believes he can get rich "servicing" lonely, wealthy women in New York City. In the Big Apple, he befriends a sickly, small-time hustler named Enrico "Ratso" Rizzo (Dustin Hoffman), who becomes his "manager," and together they struggle to survive in the heartless city.

Midnight Cowboy is a bleak look at urban life with some superb acting. Dustin Hoffman gives one of his finest performances as Rizzo, a desperate, dying bottom-dweller whose big dream is to move to sunny Florida. To facilitate the character's defining limp, Hoffman placed pebbles in his shoe to make walking painful.

Because it contained mature themes and adult situations unsuitable for children under 17, *Midnight Cowboy* was branded with an X rating. This was in the late 1960s, before the X rating became synonymous with pornography. Despite its rating, *Midnight Cowboy* was nominated for seven Academy Awards and took home Oscars for Best Picture, Best Director, and Best Writing, Screenplay Based on Material from Another Medium. Hoffman and Voight were both nominated for Best Actor, though neither won.

After *Midnight Cowboy*'s impressive Academy Award showing, United Artists resubmitted the movie to the MPAA ratings board in hopes of getting it downgraded to an R rating. Mainstream films did not want to be associated with the X rating, partly due to that rating's burgeoning association with the pornography industry, which had co-opted the letter to hype the sexual content of porn films. In January 1971, *Midnight Cowboy*'s rating was changed from an X to an R, the rating it retains today.

Hollywood on Hollywood

Movies can take audiences to an amazing range of places—far-flung jungles, the dramatic world of crime and law enforcement, or the compelling inner lives of everyday people. But equally exciting to viewers is a peek inside the glamorous world of Hollywood itself, whether capitalizing on the allure of the creative process or exposing the darker side of what can be a bare-knuckle business. Here's a snapshot of films in which Hollywood turns the cameras on itself.

Sullivan's Travels (1941)
John L. Sullivan is a Hollywood director beloved by his studio bosses for his successful string of comedies and light romances, but he is determined to make a serious film that chronicles the struggles of the common man during the Great Depression. He takes to the road as a hobo to research the story, with a pesky crew of studio flunkies in tow to keep an eye on him. Directed by Preston Sturges, a master at combining humor and social commentary, this complex film offers both laughs and a discomforting look at America's disenfranchised citizens, though it ends with a clear affirmation of the positive role movies can play in society.

Sunset Boulevard (1950)
Directed by Billy Wilder, this melodrama reveals the bitter consequences of fleeting and elusive fame and the lengths to which a failed screenwriter and a faded silent-era star will go to achieve it. Several famous Hollywood figures—including Cecil B. DeMille, Hedda Hopper, and Buster Keaton—appear as themselves, adding an air of authenticity to the story. Gloria Swanson became indelibly associated with her crazed portrayal of Norma Desmond, and the film also gave William Holden a new image as a world-weary cynic, which he carried over to later films such as *Stalag 17* (1953) and *The Bridge on the River Kwai* (1957). But Erich von Stroheim almost steals the show as Norma's former director, who is reduced to serving as her butler.

The Bad and the Beautiful (1952)
Like *Sunset Boulevard*, director Vincente Minnelli's *The Bad and the Beautiful* paints a memorable but unflattering picture of the movie industry. Kirk Douglas stars as a producer who fights his way to success alongside a director, screenwriter, and actress, only to betray

them all to serve his own interests. Before this film, Minnelli was known primarily for his lavish musicals, but the positive reception for *The Bad and the Beautiful* gave him the opportunity to further explore drama in films such as *Lust for Life* (1956) and *Some Came Running* (1958).

Singin' in the Rain (1952)

Generally considered one of the best musicals of all time, this lighthearted flick reveals many of the difficulties Hollywood faced during the transition from silent films to talkies. It also includes two of the most memorable dance sequences ever captured on film—Gene Kelly's carefree romp down a city street in the middle of a heavy downpour and Donald O'Connor's amazing acrobatics choreographed to the song "Make 'Em Laugh." O'Connor's number was so taxing that he was bedridden for several days after completing it, only to have to do it again when the footage from the original take was accidentally damaged.

A Star Is Born (1954)

Judy Garland stars as nightclub singer Esther Blodgett who is discovered by movie star Norman Maine, a tragic figure who is letting alcoholism ruin his career. As Esther's star rises, Norman's star falls, causing tension in their personal relationship. In this acclaimed musical drama, Hollywood is presented as a place that chews talented types up and spits them out. This film is a remake of the 1937 version, but Garland's rendition of the Oscar-winning song "The Man that Got Away" makes this one the version to see.

Nickelodeon (1976)

Peter Bogdanovich was a film critic and historian before becoming a director, and this dramedy about the earliest days of movie history is based on his knowledge of the period and his interviews with such pioneering directors as Allan Dwan and Raoul Walsh. Ryan O'Neal stars as a lawyer-turned-moviemaker in the silent era of filmmaking. With his motley crew of actors and cameramen, he learns to love the business of "picture making." A great supporting cast, including Tatum O'Neal, Burt Reynolds, John Ritter, and Brian Keith, turns in colorful performances.

Who Framed Roger Rabbit (1988)

This comical murder mystery set during Hollywood's Golden Age relies on the brilliantly fanciful concept that cartoon characters are real beings who live in a neighborhood of Hollywood called Toontown. The premise allows for zany interactions between live actors and well-known animated characters such as Bugs Bunny, Betty Boop, Donald Duck, and Woody Woodpecker. The film is a masterwork of animation, but perhaps the most remarkable thing about it is that producer Steven Spielberg was able to get so many competing studios to allow their animated stars to appear together in one film.

Barton Fink (1991)
This surreal film by Joel and Ethan Coen captures the disillusionment of a young New York playwright who is lured to Hollywood to write movie scripts in the early 1940s. Though the movie offers a blistering depiction of the film industry as all business and no art, it also lampoons the title character, a screenwriter who aspires to express the voice of the common man but understands far less about his subject than does the lonely, perhaps psychotic salesman he befriends at his run-down boardinghouse. The character W. P. Mayhew, a fellow writer that Fink greatly admires, was supposedly based on novelist and screenwriter William Faulkner.

The Player (1992)
Like many of director Robert Altman's films, *The Player* features an enormous cast of more than 60 characters, including a seemingly endless list of actors appearing as themselves—Burt Reynolds, Susan Sarandon, Jack Lemmon, Lily Tomlin, Elliott Gould, Sally Kellerman, Robert Wagner, Cher, James Coburn, Bruce Willis, Julia Roberts, and Steve Allen, to name a few. The film—a major comeback for its aging director—took a harsh swipe at Hollywood as it followed a conniving and greedy producer as he attempts to cover up the accidental murder of a screenwriter.

Bowfinger (1999)
Steve Martin and Eddie Murphy star in this bizarre Hollywood comedy about a second-rate producer (Martin) who decides to get an unwilling Hollywood actor (Murphy) to become the star of his movie by secretly filming him as he goes about his regular life. The story highlights the ego-driven, insular nature of the film industry while at the same time celebrating the passion and dedication of filmmakers. The idea for the film supposedly came from a real incident in the 1920s: Russian filmmaker Sergei Komarov took newsreel footage of a vacationing Mary Pickford and assembled a film around it called *The Kiss of Mary Pickford* (1927).

Jayne Mansfield

☆ ☆ ☆ ☆

Hollywood's other blonde bombshell also lived a tragically short life.

Going Toe to Toe

To better understand 1950s sex symbol Jayne Mansfield, it helps to know something about her chief rival, Marilyn Monroe. Pursued by men and idolized by women, Monroe inherited the role of the blonde bombshell from former Hollywood pinups like Jean Harlow and Betty Grable. With her exaggerated, breathy voice, trademark sashay, and suggestive pout, Monroe's effect on people was pronounced. Many worshipped her beauty, some were taken by her fragility, some were outraged by the sexuality she exuded, and others saw her as a tragic figure, but nobody was able to ignore her. It's a lesson that wasn't lost on budding starlet Jayne Mansfield.

Bigger Is Better

Making her move on Hollywood in the early 1950s, Jayne Mansfield had high hopes. Where Monroe was shy and insecure, platinum blonde Mansfield was anything but. The former Vera Jayne Palmer had married Paul Mansfield at 17 and divorced him eight years later. For a single mother with a young daughter to raise, an assured mind-set came with the territory. Brimming with confidence and a knack for self-promotion, Mansfield assembled her career mostly through sheer will and her willingness to trade privacy for publicity. Her physical assets belied a surprising I.Q. of 163—quite a contradiction to her "dumb blonde" image—but Mansfield instinctively knew which assets to play up. "They're more interested in 40–21–35," she once cooed with a wink and a smile. Although some have suggested that Mansfield's remarkable I.Q. was a press agent's gimmick, no one could deny that she was savvy.

Don't You Dare Peek!

Working hard to keep her publicity train rolling, the actress often experienced "accidental" clothing malfunctions. One notable incident occurred at a dinner party held to honor Italian siren Sophia

Loren. While sitting beside the seductive actress, Mansfield leaned far over the table in a low-cut dress and the inevitable happened. Loren's raised eyebrow was recorded for posterity by an alert photographer, and the American's role as world-class sex-bomb was fully assured. Not too surprisingly, such "embarrassments" seemed to occur only at the most opportune times, when the press was gathered in full force.

Gaining a Foothold

Such playfulness brought the actress a boatload of publicity, which helped open doors to future roles. And in 1955, Mansfield's big break came when she was offered the part of Rita Marlowe in the Broadway play *Will Success Spoil Rock Hunter?* The play was well received by reviewers and theatergoers alike, and Mansfield became an overnight sensation. The play was such a smash that it was remade for the silver screen in 1957, with Mansfield reprising her role.

In 1958, the actress married professional bodybuilder Mickey Hargitay, a Hungarian émigré. Their union produced three children and, according to published accounts, was the happiest time in Mansfield's life. The actress set her sights on a positively *divoon* (Jayne's unique catchword for "divine") future, both in Hollywood and at home. For a spell, all seemed to go precisely as planned. Then things started to unravel.

Bimbo Backlash

The 1960s were not at all kind to pinup girls. "Cheesecake" actresses began to lose their appeal with younger, more sophisticated audiences searching for substance over style. As a result, Mansfield's acting opportunities began to dry up. Determined to put herself back on top, Mansfield accepted show-business work wherever she could find it. This led to stints working as a cabaret singer and as an off-Broadway actress, among other lesser gigs.

Downward Spiral

Mansfield's compulsion to succeed drove a wedge between her and Hargitay, and the two divorced in 1964. By the late 1960s, Mansfield was coming off another failed marriage (this time to filmmaker Matt Cimber, who had misguidedly advised her not to take the role of

Ginger on *Gilligan's Island*) and was dating her manager Sam Brody. Furiously plying the supper-club circuit, Mansfield worked hard to resurrect her career. On June 29, 1967, Mansfield, Brody, and 22-year-old chauffer Ronnie Harrison were driving through Slidell, Louisiana, on their way to New Orleans for a television interview. Three of Mansfield's children (Mariska, 3; Zoltan, 6; and Miklos Jr., 8) and the family dogs were also on board.

An Untimely End

Just after 2 A.M., while moving through the dank Louisiana swampland, Harrison encountered a thick haze from a mosquito fogging truck. As the chauffer piloted the 1966 Buick Electra with his vision greatly impaired, he slammed into the back of an unseen tractor-trailer with astonishing force. The impact sheared off the Electra's roof, immediately killing Mansfield and her two adult companions riding up front. Mansfield was only 34 years old.

Amazingly, all three children survived with only minor injuries. They owed their luck to the fact that they were fast asleep on the back seat during the impact, with their bodies well below the carnage above them. One of the dogs wasn't so lucky. He was found dead on the floor amidst shards of glass—jagged reminders of the accident's ferocity. In short order, Hollywood's gossip mill seized upon the story and ran with it—half-cocked as usual.

Erroneous Reports and Other Fiction

Immediately, rumors began to fly. The most persistent one held that Mansfield had been decapitated in the crash, which was not true. What appeared to be her severed head in photos was actually one of her wigs. Another bit of conjecture claimed that Mansfield had died as a result of a curse placed upon her by former associate Anton LaVey, founder of the International Church of Satan. Of course, something that macabre was hard to prove or disprove. What's known for certain is that a vibrant, talented woman exited this life far too early. But Mansfield's Hollywood connection lives on through her daughter Mariska, famous in her own right for her role as Detective Olivia Benson on *Law & Order: SVU*. Her Hollywood breakthrough is a *divoon* punctuation mark to a blonde bombshell's life cut tragically short.

Pop Quiz: When Musicians Decide to Act

When musicians find themselves on the big screen, the results are often mixed. Some seem born to act, while others...well, as the saying goes, "Don't quit your day job." See if you can match the musical performer to his or her Tinseltown debut.

Performer	Film (Character)
1. Cher	A. *A Certain Sacrifice* (Bruna)
2. Bob Dylan	B. *Chastity* (Chastity)
3. Flea	C. *The Fastest Guitar Alive* (Johnny Banner)
4. Chris Isaak	D. *Jungle Fever* (Lashawn)
5. Mick Jagger	E. *La Bamba* (Eddie Cochran)
6. Queen Latifah	F. *Love Me Tender* (Clint Reno)
7. Cyndi Lauper	G. *Married to the Mob* (The Clown)
8. Courtney Love	H. *Paradise Alley* (Mumbles)
9. Lyle Lovett	I. *Pat Garrett and Billy the Kid* (Alias)
10. Madonna	J. *Performance* (Turner)
11. Roy Orbison	K. *The Player* (Detective DeLongpre)
12. Elvis Presley	L. *Quadrophenia* (Ace Face)
13. Brian Setzer	M. *Red Rock West* (Truck Driver)
14. Sting	N. *Renaissance Man* (Pvt. Haywood)
15. James Taylor	O. *Sid and Nancy* (Gretchen)
16. Tina Turner	P. *Suburbia* (Razzle)
17. Mark Wahlberg	Q. *Tommy* (The Acid Queen)
18. Tom Waits	R. *Two-Lane Blacktop* (The Driver)
19. Dwight Yoakam	S. *Vibes* (Sylvia Pickel)

Answer Key: 1. B; 2. I; 3. P; 4. G; 5. J; 6. D; 7. S; 8. O; 9. K; 10. A; 11. C; 12. F; 13. E; 14. L; 15. R; 16. Q; 17. N; 18. H; 19. M

The Pig 'n Whistle

☆ ☆ ☆ ☆

The Pig 'n Whistle is a classic restaurant with a history that's indelibly tied to the movies. For 20 years, it was one of the few places in Hollywood where average filmgoers could rub elbows with the stars they paid to see on the big screen. The family-friendly venue closed in the late 1940s, but in 2001, it was refurbished and has become one of the city's hottest hangouts.

We all think of concession stands as a fixture in movie theaters, and most moviegoers don't think twice about shelling out more for popcorn, candy, and soda than they would ever be willing to pay for it anywhere else. But in the early days of motion pictures, theater owners didn't sell food to their customers; in fact, in the spectacular movie palaces built during Hollywood's golden era, messy snacks were decidedly unwelcome.

A New Idea

In 1927, an enterprising restaurateur realized that an eatery situated next to a movie theater would benefit from the throngs of hungry people filing in and out next door. So he opened the Pig 'n Whistle right next to Sid Grauman's popular Egyptian Theater on Hollywood Boulevard—a side door actually connected the restaurant to the theater lobby. The lavishly decorated restaurant sported high ceilings, ornately carved mahogany beams, and stained glass around the booths. Near the entrance, the restaurant offered both a candy counter and a soda fountain, as well as an organ for serenading the clientele. It quickly became a favorite spot for regular moviegoers and film stars alike.

During the Pig 'n Whistle's heyday, stars such as Spencer Tracy, Cary Grant, Loretta Young, and Shirley Temple could frequently be found dining there alongside adoring fans who might have just seen one of their films at the Egyptian. The restaurant claims to have hosted the first-ever Oscars after-party following the inaugural Academy Awards ceremony in 1929, and child actress Judy Garland is said to have celebrated her 15th birthday there.

Decline and Renewal

The Pig 'n Whistle closed its doors in 1949, and over the next several decades, the Hollywood Boulevard area slid into decay. The restaurant site changed hands numerous times and was even damaged in a fire. In the 1990s, a civic effort brought new businesses and entertainment complexes to the area in an attempt to recapture its appeal as a tourist destination. As part of that effort, the Egyptian Theater was restored to its former glory as one of the centerpieces of the street. The Pig 'n Whistle also underwent a complete renovation, and much of the original finery of the 3,500-square-foot landmark has been restored, though the candy counter and soda fountain are gone.

The new incarnation, which opened its doors in 2001, still offers lunch and dinner to moviegoers but also draws a younger, hip nighttime crowd with its bar and entertainment events, such as karaoke and live music. Star sightings may be a bit less frequent than in the old days, but the Pig 'n Whistle and its neighbor the Egyptian still make the perfect location for dinner and a movie for true Hollywood film buffs. And you never know which celebrity you might find sitting at the next table.

- *Director Roman Polanski gave a nod to the Pig 'n Whistle in his classic neo-noir mystery* Chinatown *(1974), which starred Jack Nicholson and Faye Dunaway. Nicholson's character Jake Gittes, a private detective, finds a lead in the murder he is investigating when an informant shows him photographs of two characters having an explosive argument in front of the famed restaurant.*

Switcheroo!

It's hard to imagine different actors playing the characters in your favorite movies. Could anyone but Jon Heder have been the goofy title character in Napoleon Dynamite *(2004)? Who but Julia Roberts could have played opposite Richard Gere in* Pretty Woman *(1990)? Surprisingly, roles can change hands many times before a movie starts shooting—sometimes actors get switched around even after the cameras roll. Read on for a few actor "switcheroos."*

- Michael J. Fox was the original choice for Marty McFly in *Back to the Future* (1985), but his work on *Family Ties* caused scheduling conflicts, so producers went with Eric Stoltz instead. When they decided Stoltz was "miscast" as McFly, they were already six weeks into filming and had to reshoot several scenes when Fox finally came onboard.

- Director Francis Ford Coppola fired Harvey Keitel two weeks into filming *Apocalypse Now* (1979). Martin Sheen replaced Keitel as Capt. Benjamin L. Willard in the famously troubled production of this war flick.

- The villain played by Colin Farrell in Steven Spielberg's *Minority Report* (2002) was originally a character meant for Matt Damon. But Damon was busy filming *The Bourne Identity* (2002) and couldn't take the part.

- *The Godfather: Part III* (1990) presents Sofia Coppola as the daughter of mobster Michael Corleone. Sofia (the real-life daughter of *Godfather* director Francis Ford Coppola) was a replacement for Winona Ryder, who gave up the part due to exhaustion.

- Will Smith turned down the role of Neo in *The Matrix* (1999) in order to star in the flop *Wild Wild West* (1999). Although Smith admits the decision was a mistake, he feels Keanu Reeves played the role better than he would have himself.

- The Oscar-winning script for *Forrest Gump* (1994) was originally offered to directors Terry Gilliam and Barry Sonnenfeld, but Robert Zemeckis ended up taking the helm. Bill Murray was considered for the role of Forrest as was Chevy Chase, but both turned down the role that eventually went to Tom Hanks. The role of Bubba was passed up by David Alan Grier, Dave Chappelle, and Ice Cube.

- Sandra Bullock replaced Lori Petty as Lt. Lenina Huxley in *Demolition Man* (1993). The temperamental Petty—known for her roles in *A League of Their Own* (1992) and *Tank Girl* (1995)—had been on set for several days before being let go. All of her footage had to be reshot.

- Vivien Leigh made history as Scarlett O'Hara in *Gone with the Wind* (1939), but many of Hollywood's top female stars tested for the part, including Bette Davis and Paulette Goddard. Both were considered front-runners until Leigh was signed.

- Marilyn Monroe wanted to have *Breakfast at Tiffany's* (1961), but the equally iconic Audrey Hepburn was the actress who brought the beloved character of Holly Golightly to life. Monroe campaigned for the role, partly because she was encouraged by Truman Capote, who wrote the novella. She even worked on scenes for her audition in Lee Strasberg's acting class. But Paramount had no intention of hiring Monroe after her behavior on their production of *Some Like It Hot* (1959), during which she was late to the set, emotionally distraught, and unable to act some days.

- In the psychological thriller *Panic Room* (2002), Jodie Foster plays an aptly freaked-out mom. The role was first offered to Nicole Kidman, but an injured knee kept her from accepting it.

- The 1964 big-budget comedy *What a Way to Go!* featured the legendary Robert Mitchum in one of the film's five male roles, but the part changed hands several times before he got it. The studio wouldn't pay Frank Sinatra's asking price; Gregory Peck was sought but was unavailable; finally, a recommendation from costar Shirley MacLaine got Mitchum the role.

- Fred Astaire and Judy Garland sing and dance their way through *Easter Parade* (1948), but it would've been a different duo if fate hadn't interceded. Gene Kelly was supposed to be Garland's dancing partner, but a broken ankle put him out of commission and out of the running.

- Can you imagine Sylvester Stallone—Rocky himself—as Axel Foley in *Beverly Hills Cop* (1984)? Stallone was replaced by comic Eddie Murphy because Sly demanded that the writers add more action to their comedic script. Murphy made the cut and then made history as everyone's favorite 1980s funny cop.

A Love Triangle, Hollywood Style

☆ ☆ ☆ ☆

Director, actor, and screenwriter Woody Allen is famous for making movies that chronicle the bizarre struggles of his neurotic protagonists. But the very public personal saga that made headlines in the early '90s tops even the most convoluted of Allen's screenplays.

Setting the Stage

Woody Allen had built a career as a respected filmmaker with movies such as *Bananas* (1971), *Sleeper* (1973), *Manhattan* (1979), and the Oscar-winning *Annie Hall* (1977). His films were recognizably his own, and announcements of new projects were greeted with anticipation among critics and the public.

In 1980, Allen began a relationship with actress Mia Farrow, best known at the time for her roles in the movie *Rosemary's Baby* (1968) and on the TV series *Peyton Place.* Farrow already had six children, both adopted and biological, from her previous marriage to pianist Andre Previn. In 1987, Allen and Farrow had a son of their own, Satchel O'Sullivan Farrow (who later changed his name to Ronan Seamus Farrow). While she was with Allen, Farrow also adopted a boy named Moses and a girl named Dylan. Allen and Farrow never married, but in 1991, Allen also adopted Dylan and Moses.

The Rising Action

Allen and Farrow spent a dozen years leading what looked like an idyllic, if somewhat peculiar, existence. The two never lived together but kept separate residences on opposite sides of New York City's Central Park. Farrow and her roster of kids would trudge across the green, armed with sleeping bags, to spend the night at Allen's place.

But that all ended in 1992, when Farrow discovered nude photos that Allen had taken of her adopted daughter Soon-Yi Previn. It turned out that Allen had been sleeping with Soon-Yi for a while—

at least since her first year of college. Soon-Yi was 21 at the time of her mother's discovery, and Allen was 57.

Recognizing that Farrow was miles beyond peeved by this turn of affairs, Allen sued her for custody of their three children—Satchel, Moses, and Dylan. Farrow responded by accusing Allen of sexually abusing Dylan, who was seven years old at the time.

Not surprisingly, the press had a field day. The ensuing court-room drama was covered daily in newspapers in the United States and around the world. It didn't hurt that the two stars of this media circus never shied away from reporters. Allen was eager to emphatically deny the accusation of molestation, and he also revealed that he didn't regret his affair with Soon-Yi. When the story of the affair first broke, Allen responded, "It's real and happily all true."

Farrow, meanwhile, was more than open to depicting Allen as a small, sniveling, neurotic, and deeply disturbed man. Regarding Allen's relationship with their daughter Dylan, Farrow testified, "He would creep up in the morning and lay beside her bed and wait for her to wake up.... I was uncomfortable all along."

Resolution—Sort Of

In the end, Farrow was granted full custody of the three children. The judge wrote a 33-page decision in which he described Allen as a "self-absorbed, untrustworthy, and insensitive" father. He chastised Allen for not knowing the names of his son's teachers or even which children shared which bedrooms in Farrow's apartment. A state-appointed group of specialists concluded that Allen was not guilty of molesting Dylan, although the judge deemed the report "sanitized and... less credible."

Allen was disappointed to lose custody of his children, but he was happy to continue his relationship with their older adopted half-sister. Shortly after the conclusion of the court battle, Soon-Yi and Allen were spotted at trendy restaurants all across Manhattan. They married in 1997 and have since adopted two children of their own. Farrow remains estranged from Soon-Yi but is more than busy with her current activities. In her 1997 memoir, Farrow compared her relationship with Allen to her childhood battle with polio: "I had unknowingly brought danger into my family and... I might have contaminated those that I loved the most."

Best Boy, Dolly Grip, and Other Odd-Sounding Jobs

Movies take dozens of people to create, and if you've ever read a film's credits, you've probably noticed some strange-sounding job titles. Here's what those crew members really do.

Boom Operator
Ever since the silent era ended, sound has been an important part of the film industry. And if you've got sound, you need to have someone operating the microphones. The *boom* refers to the boom microphone, which is often at the end of a long pole. It can pick up sounds by hanging above the actors, just out of camera range.

Gaffer
The gaffer is the movie's chief lighting technician. This person manages the production's lighting and electrical departments and lights each scene based on direction from the cinematographer.

Best Boy
The best boy is the gaffer's primary assistant in managing the lighting and electrical crews. The best boy can be a female, but the title, which was derived from sailing terminology, remains the same.

Clapper Loader
The clapper loader, also known as the camera loader, handles one of the most recognizable pieces of filmmaking: the black-and-white clapper that marks the beginning of each new take. This person's job is simply to clap the clapper in front of the camera every time a take begins. He or she also loads the film stock into the camera's magazines.

Swing Gang
Don't be scared—the swing gang isn't a group of dancers that will force you to jump, jive, and wail across the set. This is just a fancy name for set decorators—a group that generally works at night to ready the set or soundstage for the upcoming day's filming. They also take down the set when it is no longer needed.

Armoror

If you're going to be scared of any crew member, it should probably be the armoror. This person deals with all the weapons on a movie's set and decides which weapons best suit each scene based on its era and genre, then makes sure everything goes off without a hitch. The armoror is responsible for picking out the right kinds of blanks and teaching the actors how to properly use the weapons.

Key Grip

The key grip is the leader of the grips—lighting and rigging techies who handle equipment that is not attached to the lights (which are the realm of the gaffers). Grips are essentially responsible for the entire cast and crew's safety.

Dolly Grip

A dolly is a platform on wheels that moves the camera during filming to ensure a smooth, fluid shot. The dolly grip moves the dolly around the set as needed.

Focus Puller

The focus puller measures the distance between the subject and the camera lens and uses the marking ring on the camera lens to determine where the lens needs to be set to ensure focus.

Foley Artist

You might not guess it by the name, but the foley artist is the person who makes the sound effects for a movie. The name comes from Jack Foley, one of the industry's first sound effects artists. Foley artists often use unusual objects to make the noises that accompany the film—slapping coconut shells together to make the sound of horses galloping, for example, or snapping stalks of celery to make the sound of bones breaking.

Lead Man

The lead man works with the art department to buy, borrow, or scrounge for objects to make the set more believable or atmospheric.

Wrangler

As one might expect, a wrangler deals with animals. He or she is responsible for selecting, training, and taking care of the animals used in a film, which can range from horses and cows to spiders and snakes.

Hollywood's Self-Censorship Machine

☆ ☆ ☆ ☆

Today's moviegoers are accustomed to using the letter-ratings system to decide if a film is suitable viewing for themselves or their children. Thus, the decision to view films with violent or sexual content currently rests on the shoulders of the moviegoers themselves. The Motion Picture Association of American (MPAA) began the letter-ratings system in 1968. Prior to that, Hollywood was governed by a different method of censorship, which was known as the Motion Picture Production Code, or the Hays Code.

What Is the Production Code?

The Production Code was a lengthy set of guidelines used to control the content of Hollywood movies from 1930 to 1968, though it was only strictly enforced from 1934 to the mid-1950s. Censorship via the Code occurred during the production of a movie, so by the time it was completed, it had already been through the approval process and therefore was suitable for all ages. In this system, it was the film industry that was responsible for what patrons saw on the big screen. Like the letter-ratings system, the Code is an example of self-regulation; it is not administered by the government as are censorship systems in some other countries.

Nude Hippos No Longer Allowed!

The Production Code was not just a list of forbidden acts; it was a complex system of guidelines that controlled how American institutions, values, and ideals should be depicted in Hollywood storytelling. The Code was authored by Father Daniel A. Lord, a Catholic priest and professor of drama, and Martin Quigley, a Catholic layperson who published trade magazines for the film industry. They imbued the Code with a moral agenda, which is clear from its three general principles: "No film should lower the moral standards of those who see it; the correct standards of life should be presented; and, the law should not be ridiculed, nor should sympathy be created for its violation."

The Code forbade certain behaviors, such as profanity, sexual perversion (including prostitution), white slavery, miscegenation, and nudity or partial nudity. Even animated characters were not exempt: Betty Boop was completely altered and desexualized after the advent of the Code, and Walt Disney was forced to add tutus to the dancing hippos in *Fantasia* (1940), which were originally "nude."

However, the bulk of the Code amounted to guidelines on how to deal with facets of American ideology. For example, religion was never to be condemned or criticized; democracy and the trial-by-jury judicial system could not be attacked or depicted as unfair; and outlaws and other lawbreakers could not be treated with sympathy. Gangster films such as *The Public Enemy* (1931), *Little Caesar* (1931), and *Scarface* (1932) thrived during the early 1930s, but after the strict enforcement of the Code, it became difficult to feature a criminal in a leading role for fear of treating him too sympathetically.

Separate Beds

In retrospect, the Code's most talked-about guidelines are those regarding marriage. Marriage and family were sanctified as the most righteous of social institutions and therefore should be the goal of all good female characters. Often, leading ladies in films expressed the opinion that they would gladly give up their career or goals if the right man came along, whether it was part of the plot or not. This was to appease the Code, which suggested that both career women and girls with low morals be "punished" within the story lines of films because those lifestyles did not illustrate the sanctity of marriage. Additional Code rules on marriage and sex stated that sexual relations should not be depicted in a way that suggested sex was typical behavior. The Code's administrators interpreted this to mean that even married couples in the movies had to sleep in separate beds, as in the Spencer Tracy and Katharine Hepburn classic *State of the Union* (1948).

The film industry adopted the Code after the advent of sync-sound movies in 1927, when religious groups, social groups, and children's advocacy organizations pressured Hollywood to clean up its act, or they would lobby the government to do it for them. Movie studios were already battling individual state censorship boards, who often edited out offending scenes or altered inappropriate intertitles (title cards between the scenes of silent movies) without asking the studios' permission. Because each state had its own set of guidelines, a film print making the rounds of distribution could conceivably be edited in one state, but there was no way to ensure that the footage was restored before the print was shipped to the next state. Therefore, the studios decided to adopt the Code in 1930 on a voluntary basis. As might be expected, the studios did not always adhere to the Code, so in 1934, it became mandatory. After that, no Hollywood movie could be distributed or exhibited without a seal of approval from the Code office, which was included in a film's opening credits.

Moral Compensation

Contrary to popular belief, the Code did not ban immoral behavior, crime, or even sexual situations because those behaviors are the essence of drama. Instead, it guided the depiction of those behaviors, and the Production Code Administration (PCA) worked with studios and filmmakers to ensure that the Code was followed without compromising artistic integrity. The PCA reviewed each project at script stage, at first cut, and then at final cut, so that filmmakers could address problems during the production process. The PCA strongly advocated the idea of "compensating moral values." That is, if a film featured a corrupt politician, then an honest politician needed to be included to show that democracy was a valid institution even if there was the occasional bad apple.

If a studio felt strongly about a requested change, they could appeal it. One of the most famous appeals was on behalf of *Gone with the Wind* because of the famous line, "Frankly my dear, I don't give a damn." The line was originally cut by the PCA but was reinstated after producer David O. Selznik protested, arguing that it had been made famous by the book.

The Code on Trial

During the 1950s, a series of Supreme Court decisions questioned the constitutionality of the Code, weakening its hold over Hollywood. At the same time, filmmakers such as Otto Preminger began to openly violate the Code with films such as *The Moon Is Blue* (1953) and *The Man with the Golden Arm* (1955) until it was forgotten completely by the early 1960s. Though still on the books, filmmakers paid little attention to the Code as they continued to escalate depictions of sex and violence. Finally, in 1968, the Code was discarded in favor of the letter-ratings system still used today.

Family Ties

Families with multiple generations of actors aren't uncommon, but Hollywood has plenty of little-known connections as well. Check out these celebrity ties.

- Drew Barrymore is descended from one of America's greatest acting dynasties. Her grandfather was John Barrymore, her great uncle was Lionel Barrymore, and her great aunt was Ethel Barrymore. This trio of legends from the Golden Age were descendants of 19th century actor John Drew, whose actress daughter Georgianna married actor Maurice Barrymore. Talk about having it in your genes.

- Oprah is the queen of media, and by some accounts, including a television show called *Myths and Legends of Elvis,* she's also related to "The King" himself. A genealogist claims Winfrey and Elvis Presley are distant cousins.

- Tom Hanks is Abraham Lincoln's fourth cousin, four generations removed. Lincoln's great-great-great-grandparents, William and Sarah Hanks, are also Hanks's ancestors.

- Jennifer Aniston is the daughter of actor John Aniston, a soap-opera veteran. John Aniston first appeared in daytime soaps in the mid-1970s and has held a long-running role as Victor Kiriakis on *Days of Our Lives.*

- Warren Beatty and Shirley MacLaine are siblings. MacLaine, whose birth name was Shirley MacLean Beaty, is three years older than Warren. She changed her name to make it easier to pronounce. (Perhaps that's why Warren added the extra *t* to his last name.)

- Nicolas Cage's real name is Nicholas Coppola, connecting him to one of Hollywood's greatest directors, Francis Ford Coppola. Nicolas just calls him Uncle Frank.

- In a few movies that George Clooney has directed or produced, a song by female crooner Rosemary Clooney plays as part of the background music. That's George's way of honoring his Aunt Rosemary.

- Mariel Hemingway, who played Woody Allen's much-younger girlfriend in *Manhattan* (1977), is the granddaughter of writer Ernest Hemingway.

Guess Who's Coming to Dinner

☆ ☆ ☆ ☆

Though quaint by today's standards, Guess Who's Coming
to Dinner *was a controversial shocker upon its release
in 1967. Never before had the big Hollywood studios
addressed the then-sensitive issue of interracial marriage in
a major commercial film starring a heavyweight cast.*

According to producer/director Stanley Kramer, the idea for the film
arose from a talk between himself and screenwriter William Rose as
they strolled through Beverly Hills one evening. Rose pitched the
idea of a liberal, white South African man whose daughter falls in
love with a black man. Kramer liked the idea of a liberal suddenly
forced by circumstance to face his deepest principles and suggested
setting the story in the United States, which at the time was in the
midst of a fierce battle between liberal and conservative ideologies.

Perfect Casting

Kramer, whose credits included *The
Defiant Ones* (1958), *Inherit the Wind*
(1960), and *Judgment at Nuremburg*
(1961), immediately thought of Spencer
Tracy and Katharine Hepburn to play
the film's liberal parents and secured
their participation early on. He then
contacted Sidney Poitier, who was willing to play the black man to whom their
daughter becomes engaged, though the actor expressed skepticism
that a major studio would touch such a sensitive topic. Poitier
needn't have worried: With such a notable triumvirate of actors
on board, in addition to a script by the talented William Rose,
Columbia Pictures green-lighted the movie with little hesitation.

The production went off without a hitch, though concessions had
to be made for Tracy, who was in ill health at the time. Kramer did
his best to make things as easy as possible for his old friend, including filming only in the morning, when Tracy was at his strongest.

Katharine Hepburn jumped into the production with her usual vigor, but Poitier, though himself a seasoned professional, was nervous about working with such fabled performers. "I wasn't able to get it out of my head: I am here playing a scene with Tracy and Hepburn!" he wrote in his first autobiography, *This Life*. "It was all so overwhelming I couldn't remember my lines."

Critics Have Their Say

Guess Who's Coming to Dinner generated quite a bit of discussion and criticism upon its release. Poitier, in particular, came under attack by some civil rights leaders for being almost too perfect as Dr. John Prentice—nonthreatening, charismatic, and thus acceptable to white Americans.

The movie's central love story was also derided for skirting the intimacy one would expect from a young couple in love. Indeed, there is very little physical contact between Prentice and his fiancée, Joey Drayton, played by Katharine Houghton, Hepburn's real-life niece. To Kramer's credit, several scenes were filmed of Poitier and Houghton kissing but were later dropped from the final version of the movie.

Despite these and other criticisms, *Guess Who's Coming to Dinner* was a huge success for Columbia Pictures, grossing nearly $25 million in its initial box-office run. In addition, the film was nominated for almost every major Academy Award, including Best Picture, Best Director, and Best Actor in a Leading Role (Spencer Tracy), and received Oscars for Best Actress (Katharine Hepburn) and Best Writing (Story and Screenplay) (William Rose). And though Poitier wasn't nominated for an Academy Award, *Guess Who's Coming to Dinner* helped cement his reputation as one of the most popular (and bankable) black actors in Hollywood history, making him a bona fide movie star.

Unfortunately, there's a sad footnote to *Guess Who's Coming to Dinner* Spencer Tracy was so ill during production that Hepburn and Kramer voluntarily placed their salaries in escrow as collateral for the studio because Tracy was uninsurable. He passed away just ten days after filming wrapped and never got to see his final film on the big screen.

The Best Movies About World War II

The Second World War has inspired countless retellings on the silver screen. While no short list of worthwhile movies about the war could be complete, here are a handful of particularly noteworthy titles.

Mrs. Miniver (1942)
Winston Churchill reportedly said that this American depiction of a family in wartime Britain did more for the war effort than a flotilla of battleships.

They Were Expendable (1945)
This John Ford-directed film depicts the story of American PT boats battling the Japanese in the South Pacific. On hearing the title, a PT-boat sailor had a different recollection of the boats: "It should have been called *They Were Useless*," he said.

The Bridge on the River Kwai (1957)
Alec Guinness stars as the officer in charge of a group of British prisoners of war forced to build a railway for the Japanese amid brutal jungle conditions. This David Lean production is well known for its eminently whistled theme march.

The Longest Day (1962)
This sweeping depiction of the Normandy invasion stars dozens of Hollywood heavyweights, including Robert Mitchum, Richard Burton, Henry Fonda, and John Wayne. More than 20,000 real soldiers were used as extras in the film.

Patton (1970)
Winner of seven Academy Awards, this film starring George C. Scott is fascinating both as a psychological study of General George S. Patton and as a war movie.

Tora! Tora! Tora! (1970)
A retelling of the attack on Pearl Harbor, this film features a look at the events from both an American and a Japanese perspective. To reflect the two different viewpoints, the film was shot in separate segments by directors from each country.

A Bridge Too Far (1977)
This story of Operation Market Garden, an Allied plan to capture bridges in the occupied Netherlands in 1944, is one of the more historically accurate Hollywood productions about the war.

Das Boot (1981)
Regarded as one of the greatest German films of all time, *Das Boot* follows the crew of German submarine U-96 through the course of its mission. The commander of the real U-96 was a consultant on the movie, and the result is a film that immerses the viewer in the tense, claustrophobic world of a U-boat at war.

Idi i Smotri (Come and See) (1985)
This shattering Soviet film by director Elem Klimov chronicles the disasters that befall a Russian village when it is invaded by bloodthirsty SS troops. Audiences squirm because the terror is seen through the eyes of a young boy who is driven to the brink of madness by what he witnesses.

Schindler's List (1993)
Steven Spielberg's haunting true story of how one man saved a thousand Jews from the Holocaust won seven Oscars and is consistently ranked among the greatest movies of all time by critics' associations and audiences alike.

Saving Private Ryan (1998)
Steven Spielberg directed Tom Hanks in this story of a group of eight soldiers putting their own lives at risk to save one man. The D-Day scenes are some of the most realistic ever filmed.

The Thin Red Line (1998)
This expansive look at the 1942–43 U.S. invasion of Guadalcanal was adapted by director Terence Malick from the highly regarded novel by James Jones. Although often shockingly violent, the film is oddly poetic as well, encompassing chaos, beauty, unbalanced officers, and ordinary Joes who just want to survive. The solid cast includes Sean Penn, John Cusack, Nick Nolte, Adrien Brody, Jim Caviezel, George Clooney, John Travolta, and Woody Harrelson.

The King of Pitch

☆ ☆ ☆ ☆

*Think you have a great idea for a movie? There's one person
in Hollywood who just might be interested in hearing it.*

He's Listening . . .

Robert Kosberg graduated from the UCLA film school, and he has
experience as a screenwriter, but in Hollywood circles, he's best
known as "The King of Pitch." He's a movie producer whose credits
include *12 Monkeys* (1995) with Bruce Willis and the Arnold
Schwarzenegger action movie *Commando* (1985). But unlike most
legitimate Hollywood producers, Kosberg is willing to listen to
movie ideas from people outside the film industry in the hope of
finding something fresh. Every day he receives e-mails, faxes, and
letters from ordinary folks all over the world: housewives in Wichita
Falls, accountants in Phoenix, plumbers in Newark, and, of course,
just about every waiter in L.A. He believes a great idea is a great
idea, no matter where it comes from.

We All Have a Story to . . . Sell

In 1997, a grandmother from Ozark, Arkansas, sent him an idea for
a movie about a man who lives in the Statue of Liberty. With the
title *Keeper of the Flame,* Kosberg sold it to the producers of *Fargo*
(1996) and *Notting Hill* (1999). According to Kosberg, the grandmother received a check for a five-figure sum and a contract for a
substantial bonus if the movie is ever produced.

A few years later, a housewife from the Midwest had an idea for a
comedy. She waited for hours with 200 other hopefuls at a seminar
for a chance to have 45 seconds to pitch her idea to Kosberg. He, in
turn, pitched the idea to Warner Bros., and within a month, the
housewife was on the phone to the studio striking a deal for her idea.

Things happened even faster for one penniless writer. Unable to
afford the entrance fee to a writing seminar that Kosberg attended, the
persistent writer instead cornered the producer outside the event.
Kosberg claims that he quickly rattled off his idea for a movie called
Born to Shop about a girl killed in a traffic accident who comes back as

a ghost and asks her friend to help her choose which couple she'll be reborn to. A day later, the writer had a check for $75,000 in his hand.

Unfortunately, none of these projects has yet to make it into production. It's a frustrating fact about the Hollywood machine: Most ideas, books, or screenplays developed by the studios never actually make it to film. Kosberg receives about 500 pitches a week and manages to sell about ten a year, of which one might eventually become a movie, so the odds are not great. The key to a good idea is to keep it simple yet provocative. In other words, it needs to be something that the industry refers to as "high concept." When Kosberg pitched an idea for a horror movie about a genetically enhanced guard dog that goes on a killing spree, he sold it as *Jaws on Paws!* The title didn't stick, but the idea became the 1993 movie *Man's Best Friend* starring Ally Sheedy.

An Idea Is Worth a Thousand Words . . . or Dollars

In truth, Kosberg is more interested in the idea than in the screenplay. According to the Hollywood veteran, many amateur writers have a good setup, but when breaking it down into sequences and scenes, they find that the story has no place to go. He sometimes buys a script for the concept and then has it rewritten by a veteran. Kosberg believes that writing talent is harder to find than "idea talent." Writing a script is a difficult process, and those who master it are often underestimated. According to Kosberg in an interview with *Absolute Writer Newsletter,* "There are so few good screenwriters."

In order to have the clout to pitch ideas from unknowns to the major studios, you need to be connected in Hollywood, and Kosberg has a solid track record. He and his company, Robert Kosberg Productions, are regularly involved in coproducing films, though most are low-budget or made-for-TV films. Some of the titles his company has been involved with include *One More Saturday Night* (1986), *In the Mood* (1987), and *Deep Blue Sea* (1999).

Still in the game, Kosberg is coproducing *The Hardy Men,* an updated version of the teen detective novels and popular TV show of the 1970s, which is due out in 2010. The movie began life as an equally straightforward pitch: The Hardy Boys have grown up. Sometimes, it's that simple.

Hollywood Slang

*The entertainment industry, known in Hollywood as simply "the biz,"
has developed its own language littered with oblique references,
colorful slang, and nontraditional abbreviations. Here's a brief guide
to deciphering some of the most common terms used in Hollywood:*

- Alphabet web—The ABC television network, i.e., "David E. Kelley is developing a new series for the Alphabet web."

- Ankle—To quit or be fired from a job, as in walking out the door and shutting it behind you. Director Catherine Hardwicke ankled from the sequel to *Twilight* when the studio would not allow her adequate time to prepare.

- Blurb—A TV commercial

- B.O.—Box office or box-office receipts

- Boff (or boffo, boffola)—Outstanding, usually in reference to box-office performance. "Boffo B.O." means the movie did well at the box office.

- Chopsocky—A martial arts film

- Dramedy—A film or TV show that combines both drama and comedy

- Ducats—tickets; "Some ducats for U2's Madison Square Garden gig are expected to fetch as much as $1,000 apiece."

- Eye web—The CBS television network, named after its eye-shape logo

- Green-light—To give the go-ahead for a film to be made

- Ink—To sign a contract

- In the can—When the director is satisfied with a take, it is "in the can," so to speak, because film used to be stored in flat cans.

- Kudocast—A televised awards show, i.e., "The Academy Awards ceremony is typically the highest-rated kudocast of the year."

- The Lion (or Leo)—Metro–Goldwyn–Mayer (MGM) Studios, a reference to the company's ferocious logo

- Major—A major film studio: Disney, Dreamworks, MGM, Paramount, Sony, 20th Century Fox, Universal, or Warner Bros.

- Mini-major—A film production company that is large but still smaller than the majors, i.e. New Line Cinema.

- Mouse (or Mouse House)—The Walt Disney Company, a reference to Mickey Mouse. When someone is speaking detrimentally about the company, they might refer to Disney as "the rat."

- Oater—A Western film, a reference to horse food, i.e., "Clint Eastwood's oater *Unforgiven* landed Best Picture at the Oscar kudocast."

- Peacock web—The NBC television network, named for its colorful logo

- Percentery (or tenpercentery)—A talent agency, i.e., "The actor recently switched percentery from the William Morris Agency to ICM."

- Powwow—A meeting

- Preem (or bow)—Used as a noun, meaning an opening premiere performance; used as a verb, meaning to debut a movie or show it for the first time.

- Romcom—A romantic comedy

- Scripter (or scribe)—A screenwriter

- Showrunner—The executive producer of a television series

- Suspenser—A suspense film

- Tentpole—A movie that a studio expects to be its highest-grossing blockbuster of the year, which will support the studio during the ups and downs of the rest of the year. If successful, a tentpole may begin a franchise, meaning it will instigate a successful series. In 2006, *Pirates of the Caribbean: Dead Man's Chest* was Disney's summer tentpole, meaning it made enough money to bolster the studio throughout the remainder of the year.

- U—Universal Studios

- Wrap—To finish production on a movie or TV show

- Zitcom—A TV sitcom aimed at teenagers

The Rebel and the Horror Hostess

✩ ✩ ✩ ✩

Late-night horror show hostess Vampira took 1950s America by storm. Her pale, ghoulish beauty and sex appeal hypnotized the country, including a tragic icon of the era.

Vampira Is Born

Decades before bosomy Elvira: the Mistress of the Dark became the sassy queen of late-night creature-features, another sultry siren bewitched after-hours TV audiences.

Former dancer Maila Nurmi hardly looked the part of a horror scream queen with her statuesque height and blonde locks. But as the gaunt, raven-haired Vampira, she owned the nighttime hours in the 1950s with her scandalous combination of sex, death, and sardonic wit.

When Nurmi attended a masquerade party in Los Angeles dressed in doom and gloom housewife attire, she was the talk of the ball and caught the eye of a producer from KABC television. When the station decided to spice up its Saturday night programming with horror and sci-fi films, Nurmi was hired to host, and she elevated the broadcasts to historic proportions.

Tweaking her original costume by adding elements inspired by underground bondage magazines and Hollywood divas like Gloria Swanson and Theda Bara, Nurmi created a character unlike any in television. With her black form-fitting dress, 17-inch cinched waist, long fingernails, pale skin, wild eyes, verbal double entendres, and blood-curdling scream, she was the antithesis of the repressed sexual energy and Cold War-era fear that gurgled beneath the surface of America. Viewers ate it up.

The Vampira Show was a runaway success, and in 1954, *Life* magazine devoted several pages to Vampira's beauty. This newfound fame shot Nurmi straight into celebrity circles where she encountered an unexpected kindred spirit.

It Began at Googie's

In the 1950s, Googie's was *the* place for the hip, beatnik set in L.A. Situated at the corner of Crescent Heights and Sunset Boulevard, the all-night coffeehouse was packed with Hollywood up-and-comers. Maila Nurmi was a regular, as were Marlon Brando, Anthony Perkins, and another star just beginning to shine—James Dean.

Dean was immediately drawn to Nurmi. The boyishly handsome future star of *East of Eden* (1955), *Rebel Without a Cause* (1955), and *Giant* (1956) was a notorious eccentric with a morose sense of humor. He was convinced that she shared his fascinations.

Nurmi, an evangelical Christian, was quite different from her on-screen alter ego, but Dean was drawn to her nonetheless. The feeling was mutual. Nurmi said they "shared the same neuroses."

In each other, Dean and Nurmi found a confidante free from the superficialities of Hollywood. They were inseparable, whether it was sharing a booth at Googie's, meeting at midnight to detail their respective days, or making homemade experimental 8mm films. Dean was even rumored to have appeared on *The Vampira Show,* hiding in the shadows with his back to the camera. But contrary to popular belief, the two were not romantically involved.

Nurmi was married to another Dean—Dean Eisner—who would later pen screenplays for *Dirty Harry* (1971) and *Play Misty for Me* (1971). Regardless, the press portrayed Dean and Vampira as hot-and-heavy. The tabloid fodder created rifts in their friendship, particularly as Dean's star ascended. He forcefully denied involvement with the horror hostess, often disparaging her character in the process.

Despite the ups-and-downs, the platonic pair remained close. Nurmi was a constant companion as Dean's *Rebel Without a Cause* breakthrough took shape, visiting him on the set and joining him for mischievous visits to director Nicholas Ray's bungalow at the Chateau Marmont. But the revelry was short-lived.

On September 30, 1955, just weeks before the release of *Rebel Without a Cause,* Dean was killed when his treasured Porsche Spyder collided with a truck on Highway 99 near Cholame, California. He died instantly. He was only 24 years old.

Dean's death devastated Nurmi, who had tried to dissuade him from driving the car. Unfortunately, her sarcastic mode of persuasion—a note left on the windshield exclaiming, "How could you be seen in such an awful looking thing!"—was ignored. Press attacks accusing her of placing a black magic curse on the deceased star only compounded her pain. Gossip rag *Whisper Magazine* even dubbed her "James Dean's Black Madonna." Nurmi's claims that Dean's ghost haunted her from the afterworld certainly fueled the fires of negativity.

Life After Dean

The years following Dean's death were a roller coaster for Nurmi. *The Vampira Show*'s cancellation in 1955 sunk its despondent actress. In near poverty, she resurrected Vampira for Ed Wood's infamous 1959 stinker *Plan 9 from Outer Space.* Her hilariously creepy performance as a wide-eyed corpse possessed by aliens cemented her place in pop culture history. The notoriety served Nurmi well for decades. She opened an antiques store (appropriately named Vampira's Attic) on Melrose Boulevard in Los Angeles; optioned her likeness for a series of sexy model kits; and appeared in numerous documentaries detailing her life on the wilder side of showbiz. She even sued Cassandra Peterson (better known as Elvira) for stealing her style—a lawsuit Nurmi lost. But her most significant post-Dean spotlight came thanks to a filmmaker who truly understood her legacy.

In his 1994 film *Ed Wood,* Tim Burton detailed the life of the notorious *Plan 9* filmmaker, with Nurmi featured as a brief but significant character in the tale. Burton's former lover Lisa Marie was cast as the former scream queen. She was a perfect fit. The statuesque beauty was not only a convincing double, but she also embodied the essence of Maila Nurmi, camping-up the Vampira character while also giving voice to the troubled woman behind the macabre persona. The performance was brief, but it gave insight into an actress seen by many as merely a spooky caricature. Reevaluated and recognized, Maila Nurmi sat firm as a cultural icon alongside Dean, whom she joined on the other side on January 10, 2008, at age 86.

Steven Spielberg's Tall Tale

☆ ☆ ☆ ☆

There's an oft-repeated myth that celebrated director Steven Spielberg got his big break in the movie industry by sneaking onto the Universal Studios lot, taking over a vacant office, and pretending to be an established filmmaker. The story has evolved and gained momentum over the years due in large part to Spielberg's own frequent embellishments.

Spielberg's first version of the story has the 21-year-old future director bluffing his way past the guards at Universal in 1969, dressed in a cheap suit and carrying a briefcase. Once inside the gates, he coolly took over a vacant office for two and a half months before allegedly being chased off the lot by none other than "The Master of Suspense" himself, Alfred Hitchcock. A second take on the tale pushes the action back to 1965, with a 17-year-old Spielberg touring the studio on a tram. According to this version of the story, the young auteur-to-be simply snuck away from the tour group during a bathroom break and found an empty office. Thereafter, he took the tour every day, got off the tram, and appropriated the office, even slapping his name on the door.

As colorful as these stories are, and as much as countless film school graduates wish they were true, the real story of how Spielberg broke into the industry is far more mundane. When Steven was 16, his father arranged for him to visit the studio and spend a day with his friend Chuck Silvers, who was an assistant to the editorial supervisor. The following year, Silvers secured Spielberg a summer job on the lot as an unpaid clerical assistant working for a woman named Julie Raymond. He ran errands for her for two summers while working on his own scripts. As Raymond later told Spielberg's biographer: "He made up a lot of stories about finding an empty editing office and moving into it. That's a bunch of °@$#!" It seems that when it comes to telling compelling stories, Spielberg doesn't limit himself to his scripts.

It Came from the 1950s!

The sci-fi genre blossomed in Hollywood in the 1950s, with all the major studios offering films with alien invaders, mutation, and end-of-the-world scenarios. Film scholars suggest that these tales reflected popular fears of technology stemming from the remarkable scientific advances of the era such as nuclear power and space flight. Whatever the underlying themes, the result was a spate of imaginative and innovative sci-fi flicks.

The Day the Earth Stood Still (1951)
Generally considered one of the best sci-fi offerings of the era, this thoughtful morality tale sees a powerful alien named Klaatu come to Earth to warn humanity that it must reject war and aggression or face annihilation from alien civilizations. The film was remade in 2008 as a vehicle for Keanu Reeves.

The Thing from Another World (1951)
A group of scientists at the North Pole battle a savage alien in this sci-fi classic produced by the great Howard Hawks. The film offers an interesting take on the theme of technology, as the humans find their modern weapons and scientific devices ineffective against the creature and must resort to natural forces such as fire and electricity to defeat it. Director John Carpenter helmed *The Thing*, a successful remake of the film in 1982.

When Worlds Collide (1951)
When scientists discover that a planet is on a collision course with Earth, a privately funded group builds a rocket ship to send a few dozen men and women into space to ensure that humanity carries on. A predecessor to the second wave of sci-fi disaster films, including *Independence Day* (1996) and *Armageddon* (1998), this early entry from sci-fi producer George Pal offered state-of-the-art special effects and a thrilling story line.

The War of the Worlds (1953)
This rousing action tale, based on a story by H. G. Wells that Orson Welles famously narrated on the radio in 1938, has ruthless Martian invaders laying Earth to waste. Filmed in Technicolor and lauded for the creepy, sterile design of the Martians and their powerful war machines, it set a new standard for visual effects. Tom Cruise and Dakota Fanning starred in Steven Spielberg's 2005 remake of this sci-fi classic.

The Creature from the Black Lagoon (1954)

A small group of scientists deep in the Amazon jungle mix it up with a prehistoric man-fish. In this tightly crafted allegory of passion gone awry, the creature's interest in the sole female member of the expedition mirrors the unwanted romantic advances of the expedition's leader.

Them (1954)

Giant ants run amok in the American Southwest in one of the first films to caution against the potentially dire consequences of tampering with nuclear radiation. This memorable movie offers plenty of mystery, thrills, drama, and even a touch of humor along with its terrifying mutant insects.

Forbidden Planet (1956)

Best remembered for its amazing special effects, including Robbie the Robot, this was one of the first films with high production values and an A-level cast to be set on another planet. A retelling of Shakespeare's *The Tempest*, *Forbidden Planet* suggests that even the most futuristic technology is no match for the destructive power of the human mind.

Invasion of the Body Snatchers (1956)

This classic story, cleverly directed by Don Siegel, has emotionless aliens taking over the identities of the residents of a small town, while the one man who knows the truth desperately tries to warn authorities. Remarkably, it has been interpreted as a commentary on both the threat of Communist infiltration and on the misguided conformity demanded by the infamous Senator Joe McCarthy in response to that threat.

The Incredible Shrinking Man (1957)

After being exposed to a mysterious radioactive cloud, a man finds himself growing smaller and smaller in size, and he must learn to adjust to a world in which mousetraps and household spiders have become potentially deadly. While its subtext clearly alludes to fears about technology, the film's conclusion also offers an inspiring bit of pulp philosophy about humankind's place in the universe.

The Blob (1958)

Though shot in just a few weeks on a shoestring budget, this alien-attacks-small-town story wowed audiences and remains a much-loved sci-fi staple. The villain, a gelatinous mass that feeds on everything in its path and grows larger with every meal, is eventually stopped by the teenage hero, played by Steve McQueen in his first starring role.

Anything but Splendor:
Natalie Wood

☆ ☆ ☆ ☆

The official account of Natalie Wood's tragic death is riddled
with holes. For this reason, cover-up theorists continue
to run hog-wild with conjecture. Here's a sampling of the
questions, facts, and assertions surrounding the case.

A Life in Pictures

There are those who will forever recall Natalie Wood as the adorable
child actress from *Miracle on 34th Street* (1947) and those who
remember her as the sexy but wholesome grown-up star of movies
such as *West Side Story* (1961), *Splendor in the Grass* (1961), and
Bob & Carol & Ted & Alice (1969). Both groups generally agree that
Wood had uncommon beauty and talent.

Wood appeared in her first film, *Happy Land* (1943), in a bit part
alongside other people from her hometown of Santa Rosa, California,
where the film was shot. She stood out to the director, who remembered her later when he needed to cast a child in another film. Wood
was uncommonly mature and professional for a child actress, which
helped her make a relatively smooth transition to ingenue roles.

Although Wood befriended James Dean and Sal Mineo—her
troubled young costars from *Rebel Without a Cause* (1955)—and she
briefly dated Elvis Presley, she preferred to move in established
Hollywood circles. By the time she was 20, she was married to
Robert Wagner and was costarring with Frank Sinatra in *Kings Go
Forth* (1958), which firmly ensconced her in the Hollywood establishment. The early 1960s represent the high point of Wood's career,
and she specialized in playing high-spirited characters with determination and spunk. She added two more Oscar nominations to the one
she received for *Rebel* and racked up five Golden Globe nominations
for Best Actress. This period also proved to be personally turbulent
for Wood, as she suffered through a failed marriage to Wagner and
another to Richard Gregson. After taking time off to raise her
children, she remarried Wagner and returned to her acting career.

Shocking News

And so, on November 29, 1981, the headline hit the newswires much like an out-of-control car hits a brick wall. Natalie Wood, the beautiful, vivacious 43-year-old star of stage and screen, had drowned after falling from her yacht the *Splendour,* which was anchored off California's Santa Catalina Island. Wood had been on the boat during a break from her latest film, *Brainstorm,* and was accompanied by Wagner and *Brainstorm* costar Christopher Walken. Skipper Dennis Davern was at the helm. Foul play was not suspected.

In My Esteemed Opinion

After a short investigation, Chief Medical Examiner Dr. Thomas Noguchi listed Wood's death as an accidental drowning. Tests revealed that she had consumed "seven or eight" glasses of wine, and the coroner contended that in her intoxicated state Wood had probably stumbled and fallen overboard while attempting to untie the yacht's rubber dinghy. He also stated that cuts and bruises on her body could have occurred when she fell from the boat.

Doubting Thomases

To this day, many question Wood's mysterious demise and believe that the accidental drowning theory sounds a bit too convenient. Pointed questions have led to many rumors: Does someone know more about Wood's final moments than they're letting on? Was her drowning really an accident, or did someone intentionally or accidentally *help* her overboard? Could this be why she sustained substantial bruising on her face and the back of her legs? Why was Wagner so reluctant to publicly discuss the incident? Were Christopher Walken and Wood an item as had been rumored? With this possibility in mind, could a booze-fueled fight have erupted between the two men? Could Wood have then tried to intervene, only to be knocked overboard for her efforts? And why did authorities declare Wood's death accidental so quickly? Would such a hasty ruling have been issued had the principals not been famous, wealthy, and influential?

Ripples

At the time of Wood's death, she and Wagner were seven years into their second marriage to each other. Whether Wood was carrying on an affair with Walken, as was alleged, may be immaterial, even if it made for interesting tabloid fodder. But Wagner's perception of their relationship could certainly be a factor. If nothing else, it might better explain the argument that ensued between Wagner and Walken that fateful night.

Case Closed?

Further information about Wood's death is sparse because no eyewitnesses have come forward. However, a businesswoman whose boat was anchored nearby testified that she heard a woman shouting for help, and then a voice responding, "We'll be over to get you," so the woman went back to bed. Just after dawn, Wood's body was found floating a mile away from the *Splendour,* approximately 200 yards offshore. The dinghy was found nearby; its only cargo was a stack of lifejackets.

In 2008, after 27 years of silence, Robert Wagner recalled in his autobiography, *Pieces of My Heart: A Life,* that he and Walken had engaged in a heated argument during supper after Walken had suggested that Wood star in more films, effectively keeping her away from their children. Wagner and Walken then headed topside to cool down. Sometime around midnight, Wagner said he returned to his cabin and discovered that his wife was missing. He soon realized that the yacht's dinghy was gone as well. In his book, he surmised that Wood may have gone to secure the dinghy that had been noisily slapping against the boat. Then, tipsy from the wine, she probably fell into the ocean and drowned. Walken notified the authorities.

Was Natalie Wood's demise the result of a deadly mix of wine and saltwater as the coroner's report suggests? This certainly could be the case. But why would she leave her warm cabin to tend to a loose rubber dinghy in the dark of night? Could an errant rubber boat really make such a commotion?

Perhaps we'll never know what happened that fateful night, but an interview conducted shortly before Wood's death proved prophetic: "I'm frightened to death of the water," said Wood about a long-held fear. "I can swim a little bit, but I'm afraid of water that is dark."

Pop Quiz: Bond Girls

The James Bond series is famous for its gorgeous leading ladies. Can you match the Bond Girl with the movie in which she appeared?

1. Anya Amasova		A. *Casino Royale*	
2. Fatima Blush		B. *Diamonds Are Forever*	
3. Pam Bouvier		C. *Die Another Day*	
4. Paris Carver		D. *Dr. No*	
5. Domino		E. *For Your Eyes Only*	
6. Strawberry Fields		F. *From Russia with Love*	
7. Pussy Galore		G. *GoldenEye*	
8. Holly Goodhead		H. *Goldfinger*	
9. Melina Havelock		I. *Licence to Kill*	
10. Jinx		J. *Live and Let Die*	
11. Christmas Jones		K. *Moonraker*	
12. Vesper Lynd		L. *Never Say Never Again*	
13. Magda		M. *Octopussy*	
14. Xenia Onatopp		N. *Quantum of Solace*	
15. Plenty O'Toole		O. *The Spy Who Loved Me*	
16. Tatiana Romanova		P. *Thunderball*	
17. Honey Ryder		Q. *Tomorrow Never Dies*	
18. Solitaire		R. *A View to a Kill*	
19. Stacey Sutton		S. *The World Is Not Enough*	
20. Kissy Suzuki		T. *You Only Live Twice*	

Answer Key: 1. O; **2.** L; **3.** I; **4.** Q; **5.** P; **6.** N; **7.** H; **8.** K; **9.** E; **10.** C; **11.** S; **12.** A; **13.** M; **14.** G; **15.** B; **16.** F; **17.** D; **18.** J; **19.** R; **20.** T

Dorothy Dandridge

☆ ☆ ☆ ☆

Dorothy Dandridge should have been a superstar. But the racism so prevalent in Hollywood when Dandridge was at her peak, coupled with her own inner demons, prevented her from achieving the stardom she so richly deserved.

Dorothy Dandridge was born on November 9, 1922, in Cleveland, Ohio, to actress Ruby Dandridge and the Reverend Cyril Dandridge. With her mother's encouragement, Dorothy and her sister, Vivian, started performing in the 1930s as a song-and-dance team known as the Wonder Children. By the end of the decade, they had teamed up with Etta Jones to form a trio known as the Dandridge Sisters.

By this time, the Dandridge family had moved to Los Angeles, where job opportunities were more plentiful. In Hollywood, Dorothy landed roles in films such as *A Day at the Races* (1937), *Sun Valley Serenade* (1941), and *Drums of the Congo* (1942).

In 1945, Dandridge wed dancer Harold Nicholas, with whom she had performed in *Sun Valley Serenade*. Marrying Harold should have been a step toward a better Hollywood career for Dandridge, but obtaining roles that were dignified was difficult for both of them. The rocky marriage lasted for six years, and during that time, Dandridge gave birth to a daughter, Harolyn, who was born with severe brain damage. Unable to care for her, Dandridge had no choice but to place the girl in an institution.

A Star on the Rise

After divorcing Nicholas, Dandridge pursued a solo singing career on the nightclub circuit. She performed with Desi Arnaz's band at the Mocambo Club in Hollywood, then did a well-received 14-week stint at La Vie en Rose in New York City. From there, she toured the world, performing in San Francisco, London, and Rio de Janeiro.

With her popularity on the rise and more doors opening for black actors, Dandridge was suddenly in demand in Hollywood as well. Her breakthrough in a dramatic role came in 1951 when she costarred as an African princess in *Tarzan's Peril*. In 1953, she received her first starring role as a dedicated schoolteacher in *Bright Road*, performing opposite Harry Belafonte. A year later, Dandridge landed her best-known film role, the lead in *Carmen Jones*, again opposite Belafonte.

Carmen Jones made Dandridge the talk of the town, and she became the first black performer to be nominated for a Best Actress Oscar. However, she lost to Grace Kelly for *The Country Girl* (1954). Despite the loss, Dandridge's star continued to rise. She found herself on the cover of *Life* magazine in 1955 and was joyously received at the Cannes International Film Festival. In 1957, she made history when she was cast as the romantic lead opposite a white actor in *Island of the Sun*. Dandridge gained a lot of attention, but the film was flawed and harshly judged by critics. Still, she was a bona fide Hollywood celebrity—the industry's first black female star.

Sadly, *Carmen Jones* would prove to be the pinnacle of Dandridge's acting career. She declined the role of Tuptim in *The King and I* (1956) because she didn't want to play a slave. In the years that followed, she was offered few quality roles, save for *Porgy and Bess* (1959), in which she played opposite Sidney Poitier. She was nominated for a Golden Globe for Best Actress in a Comedy or Musical for her performance, which marked another milestone.

Career in Decline

From there, Dandridge found herself in an unstoppable downward spiral. She appeared in a handful of films in the late '50s and early '60s, but they failed to advance her career in any significant way.

Dandridge married restaurateur Jack Denison in 1959, but again happiness eluded her. Denison was abusive and squandered most of Dandridge's savings in a failed business venture. With Dandridge no longer of use to him, he bailed on the marriage soon after. Severely depressed, Dandridge began drinking heavily and taking antidepressants. On the verge of bankruptcy and with the IRS hounding her for money, she tried to resume her nightclub career, but the audiences that had packed her performances in years past just weren't there.

With the bills piling up and her career in tatters, Dandridge suffered a nervous breakdown from which she never recovered. She was found dead in her Hollywood home on September 8, 1965, the apparent victim of an intentional drug overdose.

Left Behind on the Cutting Room Floor

Filmmakers face tough calls while editing films, and sometimes, deleting a scene can completely change the final product. Would these flicks still have been box-office gold if the following scenes had been left in?

The Wizard of Oz (1939)

Talk about a different path for the yellow brick road: The original treatment of *The Wizard of Oz* included a massively expensive musical scene called "The Jitterbug." The scene—which took five weeks to shoot and cost producers a whopping $80,000—had Dorothy, the Scarecrow, the Tin Man, and the Cowardly Lion being attacked by a group of jitterbugs as they enter the Haunted Forest. What is a jitterbug, you ask? It's commonly described by film buffs as a "furry pink and blue mosquitolike rascal" that buzzes around people, giving them the jitters.

Despite the work that went into the elaborate scene and accompanying song, MGM decided it made the movie too long. Legend has it that studio execs were also concerned that viewers would associate the scene with the then-popular dance of the same name, which could ruin the idea that Oz was a fantasy world and would one day make the movie seem dated.

King Kong (1933)

These days, it's hard to imagine that the 1933 classic *King Kong* was ever too scary to sit through. For audiences back then, however, the giant gorilla was a frightful sight—so much so that producers had to slice a scene out of the movie just to make it more tolerable.

The original *King Kong* included a scene in which Kong shook a log bridge, sending several sailors falling into a ravine below, where giant spiders were waiting to eat them alive. Yikes! During the initial preview, the scene supposedly caused people to scream and even get up and leave the theater. According to producer Merian C. Cooper, it "stopped the picture cold," so the human-eating spiders were removed from the scene.

Dr. No (1962)

James Bond's initial introduction to the world wasn't as the character's creators originally intended. *Dr. No*, the first installment in the James Bond franchise, saw several chops before hitting the big screen, including one major change to the movie's climax. The original version showed Honey Ryder, the first Bond girl, being attacked by giant crabs just before 007 swoops in to rescue her. The consensus, though, was that the crabs weren't creepy enough. Apparently, their crawling was a bit too slow to be truly scary, so the crustaceans got the ax.

Other modifications were made to tone down the violence in *Dr. No*. One scene, for example, was meant to have Bond shooting the villain six times, but the British Board of Film Classification thought that was a bit excessive, so it asked producers to pare it down to two gunshots instead.

Big (1988)
This blockbuster starring Tom Hanks got a big change before its debut. In the movie, Hanks plays a 12-year-old boy who magically transforms into an adult after making a wish on a carnival machine. But the final product featured a drastically different ending from what test audiences first saw.

Hanks's character, Josh, falls in love with a woman when he is living the life of an adult male. The version we know ends with Josh deciding to leave her behind when he wishes to become a child again. The woman, it appears, accepts this fate and moves on with her life.

But it's been rumored that the first version of the film didn't end there. A supposed subsequent scene showed Josh, back as a child and back in school, meeting a new girl in his class. And, you guessed it, that new girl is his former adult flame, who had gone to the carnival machine and wished to become a child herself so the two could stay together. However, that ending has never shown up on DVD releases and may have been wishful thinking on the part of fans who wanted a fairy-tale ending.

Titanic (1997)
The historical epic that broke box-office records and won 11 Academy Awards almost missed out on its dramatic ending. The movie ends with the elderly Rose—played by Gloria Stuart—throwing her "Heart of the Ocean" diamond necklace over the side of the research ship and into the ocean. Simple and beautiful, right? It almost wasn't.

Titanic originally went on for another nine minutes during which crew members approached Rose, thinking she was going to jump over the edge and end her life. They tried to talk her out of committing suicide, and then, when they realized she was just throwing the necklace over-board, they tried to convince her to keep it. Not quite as poetic, is it?

Hollywood Forever Cemetery

☆ ☆ ☆ ☆

*They say that if you make it in Hollywood, you'll live forever.
That might be true in terms of living in the hearts of your fans,
but unless you've managed to find the Fountain of Youth, no
matter how famous you are, your body is eventually going to give
out. It was with that realization that in 1899 nearly 100 acres
in the heart of Hollywood were set aside for use as a cemetery.
Originally called Hollywood Memorial Park Cemetery, the area
soon became the place for Hollywood's elite to spend eternity.*

Over the years, despite the fact that the cream of the
Hollywood crop were interred there, the cemetery
began to look very run-down. Things got so
bad that in 1998, amid rumors of an impending
bankruptcy, the cemetery was put up for sale.
It was quickly purchased by Tyler Cassity,
whose family had been in the funerary and
cemetery business for more than 25 years.
Cassity wasted no time spending millions of
dollars refurbishing the cemetery, restoring
it to its former glory. But some of his
methods raised a few eyebrows: For instance,
he implemented movie nights in the graveyard, where spectators
(and specters, presumably) could bring their lawn chairs and blan-
kets and plop down to watch a movie projected onto one of the
buildings. In the end, the cemetery, which Cassity renamed Hollywood Forever, has never been more popular and continues to attract
visitors from all over the world.

Hollywood Forever sits directly behind the famed Paramount
Studios lot, under the gaze of the Hollywood sign. The picturesque
cemetery has been used in numerous motion pictures, including
Steve Martin's *L.A. Story* (1991) and Robert Altman's *The Player*
(1992), and is now listed on the National Register of Historic Sites.
Hollywood Forever is also the final resting place for more celebrities
than any other place on earth.

So Who's Everyone Coming to See?

It's the stars that lit up Hollywood in the 1930s, '40s, and '50s who fill most of the cemetery's plots, including Tyrone Power, Peter Lorre, and Fay Wray of *King Kong* (1933) fame. Actor Douglas Fairbanks and his son, Douglas Fairbanks Jr., are also buried there, as are *Our Gang* sweethearts Darla Hood and Carl "Alfalfa" Switzer. And even though he died more than 80 years ago, women still flock to the crypt where Rudolph Valentino is interred.

If you're looking for the graves of people who were more "behind the scenes" in movies, Hollywood Forever is the final resting place of legendary directors John Huston (*The Maltese Falcon,* 1941; *The Treasure of the Sierra Madre,* 1948; *The African Queen,* 1951) and Victor Fleming (*The Wizard of Oz,* 1939; *Gone with the Wind,* 1939). And as long as you're in the neighborhood, you can swing by and let famous director and producer Cecil B. DeMille (*The Greatest Show on Earth,* 1952; *The Ten Commandments,* 1956) know that you're ready for your close-up.

And what would Hollywood be without a juicy scandal? It's fitting that infamous gangster Bugsy Siegel is buried in the cemetery, as is Virginia Rappe, who was reportedly killed by Fatty Arbuckle in 1921. Although Arbuckle was found not guilty, his trial is considered by many to have been one of Hollywood's first major scandals.

One tombstone inside Hollywood Forever that everyone wants to see belongs to Mel Blanc, the voice of Bugs Bunny, Daffy Duck, Porky Pig, and many other Looney Tunes characters. Blanc's epitaph reads, in part: "That's All, Folks."

There are many who say that a trip to Hollywood just isn't complete without paying respect to the legends of the silver screen at Hollywood Forever Cemetery. And where else in the world can you kick back and enjoy a classic film starring some of your favorite vintage actors and actresses... who just happen to be buried right next to your lawn chair?

• *Hollywood Forever features an interactive exhibit called the Library of Lives where visitors can look up famous people interred at the cemetery and then access video, audio, and written accounts of their lives and careers.*

Hispanic Hollywood

Hispanic actors have been prominent in Hollywood since the silent era. In the early years, many complained of typecasting and discrimination, and some even went so far as to hide their ethnicity in order to further their careers. While these issues may remain problematic even today, some of the most successful and admired stars in Hollywood history have been of Hispanic heritage.

Antonio Banderas

Banderas became a top box-office star in Spain through his work with respected director Pedro Almodovar and made his Hollywood debut in *The Mambo Kings*, a 1992 film about two Cuban brothers who become prominent musicians in New York City. His striking good looks and emotional intensity made him a favorite of female moviegoers in films such as *Interview with the Vampire* (1994), *Evita* (1996), and *The Mask of Zorro* (1998).

Penelope Cruz

Like Antonio Banderas, Cruz became an international superstar through her work with Spanish director Pedro Almodovar. She brought her fashion-model looks and considerable acting talent to Hollywood in films including *Vanilla Sky* (2001) and *Vicky Cristina Barcelona* (2008), for which she won an Oscar for Best Supporting Actress. Cruz drew much attention for her penchant for flings with hunky costars, including Tom Cruise, Matthew McConaughey, and Javier Bardem.

Dolores Del Rio

Often cited as one of the most beautiful actresses of her era, Del Rio made her Hollywood debut in 1925. She was popular with audiences throughout the 1930s but was frustrated by the stereotypical roles she was relegated to. After returning to her native Mexico in the 1940s, she became a major star there, occasionally coming back to the States to appear in a Hollywood film.

Benicio Del Toro

Though not a top box-office draw, Del Toro cultivated a loyal audience through his distinctive portrayals of likable crooks in *The Usual Suspects* (1995) and *Snatch* (2000). He also earned the Best Supporting Actor

Oscar for his sensitive performance as a conflicted Mexican cop in director Steven Soderbergh's *Traffic* (2000). Soderbergh directed Del Toro again in the title role of 2008's *Che,* a two-part, four-hour biopic about famed Argentine revolutionary Che Guevara.

Jose Ferrer
Ferrer was a respected actor, director, and producer in both theater and film. His urbane manner and distinctly resonant voice made him perfect for portraying haughty men of refinement. The Puerto Rican native earned a Best Supporting Actor nomination for his film debut in *Joan of Arc* (1948) and won the Best Actor Oscar for his sensitive but dashing portrayal of *Cyrano de Bergerac* (1950).

Andy Garcia
Garcia appeared in a number of minor film and television roles in the 1970s and '80s before getting his big break in *The Untouchables* (1987) and then *The Godfather: Part III* (1990). Ironically, in both films he portrayed an Italian American, but he would go on to celebrate his Cuban heritage in films such as *The Lost City* (2005), an homage to Havana's vibrant pre-Castro days that Garcia starred in, produced, and directed.

Rita Hayworth
Born in New York City to a Spanish father and an Irish mother, Rita Hayworth would become one of the best-known box-office stars of Hollywood's Golden Age. Though she made more than two dozens films in the 1930s, she vaulted to prominence after assuming the image of a provocative vamp in *Blood and Sand* (1941) opposite Tyrone Power. After that, she quickly became one of the most ogled pinup girls of the era. Her signature role in *Gilda* (1946) cemented her star image as a love goddess.

Salma Hayek
In the early 1990s, Salma Hayek left a successful career as a soap opera star in Mexico to take her chances in Hollywood. Director Robert Rodriguez recognized her star quality and gave Hayek her breakthrough role in *Desperado* (1995), opposite Antonio Banderas. Hayek parlayed her stardom into a career behind the camera as well. In 2002, she starred in and coproduced *Frida,* a biopic about Mexican painter Frida Kahlo. In addition to coproducing films, Hayek has served as executive producer on the groundbreaking TV comedy *Ugly Betty.*

Jennifer Lopez

A multitalented celebrity, Lopez has made her mark as a dancer, singer, and actress. Her film career has had its ups—*Selena* (1996), *Out of Sight* (1998), *Shall We Dance?* (2004)—and downs—*The Cell* (2000), *Enough* (2002), *Gigli* (2003)—but she has always remained prominent in the public eye as a favorite subject of the supermarket tabloids.

Anthony Quinn

A charismatic man's man with a much-admired passion for life, Quinn appeared in more than 100 films in his 65-year career and won two Oscars. Born in Mexico in 1915, he was noted for his remarkable ability to convincingly portray characters of almost any ethnicity— Italian (*La Strada*, 1954), Inuit (*The Savage Innocents*, 1961), Arab (*Lawrence of Arabia*, 1962), Greek (*Zorba the Greek*, 1964), or Ukrainian (*The Shoes of the Fisherman*, 1968).

Cesar Romero

Cesar Romero was born in New York City in 1907 and began appearing on Broadway in the 1930s. Elegant, imposing, and handsome, he soon moved to film where he typically played a carefree playboy who lost the girl to the male lead in light romances, but he also appeared in many musicals and was known for his grace as a dancer. He shifted to television roles later in his career and is well remembered for his outlandish portrayal of The Joker on the 1960s series *Batman*.

Martin Sheen

Born in Dayton, Ohio, Sheen began acting in the theater in the late 1950s. His film career started in the 1960s with portrayals of rebels and outsiders, culminating in his breakthrough role as a killer in *Badlands* (1973). His visceral performance as military assassin Benjamin Willard in *Apocalypse Now* (1979) remains his most memorable film role, though he is also well known for his TV work on *The West Wing*.

Lupe Velez

Velez emigrated from Mexico to the United States in the mid-1920s and by 1926 was starring opposite matinee idol Douglas Fairbanks in the silent romantic adventure *The Gaucho*. Petite, beautiful, and feisty, Velez had a natural flair for physical comedy and became best known for a formulaic series of domestic comedies in which she played "The Mexican Spitfire." Tragically, she committed suicide in 1944 after a failed romance.

The *Poltergeist* Curse

☆ ☆ ☆ ☆

Considering its paranormal story line and the number of tragic and untimely deaths it's been associated with, it's not surprising that rumors of a curse have become attached to Poltergeist *(1982).*

Cowritten and coproduced by Steven Spielberg, *Poltergeist* was one of the most successful movies of the 1980s, earning three Academy Award nominations. However, a few months after the movie's release, Dominique Dunne, who played the older sister, died under brutal circumstances. The 22-year-old actress's ex-boyfriend choked her to death in her Los Angeles home.

In 1986, the first sequel, appropriately titled *Poltergeist II*, hit movie theaters. By that time, veteran actor Julian Beck, who played Kane, had already died of stomach cancer. It was hardly unexpected, though, as the 60-year-old actor had been battling the disease for 18 months, including during the movie's production. A second member of the *Poltergeist II* cast passed away in 1987. Will Sampson, best known for his role as the Native American patient in *One Flew Over the Cuckoo's Nest* (1975), died in a Houston hospital six weeks after undergoing a heart-lung transplant. He was 53.

Then, in 1988, the rumor of a curse really took off following the tragic death of 12-year-old Heather O'Rourke, who starred in all three movies. O'Rourke played Carol Anne, the little girl who first encountered the poltergeist and made "They're heeeere!" the catchphrase of 1982. A few months before the release of *Poltergeist III*, she suffered septic shock from a bowel obstruction and died on the operating table at Children's Hospital in San Diego.

While a number of deaths have occurred among the cast of the three *Poltergeist* movies, the idea that there is a curse on the franchise is about as believable as a young girl disappearing inside a television set. The truth is that four actors who appeared in one or more of the movies have since died, but only two were untimely and unexpected deaths. Most of the cast members, including Craig T. Nelson and JoBeth Williams who headlined the original 1982 release and the first sequel, are still alive and well.

The Rest of the Best

It can take hundreds of people to bring a motion picture to life, but the person most responsible for how a movie turns out is the director. He or she decides how a scene will be shot, guides the actors through the nuances of the script, and determines the movie's final look. Many directors are skilled at their craft, but only a handful can accurately be called geniuses. Here are a few who make the grade.

Francis Ford Coppola (1939–)

Coppola got his start working for low-budget exploitation producer Roger Corman, who taught him the ins and outs of moviemaking. *The Godfather* (1972) and *The Godfather: Part II* (1974) demonstrated Coppola's skill behind the camera, which he proved yet again with *The Conversation* (1974) and *Apocalypse Now* (1979), an ambitious film about the horrors of the Vietnam War that was loosely based on Joseph Conrad's novel *Heart of Darkness*. Over the years, Coppola has written, directed, and produced dozens of films and has won every major film award, including Best Director Oscars for *The Godfather* and *The Godfather: Part II*.

Cecil B. DeMille (1881–1959)

Any discussion of historical or biblical epics begins and ends with DeMille, who almost single-handedly defined the genre. His directing career began in 1914 with *The Squaw Man* and ended in 1956 with *The Ten Commandments*, arguably his greatest epic of all. During the intervening years, he directed scores of movies, including classics such as *The King of Kings* (1927), *Cleopatra* (1934), *Samson and Delilah* (1949), and *The Greatest Show on Earth* (1952). In addition to directing, DeMille frequently produced and wrote the screenplays for the movies he made and even performed the prologue narration for some.

John Ford (1895–1973)

"I make Westerns," Ford once said of his career as a director, but the iconic filmmaker was selling himself short. Ford began making Westerns during the silent era, understanding America's obsession with the Wild West. He honed the conventions and themes of the genre, particularly during the Golden Age, with classics such as *Stagecoach* (1939) and *She Wore a Yellow Ribbon* (1949). Over the course of his stellar career, he also directed historical dramas (*Young Mr. Lincoln*, 1939) and war films (*They Were Expendable*, 1945). Ford won the Best Director Oscar three times, and his war documentary *The Battle of Midway* (1942) won a special Academy Award. Ford is credited with discovering John Wayne, whom he cast in more than 25 of his films.

D. W. Griffith (1875–1948)
Known as "the Father of Film," D. W. Griffith was an early master of many of the filmmaking techniques still used today. In addition, he and his actors developed a credible style of acting for the big screen, and he was instrumental in pushing for feature-length films—all before Hollywood became the filmmaking capital of the world. In New York, during the first five years of his career, Griffith directed an estimated 485 one- and two-reelers for American Biograph, quick jobs that allowed him to perfect his filmmaking technique. It was after Griffith left Biograph in 1914, however, that he directed many of the movies for which he is best remembered, including his most famous film, *The Birth of a Nation* (1915), which he cowrote, *Intolerance* (1916), and *Broken Blossoms* (1919). Griffith was a controversial director, but his influence as a filmmaker cannot be denied.

John Huston (1906–1987)
A man of many talents, Huston was, among other things, an actor and a journalist before turning to scriptwriting and, with *The Maltese Falcon* (1941), directing. Featuring Humphrey Bogart in one of his most iconic roles, *The Maltese Falcon* immediately established Huston as a director to be reckoned with. Over the course of his career, the hard-drinking Irishman, who was the son of respected actor Walter Huston and the father of Oscar-winning actress Angelica Huston, made dozens of critically acclaimed features, including *The Treasure of the Sierra Madre* (1948), *Key Largo* (1948), *The Red Badge of Courage* (1951), *The African Queen* (1951), *The Man Who Would Be King* (1975), and *Prizzi's Honor* (1985).

Spike Lee (1957–)
A graduate of NYU's prestigious film school, Lee caught Hollywood's eye with his directorial debut, *She's Gotta Have It* (1986), which won the Prix de Jeunesse at the Cannes Film Festival. Since then, Lee has helmed an eclectic array of movies, many of which—such as *Do the Right Thing* (1989)—address the issue of race in American society. Some of Lee's other well-received films include *School Daze* (1988), *Jungle Fever* (1991), *Malcolm X* (1992), and *Inside Man* (2006). Lee also produced the Emmy-winning documentary *When the Levees Broke: A Requiem in Four Acts* (2006) about New Orleans in the aftermath of Hurricane Katrina.

Oscar Micheaux (1884–1951)

Few people today remember Micheaux, which is a shame because he holds a historic place in American popular culture. Like all black filmmakers in the old days, Micheaux was completely shut out of the Hollywood film industry, which relegated African Americans to supporting roles as household help or comic relief. For more than 30 years, Micheaux secured his own financing for his films with all-black casts playing a variety of roles. Micheaux is believed to have been the first black filmmaker to produce a feature-length film (*The Homesteader*, 1919) and a feature-length film with sound (*The Exile*, 1931). He was also one of cinema's first independent filmmakers. The son of former slaves, Micheaux directed more than 30 films over the course of his career, including musicals, comedies, Westerns, and even gangster movies.

Martin Scorsese (1942–)

A prominent filmmaker since the late 1960s, Scorsese is a difficult director to pigeonhole. Part of the Film School Generation, Scorsese uses his films to explore the conventions of filmmaking, both visually and narratively. He is most commonly associated with gangster movies (*Mean Streets*, 1973; *GoodFellas*, 1990; *Casino*, 1995; *The Departed*, 2006), but over the course of his career he has also directed historical dramas (*Gangs of New York*, 2002), biopics (*Raging Bull*, 1980), and documentaries (*The Last Waltz*, 1978; *Shine a Light*, 2008). But this Oscar-winning filmmaker will probably be best remembered as the director of the movie that made Robert De Niro a star—*Taxi Driver* (1976).

Billy Wilder (1906–2002)

A triple threat as a director, writer, and producer, Billy Wilder may have been the most literate filmmaker of Hollywood's studio era. Born in Austria, he immigrated to Hollywood from the German film industry, eventually landing a job as a scriptwriter. In 1942, he parlayed his screenwriting success into the director's chair with the comedy *The Major and the Minor*. Wilder's now-classic *Sunset Boulevard* (1950) kicked off a decade in which the director gained maximum control over his films through his own production company. He became renowned for his sexually tinged farces with clever banter, such as *The Seven Year Itch* (1955) and *Some Like It Hot* (1959), and for his unsentimental dramas that subtly pointed out the foibles of American society, including *Ace in the Hole* (1951), *Stalag 17* (1953), and *The Apartment* (1960).

How to Become a Stunt Person

Q: When does a movie need a stunt person?

A: A stunt person stands in for an actor or actress when the scene involves physical danger—anything from fighting or falling from a bicycle to hanging from a skyscraper or driving a car through a burning building. A movie production's insurance company will insist that an actor is never exposed to unnecessary danger. If a lead gets injured, for example, production has to stop and a studio or the investors financing the movie will lose money. It's also quicker and less expensive to employ a skilled stunt double rather than train an actor to perform his own stunts.

Q: Is this a profession for thrill-seekers?

A: Absolutely not! A stunt person needs to be gutsy but not reckless. Performing a stunt involves attention to detail and lots of planning. Those just looking for an adrenaline rush are a danger to themselves and to others on the set.

Q: So what skills are required?

A: You need to be in good physical shape, and it helps to be skilled at sports such as gymnastics or martial arts or even have some military training. There are also workshops that provide basic stunt training. As with acting, aspiring stunt people also need to be good at networking.

Q: How do you break into the business?

A: Landing that first role can be harder than most of the stunts! Serious parties should check out the two largest stunt associations: the United Stuntmen's Association (www.stuntschool.com) and the Stuntmen's Association of Motion Pictures (www.stuntmen.com). You also need to be a member of the Screen Actor's Guild (SAG). You can become a member of this actor's union by working as a movie extra. Then write to stunt coordinators who work in Hollywood regularly. Try to hang out on movie sets, and take any opportunity to introduce yourself to the stunt people.

Q: How much does a stunt person earn?

A: The base rate for SAG members is $500 per day plus extras for repeating a stunt. But remember, employment is often sporadic and the work is dangerous. A desk job might not be as exciting, but it's a lot safer.

Fast Facts: Audrey Hepburn

- *Audrey Hepburn was born in Belgium in 1929. She later moved to London, where she practiced ballet and modeling.*

- *Hepburn was born Audrey Kathleen Ruston. After World War II, her father discovered documents indicating that he had ancestors named Hepburn, so he had the surname legally changed. Audrey became Audrey Kathleen Hepburn-Ruston.*

- *Audrey Hepburn's first film appearance came in 1948, during her modeling years, when a producer offered her a small part in the European film* Nederlands in 7 Lessen.

- *In the early 1950s, Hepburn moved to America to play the lead role in the Broadway play* Gigi. *It didn't take long for her to succeed—she snagged an Oscar for Best Actress for* Roman Holiday *(1953), her first role as a leading lady.*

- *Audrey Hepburn was paid $12,500 for her role in* Roman Holiday. *In her final film—Steven Spielberg's* Always *(1989)—she reportedly made $1 million.*

- *Audrey Hepburn's best-known movies include* Sabrina *(1954),* Funny Face *(1957),* Love in the Afternoon *(1957),* The Nun's Story *(1959),* Breakfast at Tiffany's *(1961),* Charade *(1963), and* My Fair Lady *(1964).*

- *Hepburn said that she didn't think she was right for the part of Holly Golightly in* Breakfast at Tiffany's.

- *In 2006, the black dress Audrey Hepburn wore in* Breakfast at Tiffany's *sold at auction for $800,000.*

- *Audrey Hepburn turned down the lead role in* The Diary of Anne Frank *(1959), stating that it would have been too painful for her because as a young girl in Holland, she had secretly smuggled messages to the Dutch Resistance during the Nazi occupation.*

- *Hepburn ranks third among all actresses (behind Katharine Hepburn and Bette Davis) in the American Film Institute's list of Greatest American Female Screen Legends. She's also on* Empire *magazine's list of Top 100 Movie Stars of All Time (#50) and 100 Sexist Stars in Film History (#8) and has been named one of* People *magazine's 50 Most Beautiful People in the World.* Harper's *and* Queen *named her the most fascinating woman of modern time.*

- *Audrey Hepburn often downplayed her own fame. "I never think of myself as an icon," she once said. "I probably hold the distinction of being one movie star who, by all laws of logic, should never have made it."*

- *Hepburn was fluent in five languages: Dutch (Flemish), English, French, Italian, and Spanish.*

- *Audrey Hepburn was always self-conscious about the size of her feet. She wore a size 10 shoe.*

- *You've probably heard Marilyn Monroe's birthday song to President John F. Kennedy, but Audrey Hepburn reportedly sang one, too— in 1963, on JFK's final birthday.*

- *A breed of tulip is named after Audrey Hepburn.*

- *Hepburn holds the record among actresses for most presentations of the Best Picture Oscar at the Academy Awards. She presented the honor four times.*

- *Audrey and Katharine Hepburn—who are not related—are the only two winners of a Best Actress Oscar to share a last name.*

- *Audrey Hepburn died on January 20, 1993, from complications stemming from cancer of the appendix, which spread to her colon.*

- *Hepburn received an Oscar after her death: the Jean Hersholt Humanitarian Award for her work as a goodwill ambassador to UNICEF—a role she played from 1988 until her death.*

The Film School Generation

☆ ☆ ☆ ☆

The 1960s was a tumultuous time for the American film industry, as the old Hollywood studios lost their ironclad grip over it. At the same time, a new generation of edgy, provocative filmmakers moved in and shook things up, bringing an artistic vision that produced some of America's most remarkable films. These trendsetters were known as the Film School Generation.

During the 1930s and '40s, the Hollywood film industry operated under what would become known as the studio system. A handful of studios dominated the industry, holding stars under long-term contracts and employing armies of writers, costumers, camera operators, and other professionals  to crank out films using a factorylike system as their model. Producers had creative control of films, overseeing every decision from casting to script approval to set design. And although the system produced some of the most memorable movies the world has ever seen, it began to crumble in the 1950s. Competition from television hurt the studios, as did court rulings that weakened the studios' grip over the marketplace and gave a boost to the growing ranks of independent filmmakers. Censorship standards were also loosening, so that the generally wholesome fare that had been Hollywood's standard began to seem unsophisticated. By the 1960s, the studio system was essentially gone, and Hollywood turned to a new breed of filmmaker. The Film School Generation had arrived.

The New Filmmakers
Actors such as Jack Nicholson, Dustin Hoffman, Warren Beatty, and Faye Dunaway and directors such as Woody Allen, Roman Polanski, Martin Scorsese, Mike Nichols, and William Friedkin brought a unique frankness and realism to film. They arrived at a time when new technologies allowed for more location shooting and freer movement of the camera, and they used this to give their work a

distinctly new look. As a group, they shared two things that Golden Age filmmakers lacked—a counterculture sensibility and a formal university education in film. The former trait led them to create films that tackled sensitive social issues head-on, while criticizing the institutions and values that old-school Hollywood films often reinforced. Their study of film history in an academic setting gave them an abiding respect for and deep knowledge of the techniques and accomplishments of the great filmmakers that preceded them. In fact, one of the hallmarks of the Film School Generation is that they frequently include tributes to earlier films in their work—they might duplicate the imagery, props, or camera angles of a specific shot or use the name of a character from an old film.

The 1960s saw the Film School Generation create seminal films such as *Bonnie and Clyde* (1967), *The Graduate* (1967), *Midnight Cowboy* (1969), and *Easy Rider* (1969), which offered gritty antiheroes and frank treatments of sex and violence. In the 1970s, Francis Ford Coppola became one of the group's most accomplished directors with his masterworks *The Godfather* (1972) and *Apocalypse Now* (1979). Similarly, Robert De Niro became a leading actor of his time through his frequent collaborations with Martin Scorsese in films such as *Taxi Driver* (1976) and *Raging Bull* (1980).

Reining Them In

The successes of these filmmakers allowed them to command more creative control over their films than directors from previous generations were typically allowed. Studios may have been uneasy with the new direction in which they were being taken, but there was no denying that the work was artful, and more importantly, it made money. Any lingering questions about that were laid to rest when Steven Spielberg virtually invented the blockbuster with his 1975 film *Jaws*.

Some directors took their pursuit of artistry a bit too far, however, letting schedules and budgets spiral out of control in the name of achieving their vision. After a number of high-profile financial failures, most notably Michael Cimino's *Heaven's Gate* (1980), studios began requiring more accountability and control over their projects and the era of the Film School Generation essentially came to an end. While many of these filmmakers remain active today, they no longer enjoy the autonomy they had at the peak of their power.

From the Playing Field to the Silver Screen

Athletes and actors both showcase their abilities on the highest stage, often receive impressive compensation for their efforts, and bask in the adulation of an adoring public. Here are a few athletes who transferred their talents to the silver screen. In some cases, their acting talents equaled or surpassed their athletic accomplishments.

Jim Brown (1935–)

One of the greatest running backs to ever lug the loaf, Brown was named first team All-Pro in eight of the nine seasons he played with the Cleveland Browns from 1957 to 1965. Brown brought the same intensity and determined professionalism to Hollywood, appearing in more than 30 films including The *Dirty Dozen* (1967), *The Running Man* (1987), and *Mars Attacks* (1996).

Chuck Connors (1921–1992)

A center for the Boston Celtics (1946) and an outfielder with the Brooklyn Dodgers (1949) and Chicago Cubs (1951), Connors shifted his focus from sports to the silver screen. From 1958 to 1963, Connors was better known as the star of TV's *The Rifleman*. He was also a well-respected movie actor who appeared in acclaimed films such as *Pat and Mike* (1952), *Old Yeller* (1957), *The Big Country* (1958), *Flipper* (1963), and *Soylent Green* (1973).

Sonja Henie (1910–1969)

The winner of three Olympic gold medals in figure skating, Sonja Henie translated her success on the ice into a dignified film career that made her a major box-office attraction. Signed by renowned Hollywood studio head Darryl Zanuck to a long-term contract in 1936, Henie appeared in films including *One in a Million* (1936), *Sun Valley Serenade* (1941), and *The Countess of Monte Cristo* (1948).

Chuck Norris (1939–)

A professional karate champion who held the middleweight world title from 1968 to 1974, Norris brought his martial arts skills to Hollywood and opened a school frequented by stars. This opened the door to a film career. In the 1980s, he starred in a string of successful films including *Missing in Action* (1984), *Code of Silence* (1985), *Firewalker* (1986), and *The Delta Force* (1986). He also played the title character in the TV series *Walker: Texas Ranger*, which ran from 1993 to 2001.

Paul Robeson (1898–1976)
Prior to carrying films such as *Show Boat* (1936) and *Song of Freedom* (1936) with his sonorous, booming baritone, Paul Robeson studied law at Columbia University and played for the Milwaukee Badgers, one of the founding franchises of the NFL. A member of the College Football Hall of Fame, Robeson also appeared in films such as *Jericho* (1937), *King Solomon's Mines* (1937), and *The Proud Valley* (1940).

O. J. Simpson (1947–)
He's now notorious for activities not related to sports or cinema, but it's hard to ignore the impact Simpson had on his two chosen pursuits. A Hall of Fame running back with the Buffalo Bills and San Francisco 49ers from 1969 to 1979, Simpson brought his acting skills to the silver screen in films such as *The Cassandra Crossing* (1976), *Capricorn One* (1978), and *The Naked Gun* series, in which he exhibited a flair for comedy.

Woody Strode (1914–1995)
One of the first African Americans to play in the NFL when he suited up with the Los Angeles Rams in 1946, Strode found even greater fame as an actor, earning a Golden Globe award nomination for *Spartacus* (1960). A favorite of legendary director John Ford, Strode appeared in four of Ford's films, including *Two Rode Together* (1961) and *The Man Who Shot Liberty Valance* (1962), but he gave the performance of his career in the great director's *Sergeant Rutledge* (1960).

Carl Weathers (1948–)
Before trading body blows with Sylvester Stallone in the *Rocky* film franchise, Weathers played professional football with the NFL's Oakland Raiders (1970) and the CFL's British Columbia Lions (1971–1973). Weathers, who also has a flair for comedy, has shared the screen with Adam Sandler in *Happy Gilmore* (1996) and *Little Nicky* (2000).

Johnny Weissmuller (1904–1984)
The winner of five Olympic gold medals in swimming, Weissmuller set 51 world records and retired from his amateur swimming career undefeated. He was able to translate his success in the pool into a stellar Hollywood career, appearing in more than 30 films including 12 *Tarzan* flicks and another dozen entries in the *Jungle Jim* franchise.

Inside Pixar:
The Makings of Modern Animation

Pixar has become a driving force in modern computer-based animation, creating hits such as Toy Story *(1995),* A Bug's Life *(1998), and* Finding Nemo *(2003). The company that started as a small brainstorm by George Lucas has exploded into a blockbuster-producing giant. But it was hardly an overnight occurrence.*

Technical Beginnings

These days, it's hard not to know the name Pixar. The animation giant has enjoyed phenomenal success with films ranging from *Cars* (2006) to *WALL-E* (2008) and beyond. Long before the talking vehicles and rolling robots, however, Pixar was just an idea in the mind of the guy behind *Star Wars* (1977). And it took some support from the guy behind Apple to really get things moving.

The first signs of Pixar popped up back in 1979, when George Lucas decided to start a computer-based graphics group to work within his existing Lucasfilm production house. He called it simply the Graphics Group. That same year, he met and hired computer scientist Ed Catmull, and the two hit it off. Both believed that, in the future, animation and special effects would be primarily computer generated. In 1986, Apple founder Steve Jobs paid $10 million to buy the division and spin it into its own company, which he called Pixar. Catmull came along with the deal, and animator John Lasseter was on board as creative leader.

Stepping into Animation

The Pixar team initially created and sold computer software and hardware, including the expensive Pixar Image Computer, which generated three-dimensional images. Animation was only a small part of the group's early work, and it was done primarily for showing off what the hardware and software could do. In fact, at this early juncture in Pixar's history, John Lasseter was the fledgling company's only animator.

The first film that Pixar released was a cartoon short called *Luxo Jr.* (1986). It was exhibited at a computer graphics conference, and it featured the hopping desk lamp that is still used in the Pixar logo today. *Luxo Jr.* was nominated for an Oscar, but it didn't win.

Fast-forward a couple of years, and Pixar's luck began to change dramatically. The next short that the company released, *Tin Toy* (1988), won an Oscar for Best Animated Short Film—and went on to provide the inspiration for the studio's first feature film.

The Leap to Feature Films

The move from *Tin Toy* to *Toy Story* wasn't instantaneous. Pixar spent several years using its animation techniques to create TV commercials for companies such as LifeSavers and Listerine. By the early 1990s, animation systems built by Pixar were being used to create intricate scenes within Disney hits such as *Beauty and the Beast* (1991), *Aladdin* (1992), and *The Lion King* (1994). Those successes led Pixar to the idea of producing its own feature film.

By 1995, *Toy Story* was ready to hit the big screen. The film took more than 100 computers to create, with some frames requiring as much as 13 hours to render. It took more than 400 computer models to make the film, with the help of 27 animators. It was a long way from *Luxo Jr.* As the world's first fully computer-generated feature film, *Toy Story* was the number-one film at the box office in 1995, and John Lasseter earned a special Academy Award for leading the Pixar creative team on the project.

The Story After *Toy Story*

Following the success of *Toy Story*, Pixar produced a number of other popular animated movies, including *Toy Story 2* (1999), *Monsters, Inc.* (2001), *Finding Nemo* (2003), *The Incredibles* (2004), *Cars* (2006), *Ratatouille* (2007), *WALL-E* (2008), and *Up* (2009).

In 2006, the Walt Disney Company acquired Pixar for $7.4 billion, and the company is now officially a part of the Disney family.

- *Since* A Bug's Life, *Pixar has created an animated short to go along with each of its feature films in the spirit of the Golden Age, when most features were accompanied by a short film or cartoon.*

Child Actors Who Made It Big as Adults

Too many times, child actors shine during their youth only to fizzle out when they mature. But these stars defied the odds and managed to burn ever brighter.

Christian Bale

This intense star of the rebooted *Batman* series was just as serious and focused as a child actor. Steven Spielberg jumpstarted Bale's career by casting him in *Empire of the Sun* (1987). Bale successfully transitioned to teen parts with *Little Women* (1994), then began an impressive career as an adult actor in *American Psycho* (2000) and *The Machinist* (2003). Currently, Bale is able to effortlessly move back and forth between challenging small roles and moneymaking blockbusters.

Drew Barrymore

Spawning from the Barrymore acting dynasty, young Drew began her acting career with an ethereal bang in *E.T.: The Extra-Terrestrial* (1982). Only seven at the time, she would soon succumb to Hollywood's grown-up temptations. By the time she reached adolescence, a reputation for drinking, drug use, and heavy partying dogged Drew, and acting offers quickly dried up. But she wasn't quite finished. No longer wishing to be fodder for the Hollywood gossip mill, the talented actress cleaned up her act and got busy. Turns in *Boys on the Side* (1995), *The Wedding Singer* (1998), and *Charlie's Angels* (2001) proved that she possessed the family's "chops." A reflective Barrymore described her convoluted journey this way: "Never regret anything. Because every little detail of your life is what made you into who you are in the end."

Peter Billingsley

Though few recognize his name, millions of people enjoy Peter Billingsley in *A Christmas Story* (1982) each holiday season. Billingsley starred as Ralphie in this Christmas classic, which is rerun on cable TV every year. He costarred in several other films as an adolescent, though none have endured like this popular family film. Like Ron Howard, Billingsley opted for a career behind the camera as an adult, becoming first a television and then a film producer, most notably on *The Break-Up* (2006) and *Iron Man* (2008). Recently, he turned to directing with *Couples Retreat* (2009).

Jodie Foster

Performing since the age of three, including stints on the wholesome TV series *Mayberry R.F.D.* and *Wonderful World of Disney* at six, Jodie Foster eventually shook her goody-two-shoes image in favor of more sophisticated roles. *Taxi Driver* (1976) found the teenager portraying a prostitute, a performance that earned her an Oscar nomination for Best Supporting Actress. In 1985, the multitalented Foster graduated from Yale University with a degree in English literature. Proving that her earlier nomination was no fluke, Foster has won not one but two Academy Awards, the first for her portrayal of Sarah Tobias in *The Accused* (1988) and the next for her turn as Clarice Starling in *The Silence of the Lambs* (1991). In 1991, she directed her first feature film, *Little Man Tate*, in which she also starred.

Judy Garland

As the breakout star of *The Wizard of Oz* (1939), young Judy Garland became MGM's newest sensation. While under long-term contract with Hollywood's biggest studio, she was completely in their hands. After *Oz*, Garland starred in a number of cheerful films with Mickey Rooney under the MGM banner. When her contractual obligation to MGM ended, Garland delivered a masterful performance as Vicki Lester in *A Star Is Born* (1954). Then, in 1961, the actress/singer took Manhattan by storm with a singing engagement at Carnegie Hall. To this day, it is considered one of the greatest nights in show business history. Tragically, Garland's life ended abruptly when she overdosed on sleeping pills in 1969.

Ron Howard

The Ron Howard story is a classic good-boy-makes-good tale in which an unassuming freckled-faced lad takes on Hollywood and wins. Starting his on-screen career at the improbable age of 18 months in *Frontier Woman* (1956), the red-headed boy became best known for his sensitive portrayal of Opie Taylor on *The Andy Griffith Show* (1960–1968). A starring role in the breakout TV hit *Happy Days* raised the actor's stock higher still, but Howard was now looking toward directing as his life's goal. With *Grand Theft Auto* (1977), Howard found his first hit *behind* the camera. Since then he has been nominated twice for a Best Director Oscar, winning for *A Beautiful Mind* (2001). "One of the great things about being a director as a life choice is that it can never be mastered," explains Howard. "Every story is its own kind of expedition, with its own set of challenges."

Mickey Rooney

After his stint as a child actor, "The Mick" took the adult acting world by storm. Starting in silent films as Mickey McGuire, Rooney signed on with MGM Studios in 1934. At just 5'2" tall, the young actor won the hearts of America in the *Andy Hardy* series of sentimental films that often cast him beside the equally beloved Judy Garland. Rooney would later say of the times, "I was a 14-year-old boy for 30 years." Nevertheless, Rooney managed to break free and branched out into meatier, adult roles. With movies like *The Adventures of Huckleberry Finn* (1939) and *National Velvet* (1944), the impish actor's transition was nearly complete. Rooney would work in hundreds of films during his long career and would marry some eight times along the way. The actor was presented with special Oscars at both the beginning and twilight of his career. In 1939, he shared a special Oscar with juvenile actress Deanna Durbin; in 1983, he was presented with a well-deserved lifetime achievement Oscar.

Kurt Russell

Acting in a brief scene with Elvis Presley in *It Happened at the World's Fair* (1963) gave a cute 11-year-old named Kurt Russell a taste for the big time, and a ten-year contract with Walt Disney Studios secured his place as a child star. By the early 1970s, however, Russell had turned his back on Hollywood in favor of a career in baseball. He reached the minor leagues before hanging up his cleats and returning to his first career. Then, in 1979, Russell brought things full circle with a brilliant portrayal of Elvis Presley in a well-received made-for-TV movie. This pivotal role led to a string of big-screen successes including *Escape from New York* (1981), *Silkwood* (1983), *Backdraft* (1991), and *Tombstone* (1993). These days, Russell acts in feature films and enjoys a long-enduring, albeit famously unwed, relationship with actress Goldie Hawn.

Elizabeth Taylor

As Velvet Brown in *National Velvet* (1944), 12-year-old Elizabeth Taylor already exhibited the breathtaking beauty that would become her hallmark. Like Judy Garland's, Taylor's career was carefully handled by MGM to ensure her continued stardom in adulthood. By the late 1950s, after acting in such well-received grown-up movies as *Cat on a Hot Tin Roof* (1958) and *Suddenly Last Summer* (1959), Taylor's place as a screen legend was cemented. Her personal life, which includes eight marriages, seven divorces, and one widowhood, reflects both the excess and price of superstardom.

It Wasn't Always a Wonderful Life

☆ ☆ ☆ ☆

For many, watching It's a Wonderful Life *(1946) is as much a part of the Christmas season as listening to carols and exchanging gifts. Spend the holiday without George and Mary Bailey, Clarence Oddbody, and Zuzu's rose petals? Why, you might as well not bother putting up a tree! But when this beloved holiday classic was initially released, it proved an uncharacteristic flop at the box office.*

During the 1930s, director Frank Capra could seemingly do no wrong. Starting with the classic screwball comedy *It Happened One Night* in 1934, he created a series of wildly successful films that won acclaim from critics and devotion from audiences while vaulting the fledgling Columbia Pictures into the ranks of Hollywood's top studios. In hits such as *Mr. Deeds Goes to Town* (1936), *You Can't Take It with You* (1938), and *Mr. Smith Goes to Washington* (1939), Capra spun tales of idealistic individuals who defended the moral high ground and protected our social institutions against greed and corruption. Though the themes of his films were viewed by some as simplistic, they resonated with audiences who saw in them the same struggles they faced during the long years of the Great Depression.

But in 1946, when Capra released the story of George Bailey, a common man who sees himself as a failure but comes to understand the value of his life through a bit of divine intervention, it marked the start of a long slide in popularity for the famous director. Movie-goers rejected the film at the box office, and it lost money despite being nominated for five Oscars. Some hold that the audiences who embraced the filmmaker's uplifting messages in the previous decade had become jaded and weary after the horrors of World War II and found no use for what they now saw as Capra's naive encouragement. Others contend that George Bailey's discovery of what might have been is depicted as a nightmare of loss and bitterness that survivors of war and hard times didn't want to be reminded of. Whatever the reason for its failure, it wasn't until the 1970s, when *It's a Wonderful Life* became a staple of holiday television programming, that Americans finally embraced Capra's heartwarming Christmas flick.

Best Westerns

*During the heyday of Westerns, Hollywood produced 300 oaters every
year. Many of these films were formulaic, but many others were superb
examples of the genre, featuring some of the greatest stars in the
Hollywood corral. Here are a few must-see flicks from the Western stable.*

Fort Apache (1948)

Fort Apache, starring John Wayne and Henry Fonda, is the first of
director John Ford's superb "cavalry trilogy," which also includes *She
Wore a Yellow Ribbon* (1948) and *Rio Grande* (1950). *Fort Apache*
is a variation of the Custer story, and in a cast dominated by males,
a grown-up Shirley Temple is delightful as the colonel's daughter.

High Noon (1952)

Gary Cooper plays the iconic sheriff of a town
about to be sieged by outlaws, except in this
case, the townspeople won't help save their
community—a controversial twist at the
time. Famous for unfolding in real time,
which increases the suspense as we all
wait for 12 o'clock high, *High Noon*
won four Oscars, including a Best Actor
award for Coop.

Shane (1953)

Based on Jack Schaefer's best-selling novel, *Shane* stars Alan Ladd and
Van Heflin in a story of cattle barons vs. homesteaders representing the
key Western theme of civilization vs. the wilderness. Jack Palance was
nominated for an Academy Award for his chilling portrayal of a hired killer.

The Searchers (1956)

This Western masterpiece by director John Ford explores the theme of
racism in its story of a young girl who is kidnapped by Native Americans.
At first, Ethan Edwards, played by John Wayne, hopes to rescue her, but
he later wants to kill her instead. A complex film with a dark view of
civilization, *The Searchers* was an incredible influence on the Film School
Generation. Wayne is magnificent in his role, and costar Ward Bond is
powerful as a Texas Ranger who doubles as a frontier preacher.

The Magnificent Seven (1960)
The rousing score is unforgettable, the action nonstop, and the cast charismatic in this Western based on Akira Kurosawa's *Seven Samurai*. The era's best young actors made up the seven, with each representing a facet of the masculine character. Look for Yul Brynner, James Coburn, Steve McQueen, and Charles Bronson in their prime.

Butch Cassidy and the Sundance Kid (1969)
With humor, history, romance, and a great chase, not to mention Paul Newman and Robert Redford, *Butch Cassidy and the Sundance Kid* is one of the most charming Westerns ever made.

Dances with Wolves (1990)
Kevin Costner directed and starred as a frontier army officer who interacts with a tribe of Native Americans. In one of cinema's finest portrayals of Native Americans to date, *Dances with Wolves* inverts the traditional Western's idea of who represents civilization and who represents the wilderness. The film won seven Oscars, including Best Picture.

Unforgiven (1992)
Clint Eastwood and Morgan Freeman star as retired gunfighters who strap on their holsters one last time to avenge the death of a prostitute. Their quest pits them against a brutal lawman, played by Gene Hackman. Directed by Eastwood, *Unforgiven* won four Academy Awards, including Best Picture, Best Director, and Best Supporting Actor (Hackman).

Tombstone (1993)
In this updated version of *Gunfight at the O.K. Corral* (1957), the mythic overtones of the West's most famous story take center stage. Kurt Russell is actor enough to play a mythic version of Wyatt Earp, but Val Kilmer steals the show with his unexpectedly poignant interpretation of tragic Doc Holliday, who chased death as a way to kill the pain of life. An engaging story provides the entertainment, while the thoughtful theme offers a message about the personal price of a life of violence.

Open Range (2003)
Kevin Costner directed this beautifully shot, character-driven story of open range drovers about to be made obsolete in a changing West. Robert Duvall is captivating as an aging trail boss, while cowboy/gunfighter Costner strikes up an unlikely romance with Annette Bening. The climactic shootout is one of the best ever filmed in a Western.

Bugsy Siegel's "Screen Test"

☆ ☆ ☆ ☆

When mobster Bugsy Siegel acted out a scene at the behest of actor pal George Raft, the results proved eye-opening. Much to the surprise of all, the gangster could really act. Unfortunately, Siegel never pursued acting, choosing instead to remain on his murderous course. This begs the rather obvious question: "What if?"

In the annals of the underworld, there was perhaps no one more dapper, or more ruthless, than Benjamin "Bugsy" Siegel (1906–1947). Nearly six feet tall, with piercing blue eyes that melted the heart of many a woman, Siegel had movie-star looks and savoir faire that disguised a temperament that could easily be described as hair-triggered. During his hard-lived life, Siegel committed nearly every crime in the book and was implicated by the FBI for more than 30 murders.

Born Benjamin Hymen Siegelbaum, the up-and-coming mobster picked up the nickname "Bugsy" (the slang term *bugs* means "crazy") for his high level of viciousness. Siegel hated the tag, considering it a low-class connection to his hardscrabble youth, and threatened to kill anyone who used it in his presence. Still, the mobster was said to be a natural born charmer who never seemed at a loss for companionship, female or otherwise.

One of Siegel's closest friends was Hollywood actor George Raft, who was known for such memorable films as *Scarface* (1932), *I Stole a Million* (1939), and *They Drive by Night* (1940). The two had both grown up on the gritty streets of New York City's Lower East Side. Throughout their lives, the pair would engage in a form of mutual admiration. For example, Raft's movie career featured many mob-related roles. So, when he needed the proper tough-guy "inspiration," the actor would mimic mannerisms and inflections that he picked up from his real-life mobster pals. Siegel, on the other hand, made no secret of the fact that he was starstruck by Hollywood and sometimes wished that he too had become an actor. He viewed Raft as the Real McCoy in this arena and gave him due respect. Hoping to get ever closer to the Hollywood action, while at the same time expanding his "operations," Siegel moved to California in 1937.

A Natural Born . . . Actor?

In no time, Siegel was hobnobbing with major celebrities even as his deadly business dealings escalated. In 1941, Raft was shooting *Manpower* with the legendary Marlene Dietrich, when Siegel showed up on the set to observe. After watching Raft go through a few takes before heading off to his dressing room, Siegel told his buddy that he could do the scene better. An amused Raft told his friend to go ahead and give it a shot. Over the course of the next few minutes, the smirk would leave Raft's face.

Siegel reenacted Raft's scene perfectly. He had not only memorized the dialogue line for line, but he interpreted Raft's nuanced gestures as well. This was no small feat given the fact that Siegel had absolutely no training as an actor. A stunned Raft told Siegel that he just might have what it takes to be an actor.

A Dream Unfulfilled

But such Tinseltown dreams were not to be. Despite his demonstrated talent, moviemakers probably wouldn't have used him. And who could blame them? What if Siegel decided to go "Bugsy" on them for not awarding him a role, for critiquing his performance, or for changing his lines? Temperamental actors are one thing; homicidal ones, quite another.

History shows that Siegel played it fast and loose from that point forward, putting most of his energies into creating the Flamingo Hotel and, along with it, the gaming capital of the world—Las Vegas. Siegel's mob associates from the East Coast put him in charge of construction of the opulent hotel. Siegel envisioned an extravagent hotel and, at least for him, money was no object. But when costs soared to $6 million—four times the original budget—Siegel's associates became concerned.

On June 20, 1947, Siegel's dreams of a life on the silver screen came to an abrupt end when a number of well-placed rounds from an M-1 Carbine sent the Hollywood gangster into the afterworld at age 41. It is believed that Siegel was killed by his own mob associates who were convinced that he was pilfering money from the organization. Siegel's life and grisly end are grand pieces of mob drama that got their due on the silver screen in the 1991 flick *Bugsy*, which starred Warren Beatty as the doomed mobster.

A Few of Oscar's Most Memorable Moments

Oscar night has become the most anticipated evening in Hollywood, and over the decades, the stars have kept us watching for fashion faux pas, bizarre acceptance speeches, and all the drama that comes when winners, losers, and egos collide. Here are a some of the most unforgettable Oscar moments.

- During the April 1974 Oscar broadcast, actor David Niven was innocently introducing Best Picture presenter Elizabeth Taylor when a streaker ran across the stage totally nude, throwing the two-finger "peace" sign. Live television caught it all, including Niven's slick response: "Just think...the only laugh that man will probably ever get in his life is for stripping and showing off his shortcomings."

- In 1933, director Frank Capra was so sure he was going to win Best Director for *Lady for a Day* that he stood up too soon when he heard his first name called. But the spotlight didn't shine on Capra when Will Rogers said, "Come on up and get it, Frank." It turns out that Frank Lloyd had won Best Director for his film *Cavalcade*. Capra walked back to his seat dazed, confused, and more than a little humiliated.

- When Marlon Brando won the Best Actor award for *The Godfather* (1972), he sent an Apache woman named Sacheen Littlefeather to refuse the award and chastise the Academy for its treatment of Native Americans in film. It was later revealed that "Littlefeather" was an actress named Maria Cruz, who was of Mexican descent.

- Marlon Brando isn't the only person to use an Oscar acceptance speech as a political platform. Vanessa Redgrave gave a pro-Palestine speech when she won for *Julia* (1977), and Michael Moore took the opportunity to shout, "Shame on you, Mr. Bush!" after winning his statue for *Bowling for Columbine* (2002). On both occasions, the winners received both cheers and jeers from the audience.

- Host Jerry Lewis found himself with 20 minutes to kill in 1959 when the show ran short—a rare occurrence, as the Oscars are known to drag on for hours. Lewis attempted to fill the time with some off-the-cuff jokes and comic bits, but they went over so poorly that NBC stopped the broadcast and just aired a short film about handguns.

- Singer/actress Cher won the Oscar for Best Actress for her role as a lonely woman who falls in love with a younger man in *Moonstruck* (1987). Known for her wild sense of style, Cher shocked millions when she accepted her award in a virtually translucent Bob Mackie gown. A few sequins were the only things keeping millions of viewers from seeing Cher's entire "body of work."

- In 1988, comedian Chevy Chase opened the Oscars by saying, "Good evening, Hollywood phonies!" He never hosted the show again.

- At age 73, Jack Palance showed the Academy—and the rest of the world—that he still had "it" when he dropped to the floor and did several one-armed push-ups after winning the Best Supporting Actor award for his role as a rugged cowhand in *City Slickers* (1991).

- In 2000, before she was one half of "Brangelina," actress Angelina Jolie made headlines when she took her brother as her date to the Oscars. At one point during the preshow festivities, Angelina and brother James shared a kiss. Like, a *kiss* kiss. Jolie denies that she and her brother are anything but loving siblings, but few can forget the weird level of intimacy they showed the cameras that night.

- When longtime rival Bette Davis was nominated for Best Actress for *What Ever Happened to Baby Jane?* (1962), and Joan Crawford was passed up for *her* role in the same film, Crawford got crafty. She contacted the other actresses nominated that year and kindly offered to accept the award in their place, in case one of them couldn't attend. Sure enough, Anne Bancroft won that year and Crawford took the stage, basking in the spotlight while Davis fumed in her seat.

- Actor George C. Scott called the Oscars "a two-hour meat parade" and swore that if he won for *Patton* (1970), he wouldn't be there to collect. Scott *was* named the winner that year and refused the "honor," becoming the first actor to do so.

- In 1989, during the opening number, Rob Lowe sang a ridiculously bad version of "Proud Mary" with an actress dressed as Snow White. Just one year prior, Lowe had been involved in a scandal for engaging in illicit activities with a minor, and this certainly didn't help his career. In addition, the Academy never got permission to use the Snow White character in the show and was summarily sued by Disney. Whoops! Disney dropped the suit after the Academy apologized.

Chaplin's Coffin Held for Ransom

☆ ☆ ☆ ☆

In the silent era, he entertained millions without ever uttering a single word. During his career, he produced and starred in nearly 100 movies, making him a millionaire at an early age. Perhaps that's why after his death, two men thought Charlie Chaplin's casket was worth more than half a million dollars in ransom.

The Life and Death of a Silent Star

Born in London on April 16, 1889, Charles Spencer Chaplin had his first taste of show business at age 5 when his mother, a failing music hall entertainer, could not continue her act, and little Charlie stepped up and finished her show. After years of moving back and forth between his separated parents, workhouses, and school, he officially entered show business in 1898 (at age 9) when he became one of the Eight Lancashire Lads, a musical comedy act that worked the lower-class music halls in London. After a couple of years, he was seeking employment in various offices, factories, and households to support his mentally ill and sick mother. Finally, around age 12, he reentered the music hall scene, joining Fred Karno's London Comedians, a traveling music hall act.

Chaplin continued working with traveling shows until he signed his first contract with the legendary Keystone Studio, in late 1913, at age 24. In February 1914, Chaplin's first movie, *Making a Living*, premiered. It would be the first of more than 30 shorts that Chaplin made in 1914 alone. In fact, from 1915 until the end of his career, Chaplin was featured in nearly 100 movies, mostly shorts. No small feat considering that he wrote, starred in, directed, produced, and even scored all of his own movies. All of this not only made Charlie Chaplin a household name but also a very rich man.

But not everything was wine and roses for Chaplin. After three failed marriages, the 54-year old actor caused quite a stir in 1943 when he married his fourth wife, Oona O'Neill, who was just 17 at the time. More scandal found Chaplin in the early 1950s when the U.S. government began to suspect that he and his family might be Communist sympathizers. There seemed to be very little to support their suspicions other than the fact that Chaplin had simply chosen to live in the United States while not declaring U.S. citizenship. Regardless, Chaplin soon tired of what he deemed harassment and moved to Switzerland, where he lived with his wife and their eight children until his death on Christmas Day 1977. Shortly thereafter, perhaps the strangest chapter in Charlie Chaplin's story began.

Grave Robbers

On March 2, 1978, visitors to Charlie Chaplin's grave were shocked to discover a massive hole where the actor's coffin had been. It soon became clear that sometime overnight, someone had dug up and stolen Chaplin's entire casket. But who would do such a thing? And why? It didn't take long to find the answer. Several days later, Oona began receiving phone calls from people claiming to have stolen the body and demanding a portion of Chaplin's millions in exchange for the casket. Oona dismissed most of the callers as crackpots, with the exception of one. This mysterious male caller seemed to know an awful lot about what Chaplin's coffin looked like. But because he was demanding the equivalent of $600,000 U.S. dollars in exchange for the coffin's safe return, Oona told the caller she needed more proof. Several days later, a photo of Chaplin's newly unearthed casket arrived in her mailbox, and Oona alerted Swiss police.

The Arrests

When Oona Chaplin first met with Swiss authorities, she could only show them the photo and tell them that the caller was male and that he spoke with a Slavic accent. She also told them that she had no intention of paying the ransom. But the police convinced Oona that the longer she pretended to be willing to pay the ransom, the better chance they had of catching the thief. Oona was emotionally unable to deal with the fiasco, so Chaplin's daughter Geraldine complied with the investigators' request.

During the next few weeks, Geraldine did such a convincing job that she talked the caller's ransom price down from $600,000 to $250,000, though the Chaplin family still did not plan to pay it. In the meantime, Swiss police were desperately trying to trace the calls. Their first big break came when they established that the calls were coming from a local Lausanne pay phone. However, there were more than 200 pay phones in the town. Undaunted, police began staking out all of them. Their hard work paid off when they arrested 24-year-old Roman Wardas, who admitted to stealing Chaplin's coffin, stating that he had gotten the idea after reading about a similar body "kidnapping" in an Italian newspaper. Based on information Wardas provided police, a second man, 38-year-old Gantcho Ganev, was also arrested. Like Wardas, Ganev admitted to helping take the casket but claimed that it was all Wardas's idea and that he just helped out.

So Where's the Body?

Of course, once the two suspects were in custody, the question on everyone's minds was the location of Chaplin's casket. Ganev and Wardas claimed that after stealing the casket from the cemetery, they drove it to a field and buried it in a shallow hole.

Following directions provided by both suspects, Swiss police descended upon a farm about 12 miles from the Chaplin estate. Spotting a mound of what appeared to be freshly moved dirt, they began digging, and on May 17, 1978, in the middle of a cornfield, Chaplin's unopened coffin was recovered.

Once word got out, people began flocking to the farm, so the farmer placed a small wooden cross, ornamented with a cane, over the hole where the casket had been buried. For several weeks, people brought flowers and paid their respects to the empty hole.

The Aftermath

After a very short trial, both men were convicted of extortion and disturbing the peace of the dead. As the admitted mastermind of the crime, Wardas was sentenced to nearly five years of hard labor. Ganev received only an 18-month suspended sentence.

As for Chaplin's unopened casket, it was returned to Corsier-Sur-Vevey Cemetery and was reburied in the exact spot where it had originally been interred. Only this time, to deter any future grave robbers, Oona ordered it buried under six feet of solid concrete. And when she passed away 14 years later, her will stipulated that she also be buried under at least six feet of concrete. She was.

Famous Last Words: Celebrity Tombstone Inscriptions

Everyone loves to get the last word in, and celebrities are no exception. We dug up some of the most original inscriptions found on celebrity tombstones. Your graveyard tour starts now.

Jack Lemmon
The comedy actor known for decades of laughs may not have been succinct in life, but his epitaph gets straight to the punch line. It reads "Jack Lemmon: In."

Rodney Dangerfield
Dangerfield was famous for self-deprecating humor during his life, so it's only fitting that he continued the theme with his passing. The comedian's grave is inscribed with the phrase: "There Goes the Neighborhood."

Billy Wilder
Keeping up with the self-directed jabs, legendary filmmaker Billy Wilder—the man behind movies such as *Some Like It Hot* (1959) and *Casino Royale* (1967)—also belittled himself one final time on his tombstone, which simply says: "I'm a Writer but then Nobody's Perfect."

Ed Wynn
Ed Wynn provided the voice for the Mad Hatter in Disney's *Alice in Wonderland* (1951). He also appeared in a number of films, including *Babes in Toyland* (1961) and *Mary Poppins* (1964). Wynn left the world with a message of gratitude on his marker: "Dear God: Thanks."

Frank Sinatra
Ol' Blue Eyes graced the world of music and film—and, judging by his epitaph, he may not be finished yet. Sinatra's grave reads: "The Best Is Yet to Come," which is also the title of the last song he sang in public.

Mel Blanc
There was only one way that the man who gave a voice to Bugs Bunny and countless other Looney Tunes characters could sign off. Blanc left instructions in his will to have his tombstone inscribed with his most famous phrase: "That's All Folks."

In Conclusion . . .

Here's one last chance to prove your movie mettle.
Match these last lines to the movies they ended.

1. "...All right, Mr. DeMille, I'm ready for my close-up."

2. "Eliza? Where the devil are my slippers?"

3. "Hey, Stella! Hey, Stella!"

4. "I do wish we could chat longer, but I'm having an old friend for dinner. Bye."

5. "I'm not a cabdriver. I'm a coffeepot."

6. "Life is a state of mind."

7. "Louie, I think this is the beginning of a beautiful friendship."

8. "Love means never having to say you're sorry."

9. "Mein Fuehrer, I can walk!"

10. "Oh, no! It wasn't the airplanes. It was Beauty killed the Beast."

11. "Shut up and deal."

12. "...Tara! Home. I'll go home, and I'll think of some way to get him back! After all, tomorrow is another day!"

13. "The greatest trick the Devil ever pulled was convincing the world he didn't exist. Like that, he's gone."

14. "The horror. The horror."

15. "Wanna dance, or would you rather just suck face?"

16. "Well, nobody's perfect."

17. "You know somethin', Utivich? I think this might just be my masterpiece."

18. "You know, they're totally irrational and crazy and absurd and—but uh, I guess we keep going through it...because...most of us need the eggs."

19. "You're still here? It's over! Go home. Go!"

Answer Choices

A. *Annie Hall* (1977)

B. *The Apartment* (1960)

C. *Apocalypse Now* (1979)

D. *Arsenic and Old Lace* (1944)

E. *Being There* (1979)

F. *Casablanca* (1942)

G. *Dr. Strangelove* (1964)

H. *Ferris Bueller's Day Off* (1986)

I. *Gone with the Wind* (1939)

J. *Inglourious Basterds* (2009)

K. *King Kong* (1933)

L. *Love Story* (1970)

M. *My Fair Lady* (1964)

N. *On Golden Pond* (1981)

O. *The Silence of the Lambs* (1991)

P. *Some Like It Hot* (1959)

Q. *A Streetcar Named Desire* (1951)

R. *Sunset Boulevard* (1950)

S. *The Usual Suspects* (1995)

The End

Index

☆ ☆ ☆ ☆

Harris, Richard, 173, 254
Harryhausen, Ray, 164, 362
Hartman, Phil, 369
Harvey, Laurence, 62
Hasselhoff, David, 174
Haunted locales, 40–41, 367–68
Hawke, Ethan, 83, 125
Hawn, Goldie, 99, 262
Hayek, Salma, 459
Hays Office, 22, 188
Hayworth, Rita, 296, 459
Head, Murray, 400
Hearst, William Randolph, 72–73, 91, 373–74
Heaven's Gate, 102–3, 191, 469
Hefner, Hugh, 29, 112, 343
He Got Game, 381
Hell's Angels, 34
Hemingway, Mariel, 433
Henie, Sonja, 470
Hepburn, Audrey, 400, 425, 466–67
Hepburn, Katharine, 34, 63, 78, 79, 121, 122, 132, 161, 163, 186–87, 203, 254, 302–3, 326, 399, 434–35
Hercules, 220
Heston, Charlton, 229, 259
Hidalgo, 323
Hidden Fortress, The, 283
High Noon, 478
Hilton, Perez, 375
His Girl Friday, 131, 161
Hispanic actors, 458–60
Historical errors in films, 86, 114–16, 268–69, 394–95
Hitchcock, Alfred, 42–43, 134–36, 234–35, 319
Hockey movies, 296–97
Hoffman, Dustin, 97, 293, 340, 388, 414, 468
Hogan, Paul, 57
Holden, William, 159, 246, 386, 415
Holliday, Judy, 148
Hollywood, founding of, 15–17, 80
Hollywood Forever Cemetery, 456–57
Hollywood landmarks, 111–13, 182–84, 213, 246–47, 298, 366–68, 422–23, 456–57
Hollywood sign, 76, 111–13
Hollywood Ten, 285–86
Hollywood Walk of Fame, 392–93
Holmes, Katie, 63, 259
Home Alone, 265

Homosexuality, 69, 129–31
Hood, Darla, 166, 457
Hoop Dreams, 380
Hoosiers, 133, 380
Hope, Bob, 184, 274–75
Hopper, Dennis, 51, 133
Hopper, Hedda, 130, 374–75
Horror movies, 66–67, 156–57, 239, 295–96, 346, 403–5
Horses in movies, 190–91, 322–23
Horse Soldiers, The, 159
Horse Whisperer, The, 323
Houdini, Harry, 41
House Un-American Activities Committee (HUAC), 284–86
Howard, Leslie, 158, 188
Howard, Ron, 86, 211–12, 226, 475
Howard, Sidney, 187
Howard, Sydney, 388
How to Lose a Guy in 10 Days, 289
Hudson, Rock, 69, 148–49, 161, 184
Hughes, Howard, 33–35, 247
Hunchback of Notre Dame, The, 40, 82, 156
Hunt, Linda, 388
Huston, John, 457, 463
Hutchins, Bobby, "Wheezer," 166–67

I
I Am Legend, 44
Ice-skating movies, 296–97
Idol of the Crowds, 296
I'll Never Forget Whatshisname, 19
Illustrated Man, The, 163
Imperioli, Michael, 257
Ince, Thomas, 72–73
Incident at Loch Ness, 172
Incomparable Atuk, The, 369
Inconvenient Truth, An, 365
Incredibles, The, 180, 181
Incredible Shrinking Man, The, 447
Indiana Jones and the Temple of Doom, 64, 100, 282
Inside jokes in animation, 180–81
Intolerance: Love's Struggles Throughout the Ages, 127
Invasion of the Body Snatchers, 447
Invasion of the Saucer Men, 357
Invincible, 201, 395
Invisible Man, The, 157, 225
Irons, Jeremy, 23
It's a Wonderful Life, 43, 263, 477

Contributing Writers

Often compared to a young Ernest Borgnine (minus the actor's looks, talent, and sex appeal), **Jeff Bahr** decided to make his Hollywood debut in print—not on the silver screen. Can Tinseltown endure such a crushing betrayal?

Film historian **Susan Doll** teaches cinema studies and writes about film and popular culture. She is a regular blogger for the Turner Classic Movies blog and the author of several books, including *Elvis: American Idol, Understanding Elvis, Elvis for Dummies*, and *Marilyn: Her Life and Legend.* She is also the coauthor of *Florida on Film.* Now, she's ready for her close-up, Mr. DeMille!

Actor-turned-author **James Duplacey** has contributed wise and witty pearls of wisdom to six books in the *Armchair Reader*™ series. Currently residing in Alberta, Canada, James did not appear in *Unforgiven* or *Brokeback Mountain,* two movies filmed in his "backyard" that somehow became classics without his participation.

Mary Fons-Misetic writes books, plays, magazine articles, and a daily blog titled "PaperGirl." She also spends a lot of time onstage, performing solo and with Chicago's Neo-Futurist ensemble. Her favorite movie is *Tootsie,* her favorite director is Ingmar Bergman, and her favorite Oscar outfit was the swan dress Bjork wore in 2001.

Bill Martin is a freelance writer who has contributed to eight *Armchair Reader*™ volumes. Bill lives in Toronto, Ontario—the city dubbed "Hollywood North" for its bustling moviemaking scene. Filmmakers have yet to discover Bill's rugged good looks and star potential, but he plays a starring role with his wife Marianna in raising their three drama queen daughters Samantha, Paige, and Erica.

David Morrow cowrote *Florida on Film* and has contributed dozens of articles to the *Armchair Reader*™ series. His philosophy on film is best summed up by the slogan, "Movies are a theatrical release." In that vein, if he were to switch places with any movie star, it would be Dean Martin; handsome, suave, and perpetually inebriated—what could be better?

JR Raphael is a star of stage and screen—if by "stage and screen," you mean "his own egomaniacal fantasies." When not stalking minor celebrities, JR runs the humor site eSarcasm and writes for *PC World* and other tech publications.

Lawrence Robinson is a Los Angeles-based novelist and screen-writer. His thriller *Psych 9,* starring Cary Elwes and Sara Foster, is due to be released by Universal Pictures (UK) in 2010. He hopes it will warrant a mention in any future volumes of *Armchair Reader™ Goes Hollywood,* although preferably not in an article about movie goofs or box-office disasters.

Peter Suciu is a New York-based freelance writer and lifelong film buff, who has reviewed movies for more than a dozen magazines and Web sites including *Home Theater* and BigPictureBigSound.com. He can quote from hundreds of films but never does so in public. And although he is a member of Generation X, he prefers the *Star Wars* prequels to the original films of his youth, which is likely because he thinks that, deep down, Darth Vader is really a good guy.

Donald Vaughan has written, cowritten, ghosted, or contributed to more than 30 books, including two celebrity autobiographies. He grew up near Hollywood (Florida, that is, not California), where he worked as a poorly paid extra in *The Pilot* (1980), *Body Heat* (1981), and *The Funhouse* (1981). Vaughan is currently between acting gigs, which allows him plenty of time to plow through his massive DVD collection. A film purist, he has never seen the remake of *Psycho,* and doesn't plan to.

James A. Willis is the founder and director of The Ghosts of Ohio and has been a contributing author on ten books about all sorts of strange and spooky things. An avid film buff, James has been known to spontaneously reenact key scenes from movies, much to the chagrin of his wife, Stephanie, and their menagerie of pets. He also believes that Adam West is the one true Batman.

Additional Contributions: Rhonda Markowtiz, Phil Morehart, Bill O'Neal, Stephen Ryder, Jennifer Plattner Wilkinson